SUSE Linux® 9.3 For Dummies®

SUSE Linux Installation

1. Boot the PC from the DVD-ROM.
2. Go through the graphical installation steps.
3. Configure the other hardware after the initial system restart.

GNOME and KDE Desktops

- Click the Main Menu button in GNOME or KDE and then select the applications to run
- Always right-click for a pop-up menu of options
- Right-click the panel to add applets to the panel
- To run OpenOffice.org applications: Main Menu⇨Office

System Administration

Manage user accounts: YaST Control Center⇨Security and Users⇨Edit and Create Users

Manage packages: YaST Control Center⇨Software⇨Install and Remove Software

Configure services: YaST Control Center⇨System⇨Runlevel Editor

Install RPM packages: `rpm -Uvh packagefile`

Check if RPM is installed: `rpm -q rpmname`

Unpack compressed tar files: `tar zxvf filename.tgz`

Unpack bz2 compressed files: `bzip2 -d filename.bz2`

SUSE Linux Configuration

- Start the YaST Control Center (select Main Menu⇨System⇨YaST in KDE or System Menu⇨YaST in GNOME)
- To configure the X Window System, log in as `root` and type **sax2** in a terminal window or text console
- Printer setup: YaST Control Center⇨Hardware⇨Printers
- Sound card setup: YaST Control Center⇨Hardware⇨Sound

Network Configuration

- **Network configuration:** YaST Control Center⇨Network Devices⇨Network Card
- **Internet connection:** Choose the network device (DSL, Modem, and so on) from YaST Control Center⇨Network Devices

Commands:

- `ping` — Checks network connectivity
- `ifconfig` — Configures network interface
- `iwconfig` — Configures wireless network interface
- `netstat` — Displays network status

Copyright © 2005 Wiley Publishing, Inc. All rights reserved.
Item 9615-2.
For more information about Wiley Publishing, call 1-800-762-2974.

Wiley, the Wiley Publishing logo, For Dummies, the Dummies Man logo, the For Dummies Bestselling Book Series logo and all related trade dress are trademarks or registered trademarks of John Wiley & Sons, Inc. and/or its affiliates. All other trademarks are property of their respective owners.

For Dummies: Bestselling Book Series for Beginners

SUSE Linux® 9.3 For Dummies®

Cheat Sheet

Bash Shell

- Pipe:
  - `command1 | command2`
- Redirections:
  - `command > file` (output goes to file)
  - `command < file` (input from file)
  - `command > file` (append to file)
  - `command 2> file` (errors go to file)
- Commands:
  - `alias` (defines shortcut for a long command)
  - `apropos` (searches the man pages for keywords)
  - `history` (displays most recent commands)
  - `locate` (finds files)
  - `whereis` (finds executable files for a command)
  - `which` (shows full pathname for a command)
  - `man` (displays online help)
  - `printenv` (displays the environment variables)
- Environment variables:
  - `HOME` (user's home directory)
  - `PATH` (directories to search for commands)
  - `TERM` (name of terminal type)

File System

- Key directories in the file system:
  - `/` Root directory (base of file system)
  - `/bin` (essential user commands)
  - `/boot` (Linux kernel and boot loader)
  - `/dev` (special device files)
  - `/etc` (system configuration files)
  - `/home` (home directories of all users)
  - `/lib` (library files for programs)
  - `/media` (mount points for CD-ROM, floppy)
  - `/opt` (application software packages)
  - `/root` (home directory of the root user)
  - `/sbin` (system-administration commands)
  - `/srv` (files for services such as Web and FTP)
  - `/tmp` (temporary directory)
  - `/usr` (shareable, read-only data)
  - `/var` (variable system files, such as logs)
- File System Commands:
  - `cat`   Copies a file to the standard output
  - `cd`   Changes the current directory
  - `chmod`   Changes file permissions
  - `chown`   Changes file ownerships
  - `cp`   Copies files
  - `dd`   Copies blocks of data
  - `df`   Reports disk space usage by device
  - `diff`   Compares two text files
  - `du`   Reports disk space usage by directory
  - `file`   Displays the type of data in a file
  - `find`   Finds files based on specified criteria
  - `grep`   Searches for text in a file
  - `ln`   Links a filename to a link name
  - `ls`   Displays the contents of a directory
  - `mkdir`   Creates a directory
  - `more`   Displays a text file, one page at a time
  - `mount`   Mounts a file system
  - `mv`   Renames or moves file
  - `pwd`   Displays the current directory
  - `rm`   Deletes files
  - `rmdir`   Deletes directories
  - `sort`   Sorts lines in a text file
  - `split`   Splits a file into smaller parts
  - `umount` Unmounts a file system
  - `wc`   Counts words and lines in a file
- File permissions:
  - `rwxrwxrwx`: Three groups of `rwx`, leftmost is for owner, middle for group, rightmost for others; `rwx` stands for read (`r`), write (`w`), execute (`x`); a dash (-) means no permission
  - `rwx------`: Only owner can read, write, execute
  - `rw-r--r--`: Everyone can read, owner can write
  - `rw-------`: Only owner can read and write
  - `r--r--r--`: Read-only file (everyone can read)

For Dummies: Bestselling Book Series for Beginners

SUSE Linux® 9.3 FOR DUMMIES®

SUSE Linux® 9.3 FOR DUMMIES®

by Naba Barkakati

Wiley Publishing, Inc.

SUSE Linux® 9.3 For Dummies®

Published by
Wiley Publishing, Inc.
111 River Street
Hoboken, NJ 07030-5774

www.wiley.com

Copyright © 2005 by Wiley Publishing, Inc., Indianapolis, Indiana

Published by Wiley Publishing, Inc., Indianapolis, Indiana

Published simultaneously in Canada

No part of this publication may be reproduced, stored in a retrieval system or transmitted in any form or by any means, electronic, mechanical, photocopying, recording, scanning or otherwise, except as permitted under Sections 107 or 108 of the 1976 United States Copyright Act, without either the prior written permission of the Publisher, or authorization through payment of the appropriate per-copy fee to the Copyright Clearance Center, 222 Rosewood Drive, Danvers, MA 01923, (978) 750-8400, fax (978) 646-8600. Requests to the Publisher for permission should be addressed to the Legal Department, Wiley Publishing, Inc., 10475 Crosspoint Blvd., Indianapolis, IN 46256, (317) 572-3447, fax (317) 572-4355, or online at http://www.wiley.com/go/permissions.

Trademarks: Wiley, the Wiley Publishing logo, For Dummies, the Dummies Man logo, A Reference for the Rest of Us!, The Dummies Way, Dummies Daily, The Fun and Easy Way, Dummies.com, and related trade dress are trademarks or registered trademarks of John Wiley & Sons, Inc. and/or its affiliates in the United States and other countries, and may not be used without written permission. Linux is a registered trademark of Linus Torvalds. All other trademarks are the property of their respective owners. Wiley Publishing, Inc., is not associated with any product or vendor mentioned in this book.

> **LIMIT OF LIABILITY/DISCLAIMER OF WARRANTY:** THE PUBLISHER AND THE AUTHOR MAKE NO REPRESENTATIONS OR WARRANTIES WITH RESPECT TO THE ACCURACY OR COMPLETENESS OF THE CONTENTS OF THIS WORK AND SPECIFICALLY DISCLAIM ALL WARRANTIES, INCLUDING WITHOUT LIMITATION WARRANTIES OF FITNESS FOR A PARTICULAR PURPOSE. NO WARRANTY MAY BE CREATED OR EXTENDED BY SALES OR PROMOTIONAL MATERIALS. THE ADVICE AND STRATEGIES CONTAINED HEREIN MAY NOT BE SUITABLE FOR EVERY SITUATION. THIS WORK IS SOLD WITH THE UNDERSTANDING THAT THE PUBLISHER IS NOT ENGAGED IN RENDERING LEGAL, ACCOUNTING, OR OTHER PROFESSIONAL SERVICES. IF PROFESSIONAL ASSISTANCE IS REQUIRED, THE SERVICES OF A COMPETENT PROFESSIONAL PERSON SHOULD BE SOUGHT. NEITHER THE PUBLISHER NOR THE AUTHOR SHALL BE LIABLE FOR DAMAGES ARISING HEREFROM. THE FACT THAT AN ORGANIZATION OR WEBSITE IS REFERRED TO IN THIS WORK AS A CITATION AND/OR A POTENTIAL SOURCE OF FURTHER INFORMATION DOES NOT MEAN THAT THE AUTHOR OR THE PUBLISHER ENDORSES THE INFORMATION THE ORGANIZATION OR WEBSITE MAY PROVIDE OR RECOMMENDATIONS IT MAY MAKE. FURTHER, READERS SHOULD BE AWARE THAT INTERNET WEBSITES LISTED IN THIS WORK MAY HAVE CHANGED OR DISAPPEARED BETWEEN WHEN THIS WORK WAS WRITTEN AND WHEN IT IS READ. FULFILLMENT OF EACH COUPON OFFER IS THE SOLE RESPONSIBILITY OF THE OFFEROR.

For general information on our other products and services, please contact our Customer Care Department within the U.S. at 800-762-2974, outside the U.S. at 317-572-3993, or fax 317-572-4002.

For technical support, please visit www.wiley.com/techsupport.

Wiley also publishes its books in a variety of electronic formats. Some content that appears in print may not be available in electronic books.

Library of Congress Control Number: 2005923238

ISBN-13: 978-07645-9615-5

ISBN-10: 0-7645-9615-2

Manufactured in the United States of America

10 9 8 7 6 5 4 3 2 1

1B/QT/QV/QV/IN

About the Author

Naba Barkakati is an electrical engineer and a successful computer-book author who has experience in a wide variety of systems, ranging from MS-DOS and Windows to UNIX and Linux. He bought his first personal computer — an IBM PC-AT — in 1984 after graduating with a PhD in electrical engineering from the University of Maryland at College Park. While pursuing a full-time career in engineering, Naba dreamed of writing software for the emerging PC software market. As luck would have it, instead of building a software empire like Microsoft, he ended up writing successful computer books. Currently, Naba is a Senior Level Technologist at the Center for Technology and Engineering in the U.S. Government Accountability Office (GAO).

Over the past 16 years, Naba has written over 25 computer books on a number of topics, ranging from object-oriented programming with C++ to Linux. He has authored several best-selling titles, such as *The Waite Group's Turbo C++ Bible, Object-Oriented Programming in C++, X Window System Programming, Visual C++ Developer's Guide, Borland C++ 4 Developer's Guide,* and *Linux Secrets*. His books have been translated into many languages, including Spanish, French, Polish, Greek, Italian, Chinese, Japanese, and Korean. Naba's most recent book is *Linux All-in-One Desk Reference For Dummies*, also published by Wiley Publishing, Inc.

Naba lives in North Potomac, Maryland, with his wife Leha, and their children, Ivy, Emily, and Ashley.

Dedication

I would like to dedicate this book to my wife Leha, and daughters Ivy, Emily, and Ashley.

Author's Acknowledgments

I am grateful to Terri Varveris for getting me started on this book — a *For Dummies* guide about the up and coming SUSE Linux. As the project editor, Linda Morris guided me through the manuscript-submission process and kept everything moving. I appreciate the guidance and support that Terri and Linda gave me during this project.

I would like to thank Susan Douglas for reviewing the manuscript for technical accuracy and providing many useful suggestions for improving the book's content.

Thanks to everyone at Wiley Publishing for transforming my raw manuscript into this well-edited and beautifully packaged book.

Of course, there would be no reason for this book if it were not for Linux. For this, we have Linus Torvalds and the legions of Linux developers around the world to thank. Thanks to Christian Egle, Andreas Jaeger, and others at Novell for providing beta copies of SUSE Linux and for the Special Edition DVD that's bundled with this book.

Finally, and as always, my greatest thanks go to my wife, Leha, and our daughters, Ivy, Emily, and Ashley — it is their love and support that keeps me going. Thanks for being there!

Publisher's Acknowledgments

We're proud of this book; please send us your comments through our online registration form located at www.dummies.com/register/.

Some of the people who helped bring this book to market include the following:

Acquisitions, Editorial, and Media Development

Project Editor: Linda Morris

Acquisitions Editor: Terri Varveris

Copy Editor: Linda Morris

Technical Editor: Susan Douglas

Editorial Manager: Carol Sheehan

Media Development Manager: Laura VanWinkle

Media Development Supervisor: Richard Graves

Editorial Assistant: Amanda Foxworth

Cartoons: Rich Tennant, www.the5thwave.com

Composition Services

Project Coordinator: Shannon Kepshire

Layout and Graphics: Carl Byers, Andrea Dahl, Lauren Goddard, Joyce Haughey, Heather Ryan

Proofreaders: Leeann Harney, Jessica Kramer, Carl William Pierce, Charles Spencer, TECHBOOKS Production Services

Indexer: TECHBOOKS Production Services

Publishing and Editorial for Technology Dummies

    Richard Swadley, Vice President and Executive Group Publisher

    Andy Cummings, Vice President and Publisher

    Mary Bednarek, Executive Acquisitions Director

    Mary C. Corder, Editorial Director

Publishing for Consumer Dummies

    Diane Graves Steele, Vice President and Publisher

    Joyce Pepple, Acquisitions Director

Composition Services

    Gerry Fahey, Vice President of Production Services

    Debbie Stailey, Director of Composition Services

Contents at a Glance

Introduction 1

Part I: Getting to Know SUSE 7
Chapter 1: What Is SUSE Linux? 9
Chapter 2: Installing SUSE Linux 23
Chapter 3: Starting SUSE for the First Time 39
Chapter 4: Taking Stock of What's in SUSE 55

Part II: Test Driving SUSE 63
Chapter 5: Exploring the SUSE Desktops 65
Chapter 6: Finding and Organizing Files 81
Chapter 7: I Want My Internet, Now! 105
Chapter 8: Setting Up an Ethernet LAN with Wireless Access 123

Part III: Doing Stuff with SUSE 139
Chapter 9: Browsing the Web 141
Chapter 10: E-Mailing and Instant Messaging in SUSE 155
Chapter 11: Reading Newsgroups 169
Chapter 12: Preparing Documents and Spreadsheets in SUSE Linux 183
Chapter 13: Doing Even More Office Stuff in SUSE Linux 205
Chapter 14: Playing Music and Burning CDs 217
Chapter 15: Working with Photos and Images 227
Chapter 16: What's a Shell and Why Do I Care? 243

Part IV: Becoming a SUSE Wizard 253
Chapter 17: Look Ma, I'm a Sysadmin! 255
Chapter 18: Updating SUSE and Adding New Software 273
Chapter 19: Securing SUSE Linux 287

Part V: The Part of Tens 309
Chapter 20: Ten Frequently Asked Questions about SUSE 311
Chapter 21: The Ten Best Things about SUSE 321
Chapter 22: Ten Great Web Sites for SUSE Maniacs 327
Chapter 23: Ten Most Commonly Used SUSE Commands 331
Appendix: About the DVD-ROM 341

Index 345

Table of Contents

Introduction 1
About This Book 2
Conventions Used in This Book 2
What You Don't Have to Read 3
Who Are You? 3
How This Book Is Organized 3
What's on the DVD? 4
Icons Used in This Book 4
Where to Go from Here 5

Part I: Getting to Know SUSE 7

Chapter 1: What Is SUSE Linux? 9
Getting a Handle on Linux 9
    Discovering SUSE Linux 12
    Making sense of Linux version numbers 12
What's in SUSE Linux? 13
    GNU software 13
    GUIs and applications 14
    Networks 15
    Internet servers 16
    Software development 16
    Online documentation 17
Figuring Out What You Can Do with SUSE Linux 17
    Disks, CD-ROMs, and DVD-ROMs 19
    Peripheral devices 19
    File systems and sharing 20
    Networking 20
Getting Started with SUSE Linux 21
    Install and configure SUSE Linux 21
    Explore SUSE Linux 22
    Use SUSE Linux 22

Chapter 2: Installing SUSE Linux 23
Introducing the Installation Steps 23
Checking Your PC's Hardware 24
Installing SUSE Linux 26
    Booting your PC from the DVD/CD-ROM drive 26
    Installing SUSE Linux from CDs or DVD 26

SUSE Linux 9.3 For Dummies

Chapter 3: Starting SUSE for the First Time 39
Powering Up SUSE Linux 39
Getting GUI 41
Setting Up Printers 45
Managing DVDs and CD-ROMs 48
Playing with the Shell 48
    Starting the bash shell 48
    Understanding shell commands 49
    Trying a few Linux commands 50
Shutting Down 52

Chapter 4: Taking Stock of What's in SUSE 55
Discovering the Internet Applications 55
Introducing the Office Applications 57
Exploring the Multimedia Applications 58
Cataloging the Image and Graphics Applications 60

Part II: Test Driving SUSE 63

Chapter 5: Exploring the SUSE Desktops 65
Discovering the Common Features of the Desktops 65
    Desktop context menus 67
    Icon context menus 68
    The panels 69
    The Main Menu or Programs Menu 70
Exploring KDE 74
Getting to Know GNOME 76

Chapter 6: Finding and Organizing Files 81
Figuring Out the Linux File System 81
Using GUI File Managers 85
    Conquering the file system with Konqueror 85
    Roaming the file system with Nautilus 88
Using Linux Commands to Manipulate Files and Directories 93
    Commands for directory navigation 94
    Commands for directory listings and permissions 95
    Commands for working with files 98
    Commands for working with directories 99
    Commands for finding files 100
    Commands for mounting and unmounting 101
    Commands for checking disk-space usage 102

Chapter 7: I Want My Internet, Now! 105
What Is the Internet? 105
Deciding How to Connect to the Internet 106

Table of Contents

Connecting to the Internet with DSL 108
    How DSL works 108
    Stirring the DSL alphabet soup: ADSL, IDSL, SDSL 110
    Typical DSL setup 110
Connecting to the Internet with a Cable Modem 114
    How cable modems work 114
    Typical cable modem setup 116
Dialing Up the Internet 119
    Connecting the modem 120
    Configuring the modem 121

Chapter 8: Setting Up an Ethernet LAN with Wireless Access 123

Getting a Handle on Ethernet 123
Connecting PCs to an Ethernet LAN 124
Configuring the Ethernet Network 125
Connecting Your LAN to the Internet 126
Extending Your LAN with a Wireless Network 128
    Understanding wireless Ethernet networking 128
    Understanding infrastructure and ad hoc modes 129
    Understanding Wired Equivalent Privacy (WEP) 130
    Setting up the wireless hardware 130
    Configuring the wireless access point 131
    Configuring wireless networking 132
Checking whether Your Network Is Up 135
    Checking the network interfaces 135
    Checking the IP routing table 136
    Checking connectivity to a host 136

Part III: Doing Stuff with SUSE *139*

Chapter 9: Browsing the Web 141

Understanding the World Wide Web 142
    Links and URLs 142
    Web servers and Web browsers 145
Web Browsing in SUSE Linux 146
Web Browsing with Konqueror in KDE 147
Web Browsing with Mozilla in GNOME 149
    Getting familiar with the Mozilla interface 150
    Changing your home page 152
Introducing Epiphany and Firefox 153

Chapter 10: E-Mailing and Instant Messaging in SUSE 155

Understanding E-Mail 156
    How MUA and MTA work 156
    Mail message enhancements 157

SUSE Linux 9.3 For Dummies

E-Mailing in SUSE Linux 158
    Introducing KMail 158
    Introducing Evolution Mail 160
Instant Messaging in SUSE Linux 163
    Using Kopete 164
    Using GAIM 166

Chapter 11: Reading Newsgroups 169

Understanding Newsgroups 169
    Newsgroup hierarchy 170
    Top-level newsgroup categories 171
    Some Linux-related newsgroups 172
Reading Newsgroups from Your ISP 173
    Taking stock of newsreaders in SUSE Linux 174
    Introducing KNode 174
    Introducing Pan 177
    Newsgroup subscriptions 179
    Posting news 179
Reading and Searching Newsgroups at Web Sites 180

Chapter 12: Preparing Documents and Spreadsheets in SUSE Linux 183

Writing with OpenOffice.org Writer 183
    Taking stock of OpenOffice.org Writer 184
    Getting started with Writer 185
    Setting up Writer 187
    Preparing documents in Writer 187
    Editing and reviewing documents 188
    Using styles and templates 189
    Doing page layout 192
    Creating and inserting graphics 194
    Using fields 195
    Working with large documents 196
Preparing Spreadsheets with OpenOffice.org Calc 197
    Taking stock of OpenOffice.org Calc 197
    Getting started with Calc 198
    Entering and formatting data 201
    Calculating and charting data 201

Chapter 13: Doing Even More Office Stuff in SUSE Linux 205

Keeping Track of Appointments and Tasks 205
Making Calculations 207
Making Presentations with OpenOffice.org Impress 208
    Taking stock of OpenOffice.org Impress 208
    Getting started with Impress 209
    Using Impress 212

Table of Contents | xv

    Preparing presentations 213
    Adding graphics and special effects 215
    Delivering presentations 216

Chapter 14: Playing Music and Burning CDs 217

  Playing Audio CDs 217
  Playing Music Files 219
  Burning a CD/DVD 221
    Burning CD/DVDs with K3b 221
    Burning data CDs in Nautilus 225

Chapter 15: Working with Photos and Images 227

  Downloading Photos from a Digital Camera 228
  Scanning Photos and Documents 232
  Editing Images with The GIMP 237
  Viewing Images 239
  Viewing PDF and PostScript Files 241

Chapter 16: What's a Shell and Why Do I Care? 243

  Opening Terminal Windows and Virtual Consoles 243
  Exploring the Bash Shell 244
    Understanding the syntax of shell commands 245
    Combining shell commands 246
    Controlling command input and output 246
    Typing less with automatic command completion 248
    Going wild with asterisks and question marks 248
    Repeating previously typed commands 250

Part IV: Becoming a SUSE Wizard 253

Chapter 17: Look Ma, I'm a Sysadmin! 255

  What Does a Sysadmin Do? 255
  Becoming root, When You Must 257
  Resetting a Forgotten root Password 257
  Introducing Your New Friend, YaST 259
  Starting and Stopping Services 261
    Understanding how Linux boots 261
    Trying a new run level with the init command 263
    Using YaST to start and stop services 264
    Manually starting and stopping services 264
  Checking Your System's Performance 265
    Using the top utility 265

Using the uptime command 267
Checking disk performance and disk usage............................268
Managing Hardware Devices 269
Managing User Accounts..270

Chapter 18: Updating SUSE and Adding New Software 273

Updating SUSE Linux Online...274
Locating and Installing Software Using YaST..277
Using RPM Commands to Work with RPM Files..280
Using the RPM commands 281
Understanding RPM filenames...281
Querying RPMs 282
Installing an RPM 284
Removing an RPM 285
Upgrading an RPM 285

Chapter 19: Securing SUSE Linux 287

Why Worry about Security?..287
Understanding Linux Security..288
Understanding the host security issues..288
Understanding network security issues..289
Getting Familiar with Computer Security Terminology 290
Practicing Good Host Security 295
Making passwords expire..295
Protecting files and directories 296
Securing the Network 300
Securing Internet services..301
Turning off stand-alone services 301
Configuring the Internet superserver 301
Configuring TCP wrapper security..302
Using Secure Shell (SSH) for remote logins.....................................303
Setting up a simple firewall 304
Using NATs...307
Keeping Up with Security News and Updates 308

Part V: The Part of Tens 309

Chapter 20: Ten Frequently Asked Questions about SUSE 311

What Does SUSE Stand for and How Do You Pronounce It? 311
How Can I Find Answers to My SUSE Linux Questions?..........................312
When Is the Next SUSE Linux Release?...312
Can I Get ISO Files for SUSE Linux from the Internet? 313

How Do I Do an FTP Install of SUSE Linux? 313
How Can I Auto-Login into the KDE Desktop as Another User? 316
If My System Crashes, Can I Press the Reset Button to Reboot? 318
How Can I Schedule a Command to Run Every 30 Minutes? 318
How Can I Find All the Huge Files on My SUSE Linux System? 319
Where Can I Find More SUSE RPMs? 320

Chapter 21: The Ten Best Things about SUSE 321

YaST — The Super Sysadmin Tool 321
Detects All Hardware (Well, Nearly All!) 322
Smooth and Easy Installation 322
I Love YOU — YaST Online Update 323
Automatic Mounting of My Windows
   Partitions and USB Memory Stick 323
Automatic Login at the KDE Desktop 324
Good Support for Laptops 324
Easy Browsing of Windows Shares 324
That Cute Gecko Mascot 324
SUSE's Increasing Popularity 325

Chapter 22: Ten Great Web Sites for SUSE Maniacs 327

http://www.suse.com 327
http://portal.suse.com/sdb/en/index.html 328
http://distrowatch.com/table.php?distribution=suse 328
http://www.suseforums.net 328
http://www.linuxquestions.org/questions/f60 329
http://www.linuxforums.org/forum/forum-36.html 329
http://www.linux-laptop.net/ 329
http://packman.links2linux.org 329
http://www.tldp.org/ 330
http://www.linuxhq.com/guides/ 330

Chapter 23: Ten Most Commonly Used SUSE Commands 331

apropos: Finding Commands Based on a Keyword 332
man: Reading Online Man Page 332
ls: Listing Files and Directories 333
cat: Feeding Input to Commands 333
grep: Searching for Text in Files 334
locate: Finding Files and Directories the Easy Way 335
chmod: Changing Permissions 336
rpm: Taming RPM Packages 337
tar: Packing and Unpacking Archives 337
pico: Editing Text Files 339

Appendix: About the DVD-ROM 341
  System Requirements 341
  DVD Installation Instructions 342
  What You'll Find on the DVD 343
  Troubleshooting 344

Index *345*

Introduction

SUSE Linux is an increasingly popular Linux distribution that competes head-on with Red Hat's Linux versions. SUSE Linux's fortunes have been on the rise following Novell's acquisition of Germany's SUSE Linux AG for $210 million. SUSE is looking for more growth in the U.S. marketplace, helped in part by IBM's $50 million investment in Novell as part of the SUSE acquisition deal. On another positive note, after acquiring SUSE, Novell announced that SUSE's famous YaST installation and configuration tool will become open source, licensed under the GNU General Public License. All these developments have generated a distinct "buzz" around SUSE Linux as the up-and-coming Linux distribution for everyone from home users to enterprise servers.

A significant factor in SUSE Linux's increasing popularity is that unlike its competitor Red Hat's singular focus on the enterprise market, Novell continues to address both the enterprise market and Linux enthusiasts. Specifically, the SUSE Linux Professional product is aimed at small-office/home-office users as well as those wishing to experiment with the SUSE Linux as their desktop system. SUSE Linux Professional is sold as boxed sets through distributors as well as online stores. SUSE Linux Professional with a typical retail price tag of $89.95 (with lower prices for students and for those updating from a previous version) is a complete Linux distribution, suitable for small office/home office or even an enterprise. This book includes a DVD with a Special Edition version of SUSE Linux Professional, with everything you need to use it as a personal desktop system. This book also includes a coupon that you can use to purchase a copy of the full SUSE Linux Professional distribution.

If you are starting out with SUSE Linux, you need a beginner's guide that not only gets you going with the installation and setup of SUSE Linux, but also shows you how to use all the tools that come with your desktop. That's why I wrote *SUSE Linux 9.3 For Dummies* in plain English, using a breezy style, that quickly gets to the step-by-step instructions for accomplishing a task, be it installing a printer or crafting a memo with OpenOffice.org Writer. My goal is to minimize confusion and keep things as simple as possible. I present the essential steps for specific tasks, but avoid inundating you with too many details.

About This Book

SUSE Linux 9.3 For Dummies is a beginner's guide for the upcoming SUSE Linux distribution. The approach to the subject matter and the writing style is that of the successful *For Dummies* series. The focus is on introducing you to the SUSE Linux desktop with all the GUI tools, including the office productivity suite (OpenOffice.org) and multimedia applications (audio player, digital camera, CD burning, image editing, and so on). I include a chapter on connecting to the Internet using cable/DSL modems and setting up a basic home network because these have become necessities for anyone who has more than one PC and, especially, for those who plan to run SUSE Linux on a PC. I also include a part that introduces the basics of routine system administration, how to add and update software, and how to tighten up the system's security.

Here are some of the things that this book shows you how to do:

- Install and configure SUSE Linux from the DVD-ROM included with the book.
- Connect the SUSE Linux system to the Internet through a DSL or cable modem.
- Set up dialup networking.
- Add a wireless Ethernet to your existing network.
- Get tips, techniques, and shortcuts for various uses of SUSE Linux, such as
    - Using the OpenOffice.org office suite
    - Browsing the Linux file system
    - Using Linux commands
    - Using multimedia applications
- Understand the basics of system and network security.
- Perform system administration tasks.

Conventions Used in This Book

I use a simple notational style in this book. All listings, filenames, commands, and keywords are typeset in a `monospace` font for ease of reading. I *italicize* the first occurrences of new terms and concepts, and then provide a definition right there. I show typed commands in **boldface**. The output of commands and any listing of files is shown in a `monospace` font.

What You Don't Have to Read

Each chapter zeros in on a specific task area — such as using the Internet or preparing documents with OpenOffice.org — and then provides hands-on instructions on how to perform a series of related tasks. You can jump right to a section and read about a specific task. You don't have to read anything but the few paragraphs or the list of steps that relate to your question. Use the Table of Contents or the Index to locate the pages relevant to your question.

You can safely ignore text next to the Technical Stuff icons as well as the sidebars. However, if you are the kind who likes to know some of the hidden details of how Linux works, by all means, dig into the Technical Stuff and the sidebars.

Who Are You?

I assume that you are somewhat familiar with a PC — you know how to turn it on and off and you have dabbled a bit with Windows. Considering that most new PCs come preloaded with Windows, this assumption is safe, right? And I assume that you know how to use some of the Windows applications such as Microsoft Office. Most of all, you want to either experiment with or switch to SUSE Linux as your desktop of choice.

When installing SUSE Linux on your PC, you may want to retain your Windows 2000 or Windows XP installations. I assume that you are willing to accept the risk that when you try to install SUSE Linux, some things may not quite work. Problems can happen if you have some uncommon types of hardware. If you are afraid of ruining your system, try finding a slightly older spare Pentium PC that you can sacrifice and then install Linux on that PC.

How This Book Is Organized

SUSE Linux 9.3 For Dummies contains 23 chapters organized into five parts. The book's organization is that of a typical *For Dummies* title that covers an operating system such as SUSE Linux where the reader is expected to install the software and then learn to use it. The five parts cover installation and setup, test driving the system to learn the ropes, using the system to do productive work, learning to be a budding system administrator, and the mandatory "Part of Tens." Here's a quick overview of the five parts and the appendix:

  ✔ **Part I: Getting to Know SUSE** introduces the reader to SUSE Linux, provides step-by-step installation instructions, and explains what happens when you start the system for the first time.

SUSE Linux 9.3 For Dummies

- **Part II: Test Driving SUSE** is about getting started with SUSE Linux — how to use the desktop and the file manager, how to connect to the Internet (and set up a home network), and figuring out what else is there to play with.

- **Part III: Doing Stuff with SUSE** turns to doing day-to-day things with the SUSE Linux system such as browsing the Web, reading e-mail and newsgroups, using the OpenOffice.org office suite and some multimedia applications, and, finally, working with the command line shell.

- **Part IV: Becoming a SUSE Wizard** includes chapters on the basic system administration and security. In particular, Part IV explains how to add new software and keep the SUSE system up to date with the YaST (Yet another Setup Tool) installation/configuration tool and YaST Online Update (YOU).

- **Part V: The Part of Tens** is the standard Part of Tens with chapters that present ten frequently asked questions about SUSE, ten best things about SUSE, ten great SUSE-related Web sites, and ten most commonly used SUSE Linux commands.

- **Appendix: About the DVD-ROM** summarizes the contents of the book's companion DVD-ROM.

What's on the DVD?

The DVD contains a Special Edition version of SUSE Linux 9.3 Professional. You may use the DVD in accordance with the license agreements accompanying the software. To find out more about the contents of the DVD, please consult the appendix.

Sidebars

Sometimes I use sidebars to highlight interesting, but not critical, information. Sidebars explain concepts you may not have encountered before or give a little insight into a related topic. If you're in a hurry, you can safely skip the sidebars.

Icons Used in This Book

Following the time-honored tradition of the *For Dummies* series, I use icons to help you quickly pinpoint useful information. The icons include the following:

The Remember icon marks a general interesting fact — something that I think you might want to know and remember.

The Tip icon indicates things that you can do to make your job easier.

The Warning icon highlights potential pitfalls. With this icon, I'm telling you: "Watch out! This could hurt your system!"

The Technical Stuff icon marks technical information that could be of interest to an advanced user (or those of us aspiring to be advanced users).

Where to Go from Here

It's time to get started on your SUSE Linux adventure. Take out the DVD and install SUSE Linux, following the instructions in Chapter 2. Then, turn to a relevant chapter and let the fun begin. Use the Table of Contents and the Index to figure out where you want to go. Before you know it, you'll become an expert at SUSE Linux!

I hope you enjoy reading this book as much as I enjoyed writing it!

Part I
Getting to Know SUSE

The 5th Wave — By Rich Tennant

"OK—ANTIDOTE, ANTIDOTE, WHAT WOULD AN ANTIDOTE ICON LOOK LIKE? YOU KNOW, I STILL HAVEN'T GOT THIS DESKTOP THE WAY I WANT IT."

In this part...

This part is all about getting you started on your way to a lasting relationship with SUSE Linux. Before you can begin your SUSE Linux experience, I spend a chapter explaining what SUSE Linux is and what you can do with SUSE Linux (pretty much anything you can do with a PC that runs Windows).

To start using SUSE Linux, first you must install SUSE Linux on your PC's hard drive. SUSE Linux installation is quite simple, and I explain everything in Chapter 2. In Chapter 3 of this part, I guide you through a quick tour of SUSE Linux, primarily focusing on the key steps: booting the system, logging in, using the KDE and GNOME desktops, and shutting down the system.

The final chapter in this part gives you an overview of all the applications in SUSE Linux — as a precursor to using these applications to get some productive work out of your SUSE Linux system.

Chapter 1

What Is SUSE Linux?

In This Chapter
▶ Explaining what Linux is
▶ Going over what SUSE Linux includes
▶ Introducing you to what SUSE Linux helps you do
▶ Getting started with SUSE Linux

I bet you've heard about Linux, even if you may not know much about SUSE (pronounced *soo-za*) Linux. Even if you haven't, don't worry: I'll explain everything about Linux, what the different names like SUSE and Red Hat mean, what SUSE Linux includes, and how to get started with SUSE Linux.

By the way, SUSE Linux runs on computers with Intel 80x86 and Pentium processors (basically any PC that can run any flavor of Windows). If you have a PC, you can install SUSE Linux on it and experience firsthand what the fuss is all about.

Getting a Handle on Linux

You know that your PC is a bunch of *hardware* — things you can touch, like the system box, monitor, keyboard, and mouse, as shown in Figure 1-1. The system box contains the most important hardware of all — the *central processing unit* (CPU), the microchip that runs the *software* (any program that tells the computer how to do your bidding), which you actually *can't* touch. In a typical Pentium 4 PC, the Pentium 4 microprocessor is the CPU. Other important hardware in the system box includes the memory (RAM chips) and the hard drive — and one program has to run all this stuff and get it to play nice: the operating system.

Figure 1-1: A simplified view of a computer and how it runs computer programs.

Memory
Transient storage where programs are loaded and executed by the CPU

Central Processing Unit (CPU)
The computer's brain—the microprocessor—that executes the instructions contained in the program loaded into memory

Disk
Permanent storage where programs are loaded and data are stored in files

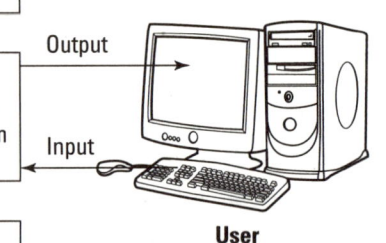

The *operating system* is software that manages all the hardware and runs other software at your command. You, the user, communicate those commands by clicking menus and icons or by typing some cryptic text. Linux is an operating system — as are UNIX, Windows 98, Windows 2000, and Windows XP. The Linux operating system — also called the *Linux kernel* — is modeled after UNIX.

The operating system is what gives a computer — any computer — its personality. For example, you can run Windows 98 or Windows XP on a PC — and on that same PC, you can *also* install and run Linux. That means, depending on which operating system is installed and running at any particular time, *the same PC* can be a Windows 98, Windows XP, or Linux system.

The primary job of an operating system is to load software (computer programs) from the hard drive (or other permanent storage) into the memory and get the CPU to run those programs. Everything you do with your computer is possible because of the operating system — so if the operating system somehow messes up, the whole system freezes up. You know how infuriating it is when your favorite operating system — maybe even the one that came with your PC — suddenly calls it quits just as you were about to click the Send button after composing that long e-mail to your friend. You try the three-finger salute (pressing Ctrl+Alt+Del), but nothing happens. Then it's time to try the Reset button (provided your computer's builders were wise enough to include one). Luckily, that sort of thing almost never happens with Linux — it has a reputation for being a very reliable operating system.

In technical mumbo jumbo, Linux is a *multiuser, multitasking operating system*. This means that Linux enables multiple users to log in, and Linux can run more than one program at the same time. Nearly all operating systems are

> **Does Linux really run on any computer?**
>
> Well, it runs on almost any computer. Let's see.... Nowadays, you can get versions of Linux for systems based on Intel 80x86, Pentium, and other Intel compatible processors; AMD's 64-bit AMD64 processors; the Motorola 68000 family; Alpha AXPs; Sun SPARCs and UltraSPARCs; Hewlett-Packard's HP PA-RISC; the PowerPC and PowerPC64 processors; the MIPS R4x00 and R5x00; even IBM mainframes.

multiuser and multitasking these days, but when Linux first started in 1994, *multiuser* and *multitasking* were big selling points.

All the different names that you hear for Linux — SUSE, Red Hat, Debian, Knoppix, Xandros, you name it — are actually the names of different Linux distributions.

A *Linux distribution* is basically the Linux *kernel* (the operating system) together with a huge collection of applications, along with an easy-to-use installation program. By the way, most people just say *Linux* to refer to a specific Linux distribution.

Many different Linux distributions exist, and each includes the standard Linux operating system and the following major packages:

- **The X Window System:** The graphical user interface.
- **One or more graphical desktops:** Among the most popular are GNOME and KDE.
- **A collection of applications:** Linux programs come in the form of ready-to-run software, but the *source code* (the commands humans use to tell the computer what to do) is included (or easily available), as is its documentation.

    Current Linux distributions include a huge selection of software — so much that it usually requires multiple CD-ROMs or a single DVD-ROM (which this book includes).

The development and maintenance of the Linux kernel, software packages in a Linux distribution, and the Linux distributions themselves are organized as open source projects. In a nutshell, *open source* means you have access to the source code and the right to freely redistribute the software without any restrictions. My succinct definition is pretty basic, so to find out more details of what *open source* means and to see some acceptable open source licenses, please visit the Open Source Initiative Web site at `www.opensource.org`.

Discovering SUSE Linux

SUSE Linux is a commercial distribution that focuses on the desktop and includes some proprietary components that prevent its redistribution. You can buy SUSE Linux online or in computer stores and bookstores. If you have heard about *open source* and the *GNU (GNU's not UNIX)* license, you may think that no one can sell Linux for a profit. Luckily for companies that sell Linux distributions, the GNU (pronounced *gah-nu*) license — also called the GNU General Public License (GPL) — does allow commercial, for-profit distribution, but requires that the software be distributed in source-code form, and stipulates that anyone may copy and distribute the software in source-code form to anyone else. Several Linux distributions are available free of charge under the GPL. For this book, SUSE has graciously provided us with a Special Edition version of SUSE Linux that's included with this book.

I tell you a lot more about SUSE in this book, but you can also visit www.suse.com for more information (especially the latest news) about SUSE Linux.

Making sense of Linux version numbers

Both the Linux kernel and a Linux distribution such as SUSE Linux have their own version numbers, not to mention the many other software programs (such as GNOME and KDE) that come with the Linux distribution. The version numbers for the Linux kernel and the Linux distribution are unrelated, but each has particular significance.

Linux kernel version numbers

After Linux kernel version 1.0 was released on March 14, 1994, the loose-knit Linux development community adopted a version-numbering scheme. Version numbers such as 1.*X.Y* and 2.*X.Y,* where *X* is an even number, are considered the stable versions. The last number, *Y,* is the patch level, which is incremented as problems are fixed. For example, 2.6.9 is a typical, stable version of the Linux kernel. Notice that these version numbers are in the form of three integers separated by periods — *Major.Minor.Patch* — where *Major* and *Minor* are numbers denoting the major and minor version numbers, and *Patch* is another number representing the patch level.

Version numbers of the form 2.*X.Y* with an odd *X* number are beta releases for developers only; they may be unstable, so you should not adopt such versions for day-to-day use. For example, when you look at version 2.5.65 of the Linux kernel, notice the odd number *5* — that tells you it's a beta release. Developers add new features to these odd-numbered versions of Linux.

You can find out about the latest version of the Linux kernel online at www.kernel.org.

SUSE Linux version numbers

Each Linux distribution has a version number as well and SUSE Linux is no exception. These version numbers are usually of the form *X.Y,* where *X* is the major version and *Y* the minor version. Unlike with the Linux kernel version numbers, no special meaning is associated with odd and even minor versions. Each version of a SUSE Linux includes specific versions of the Linux kernel and other major components, such as GNOME, KDE, and various applications.

SUSE usually releases new versions of SUSE Linux on a regular basis — every six months or so. For example, SUSE Linux 9.0 was released in October 2003, 9.1 was released in April 2004, and 9.2 came out in October 2004. Typically, each new major version of SUSE Linux provides significant new features.

What's in SUSE Linux?

A Linux distribution comes with the Linux kernel and a whole lot of software. These software packages include everything from the graphical desktops to Internet servers to programming tools to create new software. In this section, I briefly describe some major software packages that come bundled with SUSE Linux. Without this bundled software, SUSE Linux wouldn't be as popular as it is today.

When you install SUSE Linux, not all software packages are installed by default. This book's companion DVD, however, includes most of the packages I describe in the following sections.

GNU software

At the heart of SUSE Linux is a collection of software that came from the GNU Project. You get to know these GNU utilities only if you use your Linux system through a text terminal (or a graphical window that mimics one) — a basic *command line interface* that puts nothing much on-screen but a prompt that enables you to type in your commands. The GNU software is one of the basic parts of any Linux distribution.

As a Linux user, you may not realize the extent to which all Linux distributions rely on GNU software. Nearly all the tasks you perform in a Linux system involve one or more GNU software packages. For example, the GNOME graphical user interface (GUI) and the command interpreter (that is, the `bash` shell) are both GNU software programs. By the way, the *shell* is the command-interpreter application that accepts the commands you type and then runs programs in response to those commands. If you rebuild the kernel or develop software, you do so with the GNU C and C++ compiler (which is part of the GNU software that accompanies Linux). If you edit text files with the `ed` or `emacs` editor, you again use a GNU software package. The list goes on and on.

> ## The GNU Project
>
> GNU is a recursive acronym that stands for *GNU's not UNIX*. The GNU Project was launched in 1984 by Richard Stallman to develop a complete UNIX-like operating system. The GNU Project developed nearly everything needed for a complete operating system except for the operating system kernel. All GNU software was distributed under the GNU General Public License (GPL). GPL essentially requires that the software is distributed in source-code form and stipulates that any user may copy, modify, and distribute the software to anyone else in source-code form. Users may, however, have to pay for their individual copies of GNU software.
>
> The Free Software Foundation (FSF) is a tax-exempt charity that raises funds for work on the GNU Project. To find out more about the GNU Project, visit its home page at `www.gnu.org`. You can find information about how to contact the Free Software Foundation and how to help the GNU Project.

GUIs and applications

Face it — typing cryptic Linux commands on a terminal is boring. For average users, using the system through a *graphical user interface* (*GUI,* pronounced "gooey") — one that gives you pictures to click and windows (with a small *w*) to open — is much easier. This is where the X Window System, or X, comes to the rescue.

X is kind of like Microsoft Windows, but the underlying details of how X works are completely different from Windows. Unlike Windows, X provides the basic features of displaying windows on-screen, but it does not come with any specific look or feel for graphical applications. That look and feel comes from GUIs, such as GNOME and KDE, which make use of the X Window System.

SUSE Linux comes with the X Window System in the form of X.Org X11 — an implementation of the X Window System for 80x86 systems. X.Org X11 works with a wide variety of video cards used in today's PCs.

As for the GUI, SUSE Linux includes a choice of two powerful GUI desktops: KDE (K Desktop Environment) and GNOME (GNU Network Model Environment). You can choose to install either KDE or GNOME on your system. KDE and GNOME provide desktops similar to those of Microsoft Windows and Apple Mac OS. With GNOME or KDE, you can begin using your SUSE Linux system without having to know cryptic Linux commands. However, if you ever need to use those commands directly (or when you become a Linux expert and want to use commands), all you have to do is open a terminal window and type them at the prompt.

SUSE Linux also comes with many graphical applications. The most noteworthy program is The GIMP (GNU Image Manipulation Program), a program for working with photos and other images. The GIMP's capabilities are on a par with Adobe Photoshop.

Providing common productivity software — such as word-processing, spreadsheet, and database applications — is an area in which Linux used to be lacking. This situation has changed, however. SUSE Linux comes with the OpenOffice.org office productivity applications. In addition, you may want to check out these prominent, commercially available office productivity applications for Linux that are not included on the companion DVD-ROM:

- **Applixware Office:** This office package is a good example of productivity software for Linux. You can find it at www.vistasource.com.
- **StarOffice:** From Sun Microsystems (www.sun.com/staroffice), StarOffice is another well-known productivity software package.
- **CrossOver Office:** From CodeWeavers (www.codeweavers.com/site/products), you can use CrossOver Office to install your Microsoft Office applications (Office 97, Office 2000, and Office XP) in Linux.

As you can see, plenty of Linux office applications are compatible with Microsoft Office.

Networks

SUSE Linux comes with everything you need to use the system on a network so that the system can exchange data with other systems. On networks, computers that exchange data have to follow well-defined rules or protocols. A *network protocol* is a method that the sender and receiver agree upon for exchanging data across a network. Such a protocol is similar to the rules you might follow when you're having a polite conversation with someone at a party. You typically start by saying hello, exchanging names, and then taking turns talking. That's about the same way network protocols work. The two computers use the protocol to send bits and bytes back and forth across the network.

One of the most well-known and popular network protocols is Transmission Control Protocol/Internet Protocol (TCP/IP). TCP/IP is the protocol of choice on the Internet — the "network of networks" that now spans the globe. Linux supports the TCP/IP protocol and any network applications that make use of TCP/IP.

Internet servers

Some popular network applications are specifically designed to deliver information from one system to another. When you send electronic mail (e-mail) or visit Web sites using a Web browser, you use these network applications (also called Internet services). Here are some common Internet services:

- ✓ Electronic mail (e-mail) that you use to send messages to any other person on the Internet using addresses like `joe@someplace.com`.
- ✓ World Wide Web (or simply, Web) that you browse using a Web browser.
- ✓ News services, where you can read newsgroups and post news items to newsgroups with names such as `comp.os.linux.networking` or `comp.os.linux.setup`.
- ✓ File-transfer utilities that you can use to upload and download files.
- ✓ Remote login that you can use to connect to and work with another computer (the remote computer) on the Internet — assuming you have the required username and password to access that remote computer.

A SUSE Linux PC can offer these Internet services. To do so, the PC must be connected to the Internet and it must run special server software called *Internet servers*. Each of the servers uses a specific protocol for transferring information. For example, here are some common Internet servers that you find in SUSE Linux:

- ✓ Sendmail: Mail server for exchanging e-mail messages between systems using SMTP (Simple Mail Transfer Protocol).
- ✓ Apache Web server: For sending documents from one system to another using HTTP (Hypertext Transfer Protocol).
- ✓ `vsftpd`: FTP server for transferring files between computers on the Internet using FTP (File Transfer Protocol).
- ✓ `innd`: News server for distribution of news articles in a store-and-forward fashion across the Internet using NNTP (Network News Transfer Protocol).
- ✓ `sshd`: For securely logging in to the system using the SSH (Secure Shell) protocol.

Software development

SUSE Linux is particularly well-suited to software development. Straight out of the box, it's not configured for software development, but you can easily install all the necessary software-development tools such as the compiler and libraries of code needed to build programs. If you happen to know UNIX and the C programming language, you will feel right at home programming in Linux.

Chapter 1: What Is SUSE Linux? 17

As far as the development environment in SUSE Linux goes, you can use the same basic tools (such as an editor, a compiler, and a debugger) that you might use on other UNIX workstations, such as those from IBM, Sun Microsystems, and Hewlett-Packard (HP). What this means is that if you work by day on one of these UNIX workstations, you can use a Linux PC in the evening at home to duplicate that development environment at a fraction of the cost. Then you can either complete work projects at home or devote your time to writing software for fun and to share on the Internet.

Online documentation

As you become more adept at using Linux, you may want to look up information quickly — without having to turn the pages of (ahem) this great book, for example. Luckily, Linux comes with enough online information to jog your memory in those situations when you vaguely recall a command's name, but can't remember the exact syntax of what you're supposed to type.

If you use Linux commands, you can view the manual page — commonly referred to as the *man page* — for a command by using the man command. (You do have to remember that command in order to access online help.)

You can also get help from the GUI desktops. Both GNOME and KDE desktops come with Help viewers to view online help information. In KDE, choose Main Menu⇨SUSE Help Center and in GNOME choose Desktop Menu⇨SUSE Help Center from the top panel (you learn the details in Chapter 3). You can then browse the help information by clicking the links on the initial Help window. Figure 1-2 shows a typical Help window — this one from the KDE desktop.

Figuring Out What You Can Do with SUSE Linux

As an operating system, SUSE Linux acts as the intermediary through which you, the "lord of the system," control all the hardware and software in your PC. The hardware includes the system box, the monitor, the keyboard, the mouse, and anything else connected to the system box. The catchall term *peripheral* refers to any equipment attached to the system. If you use a laptop computer, all your hardware is packaged into the laptop.

Inside that system box is the system's brain — the microprocessor (Intel Pentium 4, for example) or the central processing unit (CPU) — that performs the instructions contained in a computer program. When the microprocessor is running a computer program, that program's instructions are stored in the memory or RAM. RAM stands for *Random Access Memory* (that means any part of the memory can be accessed randomly — in arbitrary order).

Part I: Getting to Know SUSE

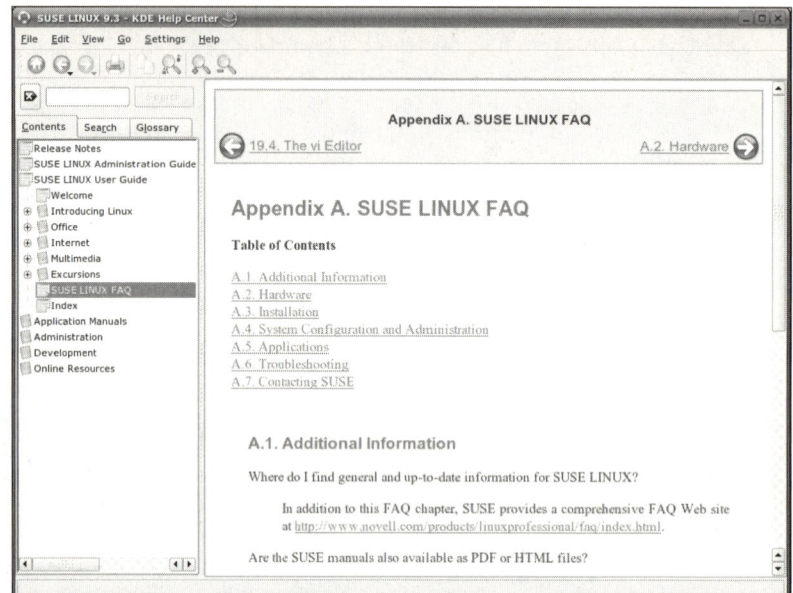

Figure 1-2: Online help is available from the GUI desktops.

The system box has another crucial component — the hard drive (or hard disk, as it is sometimes called). The hard drive is the permanent storage space for computer programs and data. It's permanent in the sense that the contents don't disappear when you power off the PC. The hard drive is organized into files, which are in turn organized in a hierarchical fashion into directories and subdirectories (somewhat like organizing papers in folders inside the drawers of a file cabinet).

To keep a Linux system running properly, you or someone else has to make sure that the hardware is working properly and that the files are backed up regularly. There is also the matter of security — making sure that only legitimate people can access and use the system. These tasks are called *system administration*.

If you are using SUSE Linux at a big facility with many computers, a full-time system administrator probably takes care of all system administration tasks. On the other hand, if you are running SUSE Linux on a home PC, you are the system administrator. Don't let the thought frighten you. You don't have to know any magic incantations or prepare cryptic configuration files to be a system administrator.

SUSE Linux includes a graphical configuration and setup tool called YaST that makes system administration a "point-and-click" job, just like running any other application. Incidentally, you first encounter YaST when you install SUSE Linux following the directions in Chapter 2.

Disks, CD-ROMs, and DVD-ROMs

SUSE Linux typically comes on a single DVD-ROM or several CD-ROMs. After installation, the Linux kernel and all the applications are stored on your hard drive — which is where your PC looks first when you tell it to do something.

Typically, the hard drive is prepared to use SUSE Linux during the installation process. After that, you usually leave the hard drive alone except to back up the data stored there or (occasionally) to install new applications.

Using CD-ROMs or DVD-ROMs in SUSE Linux is easy. While you are logged in at the GNOME or KDE desktop, just pop a CD or DVD in the drive, and the system should automatically detect the DVD/CD-ROM. A graphical file manager automatically opens and displays the contents of the DVD/CD-ROM. If all else fails, you can type a simple `mount` command in a terminal window and associate the DVD/CD-ROM with a directory on your system. This whole process of accessing the files on a CD or a DVD from Linux is called *mounting the CD or the DVD*.

Besides the hard drive and DVD/CD-ROM drive, of course, your PC may have other drives, such as a floppy disk or Zip drive, and using those disks in Linux is also simple: You insert a disk and double-click the icon that represents the disk drive on the GUI desktop. Doing so mounts the disk so that you can begin using it.

Peripheral devices

Anything connected to your PC is a peripheral device, and so are some components like sound cards that are installed inside the system box. You can configure and manage these peripheral devices in SUSE Linux with YaST.

One of the common peripherals is a printer, typically hooked up to the parallel port of your PC. YaST includes a graphical printer configuration tool that you can use to configure the printer.

Another peripheral device that needs configuration is the sound card. SUSE Linux can detect and configure the sound card during installation, just as Windows does. However, if SUSE Linux cannot detect the sound card correctly, you can use YaST to configure the sound card.

SUSE Linux configures other peripheral devices such as the mouse and keyboard at the time of installation. You can pretty much leave them alone after installation.

Nowadays, PCs come with the USB (Universal Serial Bus) interface; many devices, including printers and scanners, plug into a PC's USB port. One nice feature of USB devices is that you can plug them into the USB port and unplug them at any time — the device does not have to be connected when you power up the system. These devices are called *hot plugs* because you can plug in a device when the system is hot, meaning while it's running. SUSE Linux supports many hot plug USB devices. When you plug a device into the USB port, SUSE Linux loads the correct driver and makes the device available to applications.

SUSE Linux also supports Bluetooth, which is a low-power, short-range wireless technology for connecting devices to your PC. Devices that use Bluetooth can usually connect when they are within 10 meters of one another. (To find out more about Bluetooth, visit www.bluetooth.com.) If your PC includes Bluetooth capability, you could use a wireless keyboard and mouse that connect to the PC using Bluetooth. SUSE Linux supports such Bluetooth devices.

File systems and sharing

The whole organization of directories and files is called the *file system*. You can, of course, manage the file system using Linux. When you browse the files from the GNOME or KDE graphical desktop, you work with the familiar folder icons.

A key task in caring for a file system is to back up important files. In SUSE Linux, you can use the tar program to archive one or more directories on a floppy or a Zip drive. You can even back up files on a tape (if you have a tape drive). If you have a CD/DVD burner, you can also burn a CD or a DVD with the files you want to back up or save for posterity.

SUSE Linux can also share parts of the file system with other systems on a network. For example, you can use the Network File System (NFS) to share files with other systems on the network. To a user on the system, the remote system's files appear to be in a directory on the local system.

SUSE Linux also comes with the Samba package, which supports file sharing with Microsoft Windows systems. Samba makes a Linux system work just like a Windows file or print server. You can also access shared folders on other Windows systems on your network.

Networking

Now that most PCs are either in a local area network or connected to the Internet, you need to manage the network as well. You set up the local area network when you install SUSE Linux. For connecting to the Internet using a modem, you can use YaST.

If you connect to the Internet using DSL (that's the fast Internet connection from the phone company) or a cable modem, you need a PC with an Ethernet card that connects to the cable or DSL modem. It also means that you have to set up a local area network and configure the Ethernet card. But fortunately, these steps are typically a part of the SUSE Linux installation. If you want to do the configurations later, you can — by using a GUI network configuration tool accessible from YaST.

SUSE Linux also includes tools for configuring a *firewall,* a protective buffer that helps keep your system relatively secure from anyone trying to snoop over your Internet connection. You can configure the firewall by running a GUI firewall configuration tool accessible from YaST.

Getting Started with SUSE Linux

Based on my personal experience in learning new subjects, I recommend a three-step process to get started with SUSE Linux:

1. **Install and Configure SUSE Linux on your PC.**
2. **Explore SUSE Linux — the GUI desktop and the applications.**
3. **Use SUSE Linux for your day-to-day work.**

In the following sections, I explain this prescription a bit more.

Install and configure SUSE Linux

Your PC probably came with some flavor of Microsoft Windows. So the first step is to get SUSE Linux onto your PC. This book comes with SUSE Linux — all you have to do is follow the instructions in Chapter 2 to install it.

Just to pique your curiosity, you can keep both Windows and SUSE Linux on the PC; the SUSE Linux installer can split up the space on the hard drive into two parts — one part for Windows and the other for installing SUSE Linux. During the SUSE Linux installation, you configure many items — from the network card (if any) to the X Window System.

As you'll find out for yourself, SUSE Linux installation is very easy, especially with the graphical YaST installer.

After you install SUSE Linux, you can configure individual system components (for example, the printer) and tweak any needed settings that aren't configured during installation.

You also can configure your GUI desktop of choice — GNOME or KDE. Each has configuration tools. You can use these tools to adjust the look and feel of the desktop (background, fonts, screen saver, and even the entire color scheme).

After you're through with the configuration step, all the hardware on your system and the applications should run to your liking.

Explore SUSE Linux

With a properly configured SUSE Linux PC at your disposal, you can start exploring SUSE Linux. You can begin the exploration from the GUI desktop that you get after logging in.

Explore the GUI desktops — GNOME and KDE — and the folders and files that make up the Linux file system. You can also try out the applications from the desktop. SUSE Linux comes with office and multimedia applications and databases that you can begin using.

Also try out the *shell* — open up a terminal window and type some Linux commands in that window. You can also explore the text editors that work in text mode. Knowing how to edit text files without the GUI is a good idea. At least you won't be helpless if the GUI is unavailable for some reason.

Use SUSE Linux

After you explore the SUSE Linux landscape and know what is what, you can then start using SUSE Linux for your day-to-day work — browsing the Web, using Office applications such as a word processor and spreadsheet, listen to music, burn a music CD, and anything else you want.

Of course, you can expect to become increasingly proficient in SUSE Linux as time goes on. After all, learning is a lifelong journey.

Bon voyage!

Chapter 2
Installing SUSE Linux

In This Chapter
- Understanding the installation steps
- Checking your PC's hardware
- Installing SUSE Linux
- Configuring SUSE Linux

Most PCs come with Microsoft Windows preinstalled, so you typically never have to go through the Windows installation (except when something goes wrong, of course). To run SUSE Linux, however, you first have to install it on your PC. All you have to do to install SUSE Linux is take out the DVD that comes with this book and follow the steps in this chapter.

You can install SUSE Linux in addition to Microsoft Windows and simply select one or the other operating system after you power up the PC. The SUSE Linux installer can shrink the disk space used by Windows and create a new *disk partition* — basically set aside a part of the hard drive for SUSE Linux.

Before you get started, just take a deep breath and exhale slooowwwly. You have nothing to worry about because I explain everything in this chapter.

Introducing the Installation Steps

Before getting started with the installation, I find it helpful to go over the entire sequence of installation steps, without the gory details. In this section, I show you the road map for the installation process. Then you can follow the detailed steps and install SUSE Linux from this book's companion DVD.

Here are the general steps for installing SUSE Linux:

1. **Check your PC's hardware to make sure everything works with SUSE Linux.**

2. **Make sure that your PC can boot from the DVD/CD-ROM drive.**

You may have to get into SETUP and change the order of boot devices.

3. **Boot your PC from the DVD.**

   At the initial boot screen, use the arrow keys to select Installation and press Enter. This starts SUSE's graphical installer — YaST — that you use to complete the installation.

4. **Select the installation language and then select New Installation.**

   YaST then gathers information about your PC and displays a set of installation settings.

5. **If you are going to add SUSE Linux to a PC that already has any version of Microsoft Windows on the hard drive, edit the Partitioning setting and select the hard drive as the location where you want to install SUSE Linux.**

   Then YaST gives you the option to shrink the Windows partition. In particular, YaST can resize Windows XP partitions that use the NTFS file system. When you resize the Windows partition, everything is safe until you confirm that installation should begin.

6. **Edit any other installation settings.**

   In particular, you probably have to edit the time zone to suit your geographic location. You have to edit the software selection if you want a GNOME desktop instead of the default KDE desktop.

7. **After you have finished editing the installation settings, accept the selections and confirm that YaST should begin installing.**

   This is the point of no return. YaST formats the selected disk partition and begins copying files from the DVD onto the hard drive.

8. **After installing a minimal SUSE Linux system, YaST reboots the PC.**

   After the initial version of SUSE Linux starts again, YaST guides you through a number of configuration steps that include setting the root (superuser) password; configuring the network and firewall; setting up online updates of SUSE Linux; creating a normal user account; and configuring hardware such as a graphics card, printer, and sound card.

9. **At the end of the installation, YaST reboots the PC. When SUSE Linux runs again, you should get the GUI desktop.**

Checking Your PC's Hardware

If you are concerned that your PC may not be able to run SUSE Linux, here are some of the key components in your PC that you need to consider before you start the SUSE Linux installation:

Chapter 2: Installing SUSE Linux 25

- **Processor:** A 400 MHz Pentium II or better is best. The processor speed, expressed in MHz (megahertz) or GHz (gigahertz), is not that important as long as it's over 400 MHz, but the faster the better. Linux can run on other Intel-compatible processors such as AMD, Cyrix, and VIA processors.

- **RAM:** RAM is the amount of memory your system has. As with processing speed, the more RAM, the better. You need 256MB to install both SUSE Linux and to comfortably run a GUI desktop.

- **DVD/CD-ROM:** You must have a DVD/CD-ROM drive and the PC must be able to boot from that drive. The exact model doesn't matter. What matters is how the DVD/CD-ROM drive connects to the PC. Most new PCs have DVD/CD-ROM drives that connect to the hard drive controller (called IDE for Integrated Drive Electronics or ATA for AT Attachment). If you add an external DVD/CD drive, it most likely connects to the USB port. Any IDE/ATA or USB DVD/CD-ROM works in SUSE Linux.

- **Hard drives:** Any IDE disk drive works in SUSE Linux. Another type of hard drive controller is SCSI (Small Computer System Interface), which SUSE Linux also supports. To comfortably install and play with SUSE Linux, you need about 5GB of hard drive space.

- **Keyboard:** All keyboards work with SUSE Linux and the X Window System.

- **Mouse:** The installation program can detect the mouse. All types of mice (such as PS/2 or USB) work with SUSE Linux and the X Window System.

- **Video card:** SUSE Linux works fine with all video cards (also known as *display adapters*) in text mode, but if you want the GUI desktop, you need a video card that works with the X Window System. The installer can detect a supported video card and configure the X Window System correctly. However, if the installer cannot detect the video card, it helps if you know the make and model of your video card.

- **Monitor:** The kind of monitor is not particularly critical except that it must be capable of displaying the screen resolutions that the video card uses. The screen resolution is expressed in terms of the number of picture elements (pixels), horizontally and vertically (for example, 1024 x 768). The installer can detect most modern monitors. If it does not detect your monitor, you can select a generic monitor type with a specific resolution such as 1024 x 768. You can also specify the monitor by its make and model (which you can find on the back of the monitor).

- **Network interface card (NIC):** Not all PCs have network interface cards, but if yours does, the installer can probably detect and use it. If you have problems, try to find the make and model (such as *Linksys LNE100TX Fast Ethernet Adapter*) so that you can search for information on whether SUSE Linux supports that card or not.

- **SCSI controller:** Some high-performance PCs have SCSI controllers that connect disk drives and other peripherals to a PC. If your PC happens to have a SCSI controller, you might want to find out the make and model of the controller.

- **Sound card:** If your PC has a sound card and you want to have sound in SUSE Linux, you have to make sure it's compatible. You can configure the sound card after successfully installing SUSE Linux.
- **Modem:** If you plan to dial out to the Internet, you need a modem that Linux supports. For software-based modems, called *soft modems* or *winmodems,* you may have to download a driver from the manufacturer (it may or may not be freely available).

In addition to this hardware, you also need to find out the make and model of any printer you plan to use in SUSE Linux.

To check if your PC's hardware is compatible with SUSE Linux, visit the SUSE Linux Hardware Database at hardwaredb.suse.de.

Installing SUSE Linux

The companion DVD does not include the full SUSE Linux Professional distribution because it's a commercial product. Instead, the DVD includes a Special Edition, which is similar to the personal edition that SUSE used to sell in versions prior to 9.2. In this section, I describe the installation process for the companion DVD, but the steps are similar if you were to install SUSE Linux Professional.

Booting your PC from the DVD/CD-ROM drive

Most new PCs can boot directly from the DVD/CD-ROM drive, but some PCs may require intervention from you. Typically, the PC may be set to boot from the hard drive before the DVD/CD drive, and you have to get into SETUP to change the order of boot devices. To set up a PC to boot from the DVD drive, you have to go into SETUP as the PC powers up. The exact steps for entering SETUP and setting the boot device vary from one PC to the next, but typically they involve pressing a key such as F2. As the PC powers up, a brief message tells you what key to press to enter SETUP. When you're in SETUP, you can designate the DVD/CD drive as the boot device. After your PC is set up to boot from the DVD/CD drive, simply put the DVD in the DVD/CD drive and restart your PC.

Installing SUSE Linux from CDs or DVD

To install SUSE Linux from CDs or a DVD, simply insert the first CD or the DVD into your PC's CD/DVD drive and restart your PC (in Windows, choose

Chapter 2: Installing SUSE Linux

Start➪Shutdown and then select Restart from the dialog box). If you are using CDs, the installation steps are the same as that for the DVD except that you have to swap CDs when prompted by the installation program.

After your PC powers up, a boot loader starts and displays an initial boot screen with a menu of items. Table 2-1 lists these boot menu items and their meaning. As you can see, you can perform a number of tasks from the boot screen, including booting an existing installation from the hard drive and starting a rescue system.

Table 2-1	SUSE Installer Boot Menu Items
Select This Item	*To Do This*
Boot from Hard Disk	Boot the PC from a previously installed operating system from the hard drive.
Installation	Automatically detect hardware and then begin installing SUSE Linux.
Installation — ACPI Disabled	Disable support for ACPI (Advanced Configuration and Power Interface), but otherwise detect hardware and start SUSE installation.
Installation — Safe Settings	Disable potentially troublesome features such as ACPI, APM (Advanced Power Management), and DMA (direct memory access) for IDE interface and start installing SUSE. Select this option if the installation hangs with any of the other options.
Manual Installation	Control all aspects of installation, including loading device driver modules for your PC's hardware.
Rescue System	Start a small Linux system in memory so that you can troubleshoot by logging in as `root`.
Memory Test	Check to see if the PC's memory has any problems.

Along the bottom of the SUSE installer boot screen, you see some information about using the function keys F1 through F6. Table 2-2 explains what each of these functions does.

You can also provide other installer options — as well as Linux kernel options — at the Boot Options text box below the boot menu. The installer options control some aspects of the installer's behavior, whereas the kernel options are passed to the Linux kernel that starts when you start the installation. Typically you don't have to provide any of these options to install SUSE Linux.

Part I: Getting to Know SUSE

Table 2-2   Using Function Keys at the SUSE Installer Boot Screen

Press This Function Key	To Do This
F1	Get *context-sensitive* help — help information that depends on the currently selected item. Use the up- and down-arrow keys to read the Help screen and the left- and right-arrow keys to jump between topics. You can dismiss the Help screen by pressing Escape.
F2	Select a screen resolution that you want the YaST installer to use for its GUI. If the GUI screen fails to appear, you can select Text Mode for a text mode interface.
F3	Select the source from where you want to install. The choices are CD or DVD, network sources with different protocols such as FTP, HTTP, NFS, and SLP (Service Location Protocol). Typically you can leave this at its default choice of CD or DVD.
F4	Select the language and keyboard mapping to be used by the boot loader.
F5	View kernel messages as the Linux kernel loads. This could help you identify problems if the installation hangs.
F6	Update a driver module for new hardware for which drivers may not be on the CD or DVD. You will be prompted to insert the updated driver module on a floppy or CD-ROM after you start the installation.

TIP — The installer initially picks a rather high screen resolution for the GUI screen (typically, 1280 x 1024 pixels). To change the resolution, press F2, which brings up a menu from which you can select other screen resolutions, such as 1024 x 768 pixels.

After setting the screen resolution by pressing F2, select Installation from the boot menu and press Enter. This loads the Linux kernel from the DVD or CD. The Linux kernel starts running the YaST installation program. For the rest of the installation, you work with YaST's GUI screens.

Starting the SUSE install in YaST

YaST — the SUSE installer — displays a GUI screen (see Figure 2-1) from which you install SUSE Linux on your PC's hard drive and configure it. The left-hand side of the YaST screen shows the list of installation steps, organized into two broad categories of tasks — Base Installation and Configuration. An arrow marks the current step. For example, in Figure 2-1, the arrow marks the language selection step. After the step is complete, YaST displays a check mark next to the step.

Chapter 2: Installing SUSE Linux   29

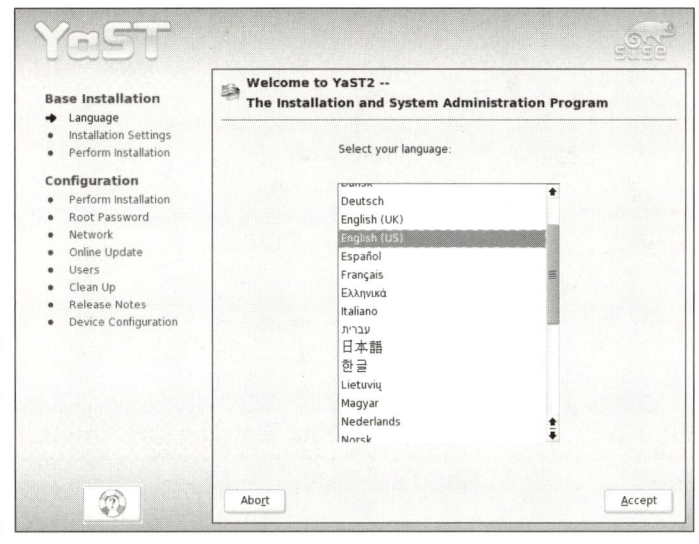

Figure 2-1:
The YaST installer's main GUI screen.

On the right-hand side of the YaST screen (see Figure 2-1), you see the options for the current step. You have to select options and then click Accept to proceed to the next installation step. You can abort the installation at any time by pressing the Abort key, up until you confirm that you want to really proceed with the installation.

TIP

At any installation step, click the life buoy button at the lower-left corner of the YaST screen (refer to Figure 2-1) to view context-sensitive help information for the current step. The help appears on the left-hand side of the YaST screen. Press the button again to return to view the list of installation steps.

Follow these steps to complete the initial installation steps in the YaST installer:

 1. **Select the language to be used during installation and for use in the installed SUSE Linux system. Then click Accept.**

    YaST probes the hardware and loads driver modules. YaST may prompt you to confirm that it should load some driver modules. Then YaST displays a dialog box (shown in Figure 2-2) that prompts you for the next step.

 2. **Assuming that you are installing SUSE for the first time, select New Installation and click OK.**

    YaST gathers information about the system and prepares a list of all the installation settings, organized by category, and displays it in the Installation Settings screen (see Figure 2-3). Table 2-3 summarizes the installation settings categories. Remember to scroll down to see all the installation settings in the screen shown in Figure 2-3.

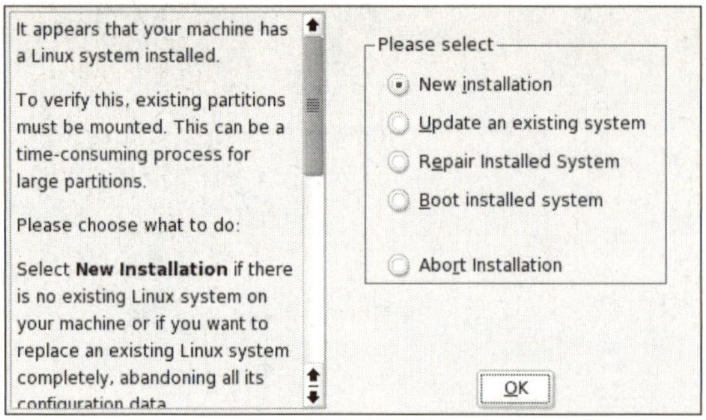

Figure 2-2:
Select New Installation and click OK.

Table 2-3	Installation Settings Categories
Category	***What These Settings Specify***
System	Information about the PC's hardware, including the processor type, amount of memory, hard drive, keyboard, mouse, graphics card, sound, and Ethernet card.
Mode	Whether this is a new installation or an update.
Keyboard Layout	Language and layout of the keyboard.
Mouse	Type of mouse (for example, PS/2 mouse).
Partitioning	Information about the hard drive partitions that will be formatted and any partitions that would be mounted on the Linux file system. You can edit this category and select the hard drive with Microsoft Windows. Then YaST offers to either delete or shrink the Windows partition. You can shrink the Windows partition and install SUSE Linux in the newly created space on the hard drive.
Software	What software YaST will install. The default is a typical system with KDE desktop and office applications. If you want, you can select a GNOME desktop by editing this category.
Booting	Information about the boot loader that takes care of starting Linux (as well as other operating systems, such as Windows XP, that may be on the hard drive) when you reboot the PC. The default is the GRUB boot loader, installed on the hard drive's master boot record (MBR).
Time Zone	Current time zone and how the hardware clock stores time. The default is the USA/Pacific time zone, which you may need to change.

Chapter 2: Installing SUSE Linux

Category	What These Settings Specify
Language	The language to be used by the installed SUSE Linux system.
Default Runlevel	What processes Linux starts after booting. The default runlevel is 5, which gives you a full multiuser system with networks enabled and a graphical login screen.

3. **Scroll down the list of installation settings and click a heading to view the settings and make any changes.**

   If you are installing on a PC that had only Windows installed, the Partitioning settings would suggest shrinking the Windows partition and creating space for SUSE Linux. If you want to change the size of the SUSE Linux partition, click Partitioning, and then click Next in the next screen. YaST then asks you whether you want to delete the Windows partition or shrink it (see Figure 2-4).

   Select Shrink Windows Partition and click Next. YaST then displays a window (Figure 2-5) where you can specify the size of the Windows and SUSE Linux partitions by clicking and dragging the slider.

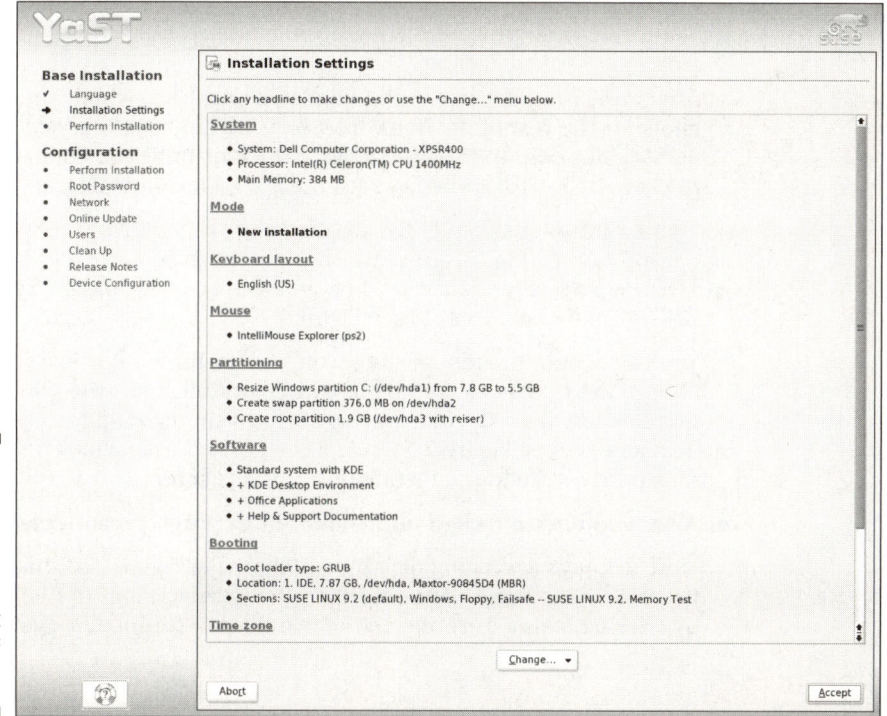

Figure 2-3: Click a heading to make changes to that category of settings.

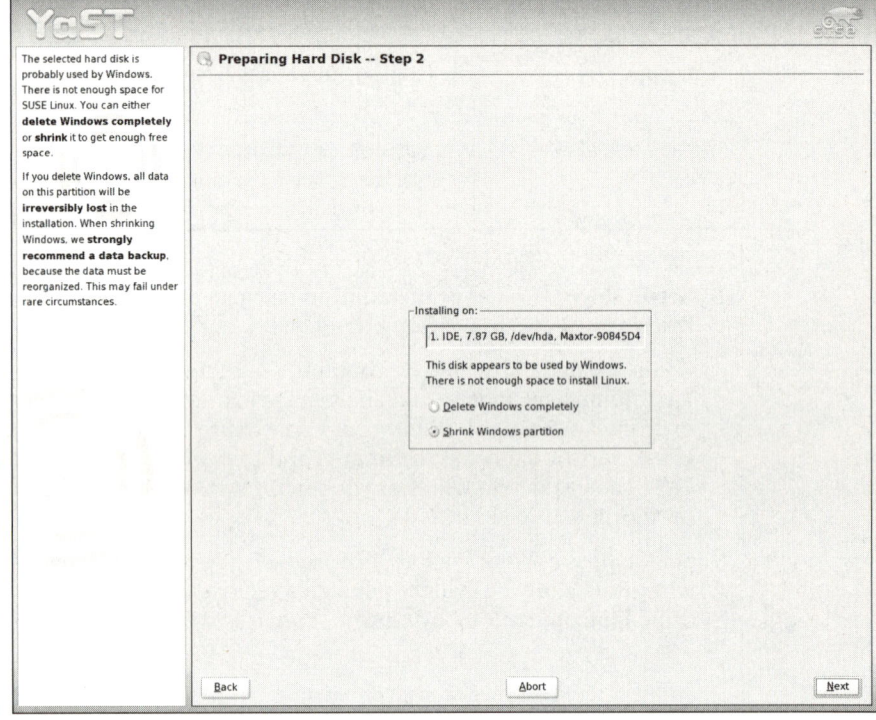

Figure 2-4: Select Shrink Windows Partition and click Next.

After indicating the size of the Windows partition (which automatically allocates the rest of the hard drive to SUSE Linux), click Next. Note that nothing happens to the hard drive partitions until you confirm that you really want YaST to proceed with the SUSE Linux installation.

If you want to change the desktop from the default KDE to GNOME, click Software in the main YaST Installation Settings screen (see Figure 2-3). YaST displays a new screen where you can select Standard System with GNOME and click Accept (see Figure 2-6).

You can accept the rest of the settings as is, but you probably need to change the time zone. To change the time zone, click the Time Zone section heading from the Installation Settings screen (Figure 2-3). From the next screen (see Figure 2-7), select the correct time zone and click Accept to return to the Installation Settings screen.

4. **After you have checked all installation settings, click Accept.**

   YaST displays a warning dialog box (shown in Figure 2-8) that tells you that this is the point of no return and you can commit to the installation by clicking Install or return to the installation settings by clicking Back.

Chapter 2: Installing SUSE Linux

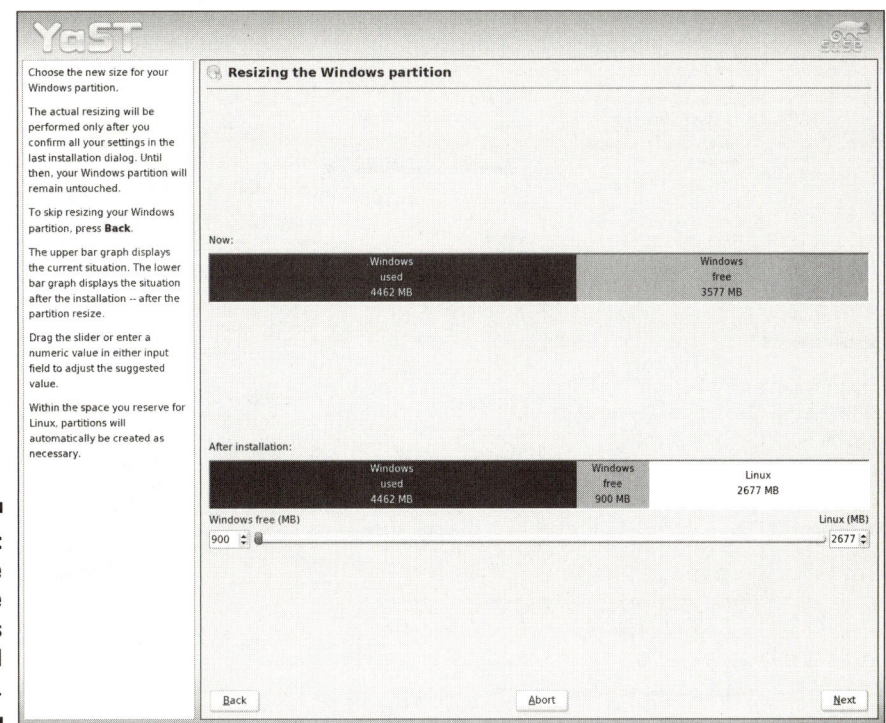

Figure 2-5: Set the size of the Windows partition and click Next.

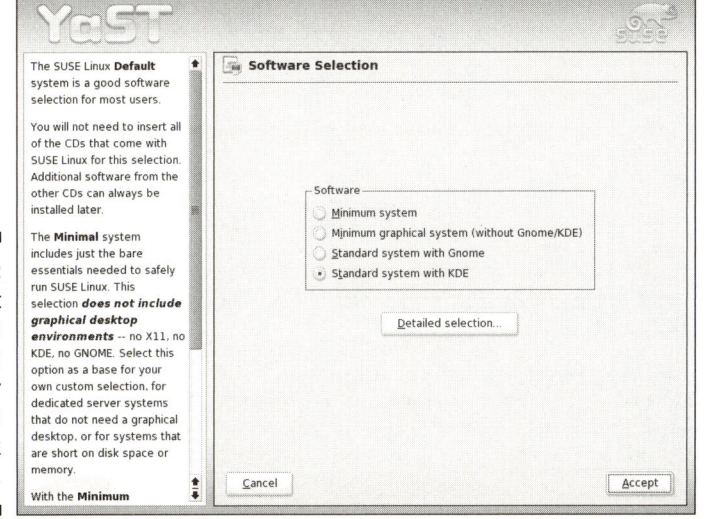

Figure 2-6: Select Standard System with KDE or GNOME and click Accept.

Part I: Getting to Know SUSE

Figure 2-7: Select the time zone and click Accept.

Figure 2-8: Click the Install button only if you are sure.

5. **If you are certain that you want to continue with the installation, click the Install button.**

   YaST then begins the installation, which includes formatting and preparing the hard drive partitions and copying SUSE Linux files to the hard drive.

   As YaST installs the software packages, it displays a slide show that introduces various features of SUSE Linux. After the base installation is complete, YaST installs the boot loader and reboots the system.

Completing the SUSE Linux configuration

After the initial SUSE Linux system boots, YaST starts again and guides you through the remaining SUSE Linux installation and configuration steps, as follows:

1. **Enter the password for the `root` user and click Next.**

    The `root` user is the administrator account that you can use to do anything on the SUSE Linux system — from installing software to adding new user accounts.

2. **Accept or change the network configuration.**

    YaST displays the current network settings (see the example in Figure 2-9). If the settings are correct (usually it's safe to assume that they are correct), you can simply click Next to continue.

3. **Test the Internet connection and update the system with the YaST Online Update (YOU) service. Then click Next.**

4. **Select whether your PC is a standalone machine or a network client and click Next.**

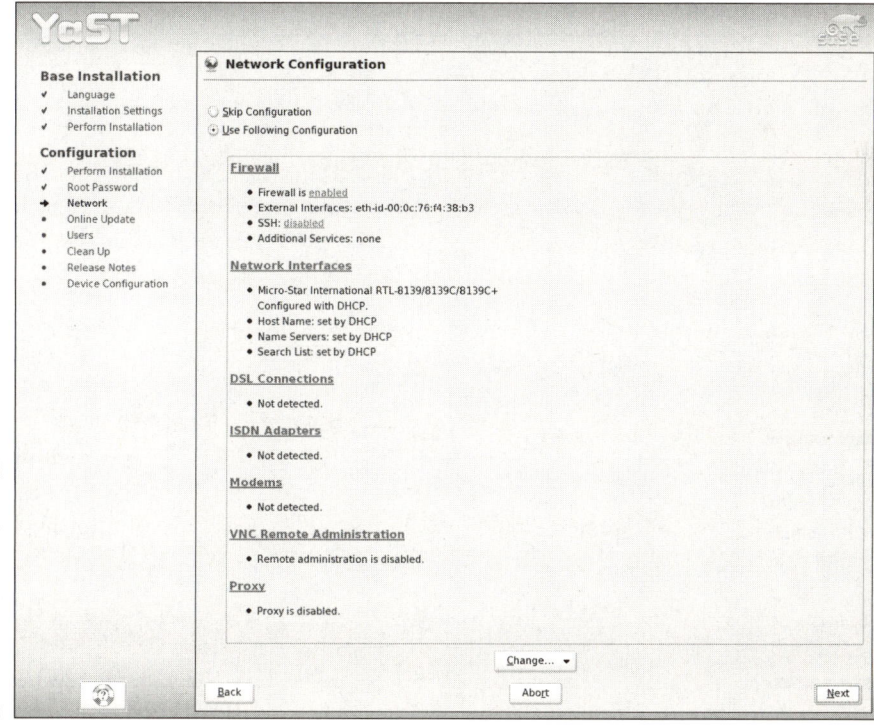

Figure 2-9: Accept or change the network configuration from this screen.

Part I: Getting to Know SUSE

If you select network client, you have to select one of two network authentication methods — NIS (Network Information System) or LDAP (Lightweight Directory Access Protocol). Typically, most PCs are stand-alone systems. (This simply means that the user accounts are authenticated on the PC and not by checking with another server on the network.)

5. **For a standalone system, add a new local user by entering the user name, password, and other settings (Figure 2-10). Click Next to continue.**

The Auto Login check box is active if you are the only user on the system and if you use KDE as the default desktop. If you mark the Auto Login check box (when it's not grayed out), SUSE Linux automatically logs in this user when it starts. Also, if you are the only user of this system, mark the Receive System Mail check box. That way mail intended for the root user would be delivered to your user account. Some programs send mail to `root` with information about any errors or problems. By receiving the system mail, you will be in the loop when it comes to any important system messages.

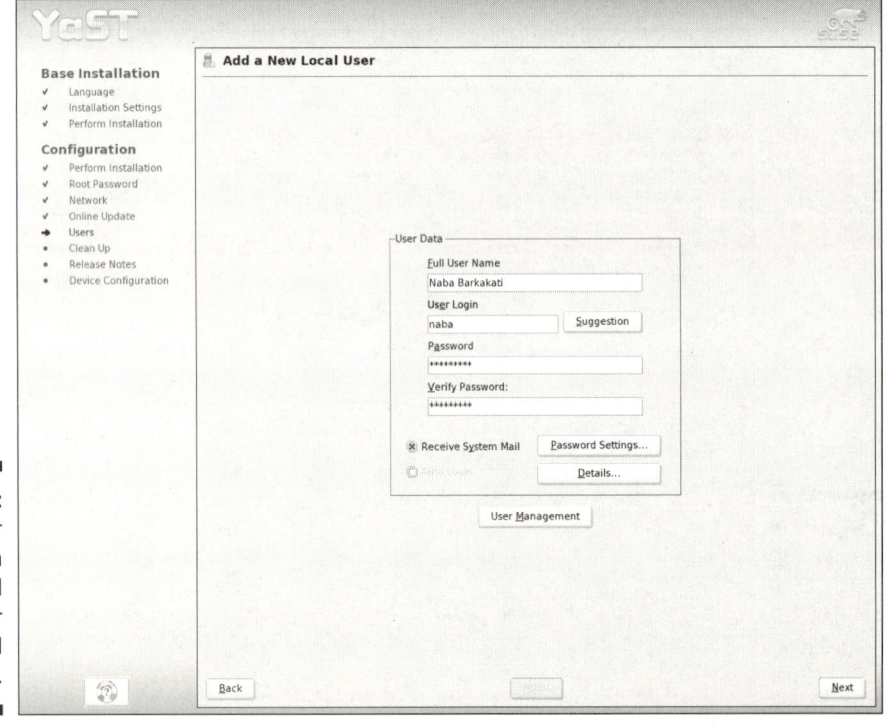

Figure 2-10: Enter information for a local user account and click Next.

Chapter 2: Installing SUSE Linux

6. **Read the release notes and click Next.**

    The release notes contain last-minute information about the SUSE Linux distribution, including any known problems and workarounds. It's worth glancing through so that you know about anything that might apply to your PC's hardware configuration. When you click Next, YaST detects all of your PC's hardware and displays a summary (Figure 2-11).

7. **Accept or change the displayed hardware configuration for your PC (Figure 2-11) and click Next.**

    The hardware configuration includes information about specific hardware such as your graphics card, monitor, sound card, printing system, and so on. Typically, the displayed configuration should be acceptable, but you should check each of the items. In particular, check the graphics card configuration to see if YaST correctly detected the monitor and graphics card. If not, you can make changes by clicking Graphics Cards (see Figure 2-11) and changing the information in a subsequent window. After the configuration steps are complete, YaST informs you that the installation is complete, as shown in Figure 2-12.

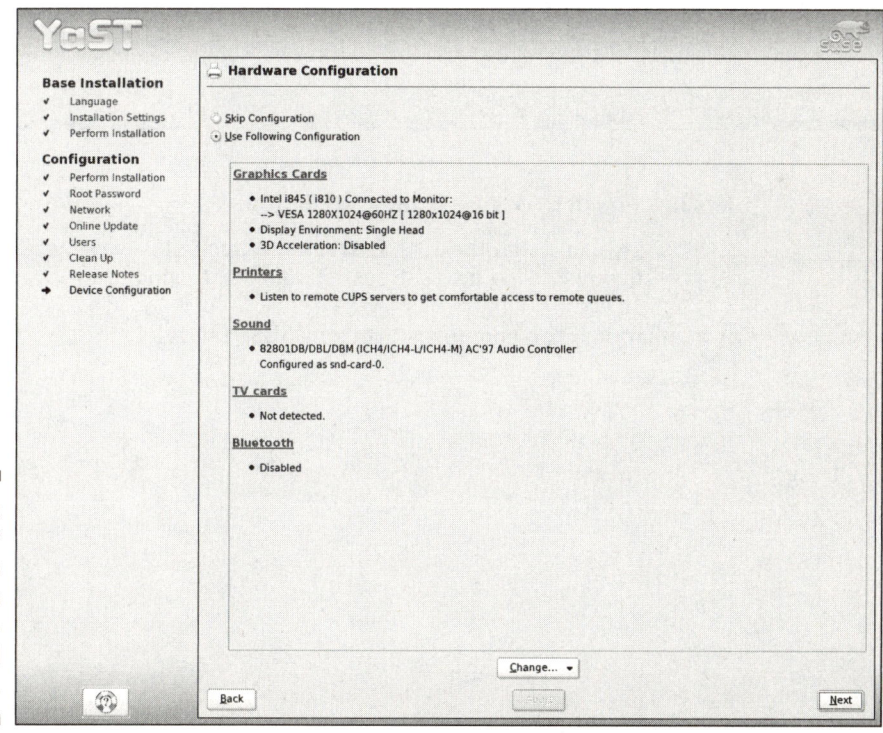

Figure 2-11: Accept or change hardware configuration and click Next.

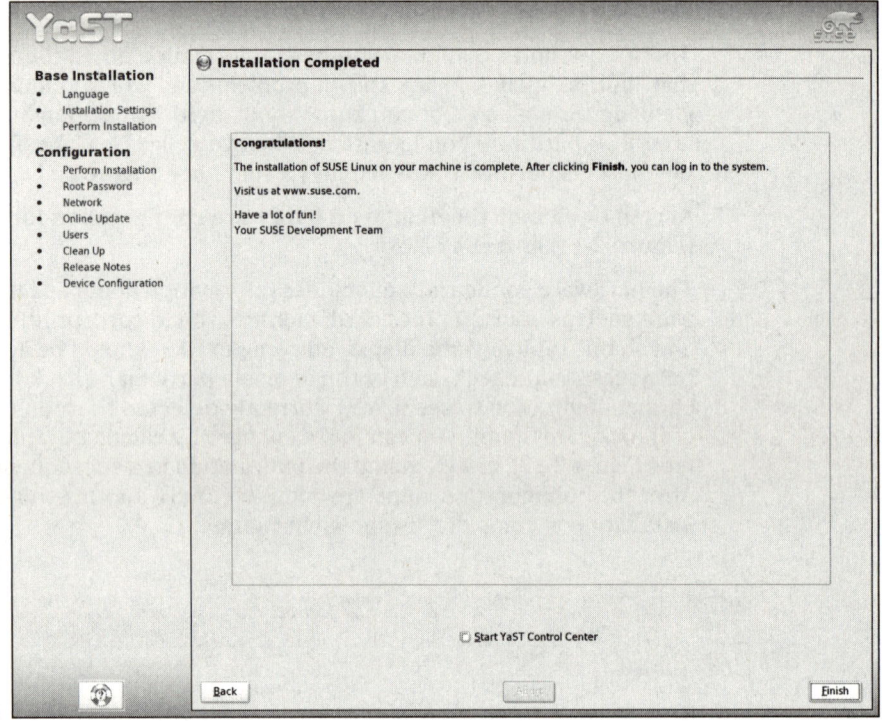

Figure 2-12: Click Finish to reboot and begin using your SUSE system.

8. **Click Finish to complete the installation.**

    The installer then reboots the system. When you see the graphical login screen, you can log into the system and start using it.

    Congratulations! You can now start using SUSE Linux.

Chapter 3

Starting SUSE for the First Time

In This Chapter

▶ Powering up SUSE Linux
▶ Logging in
▶ Checking out the GUI desktops
▶ Playing with the shell
▶ Shutting down

*Y*ou're sitting in front of your PC about to turn it on. You know that the PC has SUSE Linux installed. You're wondering what to expect when you turn it on and what you do afterward. Not to worry. If you're using SUSE Linux for the first time, this chapter shows you how to log in, check out the graphical desktops, try out some cryptic Linux commands, and finally, shut down the PC.

If this quick tour of SUSE Linux seems hurried, don't worry; I cover everything at a slower pace and with more details in later chapters.

For those of you who already know something about SUSE Linux, flip through this chapter to see if anything looks new. You never know what you may not know!

Powering Up SUSE Linux

When you power up the PC, it goes through the normal power-up sequence and loads the boot loader — called GRUB. The *boot loader* is a tiny computer program that loads the rest of the operating system from the hard drive into the computer's memory. The whole process of starting up a computer is called *booting*.

The GRUB boot loader displays a graphical screen with the names of the operating systems that the boot loader can load. For example, if your PC has both Microsoft Windows and SUSE Linux installed on the hard drive, you see both names listed. Use the up- and down-arrow keys to select the operating

Part I: Getting to Know SUSE

system you want to use and press Enter. If the PC is set up to load SUSE Linux by default, you don't have to do anything — after a few seconds the boot loader starts SUSE Linux.

You see a graphical boot screen that shows information about the progress of the system startup. If you selected KDE as your desktop and enabled automatic login during installation, you are automatically logged in and you get a KDE desktop similar to the one shown in Figure 3-1.

By the way, SUSE Linux logs you in using the normal user account that you set up during installation.

For a GNOME desktop, you get a graphical login screen, similar to the one shown in Figure 3-2.

You can log in using the account you defined during the installation. Type the username and press Enter. When prompted for it, type the password and press Enter. You then see the initial GNOME graphical user interface (GUI — pronounced *gooey* for short) appear.

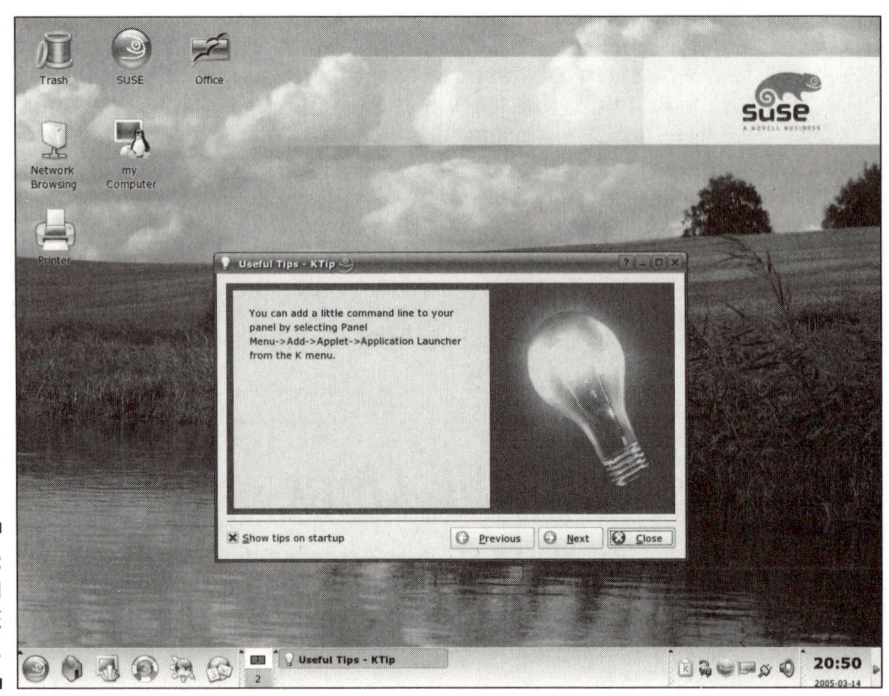

Figure 3-1: The initial KDE desktop.

Chapter 3: Starting SUSE for the First Time *41*

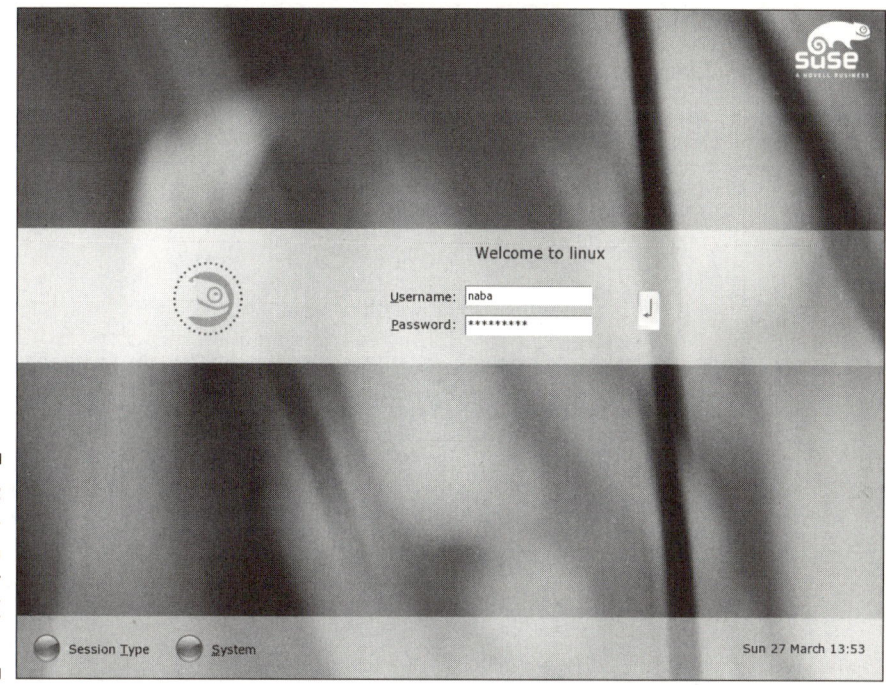

Figure 3-2: The graphical login window for the GNOME desktop.

You should not normally log in as `root`. When you log in as `root`, you could accidentally damage your system because you can do anything when you're `root`. Always log in as a normal user. When you need to perform any task as `root`, type **su -** in a terminal window and enter the `root` password. Graphical system administration tools such as YaST prompt for the `root` password when needed.

Getting GUI

When you install SUSE Linux, you can install one of two GUI desktops — GNOME or KDE. I provide a quick look at both KDE and GNOME desktops in this section.

Figures 3-3 and 3-4 provide a snapshot of KDE and GNOME desktops, respectively. In these figures, I point out the major components of each desktop.

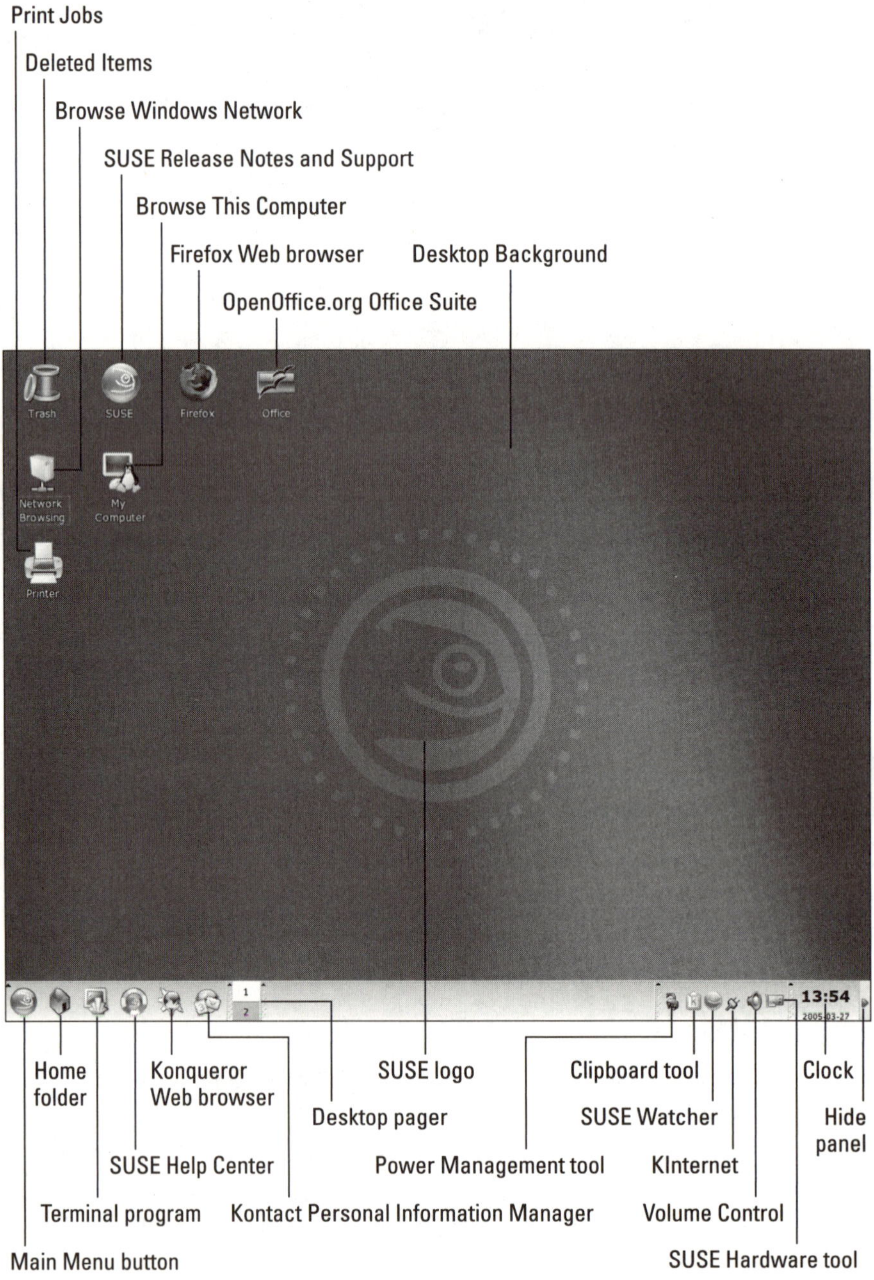
Print Jobs
Deleted Items
Browse Windows Network
SUSE Release Notes and Support
Browse This Computer
Firefox Web browser
Desktop Background
OpenOffice.org Office Suite
Trash
SUSE
Firefox
Office
Network Browsing
My Computer
Printer
13:54
Home folder
Konqueror Web browser
SUSE logo
Clipboard tool
Clock
Desktop pager
SUSE Watcher
Hide panel
SUSE Help Center
Power Management tool
KInternet
Terminal program
Kontact Personal Information Manager
Volume Control
Main Menu button
SUSE Hardware tool

Figure 3-3: Getting familiar with the KDE desktop.

Take a look at Figures 3-3 and 3-4 as I point out some of the noteworthy elements of these desktops:

Chapter 3: Starting SUSE for the First Time

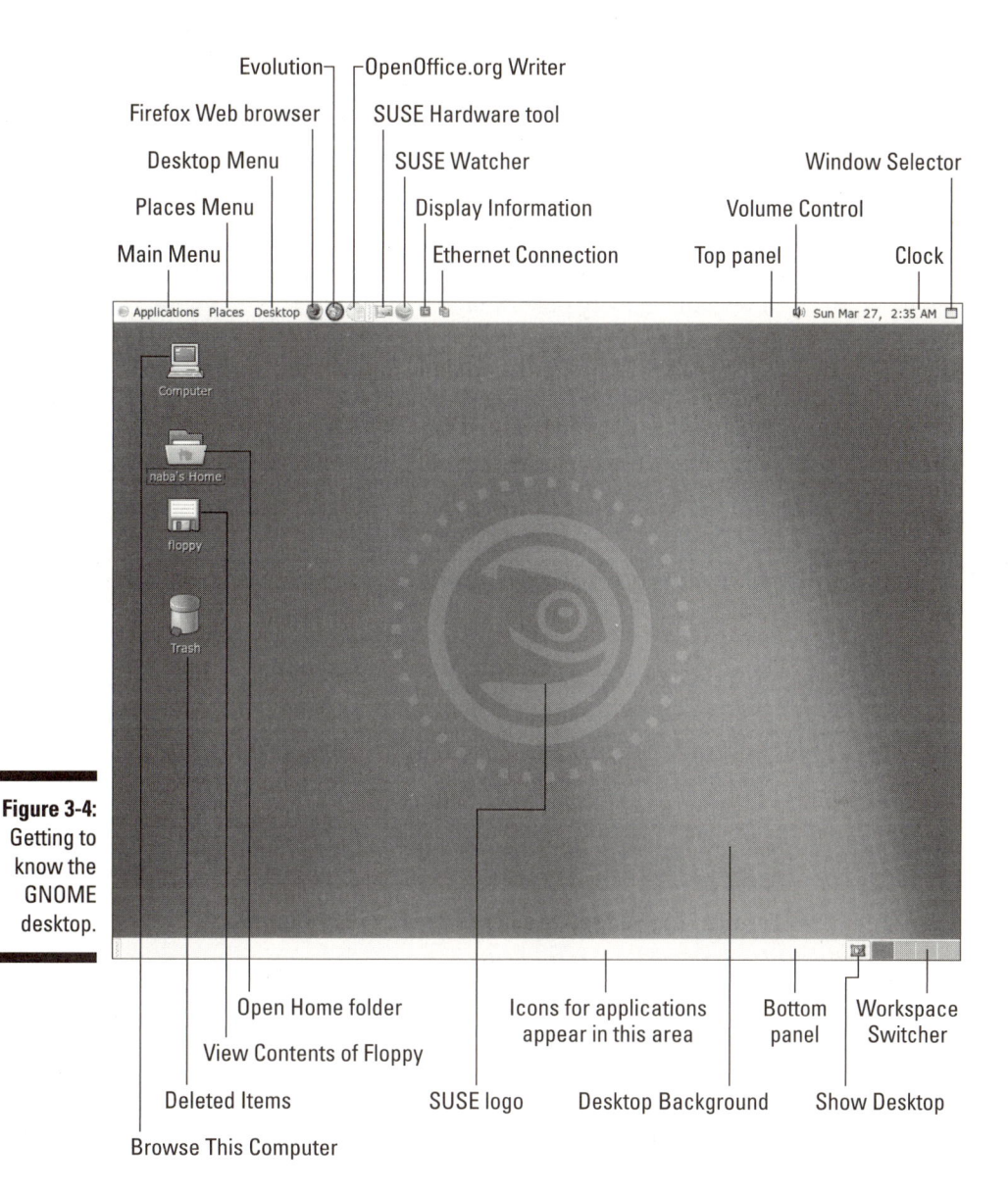

Figure 3-4: Getting to know the GNOME desktop.

Labels around the figure:
- Main Menu
- Places Menu
- Desktop Menu
- Firefox Web browser
- Evolution
- OpenOffice.org Writer
- SUSE Hardware tool
- SUSE Watcher
- Display Information
- Ethernet Connection
- Top panel
- Volume Control
- Window Selector
- Clock
- Browse This Computer
- Deleted Items
- View Contents of Floppy
- Open Home folder
- SUSE logo
- Icons for applications appear in this area
- Desktop Background
- Bottom panel
- Show Desktop
- Workspace Switcher

- ✔ **Panel:** The panel is like the Windows taskbar. KDE has one at the bottom of the screen and GNOME has one at the top and one at the bottom. The KDE panel and GNOME's top panel are the places where you can access the main menu of applications and launch programs by clicking icons on the panel. The panel also shows information such as the date and time and what applications are currently running.

- ✔ **Main Menu:** This is the leftmost button on the KDE panel and GNOME's top panel. It brings up the Main menu (refer to Figure 3-5), from which you can start applications and perform other tasks such as lock the screen, get help, switch users, or log out. In GNOME, some of these options are in separate menus — the Places menu and the Desktop menu.

- **Desktop Icons:** The desktops display the usual desktop icons — a My Computer icon for browsing the contents of the computer, a Trash icon, and icons for accessing devices such as a floppy drive and a CD/DVD drive or CD writer. The KDE desktop also has an icon for browsing the local Windows network, as well as icons for support, Print Manager, and the OpenOffice.org office suite.

- **Home Folder:** Opens your home directory in a graphical file manager.

- **Terminal Program:** Runs a program that provides a terminal window where you can type Linux commands.

- **SUSE Help Center:** Starts the SUSE Help Center, where you can get help on various aspects of SUSE Linux.

- **Web Browser:** Runs the Web browser.

- **Personal Information Manager:** Starts a mail, calendar, and contact manager. GNOME desktop provides Evolution as the personal information manager.

- **Desktop Pager or Workspace Switcher:** Click on a square to bring up a different desktop.

- **Clipboard Tool:** Click to see what has been cut and what you can paste elsewhere.

- **Power Management Tool:** Right-click to view a menu that you can use to start the YaST Power Management module that enables you to edit power-saver settings.

- **Volume Control:** Click to change the sound volume.

- **SUSE Hardware Tool:** Click to view information about devices in the PC and configure them.

- **SUSE Watcher:** Click to open a window you can use to both check for online updates as well as start online updates.

- **Clock:** Displays the current time. Clicking it brings up a calendar showing the current date.

- **Hide Panel:** Available in KDE, the end-point of the panel serves as a "hide panel" button, which means that if you click this icon, the panel slides to the right and disappears. Click again and the panel reappears. You can hide the panel to create more room for other windows.

In addition to what you see on the KDE and GNOME desktops, you have many more choices in the main menu that appears when you click Main Menu on the panel. (See Figure 3-5.) Similar to the Windows Start button, the Main Menu is where you start when you want to run an application.

Chapter 3: Starting SUSE for the First Time *45*

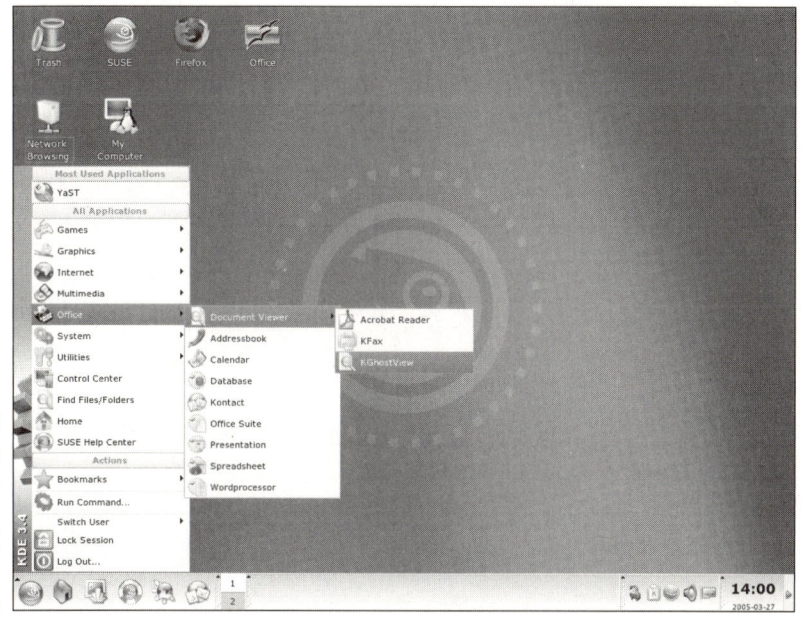

Figure 3-5: A typical Main Menu on the KDE desktop.

By the way, I refer to the menu selection shown in Figure 3-5 as Main Menu↪Office↪Document Viewer↪KGhostView. If you take a moment to compare the notation with Figure 3-5, I hope you'd agree that it's quite logical.

When you're done exploring KDE or GNOME, log out. To log out of KDE, choose Main Menu↪Logout. In GNOME, choose Desktop Menu↪Log Out. Select Log Out from the subsequent dialog box and click OK to really log out.

Setting Up Printers

During SUSE Linux installation, the installer — YaST — can detect any printer connected to your PC and provide you with the opportunity to configure the printer. If you did not configure your printer during installation, you can do so using YaST by following these steps:

 1. **Make sure that your printer is connected to the PC and powered on.**

    This step is necessary so that YaST can automatically detect the printer.

 2. **Choose Main Menu↪System↪YaST and enter the root password when prompted to do so. Then click Hardware on the left-hand side of the YaST Control Center window.**

    The YaST Control Center displays information about various hardware devices, as shown in Figure 3-6. As you can see, you can configure various hardware devices, including printers, from YaST.

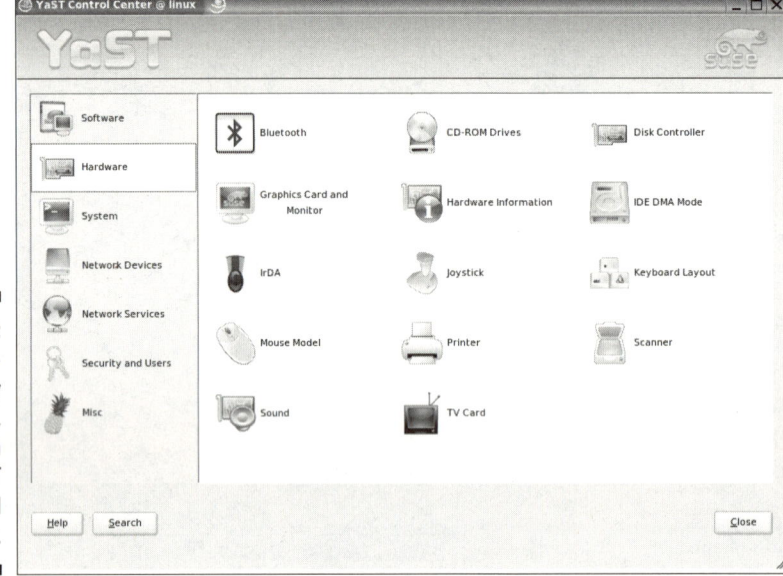

Figure 3-6: To configure any hardware, start with the YaST Control Center.

3. **Click Printer on the right-hand side of the window.**

   YaST opens the Printer Configuration window and displays information about any printers that it detects, as shown in Figure 3-7. In this case, YaST has detected an Epson Stylus printer. If YaST has correctly detected your printer, click Finish and you're all done.

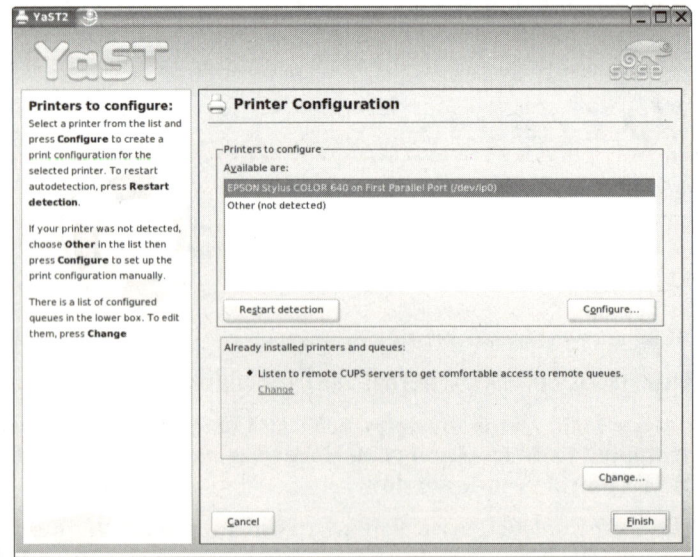

Figure 3-7: YaST displays this Printer Configuration window.

Chapter 3: Starting SUSE for the First Time   47

4. **If your printer is not detected, click Other and then click Configure.**

   YaST displays a list of printer connection types (see Figure 3-8) from which you can select how your printer is connected to your PC (through parallel, serial, USB, or network).

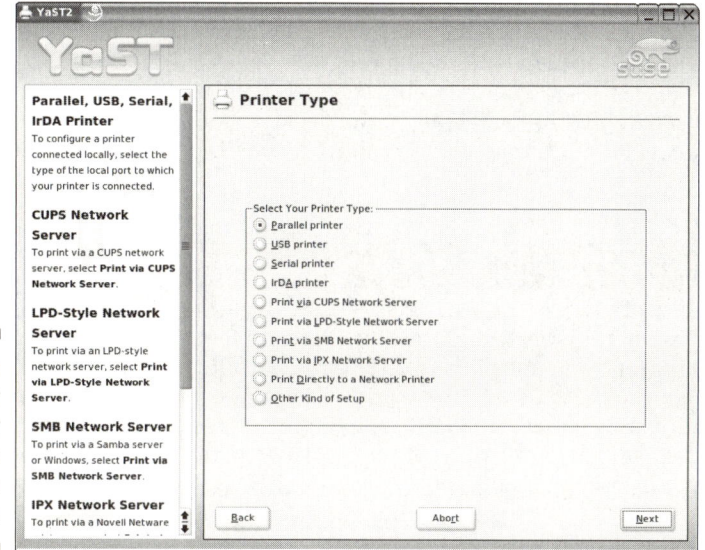

Figure 3-8: Select your printer connection type from this window.

5. **Select your printer type and click Next.**

   YaST prompts for more information, depending on the printer type you selected. For example, for a parallel printer, you have to identify the parallel port to which the printer is attached.

6. **Provide information about the printer connection and click Next.**

7. **Enter the name of the print queue as well as some descriptive information about the printer and click Next.**

   YaST displays a list of printer makes and models.

8. **Select your printer's make and model. Then click Next.**

   YaST displays the current configuration information so that you can test the configuration or edit it.

9. **Review the configuration information and click OK.**

10. **Click Finish to save the settings and finish adding the printer.**

Managing DVDs and CD-ROMs

The KDE and GNOME GUI desktops make using DVDs and CD-ROMs in SUSE Linux easy. Just place a DVD or a CD-ROM in the drive (I am assuming it's a data disc), click the My Computer icon on your desktop, and then click the icon for the DVD/CD drive. The contents of the CD or DVD data disc then appear in a GUI file manager window. If you insert a DVD movie into the DVD drive, an appropriate multimedia program opens the DVD.

If you see a DVD/CD-ROM icon on the desktop, right-click that icon for a context menu. From that menu, you can eject the CD or DVD when you are done.

Playing with the Shell

Linux is basically UNIX, and UNIX just doesn't feel like UNIX unless you can type cryptic commands in a text terminal. Although GNOME and KDE have done a lot to bring us into the world of *w*indows, *i*cons, *m*ouse, and *p*ointer (affectionately known as *WIMP*), sometimes you're stuck with nothing but a plain text screen with a prompt that looks something like this (when I log in with the username `naba`):

```
naba@linux:~>
```

You see the text screen most often when something is *wrong* with the X Window System, which is essentially the machinery that runs the windows and menus that you normally see. In those cases, your first reaction might be, "What do I do now?" And the answer is that you have to work with the shell and know some of the cryptic Linux commands.

You can prepare for unexpected encounters with the shell by trying out some Linux commands in a terminal window while you're in the GNOME or KDE GUI. After you get the hang of it, you might even keep a terminal window open, just so you can use one of those cryptic commands simply because it's faster than pointing and clicking. (Those two-letter commands do pack some punch!)

Starting the bash shell

Simply put, the *shell* is the Linux *command interpreter* — a program that reads what you type, interprets that text as a command, and does what the command is supposed to do.

Before you start playing with the shell, open a terminal window. In KDE, the panel includes an icon that looks like a monitor covered by a sea shell (for a shell, get it?). When you click that icon, a window with a prompt appears, like the one shown in Figure 3-9. That's a terminal window, and it works just like an old-fashioned terminal. A shell program is running and ready to accept any text that you type. You type text, press Enter, and something happens (depending on what you typed).

In GNOME, choose Programs Menu⇨System⇨Terminal⇨Terminal. That should then open up a terminal window.

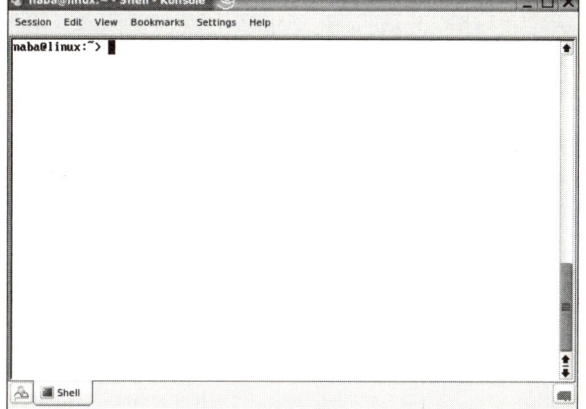

Figure 3-9: You can type Linux commands at the shell prompt in a terminal window.

The prompt that you see depends on the shell that runs in that terminal window. The default Linux shell is called `bash`.

`Bash` understands a whole host of standard Linux commands, which you can use to look at files, go from one directory to another, see what programs are running (and who else is logged in), and a whole lot more.

In addition to the Linux commands, `bash` can run any program stored in an executable file. `Bash` can also execute *shell scripts* — text files that contain Linux commands.

Understanding shell commands

Because a shell interprets what you type, knowing how the shell figures out the text that you enter is important. All shell commands have this general format:

```
command option1 option2 ... optionN
```

Such a single line of commands is commonly called a *command line*. On a command line, you enter a command followed by one or more optional parameters (or *arguments*). Such *command line options* (or command line arguments) help you specify what you want the command to do.

One basic rule is that you have to use a space or a tab to separate the command from the options. You also must separate options with a space or a tab. If you want to use an option that contains embedded spaces, you have to put that option inside quotation marks. For example, to search for two words of text in the password file, I enter the following `grep` command (`grep` is one of those cryptic commands used to search for text in files):

```
grep "SSH daemon" /etc/passwd
```

When `grep` prints the line with those words, it looks like this:

```
sshd:x:71:65:SSH daemon:/var/lib/sshd:/bin/false
```

If you created a user account in your name, go ahead and type the `grep` command with your name as an argument, but remember to enclose the name in quotes. For example, here is how I search for my name in the /etc/passwd file:

```
grep "Naba Barkakati" /etc/passwd
```

Trying a few Linux commands

While you have the terminal window open, try a few Linux commands just for fun. I guide you through some random examples to give you a feel for what you can do at the shell prompt.

To see how long the Linux PC has been up since you last powered it up, type the following (*Note:* I show the typed command in bold, followed by the output from that command.):

```
uptime
    3:52am  up 29 days 55:53,  5 users,  load average: 0.04,
         0.32, 0.38
```

The part `up 29 days, 55:53` tells you that this particular PC has been up for nearly a month. Hmmm . . . can Windows do that?

To see what version of Linux kernel your system is running, use the `uname` command like this:

```
uname -srv
```

Chapter 3: Starting SUSE for the First Time

This runs the `uname` command with three options `-s`, `-r`, and `-v` (these can be combined as `-srv`, as this example shows). The `-s` option causes `uname` to print the name of the kernel, `-r` prints the kernel release number, and `-v` prints the kernel version number. The command generates the following output on one of my Linux systems:

```
Linux 2.6.8-24-default #1 Wed Oct 6 09:16:23 UTC 2004
```

In this case, the system is running Linux kernel version 2.6.8.

To read a file, use the `more` command. Here's an example that displays the contents of the `/etc/passwd` file:

```
more /etc/passwd

root:x:0:0:root:/root:/bin/bash
bin:x:1:1:bin:/bin:/bin/bash
daemon:x:2:2:Daemon:/sbin:/bin/bash
lp:x:4:7:Printing daemon:/var/spool/lpd:/bin/bash
   ... lines deleted ...
```

To see a list of all the programs currently running on the system, use the `ps` command, like this:

```
ps ax
```

The `ps` command takes many options and you can provide these options without the usual dash (-) prefix. This example uses the `a` and `x` options — the `a` option lists all processes that you are running and the `x` option displays all the rest of the processes. The net result is that `ps ax` prints a list of all processes running on the system, as shown in the following sample output:

```
  PID TTY      STAT   TIME COMMAND
    1 ?        S      0:00 init [5]
    2 ?        SN     0:00 [ksoftirqd/0]
    3 ?        S<     0:00 [events/0]
    4 ?        S<     0:00 [khelper]
    5 ?        S<     0:00 [netlink/0]
    6 ?        S<     0:00 [kblockd/0]
   31 ?        S      0:00 [kapmd]
   ... lines deleted ...
```

Amazing how many programs can run on a system even when only you are logged in as a user, isn't it?

As you can guess, you can do everything from a shell prompt, but it does take some getting used to.

Shutting Down

When you're ready to shut down Linux, you must do so in an orderly manner. Even if you're the sole user of a SUSE Linux PC, several other programs are usually running in the background. Also, operating systems such as Linux try to optimize the way that they write data to the hard drive. Because hard drive access is relatively slow (compared with the time needed to access memory locations), data generally is held in memory and written to the hard drive in large chunks. Therefore, if you simply turn off the power, you run the risk that some files aren't updated properly.

Any user (you don't even have to be logged in) can shut down the system from the desktop or from the graphical login screen. In KDE, choose Main Menu⇨Log Out. In GNOME, choose System Menu⇨Log Out. A dialog box appears (Figure 3-10 shows the example from the KDE desktop), providing the options for restarting or turning off the system, or simply logging out. To shut down the system, simply select Turn Off Computer (or Shut Down in GNOME), and click OK. The system then shuts down in an orderly manner.

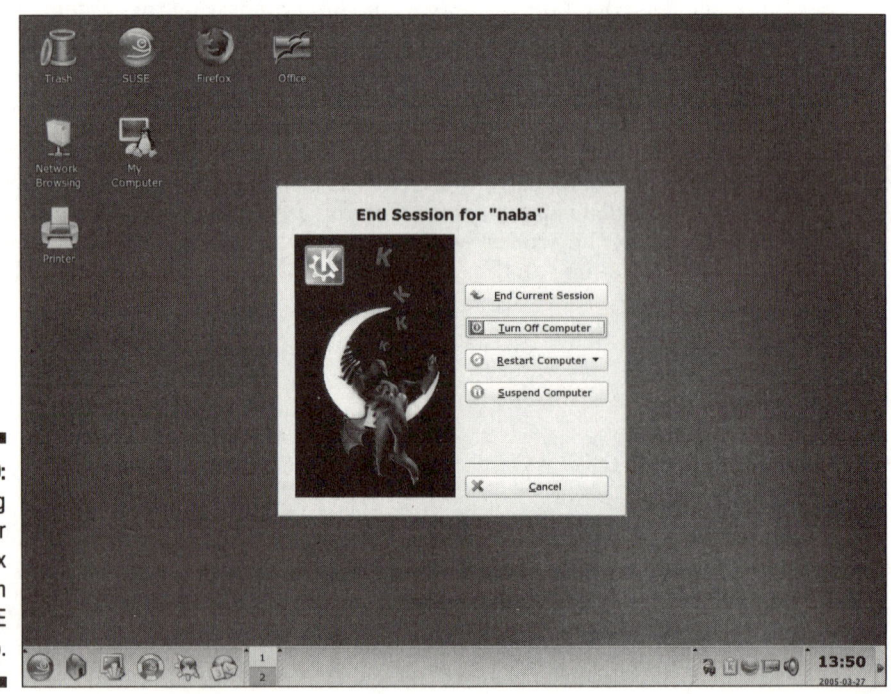

Figure 3-10:
Shutting down your SUSE Linux system from the KDE desktop.

Chapter 3: Starting SUSE for the First Time

If you are at the graphical login screen, you can shutdown the system by selecting the shutdown option from the menus available at the login screen.

As the system shuts down, you see text messages about processes being shut down. You may be surprised at how many processes exist, even when no one is explicitly running any programs on the system. If your system does not automatically power off on shutdown, you can manually turn off the power.

> **WARNING!** Note that shutting down or rebooting the system may *not* require `root` access or even the need to log into the system. This is why it's important to make sure that physical access to the console is protected adequately so that anyone who wants to cannot simply walk up to the console and shut down your system.

Chapter 4

Taking Stock of What's in SUSE

In This Chapter
▶ Discovering the Internet applications
▶ Introducing the office applications
▶ Exploring the multimedia applications
▶ Reviewing the images and graphics applications

SUSE Linux comes with a whole lot of applications. All you have to do is look at the menus on the GUI desktops to see what I mean. Often you find more than one application of the same type. For example, in the GNOME desktop, you can take your pick from three Web browsers — Firefox, Mozilla, and Epiphany.

Depending on the desktop — KDE or GNOME — that you installed by following the steps outlined in Chapter 2, you get a different set of applications. Both desktops include the OpenOffice.org office application suite with a word processor, spreadsheet, presentation software, and more. You find many choices for CD players and multimedia players, not to mention the games, utility programs, and useful tools, such as a digital camera and image editing applications.

In this chapter, I provide a quick listing of some common SUSE Linux applications. After you get familiar with these applications, you can explore them further and use them when you need them. I cover many of these applications in greater detail in Chapters 8 through 14.

Discovering the Internet Applications

Internet applications are for doing tasks such as browsing the Web, reading and sending e-mail, reading newsgroups, and downloading files. From your SUSE desktop — both KDE and GNOME — you can get to these applications by selecting the Internet menu from the Main menu.

You get different sets of default Internet applications depending on whether you installed the KDE or the GNOME desktop. Table 4-1 lists the default Internet applications for GNOME and KDE desktops.

I describe the Internet applications in detail in Chapters 8 through 11.

Table 4-1   **Typical Internet Applications on GNOME and KDE Desktops**

Application Category	GNOME Desktop	KDE Desktop
Chat (instant messaging)	GAIM, Gnome Jabber, XChat	Kopete
Web browser	Firefox, Mozilla, Epiphany	Konqueror
E-mail	Novell Evolution	KMail
News reader	Pan	KNode
Videoconference and IP telephone	GnomeMeeting	

Here's what you can do with these applications:

- **Chat (instant messaging)** applications enable you to communicate with other people on the Internet — it's like a phone call with many people at the same time, only you type your messages instead of speaking. America Online (AOL) provides a popular instant messaging (IM) service called AIM. With the chat applications in SUSE, you can talk to people on many different IM services such as AIM, ICQ, and Microsoft's MSN. On the GNOME desktop, you have a choice of several IM applications such as GAIM, Gnome Jabber, and XChat. On the KDE desktop, use Kopete for your IM needs.

- **Web browsing** applications are, well, for browsing the Web. On the GNOME desktop, you can take your pick from three Web browsers — Mozilla, Epiphany, and the up-and-coming Firefox with its reputation as the "faster, better Web browser."

- **E-mail** applications are for sending and receiving electronic mail. You need an e-mail account with an ISP to use these applications. If you use the GNOME desktop, your best bet for an e-mail inbox is Novell Evolution — a multipurpose application that integrates e-mail, calendaring, to-do lists, and contact management in a single application. On the KDE desktop, your e-mail client is KMail.

- **News readers** enable you to read Usenet newsgroups, which are like bulletin boards where people post messages. Anyone can read and respond to the messages. Like e-mail, you need access to your ISP's server to read newsgroups. The GNOME desktop provides the Pan news reader; on KDE, use the KNode application to read newsgroups.

- **Videoconference and IP telephone** applications are for making phone calls and running videoconferences (think of videoconferences as "picture phones" where you can see and be seen by other participants as you talk). The GNOME desktop includes the GnomeMeeting videoconferencing application. GnomeMeeting conforms to a standard called H.323, which means it can work with other H.323-compliant videoconferencing software such as Microsoft Netmeeting. The KDE desktop does not include any videoconferencing application by default.

Introducing the Office Applications

By *office applications,* I mean software for word processing, spreadsheets, presentations (briefing slides), calendars, and managing contacts. You can, of course, think of the Internet applications — at least e-mail and Web browser — as office applications as well, but I am differentiating between the applications that need the Internet to work versus the ones you may use on stand-alone PCs.

Regardless of your desktop — KDE or GNOME — OpenOffice.org is the primary office application suite in SUSE Linux. OpenOffice.org includes several different applications for different tasks such as word processing, working with spreadsheets, and preparing presentations. Table 4-2 summarizes the office applications available in GNOME and KDE desktops.

I describe the office applications in detail in Chapters 12 and 13.

Table 4-2	Typical Office Applications on GNOME and KDE Desktops	
Application Category	GNOME Desktop	KDE Desktop
Word processing	OpenOffice.org Writer, AbiWord	OpenOffice.org Writer
Spreadsheet	OpenOffice.org Calc, Gnumeric	OpenOffice.org Calc
Presentation	OpenOffice.org Impress	OpenOffice.org Impress
Calendar/organizer	Novell Evolution	Kontact

Here is what you can do with the office applications:

- **Word processing** applications are for preparing letters and reports and any documents, including something as big as a book like this one. In both GNOME and KDE desktops, you can use the OpenOffice.org Writer for word processing. The nice thing about Writer is that it's compatible with the popular Microsoft Word software from the Windows world.

- **Spreadsheet** applications are for creating — what else — spreadsheets. The OpenOffice.org office suite includes the Calc application for preparing spreadsheets. Calc is compatible with Microsoft Excel.

- **Presentation** software enables you to prepare slides for briefing. Perhaps the best-known presentation software is Microsoft PowerPoint. The OpenOffice.org office suite comes with the PowerPoint-compatible Impress presentation software.

- **Calendar/organizer** applications are for keeping track of your appointments and things to do. On the GNOME desktop, you can use the multipurpose Novell Evolution as the organizer, in addition to using it as your e-mail inbox. The KDE desktop comes with the Kontact application to track your calendar and to-do list. Kontact also incorporates the KMail mail reader.

Exploring the Multimedia Applications

Multimedia is audio, video, or both — as in a movie. Naturally, multimedia applications are for listening to or watching music or movies, usually from digital files or some media such as CD or DVD. I also include in the multimedia category those applications related to creating multimedia, such as video editors or CD/DVD burners. SUSE Linux comes with a good complement of multimedia applications.

When it comes to playing multimedia — audio and video in various formats such as MP3, MPEG, and QuickTime — freely available Linux distributions (including SUSE Linux on this book's companion DVD) rarely come with the appropriate decoders because of licensing restrictions on some of these decoders. The end result is that the multimedia application runs, but it can't play the MP3 file or the DVD movie because it lacks a decoder. Commercial versions of SUSE Linux usually come with some of these decoders.

Table 4-3 summarizes the multimedia applications in SUSE. I describe some of these multimedia applications in detail in Chapter 14.

Chapter 4: Taking Stock of What's in SUSE

Table 4-3   **Typical Multimedia Applications on GNOME and KDE Desktops**

Application Category	GNOME Desktop	KDE Desktop
CD player	GNOME CD Player	KsCD
CD ripper	Grip	
Audio player	XMMS, RealPlayer 10	amaroK, RealPlayer 10, juK
CD/DVD burner		K3b
Video player (needs separate decoders)	Totem Movie Player, RealPlayer 10	Kaffeine, RealPlayer 10
Video editor	kino	
TV player (needs TV card)	kdetv	kdetv

Here is a summary of what you can do with these multimedia applications:

- **CD player** applications enable you to play audio CDs on your SUSE Linux system. All you have to do is pop an audio CD into the CD/DVD drive and use one of these applications to play songs from the CD.

- **CD ripper** applications are for ripping (extracting) songs from audio CDs and converting them to a digital format such as MP3. You can rip songs from CDs and organize a digitized version of your CD collection. You can play the MP3 files using an audio player application or by downloading them into a portable MP3 player such as Apple iPod or other similar products. To convert ripped songs into MP3 format, you need an MP3 encoder that is not included with SUSE Linux.

- **Audio player** applications are used to play digital music stored in files in various formats such as MP3 or Ogg Vorbis (a patent- and royalty-free compressed audio file format). You can use amaroK as the audio player in KDE, XMMS in GNOME, and RealPlayer 10 on both KDE and GNOME desktops.

- **CD/DVD burner** applications enable you to use your CD/DVD-R (recordable) drive to burn CDs or DVDs. With these applications you can typically burn audio CDs, data CDs and DVDs, as well as CDs or DVDs from ISO image files.

- **Video player** applications are for playing movies stored in MPEG files as well as playing DVD movies. Unfortunately, these applications need decoders to decode the data from DVD movies or different format video files. Such decoders for DVDs are not available for Linux.

Part I: Getting to Know SUSE

- **Video editors** enable you to edit digital video files. The GNOME desktop comes with the kino video editor, which can capture video over a Firewire interface and provide the ability to edit the video.
- **TV player** applications enable you to watch a TV program on your SUSE Linux desktop, provided your PC has a TV card (a hardware device capable of receiving TV signals) installed. Both KDE and GNOME desktops offer the kdetv application as the TV player.

Cataloging the Image and Graphics Applications

When I talk about images and graphics, I mean applications that are meant to work with photographs or other images and those that enable you to prepare vector drawings — drawings consisting of lines and shapes — for use in various types of documents. SUSE Linux includes a number of such image and graphics applications. You can find these applications in the Main Menu⇨Graphics menu.

Table 4-4 summarizes the image and graphics applications in GNOME and KDE desktops. I describe these applications in detail in Chapter 15.

Table 4-4 Typical Image and Graphics Applications on GNOME and KDE Desktops

Application Category	GNOME Desktop	KDE Desktop
Photo or image editor	The GIMP	The GIMP
Digital camera interface		digikam
Vector drawing	Dia, OpenOffice.org Draw	OpenOffice.org Draw
Image viewer	Eye of Gnome	Gwenview
Fax viewer		KFax
PDF viewer	Acrobat Reader, GNOME PDF Viewer	Acrobat Reader, KGhostview
PostScript viewer	GGV PostScript Viewer	KGhostview

Here's what the image and graphics applications enable you to do:

- **Photo or image editor** applications are for touching up photos as well as creating and editing bitmap images in many different formats, including popular ones such as JPEG, TIFF, BMP, and PNG. Both KDE and GNOME desktops offer The GIMP as the photo and image editor application. The GIMP can do whatever Adobe Photoshop can do and it's free!

- **Digital camera interface** is for connecting a digital camera to the SUSE Linux system and downloading the photos from the camera. If the digital camera application does not support your digital camera, you can usually access it as a USB storage device after you connect the camera to the PC's USB port using the cable supplied with the camera.

- **Vector drawing** applications enable you to draw using shapes such as lines, curves, rectangles, and circles, and performing operations such as filling shapes with colors or patterns. For example, if you are drawing the plan for a room in your house, your best bet is to use a vector drawing application. OpenOffice.org Draw is a popular vector drawing application.

- **Image viewers** are for viewing image files. The GNOME desktop comes with the Eye of Gnome image viewer; the KDE desktop provides Gwenview as the default image viewer.

- **Fax viewers** enable you to view faxes stored in files. The KDE desktop offers the KFax application for viewing faxes.

- **PDF viewer** applications are for opening and reading PDF files. In both KDE and GNOME desktops, you can use the Acrobat Reader to view PDF documents.

- **PostScript viewers** enable you to view and print PostScript files.

Part II
Test Driving SUSE

The 5th Wave   By Rich Tennant

"The funny thing is he's spent 9 hours organizing his computer desktop."

In this part...

After you have installed SUSE Linux, this Part helps you begin exploring and using SUSE Linux. First, I take you on a quick tour of the GUI desktops — KDE and GNOME. I explain the similar features of GNOME and KDE and then focus primarily on the KDE desktop, which is the default in SUSE. I devote a chapter to showing you how you can locate files and applications in your system.

If I am not mistaken, you probably want your Internet access as soon as possible. You can connect your SUSE Linux system to the Internet in several different ways — by using a dial-up modem or by cable or DSL. I explain the steps in the final chapter of this part.

Chapter 5
Exploring the SUSE Desktops

In This Chapter

▶ Discovering the common features of the GNOME and KDE GUIs
▶ Introducing the KDE desktop
▶ Getting familiar with the GNOME desktop

When you install SUSE Linux following the steps I describe in Chapter 2, you can choose to install one of two popular graphical desktops — GNOME or KDE. GNOME and KDE are similar to Microsoft Windows, but they are unique in one respect. Unlike Microsoft Windows, you can pick your desktop in SUSE Linux.

You can best figure out the KDE and GNOME desktops by simply starting to use them. In this chapter, I help you get familiar with key features of the desktops. I start by introducing the common features of the two desktops and then I briefly describe each desktop individually.

Discovering the Common Features of the Desktops

From your perspective as a user, both KDE and GNOME probably seem similar because many features work similarly. Becoming familiar with these common features is helpful so that you can rely on them no matter which desktop you choose to use for your daily work.

For starters, the initial desktop for both KDE and GNOME looks like any other popular GUI desktop, such as Microsoft Windows or Apple's Mac OS desktop. For example, Figure 5-1 and Figure 5-2, respectively, show typical KDE and GNOME desktops.

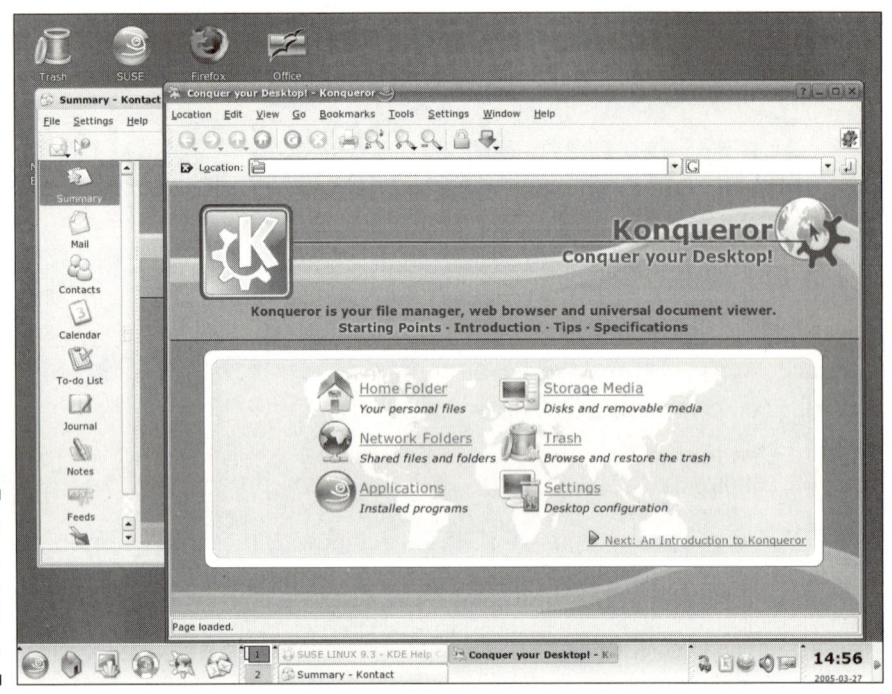

Figure 5-1: A typical KDE desktop with several applications.

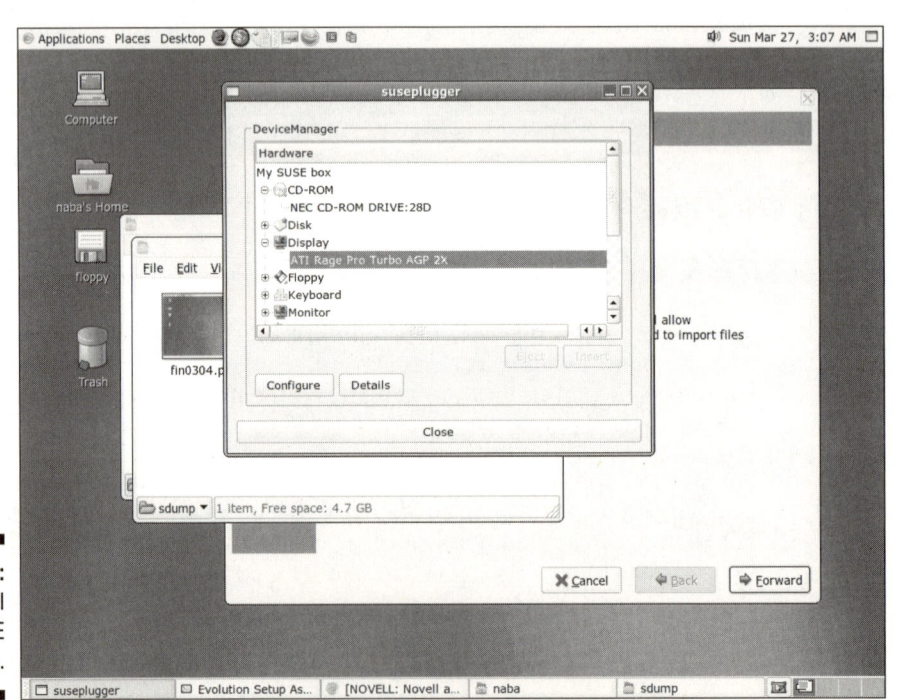

Figure 5-2: A typical GNOME desktop.

Both desktops (Figures 5-1 and 5-2) show icons for your computer, your home folder, and the trash can for deleted files. Both desktops have something similar to the Windows taskbar. On the KDE desktop, the taskbar, called the *panel,* appears along the bottom of the screen. GNOME has two such panels — one on the top and the other on the bottom of the screen. Even though the appearance may look slightly different, the panels serve the same purpose on both KDE and GNOME desktops — they provide buttons for accessing menus and starting applications, and they show buttons for any applications you've started (or were automatically started for you).

In the case of the KDE desktop, both the menu buttons and information about running applications appear on the same panel. On the GNOME desktop, the top panel provides menus and buttons for starting applications, whereas the bottom panel displays information about running applications.

Move the mouse over any icon on a panel and a small pop-up window gives a helpful hint about what you can do with that icon.

Desktop context menus

Both GNOME and KDE desktops display a context menu when you right-click a clear area on the desktop. The exact contents of that menu depends on the desktop, but it typically offers menu options that enable you to perform the following types of tasks:

- Run a command
- Create a new folder
- Create a new document
- Configure the desktop background
- Rearrange the icons on the desktop
- Lock the screen (enter your password to unlock)
- Log out

The last two options are only available on the KDE desktop's context menu.

For example, Figures 5-3 and 5-4, respectively, show the desktop context menus in typical KDE and GNOME desktops. Desktop menu options with a right-pointing arrow have other menus that appear when you put the mouse pointer over the arrow.

Part II: Test Driving SUSE

Figure 5-3: Typical right-click menu for a KDE desktop.

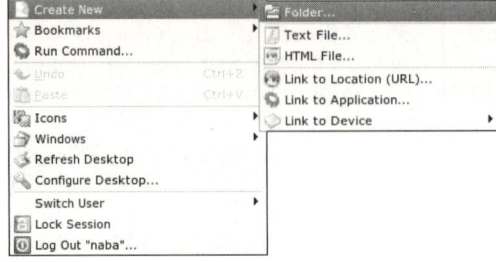

Figure 5-4: Typical right-click menu for a GNOME desktop.

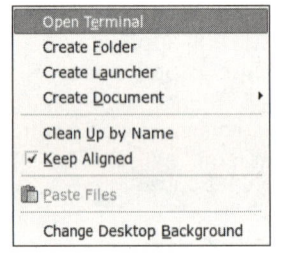

Icon context menus

Right-clicking any desktop icon in KDE or GNOME causes another menu to appear. (See Figures 5-5 and 5-6.) Many items on this context menu are the same no matter what icon you click — but right-clicking certain icons (for example, the Trash icon) produces a somewhat different menu. You can perform the following typical tasks from icon context menus:

- Open a folder in a file manager
- Open a file with an application that you choose
- Rename the icon
- Move the icon to trash
- View the properties of that icon

For the Trash icon, the icon context menu typically provides an option to permanently delete the items in the trash. (You get a chance to choose Yes or No.)

TIP: I bet you see a pattern here. It's the right-click. No matter where you are on a GUI desktop, *always right-click before you pick.* You're bound to find something useful when you right-click!

Chapter 5: Exploring the SUSE Desktops 69

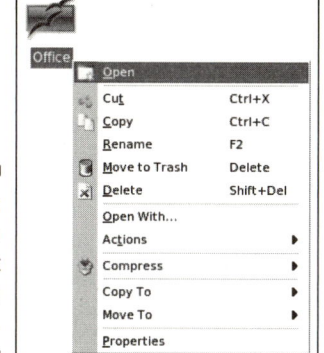

Figure 5-5: An icon context menu in KDE.

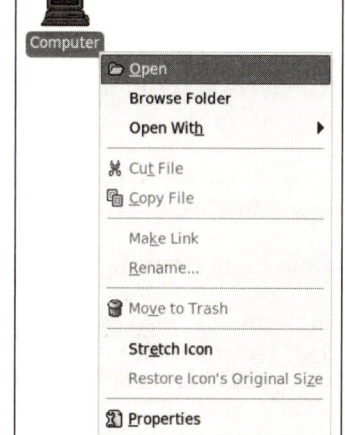

Figure 5-6: An icon context menu in GNOME.

The panels

The panel is the long bar that stretches across the bottom of the KDE desktop and both the top and bottom of the GNOME desktop. Figures 5-7 and 5-8 show typical views of the KDE and GNOME panels, respectively.

Figure 5-7: A typical view of the KDE panel.

Figure 5-8: A typical view of the top GNOME panel.

```
Applications  Places  Desktop                                    Sun Mar 27, 3:15 AM
```

The panel is a parking place for icons. Some icons open up menus from which you can select applications to run and some icons start applications when you click them. Some show the status (such as what programs are currently running) as well as other useful information such as the date and time.

Starting at the left, the first icon (regardless of what it shows) in the KDE panel and GNOME top panel is the Main Menu button — it's like the Start button in Microsoft Windows. Then come a few icons that start various programs. In GNOME, you have more menu buttons — System Menu for system tasks such as configuring the system or logging out and Help Menu for accessing online help. The date and time icon appears at the far-right edge of the panel.

By the way, if you move the mouse pointer on top of an icon, a small Help balloon pops up and gives you a helpful hint about the icon.

Now for a little bit of technical detail about these icons on the panel. The panel itself is a separate application; each icon is a button or a program called an *applet*. The applets are little applications (also called *plugins*). These panel applets can do things such as launch other programs or display the date and time. To add an applet to the panel, right-click an empty area of the panel and select the appropriate menu item to add an applet to the panel. After adding the applet, you can right-click the applet's icon to configure it or perform some task that the applet supports.

If you right-click any icon — or right-click anywhere on the panel — you get a context menu where you can do something relevant to that icon (such as move it or remove it entirely). You can also set some preferences and add more buttons and applets to the panel.

The Main Menu or Programs Menu

The leftmost icon on the KDE panel and the GNOME desktop's top panel is the *Main Menu* button. On the GNOME top panel, the button is labeled Applications (with a bright red N that signifies Novell's ownership of SUSE Linux).

Chapter 5: Exploring the SUSE Desktops 71

The Main Menu is where you typically find all the applications, organized into submenus. I provide an overview of the Main Menu and point out some interesting items. You can then further explore the menus yourself.

Click the Main Menu button to bring up the first-level menu. Then mouse over any menu item with an arrow to bring up the next level's menu and so on. You can go through a menu hierarchy and make selections from the final menu. Figures 5-9 and 5-10, respectively, show the Main Menu hierarchies in typical KDE and GNOME desktops.

A word about the way I refer to a menu selection: I use the notation Main Menu⇨Utilities⇨Desktop⇨KSnapshot to refer to the menu selection shown in Figure 5-9. Similarly, I say choose Main Menu⇨Internet⇨Web Browser⇨Firefox Web Browser to refer to the menu sequence highlighted in Figure 5-10. You get the idea.

By the way, you could refer to the menu selection in Figure 5-10 as Applications Menu⇨Internet⇨Web Browser⇨Firefox Web Browser — by using Applications Menu instead of the generic Main Menu as the name of the top-level menu. I use the generic Main Menu because it helps discuss the menu options in either the KDE or GNOME desktop. I don't think you'll ever get confused once you have used either desktop for any length of time.

Figure 5-9: The Main Menu hierarchy in a typical KDE desktop.

Part II: Test Driving SUSE

Figure 5-10: The Main Menu hierarchy in a typical GNOME desktop.

Notice in Figure 5-10 that when you point to a menu selection, a help balloon pops up with information about that selection. That's another helpful hint from the GNOME desktop. These GUI desktops do try to make it easy on us poor souls to navigate through the huge selection of menu choices!

The KDE Main Menu (refer to Figure 5-9) has three broad categories: Most Used Applications shows the icons for applications you have used recently, All Applications organizes the applications that you can access, and Actions shows buttons for some common daily tasks such as locking the screen, running a command, or logging out. You should browse the All Applications category to familiarize yourself with what SUSE has to offer as a desktop operating system.

The GNOME desktop arranges the menus a bit differently. GNOME's top panel (see Figure 5-10) provides three separate menus — the Applications Menu (or Main Menu) lists the applications by category, the System Menu includes system tasks and some actions you can take, and the Help menu provides access to help.

On both KDE and GNOME desktops, the applications listed in the top-level Main Menu are arranged in the following types of menu categories:

- **Games:** A menu of, what else, games (and quite a few of them at that — such as card games, board games, puzzles, and arcade games).
- **Graphics:** Programs such as The GIMP (an Adobe Photoshop-like program), a digital camera interface, and an Adobe Acrobat PDF file viewer.
- **Internet:** Internet applications, such as the Web browser, e-mail reader, Usenet news reader, and Instant Messenger.
- **Multimedia** or **Sound & Video:** Multimedia applications such as CD player, MP3 player, CD/DVD burner, video player, sound recorder, and volume control.
- **Office:** Office applications such as the OpenOffice.org office suite (includes Writer word processor, Calc spreadsheet, Impress slide presentation program, Draw drawing program, and much more).
- **Preferences** or **Settings:** Options to configure many aspects of the system, including the appearance and the behavior of the desktop.
- **System:** System administration tools such as YaST for configuring your SUSE Linux system.
- **Utilities:** Lots of utility programs, such as a scientific calculator, text editor, print manager, screen capture, file upload via Bluetooth connection, Palm Pilot or Handspring sync, and so on.

KDE's Main Menu and the System menu in GNOME's top panel typically also have a few menu items for some commonly performed tasks such as the following:

- SUSE help-center displays online help (this option is under the Help menu in GNOME's top panel).
- Run Command displays a dialog box where you can enter the name of a program to run and then click Run to start that program.
- Find Files (or Find Files) runs a search tool from which you can search for files.
- Lock Screen starts the screen saver and locks the screen. When you want to return to the desktop, the system prompts you for your password.
- Logout logs you out. (You get a chance to confirm whether you really want to log out or not.)

The menus in KDE and GNOME are somewhat different, but the menu organization is logical enough that you can usually find what you need.

Okay. That's all I'm telling you about the Main Menu. You'll use the Main Menu a lot as you use KDE or GNOME desktops. Even if it seems too much initially, it'll all become very familiar as you spend more time with SUSE Linux.

Exploring KDE

KDE (pronounced *Kay-dee-ee*) is the default GUI for SUSE Linux. KDE stands for the *K Desktop Environment.* From your perspective as a user, KDE provides a graphical desktop environment that includes the Konqueror Web browser and file manager, a panel with menus for starting applications, a help system, configuration tools, and many applications, including the OpenOffice.org office suite, image viewer, PostScript viewer, and mail and news reader programs.

TIP

If you want to keep up with KDE news, you can always find out the latest information about KDE by visiting the KDE home page at www.kde.org.

If you installed the KDE desktop, you see an initial KDE desktop similar to the one shown in Figure 5-1. The initial KDE session includes a window showing a helpful tip.

You will find that KDE is very easy to use and is similar in many ways to the Microsoft Windows GUI. You can start applications from a menu that's similar to the Start menu in Windows. As in Windows, you can place folders and applications directly on the KDE desktop.

You can move and resize the windows just as you do in Microsoft Windows. Also, as in the window frames in Microsoft Windows, the right-hand corner of the window's title bar includes three buttons. The leftmost button reduces the window to an icon, the middle button maximizes the window to fill up the entire screen, and the rightmost button closes the window.

KDE panel

The KDE panel (refer to Figure 5-7) appearing along the bottom edge of the screen is meant for starting applications. The most important component of the panel is the Main Menu button — the one with the cute gecko logo — on the left side of the panel. That button is like the Start button in Windows. When you click the Main Menu button, a menu appears. From this menu, you can get to other menus by moving the mouse pointer over items that display a right-pointing arrow.

You can start applications from the Main Menu. That's why the KDE documentation calls the Main Menu button the *Application Starter* (the KDE documentation refers to the button itself as the K button).

Next to the Main Menu button, the panel includes several other buttons. If you don't know what a button does, simply move the mouse pointer over the button; a small pop-up window displays a brief message about that button.

Chapter 5: Exploring the SUSE Desktops

Customizing the KDE desktop

KDE makes customizing the look and feel of the KDE desktop easy. Everything you have to decorate the desktop is in one place: the KDE Control Center. To start the KDE Control Center, choose Main Menu➪Control Center.

When the KDE Control Center starts, it displays the main window with a list of items on the left side and some summary information about your system in the workspace to the right, as shown in Figure 5-11.

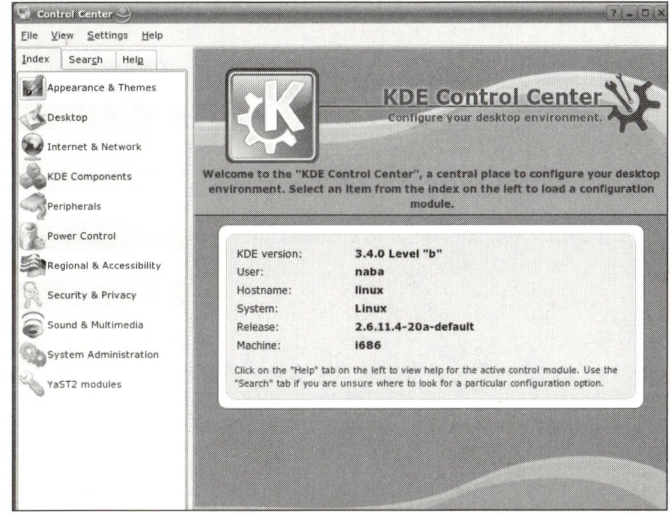

Figure 5-11: The initial window of the KDE Control Center.

The KDE Control Center's left-hand side shows the items that you can customize with this program. The list is organized into categories such as Appearance & Themes, Desktop, Internet & Network, KDE Components, Peripherals, Security & Privacy, Sound & Multimedia, System Administration, and so on. Click an item to view the subcategories for that item. Click one of the subcategory items to change it. That item's configuration options then appear on the right side of the Control Center window.

To change the desktop's background, click Appearance & Themes, and then click Background. The right side of the Control Center (see Figure 5-12) shows the options for customizing the desktop's background.

If you want to change the background of a specific desktop, click the Setting for Desktop drop-down list. From the list of desktops, you can select the desktop whose background you want to change.

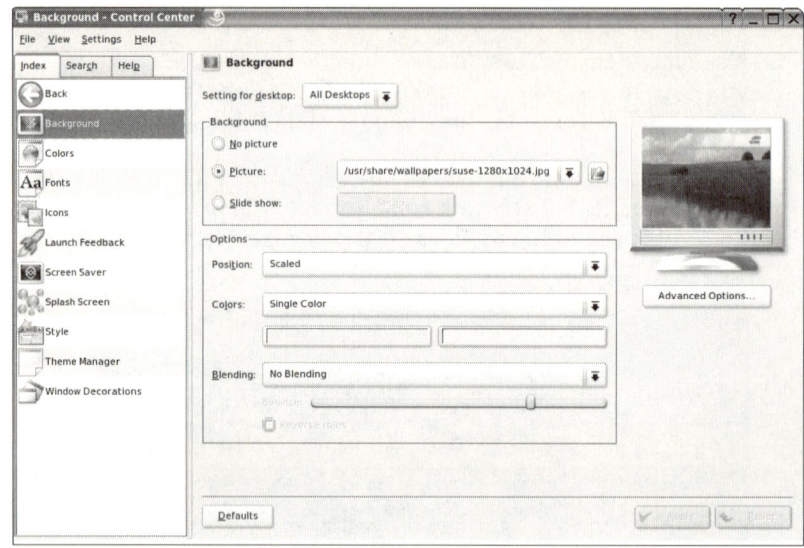

Figure 5-12: Changing the desktop background with KDE Control Center.

For a colored background, select the No Picture radio button. From the Colors drop-down list, you can select either a single color background or a variety of color gradients (meaning the color changes gradually from one color to another) or a picture (an image used as a background). You can then pick the two colors by clicking the color buttons that appear under the Colors drop-down list. After making your selections, click Apply to try out the background. (If you don't like what you get, click Reset to revert back to the previous background.)

The default KDE desktop uses a picture as the background. If you want to use a different picture as background, select the Picture radio button and then click the folder icon next to that radio button. A dialog box comes up, showing the JPEG images in the /usr/share/wallpapers directory. You can select any one of these images or pick an image from another directory and click OK. Then click the Apply button in the KDE Control Center to apply this wallpaper to the desktop. If you don't like the appearance, click Reset.

Getting to Know GNOME

GNOME (pronounced *Guh-NOME*) is another GUI for SUSE Linux. The acronym GNOME stands for *GNU Network Object Model Environment* (and GNU, as you probably know, stands for *GNU's not UNIX*). GNOME is a graphical user interface (GUI) and a programming environment. From the user's perspective, GNOME is like Microsoft Windows. Behind the scenes, GNOME has many features that allow programmers to write graphical applications that can work together well. In this chapter, I point out only some key features of the GNOME GUI, leaving the details for you to explore on your own at your leisure.

If you're curious, you can always find out the latest information about GNOME by visiting the GNOME home page at `www.gnome.org`.

If you installed GNOME as your desktop, you see the GNOME GUI desktop (see Figure 5-2) after you log in. The GNOME desktop is very similar to the Windows desktop albeit with two taskbars — one at the top and the other at the bottom of the screen, and icons for folders and applications appear directly on the desktop.

The GNOME panels

The GNOME panels are key features of the GNOME desktop. In the default configuration, the desktop has one panel at the top and the other along the bottom of the screen. You can simply drag and move the panels to any edge of the screen, but it's best to leave them alone. When you drag the panel to a side, the panel's size changes and the icons can get enlarged. That makes it hard to access the menus.

TIP

Think of the top GNOME panel as your gateway to the things you can do. From the menus and buttons on that panel you can start applications. Think of the bottom panel as information about the things you have done so far. For example, the bottom panel shows buttons corresponding to applications that you have started so far.

Figure 5-8, earlier in this chapter, shows a typical top panel that shows menus, application launcher buttons, and small panel applets. Each panel applet is a small program designed to work inside the panel. For example, the Clock applet on the panel's far right displays the current date and time.

The GNOME desktop's top panel (refer to Figure 5-8) has three menu buttons — Applications, System, and Help — at the left edge:

- Applications Menu has the menu of applications, organized by category. I refer to the Applications Menu as the Main Menu because this is the primary menu for starting applications.
- System Menu has the menu for system configuration and performing tasks such as logging out or locking the screen.
- Help Menu is for accessing online help.

The buttons to the right of the menu buttons are launcher applets. Each of these applets displays a button with the icon of an application. Clicking a button starts (launches) that application. Try clicking each of these buttons to see what happens. Move the mouse over a button and a small Help message appears with information about that button. That's how you can easily tell what each button does.

Customizing the GNOME desktop

By now, you may be itching to do a bit of decorating. After all, it's your desktop. You can set it up any way you want it. To change the GNOME desktop's background, right-click on an empty area of the desktop and select Change Desktop Background from the menu that appears. The Desktop Background Preferences dialog box appears, as shown in Figure 5-13.

Figure 5-13: Changing the GNOME desktop's background.

From this dialog box, you can select a background of a solid color, a color gradient, or a *wallpaper* (an image used as the background). A *color gradient* background starts with one color and gradually changes to another color. The gradient can be in the vertical direction (top to bottom) or horizontal (left to right).

Just for the fun of it, if you want to try out a horizontal color gradient, follow these steps:

1. **Scroll up the Desktop Wallpaper list (refer to Figure 5-13) and select No Wallpaper from the very top.**
2. **Click the Desktop Colors item, and from the drop-down list, choose the Horizontal Gradient option.**
3. **Click the Left Color button next to the drop-down list.**

   The Pick a Color dialog box comes up (shown in Figure 5-14) from which you can select a color.

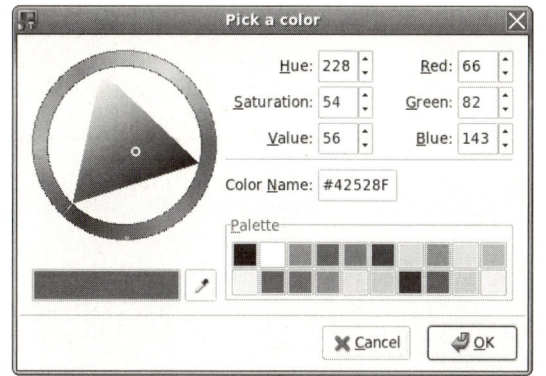

Figure 5-14: The Pick a Color dialog box.

4. **Repeat the same process to select the right color.**

After you complete these steps, the desktop shows the new background color.

To revert back to the original wallpaper, scroll down in the Desktop Wallpaper list (see Figure 5-13) and select the previous wallpaper image (or pick a different wallpaper, if that's what you want).

Click Close to get rid of the Desktop Background Preferences dialog box.

Chapter 6
Finding and Organizing Files

In This Chapter
- Understanding how Linux organizes files
- Navigating the file system with Linux commands
- Understanding file permissions
- Manipulating files and directories with Linux commands

*T*o use files and directories well, you need to understand the concept of a hierarchical file system. Even if you use the GUI file managers to access files and folders (folders are also called *directories*), you can benefit from a file system that gives you the lay of the land.

In this chapter, I introduce you to the Linux file system, and you discover how to work with files and directories with several Linux commands.

Figuring Out the Linux File System

Like any other operating system, Linux organizes information in files and directories. Directories, in turn, hold the files. A *directory* is a special file that can contain other files and directories. Because a directory can contain other directories, this method of organizing files gives rise to a hierarchical structure. This hierarchical organization of files is called the *file system*.

The Linux file system gives you a unified view of all storage in your PC. The file system has a single `root` directory, indicated by a forward slash (/). Within the `root` directory is a hierarchy of files and directories. Parts of the file system can reside in different physical media, such as a hard drive, floppy disk, and CD-ROM. Figure 6-1 illustrates the concept of the Linux file system (which is the same in any Linux system whether it's SUSE, Red Hat, or what have you) and how it spans multiple physical devices.

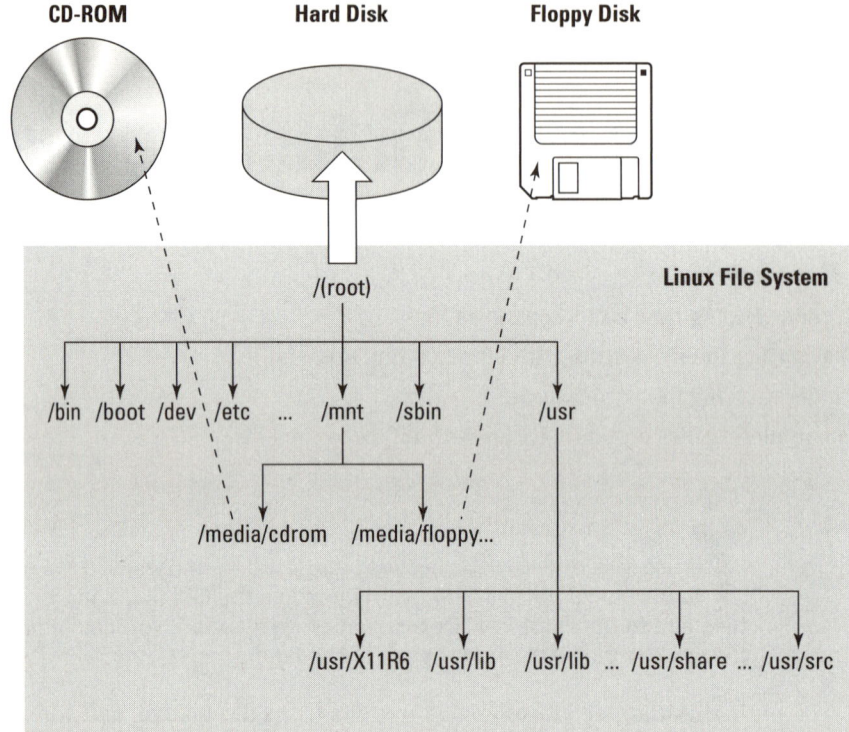

Figure 6-1: The Linux file system provides a unified view of storage that may span multiple storage devices.

If you're familiar with MS-DOS or Windows, you may find something missing in the Linux file system: You don't find drive letters such as :c and :d in Linux. All disk drives and CD-ROM drives are part of a single file system.

In Linux, filenames can be long (up to 256 characters) and are case-sensitive. Often these filenames have multiple extensions, such as `sample.tar.Z`. UNIX filenames can take many forms, such as the following: `index.html`, `Makefile`, `XF86Config.install.old`, `vsftpd-2.0.1-2.i386.rpm`, `.bash_profile`, and `apache2_src.tar.gz`.

To locate a file, you need more than just the filename. You also need information about the directory hierarchy. The extended filename, showing the full hierarchy of directories leading to the file, is called the *pathname*. As the name implies, it's the path to the file through the maze of the file system. Figure 6-2 shows a typical pathname for a file in Linux.

As Figure 6-2 shows, the pathname has the following parts:

  ✔ The `root` directory, indicated by a forward slash (/) character.
  ✔ The directory hierarchy, with each directory name separated from the previous one by a forward slash (/) character. A / appears after the last directory name.

✔ The filename, with a name and one or more optional extensions. (A period appears before each extension.)

Figure 6-2: The pathname of a file shows the sequence of directories leading to the file.

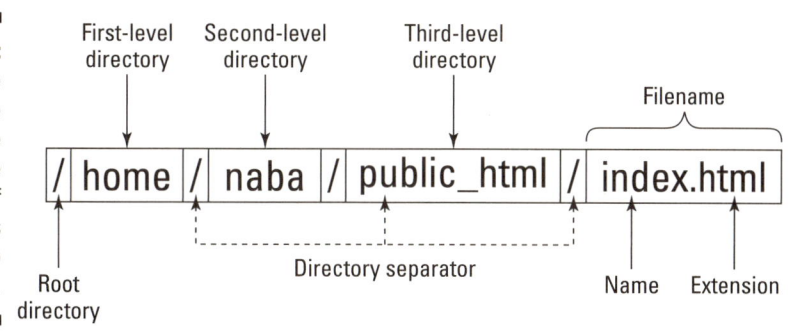

`/ home / naba / public_html / index.html`

- Root directory
- First-level directory
- Second-level directory
- Third-level directory
- Directory separator
- Filename (Name, Extension)

The Linux file system has a well-defined set of top-level directories, and some of these directories have specific purposes. Finding your way around the file system is easier if you know the purpose of these directories. You also become adept at guessing where to look for specific types of files when you face a new situation. Consult Table 6-1 for a brief description of the top-level directories in the Linux file system.

Table 6-1	Top-Level Directories in the SUSE Linux File System
Directory	**Description**
/	This `root` directory forms the base of the file system. All files and directories are contained logically in the `root` directory, regardless of their physical locations.
/bin	Contains the executable programs that are part of the Linux operating system. Many Linux commands, such as `cat`, `cp`, `ls`, `more`, and `tar`, are located in `/bin`.
/boot	Contains the Linux kernel and other files that the GRUB boot manager needs. (The kernel and other files can be anywhere, but placing them in the `/boot` directory is customary.)
/dev	Contains special files that represent devices attached to the system.
/etc	Contains most system configuration files and the initialization scripts (in the `/etc/rc.d` subdirectory).

(continued)

Table 6-1 *(continued)*

Directory	Description
/home	Conventional location of the home directories of all users. User naba's home directory, for example, is /home/naba.
/lib	Contains library files for all programs stored in /sbin and /bin directories (including the loadable driver modules) needed to start Linux.
/media	A directory for mounting file systems on removable media, such as CD-ROM drives, floppy disks, and Zip drives. Contains the /media/floppy directory for mounting floppy disks and the /media/cdrom directory for mounting the CD-ROM drive. If you have a CD recorder, you'll find a /media/cdrecorder directory instead of /media/cdrom.
/mnt	A directory for temporarily mounted file systems.
/opt	Provides a storage area for large application software packages. For example, GNOME and KDE applications are installed in the /opt directory.
/proc	A special memory-resident directory that contains various information about the processes running in the Linux system.
/root	The home directory for the root user.
/sbin	Contains executable files representing commands typically used for system-administration tasks and used by the root user. Commands such as halt and shutdown reside in the /sbin directory.
/srv	Contains data for services (such as Web and FTP) offered by this system.
/sys	A special directory that contains information about the devices, as seen by the Linux kernel.
/tmp	A temporary directory that any user can use as a *scratch* directory, meaning that the contents of this directory are considered unimportant and usually are deleted every time the system boots.
/usr	Contains the subdirectories for many important programs, such as the X Window System (in the /usr/X11R6 directory) and the online manual.
/var	Contains various system files (such as logs), as well as directories for holding other information, such as files for printers and mail messages.

Using GUI File Managers

Both GNOME and KDE desktops come with GUI file managers that enable you to easily browse the file system and perform tasks such as copying or moving files. The GNOME file manager is called Nautilus and the KDE file manager is Konqueror. I briefly introduce these GUI file managers in the following sections.

Conquering the file system with Konqueror

Konqueror is a file manager and Web browser that comes with KDE. It's intuitive to use — somewhat similar to the Windows Active Desktop. You can manage files and folders (and also view Web pages) with Konqueror.

Viewing files and folders

When you double-click a folder icon on the desktop, Konqueror starts automatically. For example, click the Home Folder icon on the KDE panel. Konqueror runs and displays the contents of your home directory (think of a *directory* as a folder that can contain other files and folders). Figure 6-3 shows a typical user's home directory in Konqueror.

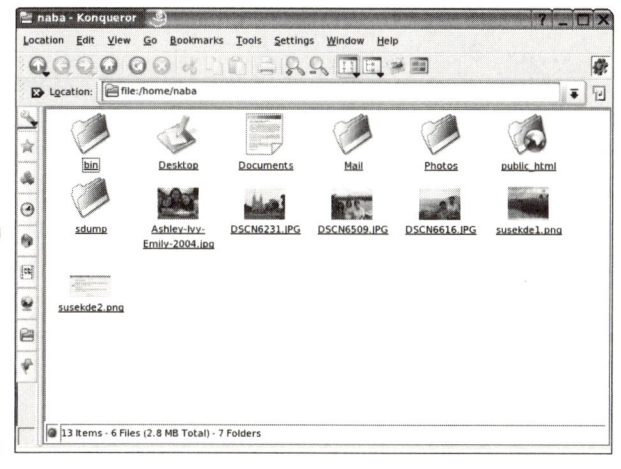

Figure 6-3: You can view files and folders in Konqueror.

If you've used Windows Explorer, you can use Konqueror in a similar manner.

The Konqueror window is vertically divided into two panes:

- A narrow left pane shows icons you can click to perform various tasks in Konqueror.
- A wide right pane uses icons to show the files and folders in the currently selected folder.

Konqueror uses different types of icons for different files and shows a preview of each file's contents. For image files, the preview is a thumbnail version of the image.

The Konqueror window's title bar shows the name of the currently selected directory. The Location text box (along the top of the window) shows the full name of the directory — in this case, Figure 6-3 shows the contents of the /home/naba directory.

Use the leftmost vertical row of buttons to select other things to browse. When you click one of these buttons, a middle pane appears with a tree menu of items that you can browse. For example, to browse other parts of the file system, do the following:

1. **From the icons in the Konqueror window's left pane (refer to Figure 6-3), click the Root Folder icon (the second icon from the bottom, the one that looks like a folder).**

    A tree menu of directories appears in a middle pane.

2. **In the tree view of directories in the middle pane, locate the folder that you want to browse and click the plus sign next to that folder to view any other folders inside that folder.**

    For example, to look inside the etc folder, click the plus sign next to the etc folder. Konqueror displays the other folders inside etc and changes the plus sign to a minus sign.

3. **To view the contents of the X11 subdirectory inside the etc folder, scroll down the middle pane and click X11.**

    The pane on the right now shows the contents of the /etc/X11 directory.

Konqueror displays the contents of a folder using different types of icons. Each directory appears as a folder, with the name of the directory shown underneath the folder icon. Ordinary files appear as a sheet of paper.

The Konqueror window has the usual menu bar and a toolbar. You can view the files and folders in other formats as well. For example, from the menu, choose View⇨View Mode⇨Detailed List View to see the folder's contents with smaller icons in a list format (see Figure 6-4), along with detailed information (such as the size of each file or directory, and at what time each was last modified).

Figure 6-4: Konqueror shows a detailed list view of the /etc/X11 directory.

If you click any of the column headings — Name, Size, File Type, or Modified, to name a few — along the top of the list view, Konqueror sorts the list according to that column. For example, if you click the Modified column heading, Konqueror displays the list of files and folders sorted according to the time of last modification. Clicking the Name column heading sorts the files and directories alphabetically by name.

Manipulating files and directories in Konqueror

Not only can you move around different folders by using Konqueror, but you can also do things such as move a file from one folder to another or delete a file. I don't outline each step here because the steps are intuitive and similar to what you do in any GUI (such as Windows or the Mac interface). Here are some things you can do in Konqueror:

- **View a text file:** Click the filename, and Konqueror displays the contents of the file in the right pane.

- **Copy or move a file to a different folder:** Drag and drop the file's icon on the folder where you want the file to go. A menu pops up and asks you whether you want to copy or simply link the file to that directory.

- **Delete a file or directory:** Right-click the icon and choose Move to Trash from the context menu. To permanently delete the file, right-click the Trash icon on the desktop and choose Empty Trash from the context menu. Of course, do this only if you really want to delete the file. When you choose Empty Trash, the deleted files are really gone forever. If you want to recover a file from the trash, double-click the Trash icon on the desktop. From that window, drag and drop the file icon into the folder where you want to save the file. When asked whether you want to copy or move, select Move. You can recover files from the trash until the moment you empty the trash.

Part II: Test Driving SUSE

- **Rename a file or a directory:** Right-click the icon and choose Rename from the context menu. Then you can type the new name (or edit the old name) in the text box that appears.
- **Create a new folder:** Choose View➪View Mode➪Icon View. Then right-click an empty area of the rightmost pane and choose Create New➪Folder from the context menu. Then type the name of the new directory and click OK. (If you don't have permission to create a directory, you get an error message.)

Viewing Web pages

Konqueror is much more than a file manager. With it, you can view a Web page as easily as you can view a folder. Just type a Web address in the Location text box and see what happens. For example, Figure 6-5 shows the Konqueror window after I type www.irs.gov in the Location text box on the toolbar and press Enter.

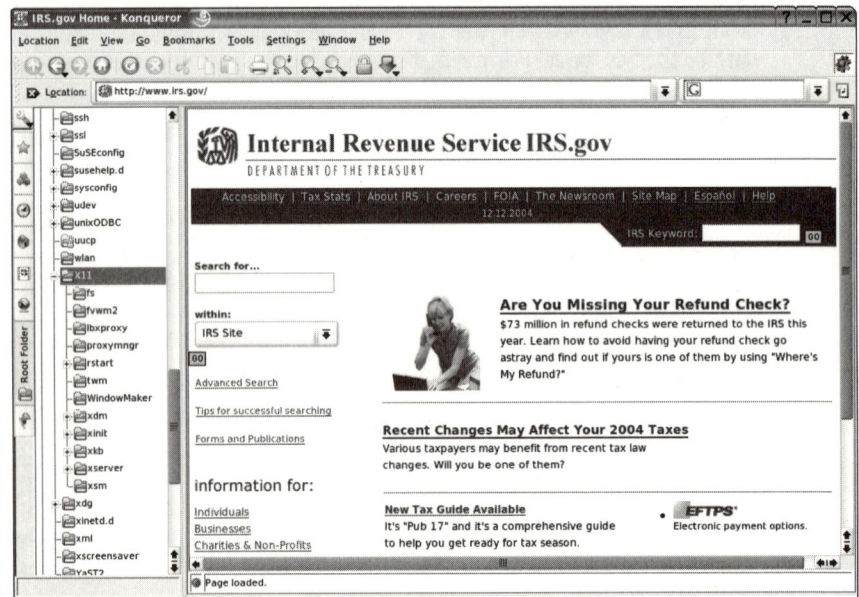

Figure 6-5: Konqueror can browse the Web as well.

Konqueror displays the Web site in the pane on the right. The left pane still shows whatever it was displaying earlier.

Roaming the file system with Nautilus

The Nautilus file manager — more accurately called a *graphical shell* — comes with GNOME. You can manage files and folders and even your system with Nautilus. In fact, you can even burn a data CD from Nautilus (I describe the CD-burning steps in Chapter 14).

REMEMBER You can browse the file system in Nautilus in two ways. By default, when you double-click any object on the desktop, Nautilus opens a new window that shows that object's contents. If you want a more Windows-like navigation window with a Web browser-like user interface, right-click a folder and choose Open➪Browse Folder from the pop-up menu.

Viewing files and folders in object windows

When you double-click a file or a folder, Nautilus opens that object in what it calls an *object window.* The object window doesn't have any Back and Forward buttons, toolbars, or side panes. For example, double-click the Home Folder icon on the GNOME desktop, and Nautilus opens an object window where it displays the contents of your home directory. (Think of a *directory* as a folder that can contain other files and folders.) If you then double-click an object inside that window, Nautilus opens another object window where that object's contents appear. Figure 6-6 shows the result of double-clicking some objects in Nautilus.

The Nautilus object window has a sparse user interface that has just the menu bar. You can perform various operations from the menu bar such as open an object using an application, create folders and documents, and close the object window.

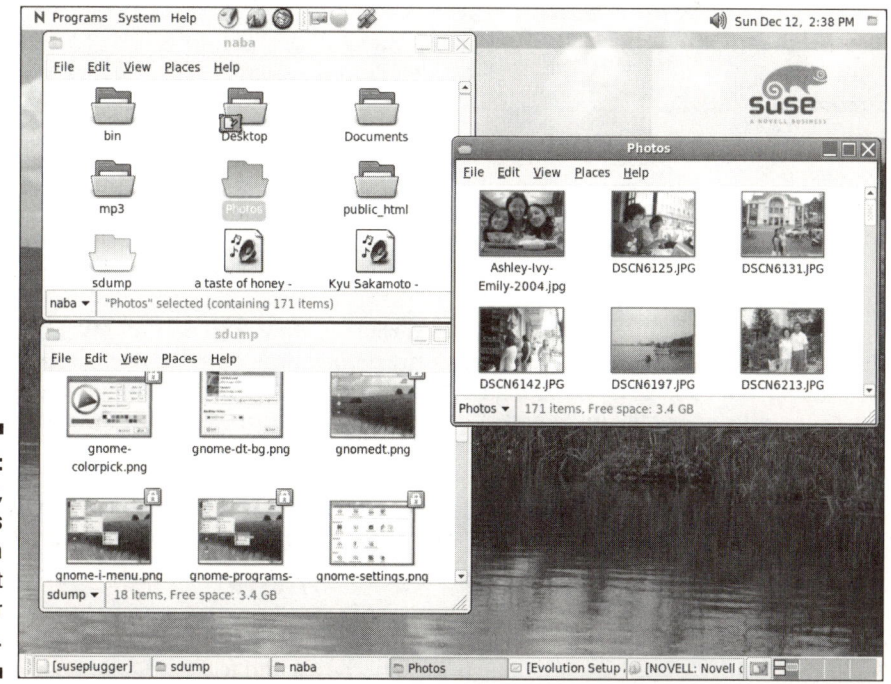

Figure 6-6: By default, Nautilus opens a new object window for each object.

Browsing folders in a navigation window

If you prefer to use the familiar navigation window for browsing folders with Nautilus, you have to do a bit of extra work. Instead of double-clicking an icon, right-click the icon and choose Browse Folder from the context menu. Nautilus then opens a navigation window with the contents of the object represented by the icon. For example, right-click the Home Folder icon on the GNOME desktop and select Browse Folder from the context menu. Nautilus opens a navigation window where it displays the contents of your home directory. Figure 6-7 shows my home directory in a Nautilus navigation window. Nautilus displays icons for files and folders. For image files, it shows a thumbnail of the image.

Figure 6-7: You can view files and folders in the Nautilus navigation window.

If you double-click any object in the window, Nautilus displays the contents of that object. If you double-click a folder, Nautilus displays the contents of that folder. On the other hand, if you double-click a document or an image or an MP3 file, Nautilus opens it with an appropriate application.

The Nautilus window's user interface is similar to that of a Web browser. The window's title bar shows the name of the currently selected folder. The Location text box along the top of the window shows the full name of the directory in Linuxspeak — for example, Figure 6-7 shows the contents of the /home/naba directory.

You can use the Nautilus navigation window in the same way you would use Windows Explorer. To view the contents of another directory, do the following:

Chapter 6: Finding and Organizing Files

1. **Press F9 to open the side pane in the Nautilus window.**

   This causes the Nautilus window to vertically divide into two parts. The left pane shows different views of the file system and other objects that you can browse with Nautilus. The right pane shows the files and folders in the currently selected folder in the left pane.

2. **Select Tree from the Information drop-down menu (located in the left window).**

   A tree menu of directories appears in that window. Initially the tree shows your home folder and the file system appears as a `FileSystem` folder.

3. **Click the right arrow that appears to the left of the `FileSystem` folder; in the resulting tree view, locate the directory you want to browse.**

   For example, to look at the `/etc` directory, click the right arrow next to the `etc` directory. Nautilus displays the subdirectories in `/etc` and changes the right arrow to a down arrow. `X11` is one of the subdirectories in `/etc` that you view in the next step. Scroll down the contents of the left pane to locate the `X11` folder.

4. **To view the contents of the `X11` subdirectory, click `X11`.**

   The window on the right now shows the contents of the `/etc/X11` directory, as shown in Figure 6-8. Notice that `/etc/X11` appears in the Location text box in the Nautilus window.

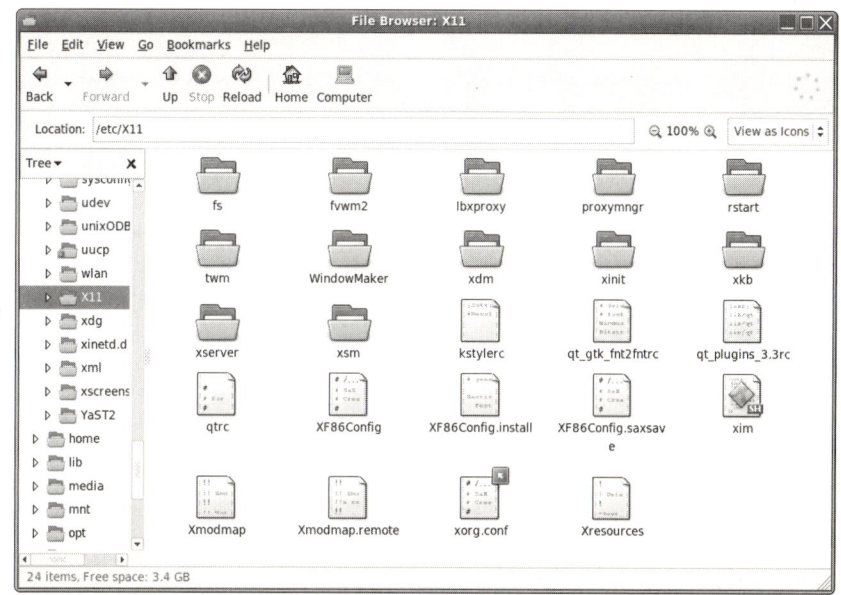

Figure 6-8: The Nautilus navigation window with an icon view of the /etc/X11 directory.

Part II: Test Driving SUSE

Nautilus displays the contents of the selected directory by using different types of icons. Each directory appears as a folder with the name of the directory shown underneath the folder icon. Ordinary files, such as XF86Config, appear as a sheet of paper.

The Nautilus navigation window has the usual menu bar and a toolbar. Notice the View as Icons button in Figure 6-8 on the right side of the toolbar. This button shows that Nautilus is displaying the directory contents with large icons. Click the button, and a drop-down list appears. Select View as List from the list, and Nautilus displays the contents by using smaller icons in a list format, along with detailed information, such as the size of each file or directory and the time when each was last modified, as shown in Figure 6-9.

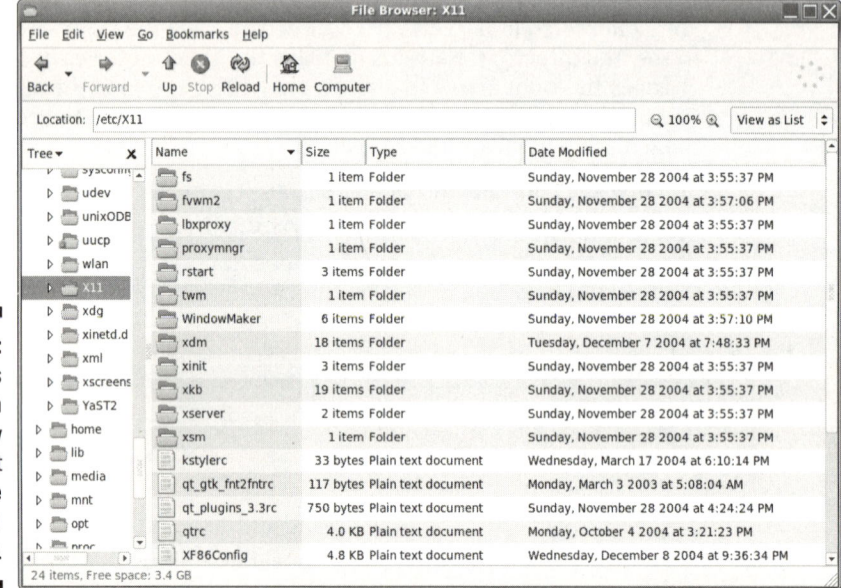

Figure 6-9: The Nautilus navigation window with a list view of the /etc/X11 directory.

If you click any of the column headings — Name, Size, Type, or Date modified — along the top of the list view, Nautilus sorts the list according to that column. For example, go ahead and click the Date Modified column heading. Nautilus now displays the list of files and directories sorted according to the time of their last modification. Clicking the Name column heading sorts the files and folders alphabetically.

Manipulating files and directories in Nautilus

Not only can you move around different folders by using the Nautilus navigation window, you can also do things such as move a file from one folder to another or delete a file. I don't outline each step — the steps are intuitive and similar to what you do in any GUI, such as Windows or Mac. Here are some of the things you can do in Nautilus:

- To move a file to a different folder, drag and drop the file's icon on the folder where you want the file.

- To copy a file to a new location, select the file's icon and choose Edit➪Copy File from the Nautilus menu. You can also right-click the file's icon and choose Copy File from the context menu. Then move to the folder where you want to copy the file and choose Edit➪Paste Files.

- To delete a file or directory, right-click the icon, and choose Move to Trash from the context menu. (You can do this only if you have permission to delete the file.) To permanently delete the file, right-click the Trash icon on the desktop and choose Empty Trash from the context menu. Of course, do this only if you really want to delete the file. Once you choose Empty Trash, you are never going to see the file again. If you have to retrieve a file from the trash, double-click the Trash icon and then drag the file's icon back to the folder where you want to save it. You can retrieve a file from the trash until you empty it.

- To rename a file or a directory, right-click the icon and choose Rename from the context menu. Then you can type the new name (or edit the name) in the text box that appears.

- To create a new folder, right-click an empty area of the window on the right and choose Create Folder from the context menu. After the new folder icon appears, you can rename it by right-clicking the icon and choosing Rename from the context menu. If you don't have permission to create a folder, that menu item is grayed out.

Using Linux Commands to Manipulate Files and Directories

Although GUI file managers such as Konqueror (in KDE) and Nautilus (in GNOME) are easy to use, you can use them only if you have a working GUI desktop. Sometimes, you may not have a graphical environment to run a graphical file manager. For example, you may be logged in through a text terminal, or the X Window System may not be working on your system. In those situations, you have to rely on Linux commands to work with files and directories. Of course, you can always use Linux commands, even in the graphical environment — all you have to do is open a terminal window and type the Linux commands.

To open a terminal window in KDE, click the terminal icon on the panel. In GNOME, choose Programs➪System➪Terminal➪Terminal.

In the sections that follow, I briefly show some Linux commands for working with the files and directories.

Commands for directory navigation

In Linux, when you log in as `root`, your home directory is `/root`. For other users, the home directory is usually in the `/home` directory. My home directory (when I log in as `naba`) is `/home/naba`. This information is stored in the `/etc/passwd` file. By default, only you have permission to save files in your home directory, and only you can create subdirectories in your home directory to further organize your files.

Linux supports the concept of a current directory, which is the directory on which all file and directory commands operate. After you log in, for example, your current directory is the home directory. To see the current directory, type the `pwd` command.

To change the current directory, use the `cd` command. To change the current directory to `/usr/lib`, type the following:

```
cd /usr/lib
```

Then, to change the directory to the `cups` subdirectory in `/usr/lib`, type this command:

```
cd cups
```

Now, if you use the `pwd` command, that command shows `/usr/lib/cups` as the current directory.

These two examples show that you can refer to a directory's name in two ways:

- An **absolute pathname** (such as `/usr/lib`) that specifies the exact directory in the directory tree
- A **relative directory name** (such as `cups`, which represents the `cups` subdirectory of the current directory, whatever that may be)

If you type `cd cups` in `/usr/lib`, the current directory changes to `/usr/lib/cups`. However, if you type the same command in `/home/naba`, the shell tries to change the current directory to `/home/naba/cups`.

TIP: Use the `cd` command without any arguments to change the current directory back to your home directory. No matter where you are, typing **cd** at the shell prompt brings you back home!

Chapter 6: Finding and Organizing Files

Technical Stuff: By the way, the tilde character (~) refers to your home directory. Thus the command `cd ~` also changes the current directory to your home directory. You can also refer to another user's home directory by appending that user's name to the tilde. Thus, `cd ~spiderman` changes the current directory to the home directory of `spiderman`.

Tip: Wait, there's more. A single dot (.) and two dots (..) — often referred to as dot-dot — (clever, huh!) also have special meanings. A single dot (.) indicates the current directory, whereas two dots (..) indicate the parent directory. For example, if the current directory is `/usr/share`, you go one level up to `/usr` by typing

```
cd ..
```

Commands for directory listings and permissions

You can get a directory listing by using the `ls` command. By default, the `ls` command — without any options — displays the contents of the current directory in a compact, multicolumn format. For example, type the next two commands to see the contents of the `/etc/X11` directory:

```
cd /etc/X11
ls
```

The output looks like this (on the console, you see some items in different colors):

```
fs                  qtrc              XF86Config.saxsave    xorg.conf
fvwm2               rstart            XF86Config.YaST2save  Xresources
kstylerc            twm               xim                   xserver
lbxproxy            WindowMaker       xinit                 xsm
proxymngr           xdm               xkb
qt_gtk_fnt2fntrc    XF86Config        Xmodmap
qt_plugins_3.3rc    XF86Config.install Xmodmap.remote
```

From this listing (without the colors), you cannot tell whether an entry is a file or a directory. To tell the directories and files apart, use the `-F` option with `ls` like this:

```
ls -F
```

Part II: Test Driving SUSE

This time, the output gives you some more clues about the file types:

```
fs/              qtrc              XF86Config.saxsave    xorg.conf@
fvwm2/           rstart/           XF86Config.YaST2save  Xresources
kstylerc         twm/              xim*                  xserver/
lbxproxy/        WindowMaker/      xinit/                xsm/
proxymngr/       xdm/              xkb/
qt_gtk_fnt2fntrc XF86Config        Xmodmap
qt_plugins_3.3rc XF86Config.install Xmodmap.remote
```

The output from `ls -F` shows the directory names with a slash (/) appended to them. Plain filenames appear as is. The *at sign* (@) appended to a file's name (for example, notice the file named `xorg.conf`) indicates that this file is a link to another file. (In other words, this filename simply refers to another file; it's a shortcut.) An asterisk (*) is appended to executable files. (`xim`, for example, is an executable file.) The shell can run any executable file.

You can see even more detailed information about the files and directories with the `-l` option:

```
ls -l
```

For the `/etc/X11` directory, a typical output from `ls -l` looks like the following:

```
total 77
drwxr-xr-x   2 root root   72 2004-11-12 20:08 fs
drwxr-xr-x   2 root root   80 2004-11-12 20:09 fvwm2
-rw-r--r--   1 root root   33 2004-03-17 18:10 kstylerc
drwxr-xr-x   2 root root   80 2004-11-12 20:08 lbxproxy
drwxr-xr-x   2 root root   72 2004-11-12 20:08 proxymngr
-rw-r--r--   1 root root  117 2003-03-03 05:08 qt_gtk_fnt2fntrc
-rw-r--r--   1 root root  868 2004-11-12 20:49 qt_plugins_3.3rc
-rw-r--r--   1 root root 4971 2004-11-23 21:51 qtrc
drwxr-xr-x   4 root root  120 2004-11-12 20:08 rstart
drwxr-xr-x   2 root root   80 2004-11-12 20:08 twm
drwxr-xr-x   2 root root  232 2004-11-12 20:09 WindowMaker
drwxr-xr-x   3 root root  552 2004-12-09 21:40 xdm
-rw-r--r--   1 root root 5741 2004-12-09 21:21 XF86Config
... lines deleted ...
```

This listing shows considerable information about every directory entry — each of which can be a file or another directory. Looking at a line from the right column to the left, you see that the rightmost column shows the name of the directory entry. The date and time before the name show when the last modifications to that file were made. To the left of the date and time is the size of the file in bytes.

Chapter 6: Finding and Organizing Files

The file's group and owner appear to the left of the column that shows the file size. The next number to the left indicates the number of links to the file. (A *link* is like a shortcut in Windows.) Finally, the leftmost column shows the file's permission settings, which determine who can read, write, or execute the file.

The first letter of the leftmost column has a special meaning, as the following list shows:

- If the first letter is l, the file is a *symbolic link* (a shortcut) to another file.
- If the first letter is d, the file is a directory.
- If the first letter is a dash (-), the file is normal.
- If the first letter is b, the file represents a block device, such as a disk drive.
- If the first letter is c, the file represents a character device, such as a serial port or a terminal.

After that first letter, the leftmost column shows a sequence of nine characters, which appear as rwxrwxrwx when each letter is present. Each letter indicates a specific permission. A hyphen (-) in place of a letter indicates no permission for a specific operation on the file. Think of these nine letters as three groups of three letters (rwx), interpreted as follows:

- The leftmost group of rwx controls the *read, write,* and *execute* permissions of the file's owner. In other words, if you see rwx in this position, the file's owner can read (r), write (w), and execute (x) the file. A hyphen in the place of a letter indicates no permission. Thus the string rw- means the owner has read and write permissions but no execute permission. Although executable programs (including shell programs) typically have execute permission, directories treat execute permission as equivalent to *use* permission — a user must have execute permission on a directory before he or she can open and read the contents of the directory.
- The middle three rwx letters control the read, write, and execute permissions of any user belonging to that file's group.
- The rightmost group of rwx letters controls the read, write, and execute permissions of all other users (collectively referred to as *the world*).

Thus, a file with the permission setting rwx------ is accessible only to the file's owner, whereas the permission setting rwxr--r-- makes the file readable by the world.

An interesting feature of the `ls` command is that it doesn't list any file whose name begins with a period. To see these files, you must use the `ls` command with the `-a` option, as follows:

```
ls -a
```

Try this command in your home directory (and then compare the result with what you see when you don't use the `-a` option):

1. **Type cd to change to your home directory.**
2. **Type ls -F to see the files and directories in your home directory.**
3. **Type ls -aF to see everything, including the hidden files.**

TIP: Most Linux commands take single-character options, each with a minus sign (think of this sign as a hyphen) as a prefix. When you want to use several options, type a hyphen and *concatenate* (string together) the option letters, one after another. Thus, `ls -al` is equivalent to `ls -a -l` as well as `ls -l -a`.

Commands for working with files

To copy files from one directory to another, use the `cp` command. For example, to copy the file `/usr/X11R6/lib/X11/xinit/Xclients` to the `Xclients.sample` file in the current directory (such as your home directory), type the following:

```
cp /usr/X11R6/lib/X11/xinit/xinitrc xinitrc.sample
```

If you want to copy a file to the current directory but retain the original name, use a period (.) as the second argument of the `cp` command. Thus, the following command copies the `Xresources` file from the `/etc/X11` directory to the current directory (denoted by a single period):

```
cp /etc/X11/Xresources .
```

The `cp` command makes a new copy of a file and leaves the original intact.

TIP: If you want to copy the entire contents of a directory — including all subdirectories and their contents — to another directory, use the command `cp -ar` *sourcedir destdir*. (This command copies everything in the *sourcedir* directory to *destdir*.) For example, to copy all files from the `/etc/X11` directory to the current directory, type the following command:

```
cp -ar /etc/X11 .
```

Chapter 6: Finding and Organizing Files

TIP: To move a file to a new location, use the `mv` command. The original copy is gone, and a new copy appears at the destination. You can use `mv` to rename a file. If you want to change the name of `today.list` to `old.list`, use the `mv` command, as follows:

```
mv today.list old.list
```

On the other hand, if you want to move the `today.list` file to a subdirectory named `saved`, use this command:

```
mv today.list saved
```

An interesting feature of `mv` is that you can use it to move entire directories — with all their subdirectories and files — to a new location. If you have a directory named `data` that contains many files and subdirectories, you can move that entire directory structure to `old_data` by using the following command:

```
mv data old_data
```

To delete files, use the `rm` command. For example, to delete a file named `old.list`, type the following command:

```
rm old.list
```

WARNING! Be careful with the `rm` command — especially when you log in as `root`. You can inadvertently delete important files with `rm`.

Commands for working with directories

To organize files in your home directory, you have to create new directories. Use the `mkdir` command to create a directory. For example, to create a directory named `Photos` in the current directory, type the following:

```
mkdir Photos
```

After you create the directory, you can use the `cd Photos` command to change to that directory.

TIP: You can create an entire directory tree by using the `-p` option with the `mkdir` command. For example, suppose your system has a `/usr/src` directory and you want to create the directory tree `/usr/src/book/java/examples/applets`. To create this directory hierarchy, type the following command:

```
mkdir -p /usr/src/book/java/examples/applets
```

When you no longer need a directory, use the `rmdir` command to delete it.

Remember: You can delete a directory only when the directory is empty.

To remove an empty directory tree, you can use the `-p` option, like this:

```
rmdir -p /usr/src/book/java/examples/applets
```

This command removes the empty parent directories of `applets`. The command stops when it encounters a directory that's not empty.

Commands for finding files

The `find` command is very useful for locating files (and directories) that meet your search criteria.

When I began using UNIX many years ago (Berkeley UNIX in the early 1980s), I was confounded by the `find` command. I stayed with one basic syntax of `find` for a long time before graduating to more complex forms. The basic syntax that I discovered first was for finding a file anywhere in the file system. Here's how it goes: Suppose you want to find any file or directory with a name that starts with `gnome`. Type the following `find` command to find these files:

```
find / -name "gnome*" -print
```

If you're not logged in as `root`, you may get a bunch of error messages. If these error messages annoy you, just modify the command as follows and the error messages are history (or, as UNIX aficionados say, "Send 'em to the bit bucket"):

```
find / -name "gnome*" -print 2> /dev/null
```

This command tells `find` to start looking at the `root` directory (`/`) for filenames that match `gnome*`, and to display the full pathname of any matching file. The last part (`2> /dev/null`) simply sends the error messages to a special file that's the equivalent of simply ignoring them.

You can use variations of this simple form of `find` to locate a file in any directory (as well as any subdirectories contained in the directory). If you forget where in your home directory you've stored all files named `report*` (names that start with `report`), you can search for the files by using the following command:

```
find ~ -name "report*" -print
```

When you become comfortable with this syntax of `find`, you can use other options of `find`. For example, to find only specific types of files (such as directories), use the `type` option. The following command displays all top-level directory names in your Linux system:

```
find / -type d -maxdepth 1 -print
```

You probably don't have to use the complex forms of `find` in a typical Linux system — but if you ever need to, you can look up the rest of the `find` options by using the following command:

```
man find
```

TIP An easy way to find all files that match a name is to use the `locate` command that searches a periodically updated database of files on your system. For example, here's a typical output I get when I type **locate Xresources** on a Debian system:

```
/etc/X11/Xresources
/etc/X11/Xresources/xbase-clients
/etc/X11/Xresources/xfree86-common
```

REMEMBER The `locate` command isn't installed by default in SUSE Linux, but it's very easy to install. See Chapter 23 for information on how to use it.

Commands for mounting and unmounting

Suppose you want to access the files on this book's companion DVD-ROM when you are logged in at a text console (with no GUI to help you). To do so, you have to first mount the DVD-ROM drive's file system on a specific directory in the Linux file system.

TIP Type **more /etc/fstab** in a terminal window to look at the `/etc/fstab` file for clues to the names of devices such as a floppy drive and DVD/CD drive. SUSE Linux distributions uses the device name `/dev/cdrom` to refer to DVD/CD-ROM drives, whereas for a DVD/CD-R drive (a CD or DVD burner), the device name is `/dev/cdrecorder`. The entry in the `/etc/fstab` file also tells you the directory where SUSE Linux mounts the DVD/CD drive. For a read-only DVD/CD-ROM drive, SUSE Linux uses `/media/cdrom` as the mount point, whereas for a DVD/CD-R drive, the mount point is `/media/cdrecorder`.

Type **su -** to become `root`, insert the DVD-ROM in the DVD drive, and then type the following command in a text console or a terminal window:

```
mount /dev/cdrom /media/cdrom
```

This command mounts the file system on the device named `/dev/cdrom` on the `/media/cdrom` directory (which is also called the *mount point*) in the Linux file system.

After the `mount` command successfully completes its task, you can access the files on the DVD-ROM by referring to the `/media/cdrom` directory as the top-level directory of the disc. In other words, to see the contents of the DVD-ROM, type

```
ls -F /media/cdrom
```

When you're done using the DVD-ROM — and before you eject it from the drive — you have to unmount the disc drive with the following `umount` command:

```
umount /dev/cdrom
```

You can mount devices on any empty directory on the file system. However, SUSE Linux has customary locations such as `/media/cdrom` and `/media/cdrecorder` for mounting DVD/CD drives.

Commands for checking disk-space usage

I want to tell you about two commands — `df` and `du` — that you can use to check the disk-space usage on your system. These commands are simple to use. The `df` command shows you a summary of disk-space usage for all mounted devices. For example, here's the result of typing **df** on one of my PCs running SUSE Linux:

```
Filesystem         1K-blocks      Used Available Use% Mounted on
/dev/hda11           6357688   1994348   4363340  32% /
tmpfs                 124004        36    123968   1% /dev/shm
/dev/hda7              43885      9749     31870  24% /boot
/dev/hdc              664234    664234         0 100% /media/cdrecorder
```

The output is a table that lists the device, the total kilobytes of storage, how much is in use, how much is available, the percentage being used, and the mount point.

To see the output of `df` in a more human-readable format, type **df -h**. Here is the output of the `df -h` command:

```
Filesystem         Size  Used Avail Use% Mounted on
/dev/hda11         6.1G  2.0G  4.2G  32% /
tmpfs              122M   36K  122M   1% /dev/shm
/dev/hda7           43M  9.6M   32M  24% /boot
/dev/hdc           649M  649M     0 100% /media/cdrecorder
```

Chapter 6: Finding and Organizing Files 103

If you compare this output with the output of plain `df` (see previous listing), you see that `df -h` prints the sizes with terms like `M` for megabytes and `G` for gigabytes. These are clearly easier to understand than `1K-blocks`.

The other command — `du` — is useful for finding out how much space a directory takes up. For example, type **du /etc/X11** to view the contents of all the directories in the /etc/X11 directory. (This directory contains X Window System configuration files.) You end up with a list that looks similar to the following:

```
4          /etc/X11/fs
4          /etc/X11/twm
84         /etc/X11/xdm/pixmaps
153        /etc/X11/xdm
372        /etc/X11/xkb/rules
44         /etc/X11/xkb/types
... lines deleted ...
40         /etc/X11/rstart
4          /etc/X11/proxymngr
2920       /etc/X11
```

Each directory name is preceded by a number — which tells you the number of kilobytes of disk space used by that directory. Thus the /etc/X11 directory, as a whole, uses 2920KB (or about 2.9MB) of disk space. If you simply want the total disk space used by a directory (including all the files and subdirectories contained in that directory), use the `-s` option and type **du -s /etc/X11**. The resulting output is as follows:

```
2920       /etc/X11
```

The `-s` option causes `du` to print just the summary information for the entire directory.

TIP Just as `df -h` prints the disk-space information in megabytes and gigabytes, you can use the `du -h` command to view the output of `du` in a more human-readable form. For example, to see the space that I'm using in my home directory (/home/naba), I type **du -sh /home/naba**. Here's a sample output from that command that tells me that I am using 645MB of space:

```
645M       /home/naba
```

Chapter 7

I Want My Internet, Now!

In This Chapter

▶ Understanding the Internet
▶ Deciding how to connect to the Internet
▶ Connecting to the Internet with DSL
▶ Connecting to the Internet with a cable modem
▶ Setting up a dialup link

*H*aving Internet access is almost a necessity nowadays. For example, if you want to access your e-mail, browse the Web, or get online updates for SUSE Linux from an Internet server, you need your PC connected to the Internet.

If your PC is not already connected to the Internet, it's a pretty safe bet for me to assume that you want to set up the Internet connection as soon as possible. In this chapter, I show you how to connect to the Internet in several different ways — depending on whether you have a DSL, cable modem, or dialup network connection.

Two of the options for connecting to the Internet — DSL and cable modem — involve connecting a special modem to an Ethernet card on your Linux system. In this chapter, I show you how to set up a DSL or a cable modem connection. I also show you another option — dialup networking — for connecting to the Internet that involves dialing up an Internet service provider (ISP) from your SUSE Linux system.

You have to turn to Chapter 8 to learn how to connect your PC to an Ethernet local area network (LAN) and add wireless capability to your LAN.

What Is the Internet?

How you view the Internet depends on your perspective. Regular folks see the Internet in terms of the services they use. For example, as a user, you might think of the Internet as an information-exchange medium with features such as

- **E-mail:** Send e-mail to any other user on the Internet, using addresses such as `mom@home.net`.
- **Web:** Download documents and images from millions of servers throughout the Internet.
- **Newsgroups:** Read newsgroups and post news items to newsgroups with names such as `comp.os.linux.networking` or `comp.os.linux.setup`.
- **Information sharing:** Download software, music files, videos, and so on. Reciprocally, you may provide files that users on other systems can download.
- **Remote access:** Log on to another computer on the Internet, assuming that you have access to that remote computer.

The techies say that the Internet is a worldwide *network of networks*. The term *internet* (without capitalization) is a shortened form of *internetworking* — the interconnection of networks. The Internet Protocol (IP) was designed with the idea of connecting many separate networks.

In terms of physical connections, the Internet is similar to a network of highways and roads. This similarity is what has prompted the popular press to dub the Internet "the Information Superhighway." Just as the network of highways and roads includes some interstate highways, many state roads, and many more residential streets, the Internet has some very high-capacity networks (for example, a 10 Gbps backbone can handle 10 billion bits per second) and a large number of lower-capacity networks ranging from 56 Kbps dialup connections to 45 Mbps T3 links. (*Kbps* is thousand-bits-per-second and *Mbps* is million-bits-per-second.) The high-capacity network is the backbone of the Internet.

In terms of management, the Internet is not run by a single organization, nor is it managed by any central computer. You can view the physical Internet as a "network of networks" managed collectively by thousands of cooperating organizations. Yes, a collection of networks managed by *thousands* of organizations — sounds amazing, but it works!

Deciding How to Connect to the Internet

So you want to connect to the Internet, but you don't know how? Let me count the ways. Nowadays you have three popular options for connecting home offices and small offices to the Internet (of course, huge corporations and governments have many other ways to connect):

- **Digital Subscriber Line (DSL):** Your local telephone company, as well as other telecommunications companies, may offer DSL. DSL provides a way to send high-speed digital data over a regular phone line. Typically,

Chapter 7: I Want My Internet, Now! 107

> DSL offers data-transfer rates of between 128 Kbps and 1.5 Mbps. You can download from the Internet at much higher rates than when you send data from your PC to the Internet *(upload)*. One caveat with DSL is that your home must be between 12,000 and 15,000 feet from your local central office (the phone-company facility where your phone lines end up). The distance limitation varies from provider to provider. In the United States, you can check out the distance limits for many providers at `www.dslreports.com/distance`.

- **Cable modem:** If the cable television company in your area offers Internet access over cable, you can use that service to hook up your Linux system to the Internet. Typically, cable modems offer higher data-transfer rates than DSL — for about the same cost. Downloading data from the Internet via cable modem is much faster than sending data from your PC to the Internet. You can expect routine download speeds of 1.5 Mbps and upload speeds of around 128 Kbps, but sometimes you may get even higher speeds than these.

- **Dialup networking:** A dialup connection is what most folks were using before DSL and cable modems came along. You hook up your PC to a modem that's connected to the phone line. Then you dial up an ISP to connect to the Internet. That's why it's called *dialup networking* — establishing a network connection between your Linux PC and another network (the Internet) through a dialup modem. In this case, the maximum data-transfer rate is 56 Kbps.

DSL and cable modem services connect you to the Internet and also act as your Internet service provider (ISP); in addition to improved speed, you pay for an IP address and your e-mail accounts. If you use a dialup modem to connect to the Internet, first you have to connect to the phone line (for which you pay the phone company) and then select and pay a separate ISP — which gives you a phone number to dial and all the other necessary goodies (such as an IP address and e-mail accounts).

Table 7-1 summarizes all these options. You can consult that table and select the type of connection that's available to you and that best suits your needs.

Table 7-1	Comparison of Dialup, DSL, and Cable		
Feature	*Dialup*	*DSL*	*Cable*
Equipment	Modem	DSL modem, Ethernet card	Cable modem, Ethernet card
Also requires	Phone service and an Internet service provider (ISP)	Phone service and location within 12,000 to 15,000 feet of central office	Cable TV connection

(continued)

Table 7-1 (continued)

Feature	Dialup	DSL	Cable
Connection type	Dial to connect	Always on, dedicated	Always on, shared
Typical speed	56 Kbps maximum	640 Kbps download, 128 Kbps upload (higher speeds cost more)	1.5 Mbps download, 128 Kbps upload
One-time costs (estimate)	None	Install = $100–$200; Equipment = $200–$300 (may be leased and may require activation cost)	Install = $100–$200; Equipment = $60–$100 (may be leased)
Typical monthly cost (2004)	Phone charges = $20/month; ISP charges = $15–$30/month	$50/month; may require monthly modem lease	$50/month; may require monthly modem lease

Note: Costs vary by region and provider. Costs shown are typical ones for U.S. metropolitan areas.

Connecting to the Internet with DSL

DSL (Digital Subscriber Line) uses your existing phone line to send digital data in addition to the normal analog voice signals (*analog* means continuously varying, whereas digital data is represented by 1s and 0s). The phone line goes from your home to a central office where the line connects to the phone company's network — by the way, the connection from your home to the central office is called the *local loop*. When you sign up for DSL service, the phone company hooks up your phone line to some special equipment at the central office. That equipment can separate the digital data from voice. From then on, your phone line can carry digital data that is then directly sent to an Internet connection at the central office.

How DSL works

A special box called a *DSL modem* takes care of sending digital data from your PC to the phone company's central office over your phone line. Your PC can connect to the Internet with the same phone line that you use for your normal telephone calls — you can make voice calls even as the line is being used for DSL. Figure 7-1 shows a typical DSL connection to the Internet.

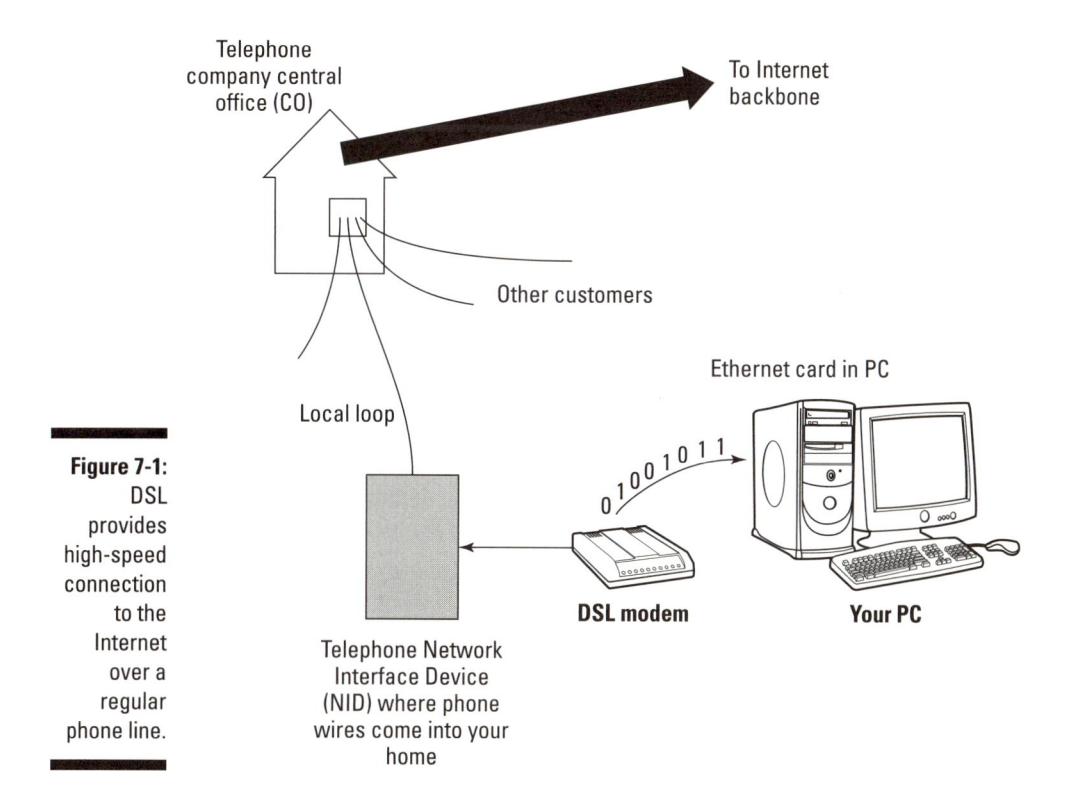

Figure 7-1: DSL provides high-speed connection to the Internet over a regular phone line.

Your PC talks to the DSL modem through an Ethernet connection, which means that you need an Ethernet card in your Linux system.

Your PC sends digital data over the Ethernet connection to the DSL modem. The DSL modem sends the digital data at different frequencies than those used by the analog voice signals. The voice signals occupy a small portion of all the frequencies that the phone line can carry. DSL uses the higher frequencies to transfer digital data, so both voice and data can travel on the same phone line.

The distance between your home and the central office — the *loop length* — is a factor in DSL's performance. Unfortunately, the phone line can reliably carry the DSL signals over only a limited distance — typically 3 miles or less, which means that you can get DSL service only if your home (or office) is located within about 3 miles of your phone company's central office. Your phone company can tell you whether your location can get DSL or not. Often, it has a Web site where you can type in your phone number and get a response about DSL availability. For example, try www.dslavailability.com for U.S. locations.

Stirring the DSL alphabet soup: ADSL, IDSL, SDSL

I have been using the term *DSL* as if there was only one kind of DSL. As you may imagine, nothing is ever that simple. DSL has in fact three variants, each with different features. Take a look:

- **ADSL:** Asymmetric DSL, the most common form of DSL, has much higher download speeds (from the Internet to your PC) than upload speeds (from your PC to the Internet). ADSL can have download speeds of up to 8 Mbps and upload speeds of up to 1 Mbps. ADSL works best when your location is within about 2½ miles (12,000 feet) of your central office. ADSL service is priced according to the download and upload speeds you want. A popular form of ADSL, called G.lite, is specifically designed to work on the same line you use for voice calls. G.lite has a maximum download speed of 1.5 Mbps and a maximum upload speed of 512 Kbps.

- **IDSL:** ISDN DSL (ISDN is an older technology called *Integrated Services Digital Network*) is a special type of DSL that works at distances of up to 5 miles between your phone and the central office. The downside is that IDSL only offers downstream (from the Internet to your PC) and upstream (from your PC to the Internet) speeds of up to 144 Kbps.

- **SDSL:** Symmetric DSL provides equal download and upload speeds of up to 1.5 Mbps. SDSL is priced according to the speed you want, with the higher speeds costing more. The closer your location is to the phone company's central office, the faster the connection you can get.

DSL speeds are typically specified by two numbers separated by a slash, like this: 1500/384. The numbers refer to data-transfer speeds in kilobits per second (that is, thousands-of-bits per second, abbreviated as *Kbps*). The first number is the download speed; the second the upload. Thus 1500/384 means you can expect to download from the Internet at a maximum rate of 1,500 Kbps (or 1.5 Mbps) and upload to the Internet at 384 Kbps. If your phone line's condition is not perfect, you may not get these maximum rates — both ADSL and SDSL adjust the speeds to suit existing line conditions.

The price of DSL service depends on which variant — ADSL, IDSL, or SDSL — you select. For most home users, the primary choice is ADSL (or, more accurately, the G.lite form of ADSL) with transfer speed ratings of 1500/128.

Typical DSL setup

To get DSL for your home or business, you have to contact a DSL provider. In addition to your phone company, you can find many other DSL providers. No matter who provides the DSL service, some work has to be done at your central office — the place where your phone lines connect to the rest of the phone network. The work involves connecting your phone line to equipment that can work with the DSL modem at your home or office. The central office equipment and the DSL modem at your location can then do whatever magic is needed to send and receive digital data over your phone line.

Because of the need to set up your line at the central office, it takes some time after you place an order to get your line ready for DSL.

The first step for you is to check out the DSL providers and see if you can actually get the service. Because DSL can work only over certain distances — typically less than 2½ miles between your location and the central office — you have to check to see if you are within that distance limit. Contact your phone company to verify. You may be able to check this availability on the Web. Try typing into Google (www.google.com) the words **DSL**, **availability**, and your local phone company's name. The search results will probably include a Web site where you can type in your phone number to find out if DSL is available for your home or office.

If DSL is available, you can look for the types of service — ADSL versus SDSL — and the pricing. The price depends on the download and upload speeds you want. Sometimes, phone companies offer a simple residential DSL (basically the G.lite form of ADSL) with a 1500/128 speed rating — meaning you can download at up to 1,500 Kbps and upload at 128 Kbps. Of course, these are the *maximums,* and your mileage may vary.

After selecting the type of DSL service and provider you want, you can place an order and have the provider install the necessary equipment at your home or office. Figure 7-2 shows a sample connection diagram for typical residential DSL service.

Here are some key points to note in Figure 7-2:

- Connect your DSL modem's data connection to the phone jack on a wall plate.
- Connect the DSL modem's Ethernet connection to the Ethernet card on your PC.
- When you connect other telephones or fax machines on the same phone line, install a *microfilter* between the wall plate and each of these devices.

Because the same phone line carries both voice signals and DSL data, you need a microfilter to protect the DSL data from possible interference. You can buy one at an electronics store or from the DSL provider.

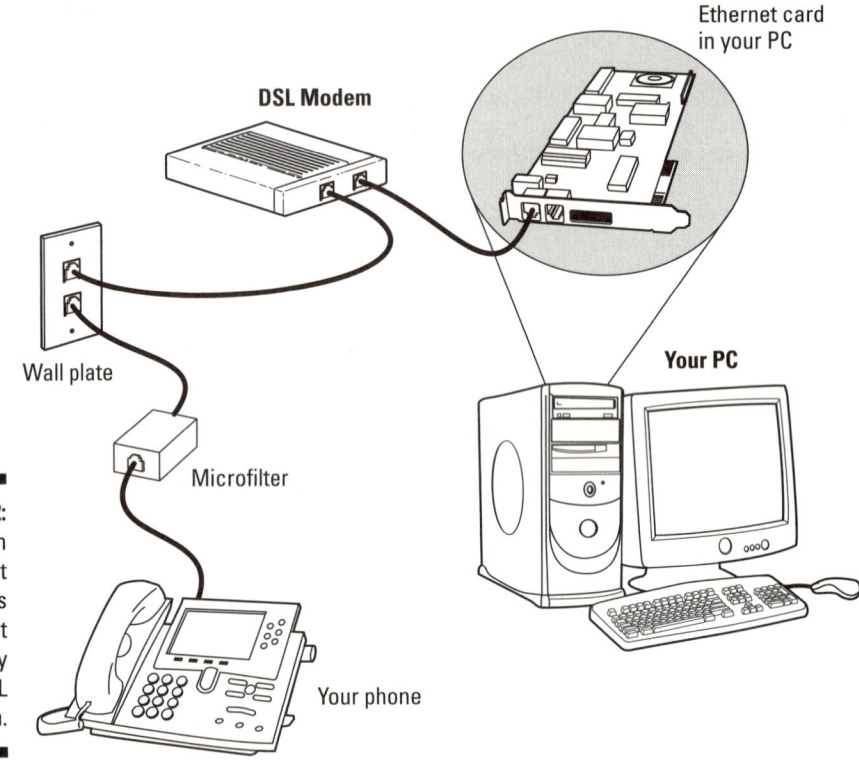

Figure 7-2: You can connect a PC's Ethernet card directly to the DSL modem.

WARNING! When you connect your Linux PC to the Internet using DSL, the connection is always on — which means a greater potential for outsiders to break into the PC.

TIP You can protect your Linux system from intruders and, as an added bonus, share the high-speed connection with other PCs in a local area network (LAN) by using a router that can perform Network Address Translation (NAT). Such a *NAT router* translates multiple private Internet Protocol (IP) addresses from an internal LAN into a single public IP address, which allows all the internal PCs to access the Internet. The NAT router acts as a gateway between your LAN and the Internet and it isolates your LAN from the Internet — this makes it harder for intruders to reach the systems on your LAN.

If you also want to set up a local area network, you need an Ethernet hub to connect the other PCs to the network. Figure 7-3 shows a typical setup that connects a LAN to the Internet through a NAT router and a DSL modem.

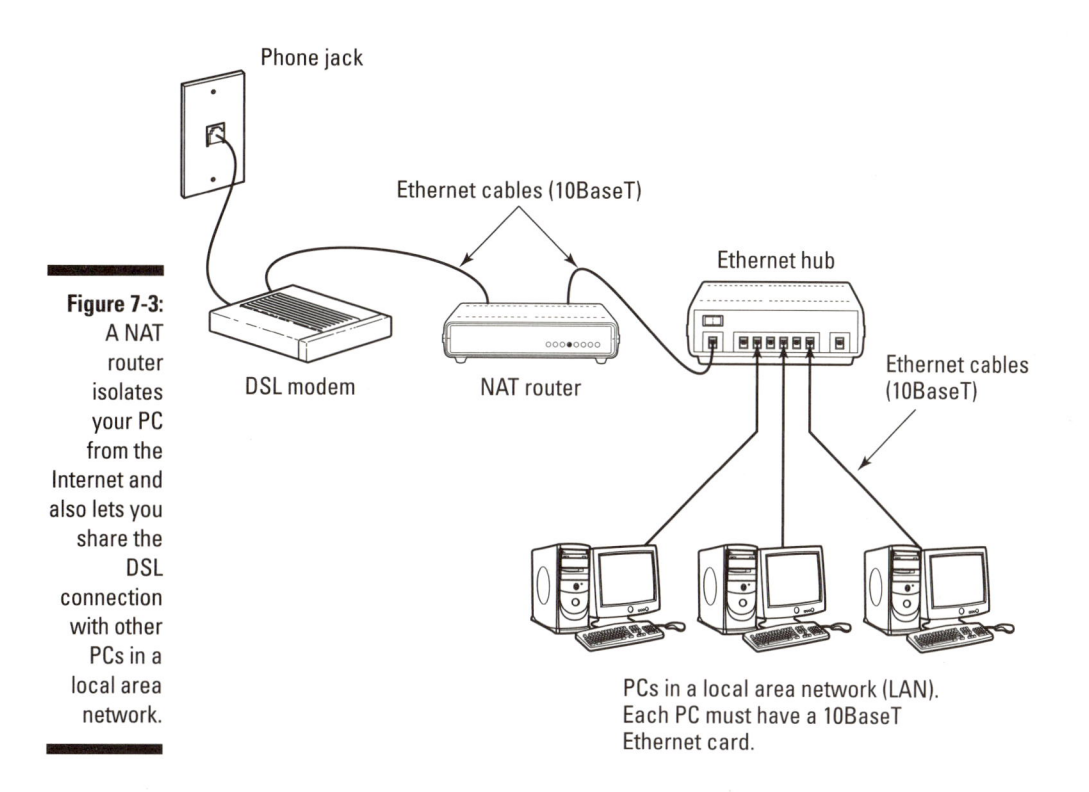

Figure 7-3:
A NAT router isolates your PC from the Internet and also lets you share the DSL connection with other PCs in a local area network.

PCs in a local area network (LAN). Each PC must have a 10BaseT Ethernet card.

Here are the points to note when setting up a connection like the one shown in Figure 7-3:

- You need a NAT router with two 10BaseT Ethernet ports (the 10BaseT port looks like a large phone jack, also known as an *RJ-45 jack*). Typically, one Ethernet port is labeled *Internet* (or *External* or *WAN* for *wide area network*) and the other one is labeled *Local* or *LAN* (for *local area network*).

- You also need an Ethernet hub. For a small home network, you can buy a 4- or 8-port Ethernet hub. Basically, you want a hub with as many ports as the number of PCs you intend to connect to your local area network.

- Connect the Ethernet port of the DSL modem to the Internet port of the NAT router using a 10BaseT Ethernet cable. (These look like phone wires with bigger RJ-45 jacks and are often labeled *Category 5* or *Cat 5* wire.)

- Connect the Local Ethernet port of the NAT router to one of the ports on the Ethernet hub, using a 10BaseT Ethernet cable.

- Now connect each of the PCs to the Ethernet hub. (Of course, to do so, you must first have an Ethernet card installed and configured in each PC.)

Tip: You can also buy a NAT router with a built-in 4- or 8-port Ethernet hub. With such a combined router-hub, you need only one box to set up a LAN and connect it to the Internet via a DSL modem. These boxes are typically sold under the name Cable/DSL router because they work with both DSL and a cable modem.

Remember: DSL providers typically use a protocol known as PPP over Ethernet (PPPoE) to establish a connection between your PC and the equipment at the provider's central office. PPPoE requires you to provide a username and password to establish the network connection over Ethernet. To set up your system for a PPPoE DSL connection, all you have to do is run YaST. (Choose Main Menu⇨System⇨YaST, click Network Devices on the left-hand window, and click DSL from the different network devices shown on the right-hand window.) YaST automatically detects the DSL modem and guides you through the configuration process.

Connecting to the Internet with a Cable Modem

Cable TV companies also offer high-speed Internet access over the same coaxial cable that carries television signals to your home. After the cable company installs the necessary equipment at its facility to send and receive digital data over the coaxial cables, customers can sign up for cable Internet service. You can then get high-speed Internet access over the same cable that delivers cable TV signals to your home.

How cable modems work

A box called a *cable modem* is at the heart of Internet access over the cable TV network. (See Figure 7-4.) The cable modem takes digital data from your PC's Ethernet card and puts it in an unused block of frequency. (Think of it as another TV channel, but instead of pictures and sound, this channel carries digital data.)

The cable modem places *upstream data* — data that's being sent from your PC to the Internet — in a different channel than the *downstream* data that's coming from the Internet to your PC. By design, the speed of downstream data transfers is much higher than that of upstream transfers. The assumption is that people download far more stuff from the Internet than they upload. (Probably true for most of us.)

Chapter 7: I Want My Internet, Now! **115**

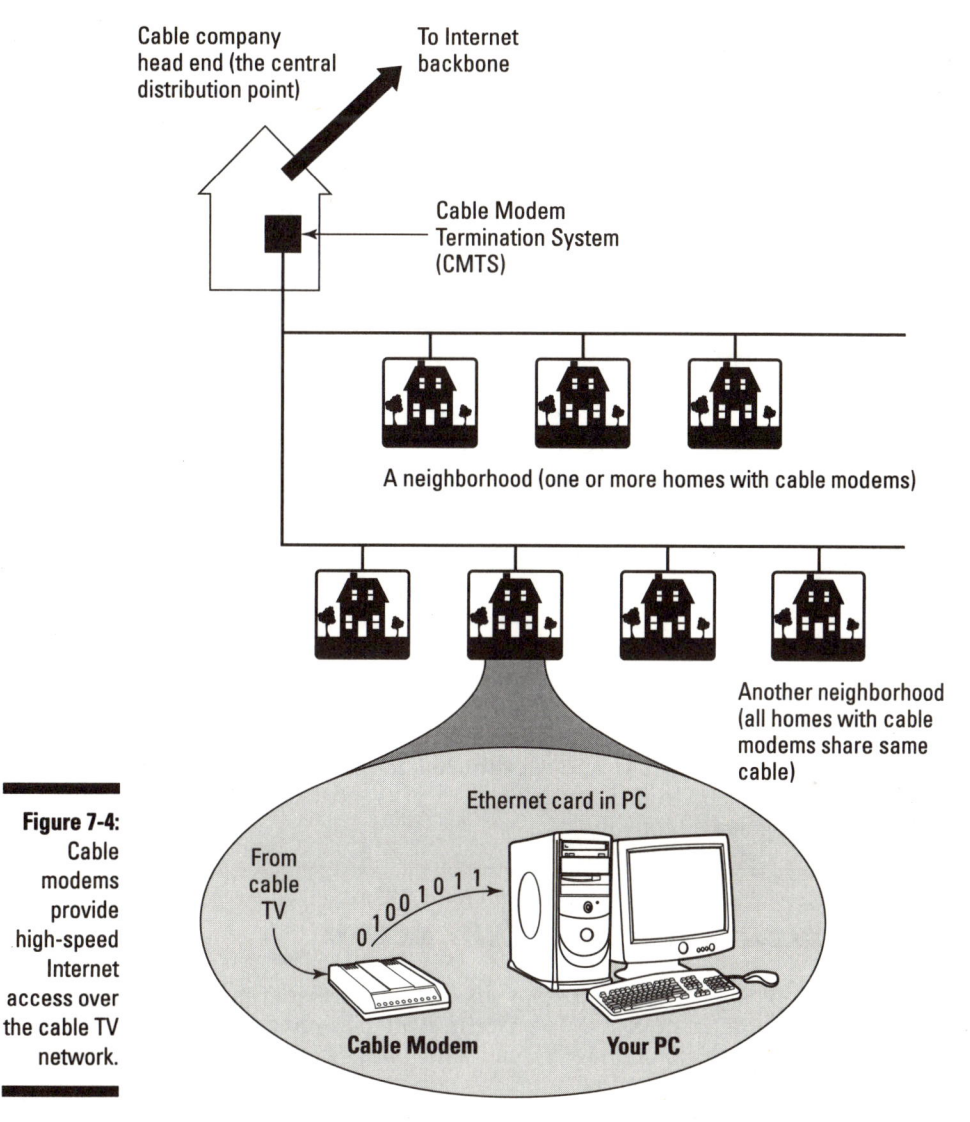

Cable company head end (the central distribution point)

To Internet backbone

Cable Modem Termination System (CMTS)

A neighborhood (one or more homes with cable modems)

Another neighborhood (all homes with cable modems share same cable)

Ethernet card in PC

From cable TV 0 1 0 0 1 0 1 1

Cable Modem   Your PC

Figure 7-4: Cable modems provide high-speed Internet access over the cable TV network.

TECHNICAL STUFF

The coaxial cable that carries all those hundreds of cable TV channels to your home is a very capable signal carrier. In particular, the coaxial cable can carry signals covering a huge range of frequencies — hundreds of megahertz (MHz). Each TV channel requires 6 MHz — and the coaxial cable can carry hundreds of such channels. The cable modem places the upstream data in a small frequency band and expects to receive the downstream data in a whole other frequency band.

Part II: Test Driving SUSE

TECHNICAL STUFF: At the other end of your cable connection to the Internet is the *Cable Modem Termination System* (CMTS) — also known as the *head end* — that your cable company installs at its central facility. (Refer to Figure 7-4.) The CMTS connects the cable TV network to the Internet. It also extracts the upstream digital data sent by your cable modem (and by those of your neighbors as well) and sends all of it to the Internet. The CMTS also puts digital data into the upstream channels so that your cable modem can extract that data and provide it to your PC via the Ethernet card.

Cable modems can receive downstream data at the rate of about 30 Mbps and send data upstream at around 3 Mbps. However, all the cable modems in a neighborhood share the same downstream capacity. Each cable modem filters out — separates — the data it needs from the stream of data that the CMTS sends out. Cable modems follow a modem standard called DOCSIS, which stands for Data Over Cable Service Interface Specification. You can buy any DOCSIS-compliant modem and use it with your cable Internet service; all you have to do is call the cable company and give them the modem's identifying information so that the CMTS can recognize and initialize the modem.

REMEMBER: In practice, with a cable modem you can get downstream transfer rates of around 1.5 Mbps and upstream rates of 128 Kbps. These are maximum rates, and your transfer rate is typically lower, depending on how many users in your neighborhood are using cable modems at the same time.

TIP: If you want to check your downstream transfer speed, go to `bandwidthplace.com/speedtest` and click the link to start the test. For my cable modem connection (for example), the tests reported a downstream transfer rate of about 1.4 Mbps.

Typical cable modem setup

To set up cable modem access, your cable TV provider must offer high-speed Internet access. If the service is available, you can call to sign up. The cable companies often have promotional offers such as no installation fee or a reduced rate for three months. Look for these offers. If you are lucky, a local cable company may have a promotion going on just when you want to sign up.

The installation is typically done by a technician, who splits your incoming cable into two — one side goes to the TV and the other to the cable modem. The technician provides information about the cable modem to the cable company's head end for setup at its end. When all that is done, you can plug in your PC's Ethernet card to the cable modem and you're all set to enjoy high-speed Internet access. Figure 7-5 shows a typical cable-modem hookup.

Chapter 7: I Want My Internet, Now! *117*

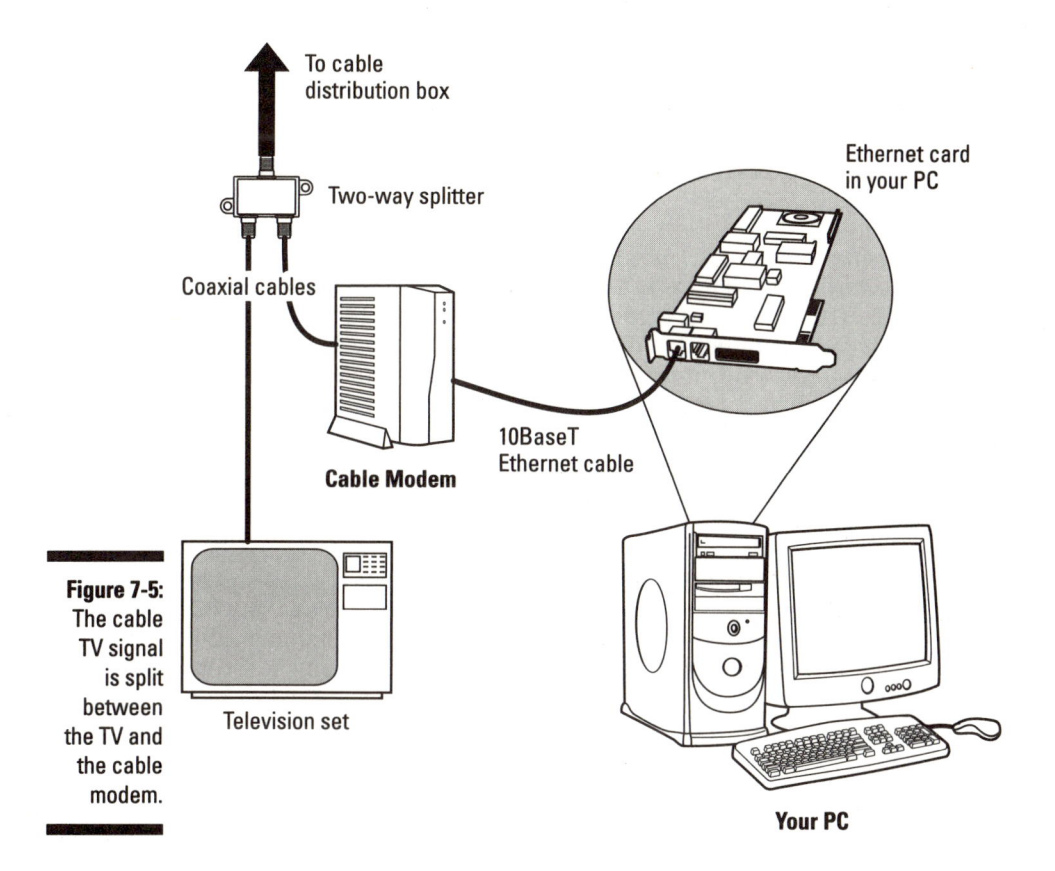

Figure 7-5: The cable TV signal is split between the TV and the cable modem.

The cable modem connects to an Ethernet card in your PC. If you don't have an Ethernet card in your PC, the cable company technician often provides one.

Here are some key points to note about the cable modem setup in Figure 7-5:

- Split the incoming cable TV signal into two parts by using a two-way splitter. (The cable company technician installs the splitter.) By the way, the two-way splitter needs to be rated for 1 GHz; otherwise, it may not let the frequencies that contain the downstream data from the Internet pass through.
- Connect one of the video outputs from the splitter to your cable modem's F-type video connector using a coaxial cable.
- Connect the cable modem's 10BaseT Ethernet connection to the Ethernet card on your PC.
- Connect your TV to the other video output from the two-way splitter.

WARNING! When you use a cable modem to directly connect your SUSE Linux PC to the Internet, the connection is always on, so you run a greater risk that someone may try to break into the PC than do dialup users. SUSE Linux includes a firewall, which you may want to use to protect your PC from unwanted Internet connections. See Chapter 19 for more information on how to enable the firewall.

TIP To isolate your SUSE Linux PC or local area network from the public Internet, you may want to add a NAT (Network Address Translation) router between your PC and the cable modem. One of the NAT router's network interfaces connects to the Internet and the other connects to your LAN — the router then acts as a gateway between your LAN and the Internet. As an added bonus, you can even share a cable modem connection with all the PCs in your own local area network (LAN) by adding an Ethernet hub. Better yet, buy a combination NAT-router-and-hub so you have only one box do the whole job. By the way, the NAT router/hubs are typically sold under the name *Cable/DSL router* because they work with both DSL and a cable modem.

The NAT router translates private Internet Protocol (IP) addresses into a public IP address. When connected through a NAT router, any PC in the internal LAN can access the Internet as if it had its own unique IP address. Result: You can share a single Internet connection among many PCs. (An ideal solution for an entire family of Net surfers!)

Figure 7-6 shows a typical setup with a cable modem connection being shared by a number of PCs in a LAN.

Here are the points to note when setting up a connection like the one shown in Figure 7-6:

- You need a Cable/DSL NAT router with two 10BaseT Ethernet ports (the 10BaseT port — also known as an RJ-45 jack — looks like a large phone jack). Typically, one Ethernet port is labeled *Internet* (or *External* or *WAN* for *wide area network*) and the other one is labeled *Local*.

- If you plan to set up a LAN, you also need an Ethernet hub. For a small home network, you can buy a 4- or 8-port Ethernet hub. Basically, you want a hub with as many ports as the number of PCs you intend to connect to your local area network.

- Consider buying a single box that acts as both a NAT router and a hub with a number of Ethernet ports.

- Connect the video cable to the video input port of the cable modem.

- Connect the Ethernet port of the cable modem to the Internet port of the NAT router using a 10BaseT Ethernet cable. (These look like phone wires, except that the Ethernet cables have bigger RJ-45 jacks and are often labeled Category 5 or Cat 5 wire.)

Chapter 7: I Want My Internet, Now! *119*

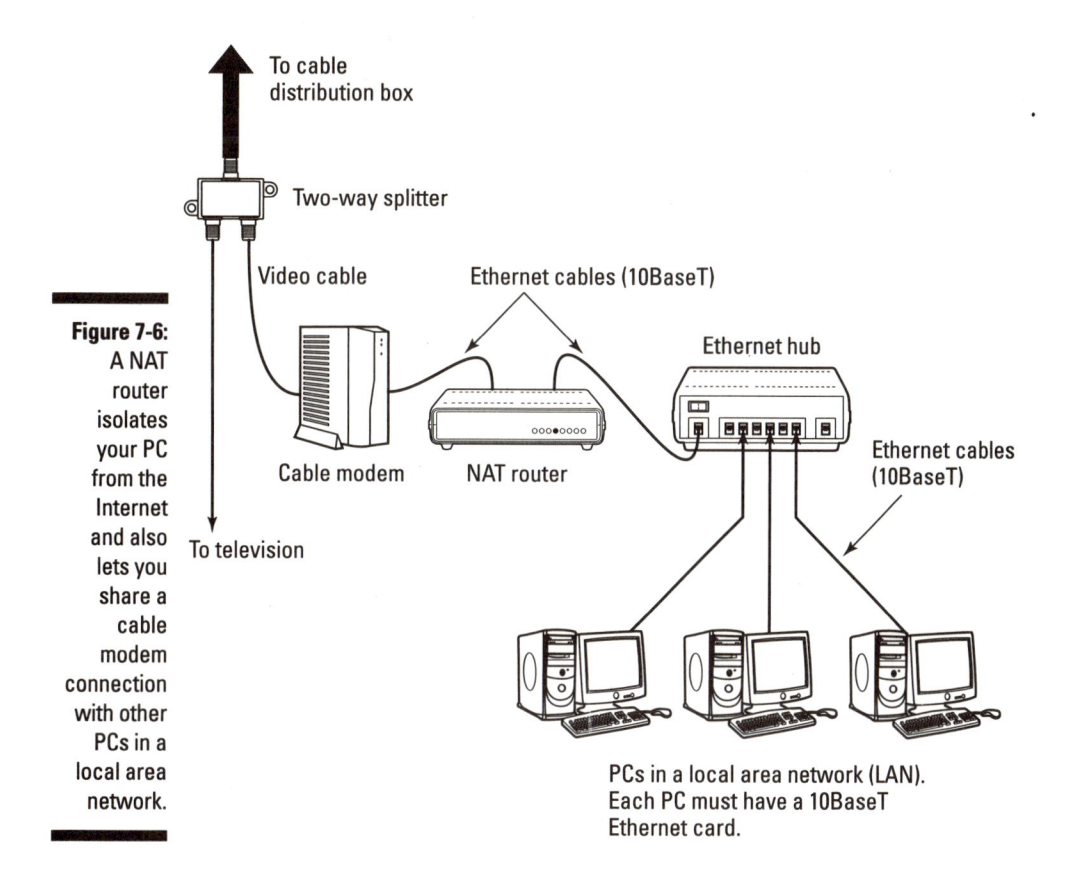

Figure 7-6: A NAT router isolates your PC from the Internet and also lets you share a cable modem connection with other PCs in a local area network.

(Diagram: Cable distribution box → Two-way splitter → Video cable to television and Ethernet path through Cable modem → NAT router → Ethernet hub → PCs in a local area network (LAN). Each PC must have a 10BaseT Ethernet card. Ethernet cables (10BaseT) connect the components.)

- Connect the Local Ethernet port of the NAT router to one of the ports on the Ethernet hub using a 10BaseT Ethernet cable.
- Now connect each of the PCs to the Ethernet hub. Of course, each PC must have an Ethernet card.

In the next section, I explain how to configure the PCs in such a LAN so that they can all access the Internet through the router.

Dialing Up the Internet

If you don't have DSL or a cable modem, you can always reach the Internet the old-fashioned way — you can just dial up your ISP using your PC's modem (you need a modem and a phone line for this to work). Connecting your PC to the Internet through a dialup modem is called *dialup networking*. In the following sections, I show you how to set up a dialup network connection to your ISP.

Part II: Test Driving SUSE

> **REMEMBER:** To use a modem to dial up and connect to the Internet, you have to first get an account with an ISP. Every ISP provides you a phone number to dial, a username, and a password. Additionally, the ISP gives you the full names of servers for e-mail and news. Typically, your system automatically gets an IP address by using a protocol known as DHCP.

Connecting the modem

Modem is a contraction of modulator/demodulator — a device that converts digital signals (string of 1s and 0s) into continuously varying analog signals that transmit over telephone lines and radio waves. Thus, the modem is the intermediary between the digital world of the PC and the analog world of telephones. Figure 7-7 illustrates the concept of a modem.

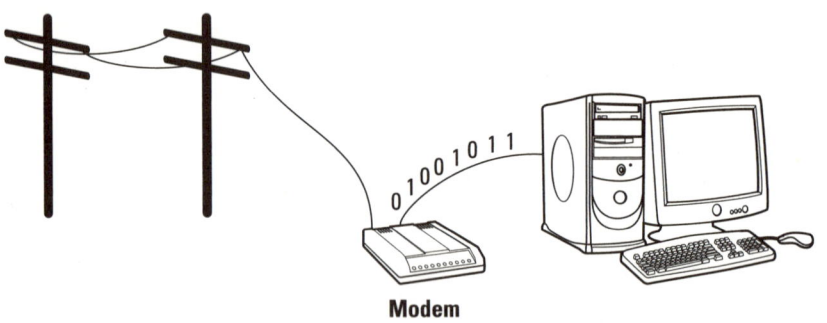

Figure 7-7: A modem bridges the digital world of PCs and the analog world of telephones.

Inside the PC, 1s and 0s are represented with voltage levels, but signals carried over telephone lines are usually tones of different frequencies. The modem sits between the PC and the telephone lines and makes data communication possible over the phone lines. The modem converts information back and forth between the voltage/no voltage representation of digital circuits and different frequency tones that are appropriate for transmission over phone lines.

Before you dial out using an external modem, make sure that the modem is powered on and properly connected to one of the serial or USB ports of your PC. You must also connect the modem to the telephone line.

Buy the right type of cable to connect the modem to the PC. You need a straight-through serial cable to connect the modem to the PC. The connectors at the ends of the cable depend on the type of serial connector on your PC. The modem end of the cable needs a male 25-pin connector. The PC end

Chapter 7: I Want My Internet, Now!

of the cable often is a female 9-pin connector. You can buy modem cables at most computer stores. Often, you can find 9-pin-female-to-25-pin-male modem cables sold under the label *AT Modem Cable.* Connect USB modems by using a USB cable.

TIP

If your PC has an internal modem, all you have to do is connect the phone line to the phone jack at the back of the internal modem card.

Whether your PC has an internal modem or you connect an external modem, you have to configure the modem.

Configuring the modem

To configure the modem for dialup networking, follow these steps:

1. **Choose Main Menu⇨System⇨YaST in KDE or System Menu⇨YaST in GNOME.**

   The YaST Control Center runs and its main window appears.

2. **Click Network Devices on the left pane of the YaST Control Center and then click Modem on the right pane.**

   YaST opens the Modem Configuration window and displays information about the modem it detects (see Figure 7-8).

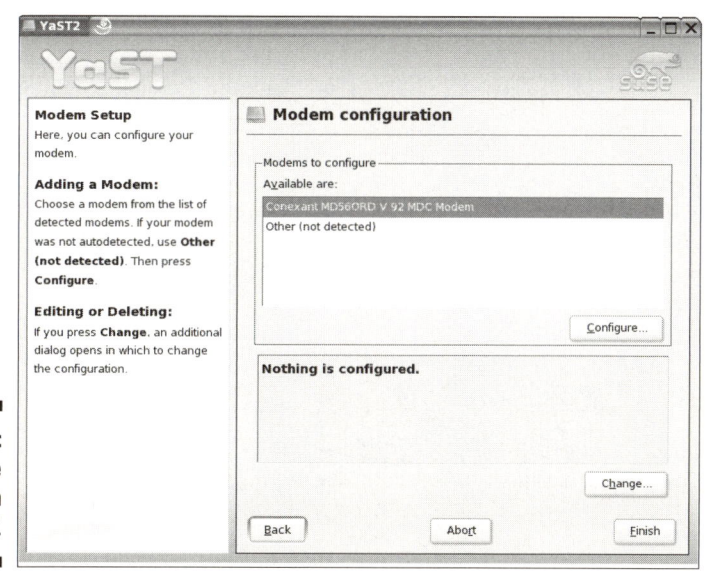

Figure 7-8: Configure the modem from YaST.

Part II: Test Driving SUSE

3. **Click the Configure button and enter any requested information (click Next to move from one screen to the next).**

   On the ISP screen, click New and then type the ISP's phone number as well as the username and password of your Internet account with the ISP. (You can guess where to enter these items; just look for the fields labeled Username, Password, and Phone Number.) Aside from these fields, you can accept the default settings from the rest of the configuration screens.

   After you finish configuring the modem, the KInternet tool starts and displays a small window with a plug icon, as shown in Figure 7-9.

Figure 7-9: Click the KInternet tool to activate a dialup connection.

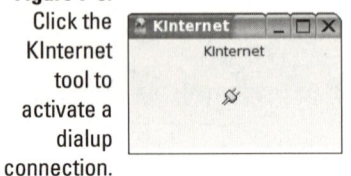

4. **Click the KInternet tool's plug icon to activate the dialup connection.**

   If the connection does not seem to come up, right-click the KInternet icon, select View Log, and look for clues about any problems.

Chapter 8

Setting Up an Ethernet LAN with Wireless Access

In This Chapter
▶ Setting up an Ethernet LAN
▶ Connecting your LAN to the Internet
▶ Extending your network's reach with wireless
▶ Checking whether your network is up and running

You might use an Ethernet network for your local area network (LAN) — at your office or even your home (if you happen to have several systems at home). Even if you have a single PC, you may need to set up an Ethernet network interface so that you can connect your PC to high-speed Internet access that uses a DSL or cable modem. (I cover DSL and cable modems in Chapter 7.) In this chapter, I explain how to set up an Ethernet network.

If you want to surf the net from anywhere in your home with your laptop PC, you can do so by adding wireless to your network. In the last part of this chapter, I show you how to set up wireless networking for connecting to an Ethernet LAN and accessing the Internet.

Getting a Handle on Ethernet

Ethernet is a standard way to move packets of data between two or more computers connected to a single hub. (You can create larger networks by connecting multiple Ethernet segments with gateways.) To set up an Ethernet local area network (LAN), you need an Ethernet card for each PC. Linux supports a wide variety of Ethernet cards for the PC.

Ethernet is a good choice for the physical data-transport mechanism for the following reasons:

- Ethernet is a proven technology that has been in use since the early 1980s.
- Ethernet provides good data-transfer rates: Typically 10 million bits per second (10 Mbps), although 100-Mbps Ethernet and Gigabit Ethernet (1,000 Mbps) are now available.
- Ethernet hardware is often built into the PC or can be installed at a relatively low cost. (PC Ethernet cards cost about $10 to $20 U.S.)
- With wireless Ethernet, you can easily connect laptop PCs to your Ethernet LAN — without having to run wires all over the place. I explain wireless Ethernet later in this chapter.

Connecting PCs to an Ethernet LAN

Any time you hear experts talking about Ethernet, you're also going to hear some bewildering terms used for the cables that carry the data. Here's a quick rundown.

Nowadays, the most popular form of Ethernet cabling is unshielded twisted-pair cable (UTP), known as 10BaseT or 100BaseT (because it can support data rates up to 100 megabits per second). The Electronic Industries Association/Telecommunications Industries Association (EIA/TIA) defines the following five categories of shielded and unshielded twisted-pair cables:

- Category 1 (Cat 1): Traditional telephone cable.
- Category 2 (Cat 2): Cable certified for data transmissions up to 4 Mbps.
- Category 3 (Cat 3): Cable that can carry signals up to a frequency of 16 MHz. Cat 3 is the most common type of wiring in old corporate networks and it normally contains four pairs of wire.
- Category 4 (Cat 4): Cable that can carry signals up to a frequency of 20 MHz. Cat 4 wires are not that common.
- Category 5 (Cat 5): Cable that can carry signals up to a frequency of 100 MHz. Cat 5 cables normally have four pairs of copper wire. Cat 5 UTP is the most popular cable used in new installations today.

To set up a 10BaseT Ethernet network, you need an Ethernet hub — a hardware box with RJ-45 jacks. (These look like big telephone jacks.) You build the network by running twisted-pair wires (usually, Category 5, or Cat5, cables) from each PC's Ethernet card to this hub. You can get a 4-port 10BaseT hub for about $20 U.S. Figure 8-1 shows a typical small 10BaseT or 100BaseT Ethernet LAN that you may set up at a small office or your home.

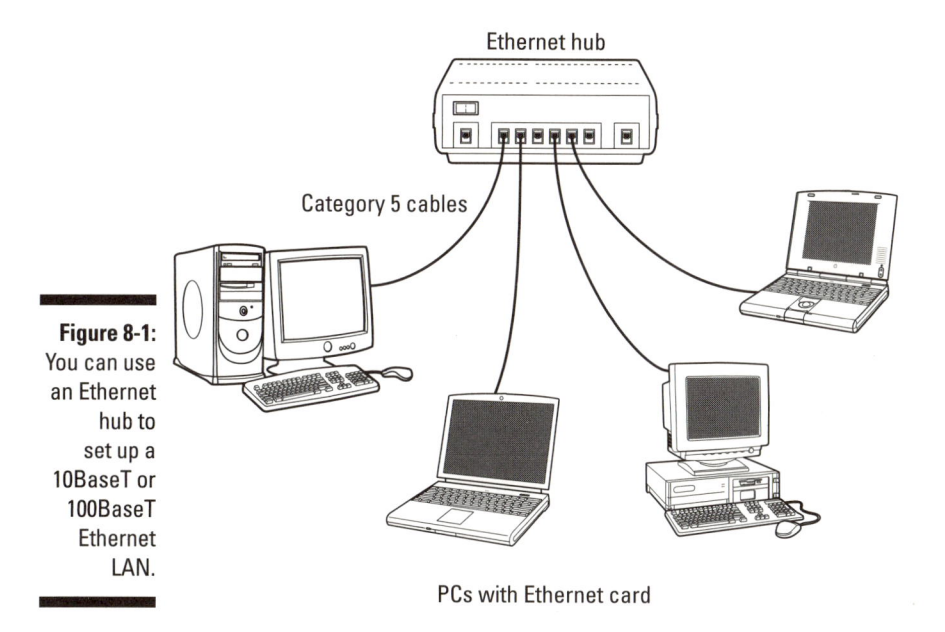

Chapter 8: Setting Up an Ethernet LAN with Wireless Access *125*

Figure 8-1: You can use an Ethernet hub to set up a 10BaseT or 100BaseT Ethernet LAN.

When you install SUSE Linux from this book's companion DVD on a PC that has an Ethernet card, the Linux kernel automatically detects the Ethernet card and installs the appropriate drivers. The SUSE Linux installer, YaST, also lets you set up TCP/IP networking.

TIP

The Linux kernel loads the driver for the Ethernet card every time it boots. To verify that the Ethernet driver is loaded, type the following command in a terminal window:

```
dmesg | grep eth0
```

On one of my PCs, I get the following output when I type that command:

```
eth0: RealTek RTL8139 at 0xd0070000, 00:0c:76:f4:38:b3, IRQ 11
eth0:  Identified 8139 chip type 'RTL-8101'
eth0: link up, 100Mbps, full-duplex, lpa 0x45E1
eth0: no IPv6 routers present
```

You should see something similar, showing the name of your Ethernet card and other related information.

Configuring the Ethernet Network

When you set up the network during SUSE Linux installation, the installation program prepares all appropriate configuration files using the information you provide. This means that you typically never have to manually configure the network. However, SUSE Linux comes with GUI tools to configure the network devices, just in case something needs changing.

To configure the Ethernet network interface, follow these steps:

1. **Choose Main Menu➪System➪YaST from the KDE desktop (choose System Menu➪YaST from the GNOME desktop).**

    This opens the YaST Control Center.

2. **Select Network Devices on the left-hand pane of the YaST Control Center window and Network Card on the right-hand pane.**

    YaST then brings up a window (shown in Figure 8-2) with information about the already configured network card and any new network cards that it detects.

3. **Select your network card (assuming it's not yet configured) and click Configure. To change an already configured card, click Change.**

    Provide the requested information such as how the IP address is obtained (typically, the answer is DHCP or dynamic).

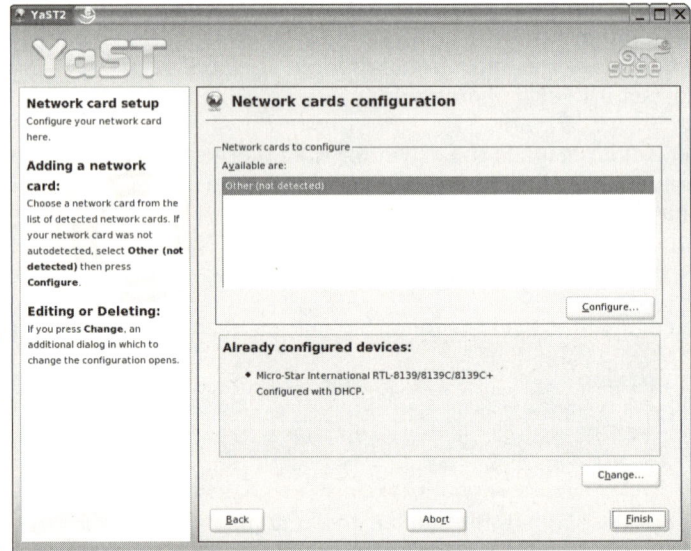

Figure 8-2: Configure the Ethernet network card with YaST.

Connecting Your LAN to the Internet

If you have a LAN with several PCs, you can connect the entire LAN to the Internet by using DSL or a cable modem. Basically, you can share the high-speed DSL or cable modem connection with all the PCs in the LAN.

Chapter 8: Setting Up an Ethernet LAN with Wireless Access   *127*

In Chapter 7, I explain how to set up a DSL or cable modem. In this section, I briefly explain how to connect a LAN to the Internet so that all the PCs can access the Internet.

The most convenient way to connect a LAN to the Internet via DSL or cable modem is to buy a hardware device called DSL/Cable Modem NAT Router with a 4- or 8-port Ethernet hub. NAT stands for *Network Address Translation* and the NAT router can translate many private IP addresses into a single externally known IP address. The Ethernet hub part appears to you as a number of RJ-45 Ethernet ports where you can connect the PCs to set up a LAN. In other words, you need only one extra box besides the DSL or cable modem.

Figure 8-3 shows how you might connect your LAN to the Internet through a NAT router with a built-in Ethernet hub. Of course, you need a DSL or cable modem hookup for this scenario to work (and you have to sign up with the phone company for DSL service or with the cable provider for cable Internet service).

When you connect a LAN to the Internet, the NAT router acts as a gateway for your LAN. The NAT router also dynamically provides IP addresses to the PCs in your LAN. Therefore, on each PC, you have to set up the networking options to obtain the IP address dynamically.

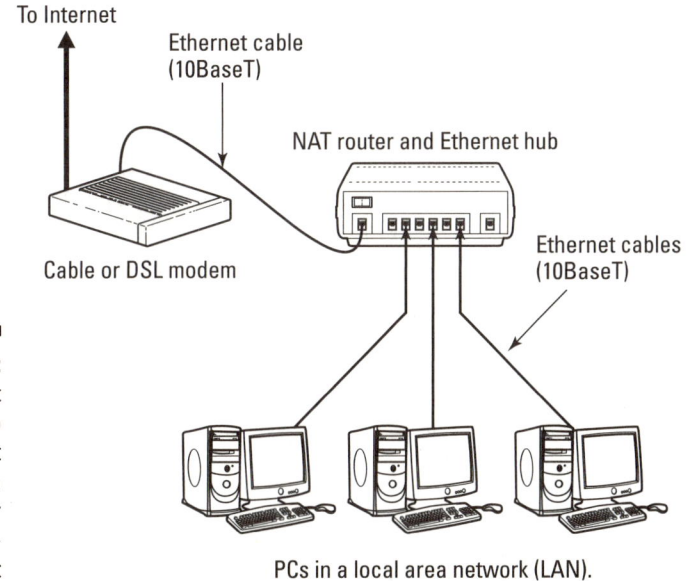

Figure 8-3: Connect your LAN to the Internet through a NAT router with a built-in Ethernet hub.

REMEMBER: Your LAN can mix and match all kinds of computers — some may be running Linux and some may be running Microsoft Windows or any other operating system that supports TCP/IP. When configuring the network settings, remember to select the option that enables Linux to automatically obtain IP address settings and DNS information with DHCP.

Extending Your LAN with a Wireless Network

If you have a laptop computer that you want to connect to your LAN — or if you don't want to run a rat's nest of wires to connect a PC to the LAN — you have the option of using a wireless Ethernet network. In a typical scenario, you have a cable modem or DSL connection to the Internet, and you want to connect one or more laptops with wireless network cards to access the Internet through the cable or DSL modem. In the following sections, I explain wireless networking and how to set it up on your network.

Understanding wireless Ethernet networking

You've probably heard about Wi-Fi. Wi-Fi stands for *Wireless Fidelity* network — a short-range wireless network similar to the wired Ethernet networks. A number of standards from an organization known as IEEE (the Institute of Electrical and Electronics Engineers) defines the technical details of how Wi-Fi networks work. Manufacturers use these standards to build the components that you can buy to set up a wireless network, also known as WLAN for short.

Until mid-2003, there were two popular IEEE standards — 802.11a and 802.11b — for wireless Ethernet networks. These two standards were finalized in 1999. A third standard — 802.11g — was finalized by the IEEE in the summer of 2003. All these standards specify how the wireless Ethernet network works over the radio waves. You don't have to fret over the details of these standards to set up a wireless network, but knowing some pertinent details is good so that you can buy the right kind of equipment for your wireless network.

The three wireless Ethernet standards have the following key characteristics:

- **802.11b:** Operates in the 2.4 GHz radio band (2.4 GHz to 2.4835 GHz) in up to three nonoverlapping frequency bands or channels. Supports a maximum bit rate of 11 Mbps per channel. One disadvantage of 802.11b is that the 2.4 GHz frequency band is crowded — many devices such as microwave ovens, cordless phones, medical and scientific equipment, as well as Bluetooth devices — all work within the 2.4 GHz frequency band. Nevertheless, 802.11b is very popular in corporate and home networks.

- **802.11a:** Operates in the 5 GHz radio band (5.725 GHz to 5.850 GHz) in up to eight nonoverlapping channels. Supports a maximum bit rate of 54 Mbps per channel. The 5 GHz band is not as crowded as the 2.4 GHz band, but the 5 GHz band is not approved for use in Europe. Products conforming to the 802.11a standard are available on the market, and wireless access points are designed to handle both 802.11a and 802.11b connections.

- **802.11g:** Supports up to 54 Mbps data rate in the 2.4 GHz band. (The same band that 802.11b uses.) 802.11g achieves the higher bit rate by using a technology called *OFDM* (orthogonal frequency-division multiplexing), which is also used by 802.11a. Although 802.11g was only recently finalized, equipment that complies with it is already on the market. That's because 802.11.g has generated excitement by working in the same band as 802.11b but promising much higher data rates and by being backward-compatible with 802.11b devices. Vendors currently offer access points that can support both the 802.11b and 802.11g connection standards.

If you are buying a new wireless access point, get an 802.11g one. An 802.11g access point can also communicate with older (and slower) 802.11b devices.

The maximum data throughput that a user actually sees is much less because all users of that radio channel share the capacity of the channel. Also, the data transfer rate decreases as the distance between the user's PC and the wireless access point increases.

To find out more about wireless Ethernet, visit `www.wi-fi.org`, the home page of the Wi-Fi Alliance — a nonprofit international association formed in 1999 to certify interoperability of wireless LAN products based on IEEE 802.11 standards.

Understanding infrastructure and ad hoc modes

The 802.11 standard defines two modes of operation for wireless Ethernet networks: infrastructure and ad hoc. *Ad hoc mode* is simply two or more wireless Ethernet cards communicating with each other without an access point.

Infrastructure mode refers to the approach in which all the wireless Ethernet cards communicate with each other and with the wired LAN through an access point. For the discussions in this chapter, I assume that you set your wireless Ethernet card to infrastructure mode. In the configuration files, this mode is referred to as *managed mode*.

Understanding Wired Equivalent Privacy (WEP)

The 802.11 standard includes Wired Equivalent Privacy (WEP) for protecting wireless communications from eavesdropping. WEP relies on a 40-bit or 104-bit secret key that is shared between a *mobile station* (such as a laptop with a wireless Ethernet card) and an *access point* (also called a *base station*). The secret key is used to encrypt data packets before they transmit and an integrity check is performed to ensure that packets are not modified in transit. The 802.11 standard does not explain how the shared key is established. In practice, most wireless LANs use a single key that is shared between all mobile stations and access points. Such an approach, however, does not scale up very well to an environment such as a college campus because the keys are shared with all users — and you know how it is if you share a "secret" with hundreds of people. That's why WEP is typically not used on large wireless networks such as the ones at universities. In such wireless networks, you have to use other security approaches such as SSH (Secure Shell) to log in to remote systems. WEP, however, is good to use on your home wireless network.

WEP has its weaknesses, but it's better than nothing. You can use it in smaller wireless LANs where sharing the same key among all wireless stations is not an onerous task.

Work is underway to provide better security than WEP for wireless networks. A standard called 802.11i is in the works that provides better security through public-key encryption. While the 802.11i standard is in progress, the Wi-Fi Alliance — a multivendor consortium that supports Wi-Fi — has developed an interim specification called Wi-Fi Protected Access (WPA) that's a precursor to 802.11i. WPA replaces the existing WEP standard and improves security by making some changes. For example, unlike WEP (which uses fixed keys), the WPA standard uses something called the Temporal Key-Integrity Protocol (TKIP), which generates new keys for every 10K of data transmitted over the network. TKIP makes WPA more difficult to break. You may want to consider wireless products that support WPA while waiting for products that implement 802.11i.

Setting up the wireless hardware

To set up the wireless connection, you need a wireless access point and a wireless network card in each PC. You can also set up an ad hoc wireless network among two or more PCs with wireless network cards, but that is a stand-alone wireless LAN among those PCs only. In this section, I focus on the scenario where you want to set up a wireless connection to an established LAN that has a wired Internet connection through a cable modem or DSL.

Chapter 8: Setting Up an Ethernet LAN with Wireless Access

In addition to the wireless access point, you also need a cable modem or DSL connection to the Internet, along with a NAT router/hub. Figure 8-4 shows a typical setup for wireless Internet access through an existing cable modem or DSL connection.

As Figure 8-4 shows, the LAN has both wired and wireless PCs. In this example, either a cable or DSL modem connects the LAN to the Internet through a NAT router/hub. Laptops with wireless network cards connect to the LAN through a wireless access point attached to one of the RJ-45 ports on the hub. To connect desktop PCs to this wireless network, you can use a USB wireless network card (which connects to a USB port).

TIP: If you have not yet purchased a NAT router/hub for your cable or DSL connection, consider buying a router/hub that has a built-in wireless access point.

Configuring the wireless access point

Configuring the wireless access point involves the following tasks:

- Setting a name for the wireless network (the technical term is ESSID).
- Setting the frequency or channel on which the wireless access point communicates with the wireless network cards. The access point and the cards must use the same channel.

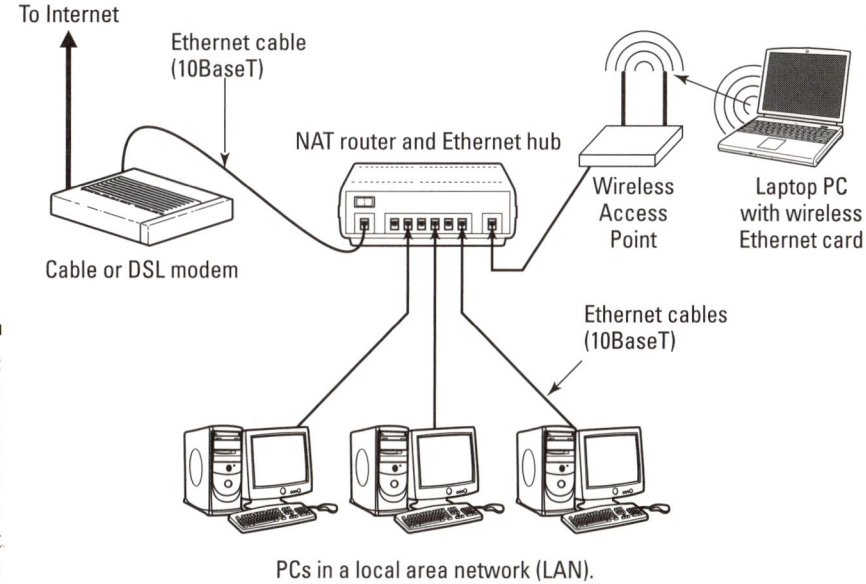

Figure 8-4: Typical connection of a mixed wired and wireless Ethernet LAN to the Internet.

- Deciding whether to use encryption.
- If encryption is to be used, setting the number of bits in the encryption key and the value of the encryption key. For the encryption key, 24 bits are internal to the access point; you specify only the remaining bits. Thus, for 64-bit encryption, you have to specify a 40-bit key, which comes to ten hexadecimal digits (a *hexadecimal digit* is an integer from 0 through 9 or a letter from A through F). For a 128-bit encryption key, you specify 104 bits, or 26 hexadecimal digits.
- Setting the access method that wireless network cards must use when connecting to the access point. You can opt for either open access or shared key. The open-access method is typical (even when using encryption).
- Setting the wireless access point to operate in infrastructure (managed) mode (because that's the way you connect wireless network cards to an existing Ethernet LAN).

The exact method of configuring a wireless access point depends on the make and model; the vendor provides instructions to configure the wireless access point. You typically work through a graphical client application on a Windows PC to do the configuration. If you enable encryption, make note of the encryption key; you have to specify that same key for each wireless network card on your laptops or desktops.

Configuring wireless networking

On your SUSE Linux laptop, the PCMCIA manager recognizes the wireless network card and loads the appropriate driver for the card (PCMCIA or PC Card is the name of the plug-in card devices). Linux treats the wireless network card like another Ethernet device and assigns it a device name such as `eth0` or `eth1`. If you already have an Ethernet card in the laptop, that card gets the `eth0` device name, and the wireless PC card becomes the `eth1` device.

When you plug in the wireless Ethernet PC Card, SUSE Linux detects the hardware and prompts you if you want to configure the network card. Click Yes and YaST prompts you for the `root` password. Then YaST opens the network card configuration window. You should see the wireless Ethernet card listed, as shown in Figure 8-5.

From the screen shown in Figure 8-5, follow these steps:

1. **Click Configure (see Figure 8-5).**

   YaST displays the Network Address Setup screen.

Chapter 8: Setting Up an Ethernet LAN with Wireless Access *133*

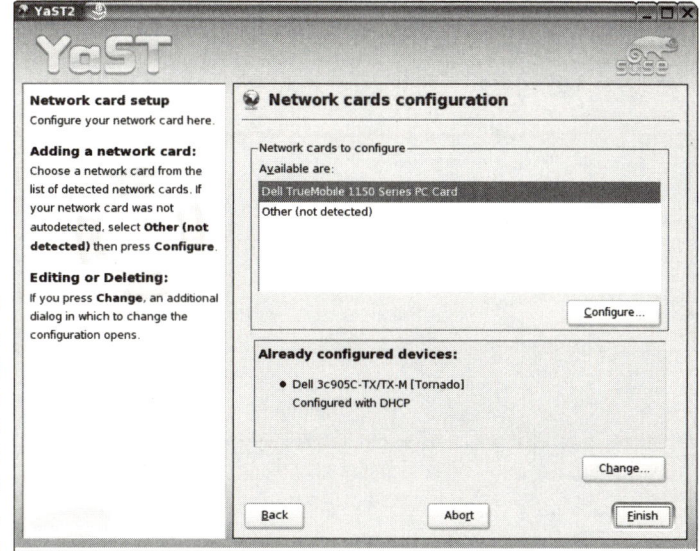

Figure 8-5:
Configuring a new wireless Ethernet card in SUSE Linux.

2. **Choose Advanced⇨Hardware Details from the Detailed Settings section.**

    YaST displays the Manual Network Card Configuration screen.

3. **Click Wireless Settings.**

    YaST displays the Wireless Network Card Configuration screen (see Figure 8-6).

4. **Enter the needed parameters and click OK.**

    You can leave the Operating Mode as Managed, but you do have to enter certain parameters to enable the wireless network card to communicate with the wireless access point. For example, you have to specify the wireless network name assigned to the access point — and the encryption settings must match those on the access point.

That should get the wireless card ready to go.

To check the status of the wireless network interface, type **su -** to become root and then type the following command:

```
iwconfig
```

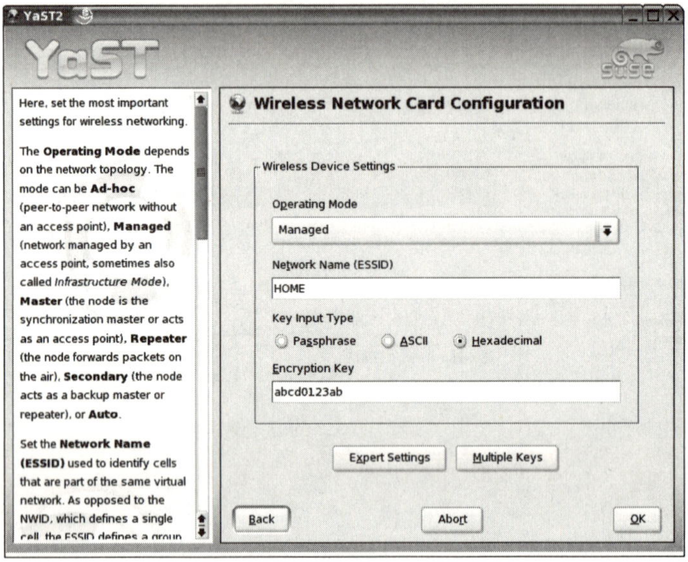

Part II: Test Driving SUSE

Figure 8-6: Enter parameters for the wireless Ethernet card in this screen.

Here's a typical output from a SUSE Linux laptop with a wireless Ethernet PC card:

```
lo        no wireless extensions.

eth0      no wireless extensions.

eth1      IEEE 802.11-DS  ESSID:"HOME"  Nickname:"linux"
          Mode:Managed  Frequency:2.437GHz  Access Point: 00:30:AB:06:2E:50
          Bit Rate:11Mb/s  Tx-Power=15 dBm  Sensitivity:1/3
          Retry limit:4  RTS thr:off  Fragment thr:off
          Encryption key:AECF-A00F-03
          Power Management:off
          Link Quality:50/92  Signal level:-39 dBm  Noise level:-89 dBm
          Rx invalid nwid:0  Rx invalid crypt:0  Rx invalid frag:0
          Tx excessive retries:0  Invalid misc:0  Missed beacon:0
```

Here the `eth1` interface refers to the wireless network card. I edited the encryption key and some other parameters to hide those details, but the sample output shows you what you'd typically see when the wireless link is working.

Checking whether Your Network Is Up

Regardless of whether you use a dialup modem or a cable modem or DSL to connect to the Internet, sometimes you need to find out whether the network is working. SUSE Linux includes several commands to help you monitor and diagnose problems. These tasks are best done by typing commands in a terminal window. I explain a few useful network commands.

Checking the network interfaces

Use the /sbin/ifconfig command to view the currently configured network interfaces. The ifconfig command is used to configure a network interface (that is, to associate an IP address with a network device). If you run ifconfig without any command line arguments, the command displays information about current network interfaces. The following is typical output when you type **/sbin/ifconfig** in a terminal window:

```
eth0      Link encap:Ethernet  HWaddr 00:08:74:E5:C1:60
          inet addr:192.168.0.6  Bcast:192.168.0.255  Mask:255.255.255.0
          inet6 addr: fe80::208:74ff:fee5:c160/64 Scope:Link
          UP BROADCAST RUNNING MULTICAST  MTU:1500  Metric:1
          RX packets:93700 errors:0 dropped:0 overruns:1 frame:0
          TX packets:74097 errors:0 dropped:0 overruns:0 carrier:0
          collisions:0 txqueuelen:1000
          RX bytes:33574333 (32.0 Mb)  TX bytes:8832457 (8.4 Mb)
          Interrupt:10 Base address:0x3000

eth1      Link encap:Ethernet  HWaddr 00:02:2D:8C:F8:C5
          inet addr:192.168.0.8  Bcast:192.168.0.255  Mask:255.255.255.0
          inet6 addr: fe80::202:2dff:fe8c:f8c5/64 Scope:Link
          UP BROADCAST RUNNING MULTICAST  MTU:1500  Metric:1
          RX packets:3403 errors:0 dropped:0 overruns:0 frame:0
          TX packets:22 errors:1 dropped:0 overruns:0 carrier:0
          collisions:0 txqueuelen:1000
          RX bytes:254990 (249.0 Kb)  TX bytes:3120 (3.0 Kb)
          Interrupt:3 Base address:0x100

lo        Link encap:Local Loopback
          inet addr:127.0.0.1  Mask:255.0.0.0
          inet6 addr: ::1/128 Scope:Host
          UP LOOPBACK RUNNING  MTU:16436  Metric:1
          RX packets:3255 errors:0 dropped:0 overruns:0 frame:0
          TX packets:3255 errors:0 dropped:0 overruns:0 carrier:0
          collisions:0 txqueuelen:0
          RX bytes:2686647 (2.5 Mb)  TX bytes:2686647 (2.5 Mb)
```

This output shows that three network interfaces — the loopback interface (`lo`) and two Ethernet cards (`eth0` and `eth1`) — are currently active on this system. For each interface, you can see the IP address, as well as statistics on packets delivered and sent. If the SUSE Linux system has a dialup link up and running, you also see an item for the `ppp0` interface in the output.

Checking the IP routing table

Another network configuration command, `/sbin/route`, provides status information when it is run without any command line argument. If you're having trouble checking a connection to another host (that you specify with an IP address), check the IP routing table to see whether a default gateway is specified. Then check the gateway's routing table to ensure that paths to an outside network appear in that routing table.

A typical output from the `/sbin/route` command looks like the following:

```
/sbin/route
Kernel IP routing table
Destination     Gateway         Genmask         Flags Metric Ref    Use Iface
192.168.0.0     *               255.255.255.0   U     0      0        0 eth0
192.168.0.0     *               255.255.255.0   U     0      0        0 eth1
169.254.0.0     *               255.255.0.0     U     0      0        0 eth1
127.0.0.0       *               255.0.0.0       U     0      0        0 lo
default         192.168.0.1     0.0.0.0         UG    0      0        0 eth0
```

As this routing table shows, the local network uses the `eth0` and `eth1` Ethernet interfaces, and the default gateway is the `eth0` Ethernet interface. The default gateway is a routing device that handles packets addressed to any network other than the one in which the Linux system resides. In this example, packets addressed to any network address other than those beginning with 192.168.0 are sent to the gateway — 192.168.0.1. The gateway forwards those packets to other networks (assuming, of course, that the gateway is connected to another network, preferably the Internet).

Checking connectivity to a host

To check for a network connection to a specific host, use the `ping` command. `ping` is a widely used TCP/IP tool that uses a series of Internet Control Message Protocol (ICMP, pronounced *eye-comp*) messages. ICMP provides for an Echo message to which every host responds. Using the ICMP messages and replies, `ping` can determine whether or not the other system is alive and can compute the round-trip delay in communicating with that system.

The following example shows how I run `ping` to see whether a system on my network is alive:

```
ping 192.168.0.1
```

Here is what this command displays on my home network:

```
PING 192.168.0.1 (192.168.0.1) 56(84) bytes of data.
64 bytes from 192.168.0.1: icmp_seq=1 ttl=63 time=0.256 ms
64 bytes from 192.168.0.1: icmp_seq=2 ttl=63 time=0.267 ms
64 bytes from 192.168.0.1: icmp_seq=3 ttl=63 time=0.272 ms
64 bytes from 192.168.0.1: icmp_seq=4 ttl=63 time=0.267 ms
64 bytes from 192.168.0.1: icmp_seq=5 ttl=63 time=0.275 ms

--- 192.168.0.1 ping statistics ---
5 packets transmitted, 5 received, 0% packet loss, time 3999ms
rtt min/avg/max/mdev = 0.256/0.267/0.275/0.016 ms
```

In SUSE Linux, `ping` continues to run until you press Ctrl+C to stop it; then it displays summary statistics showing the typical time it takes to send a packet between the two systems. On some systems, `ping` simply reports that a remote host is alive. However, you can still get the timing information by using appropriate command line arguments.

Part III
Doing Stuff with SUSE

The 5th Wave   By Rich Tennant

"It's called Linux Poker. Everyone gets to see everyone else's cards, everything's wild, you can play off your opponents' hands, and everyone wins except Bill Gates, whose face appears on the jokers."

In this part...

So what's this SUSE Linux thing good for? Can you do anything useful with it? This Part answers your questions about how to do some productive (and maybe even entertaining) work in SUSE Linux. I cover a number of things that you might want to do with a computer — browse the Web, e-mail, read newsgroups, and do office work (write reports, prepare spreadsheets, and make presentations). I also describe some fun things such as playing music, burning CDs, and using digital cameras. Finally, I introduce you to the shell and the command-line. (GUI desktops are great, but in a pinch, you need to know what to do at the command prompt.)

Chapter 9

Browsing the Web

In This Chapter

▶ Discovering the World Wide Web

▶ Understanding a URL

▶ Taking stock of Web browsers in SUSE Linux

▶ Web browsing with Konqueror in KDE

▶ Web browsing with Mozilla in GNOME

▶ Introducing Epiphany and Firefox in GNOME

*Y*ou probably already know about the Web, but did you know that the Web, or more formally the World Wide Web, made the Internet what it is today? The Internet has been around for quite a while, but it did not reach a mass audience until the Web came along in 1993.

Before the Web came along, you had to use arcane UNIX commands to download and use files, which were simply too complicated for most of us. With the Web, however, anyone can enjoy the benefits of the Internet by using a *Web browser* — a graphical application that downloads and displays Web documents. A click of the mouse is all you need to go from reading a document from your company Web site to downloading a video clip from across the country.

In this chapter, I briefly describe the Web and introduce you to the Web browsers in KDE and GNOME. In KDE, the primary Web browser is Konqueror, which also doubles as a file manager. In GNOME, you have a choice of three Web browsers — Mozilla, Firefox, and Epiphany. I introduce you to all of these Web browsers in this chapter, but after you have used one Web browser, you can easily use any other Web browser.

Understanding the World Wide Web

If you have used a file server at work, you know the convenience of sharing files. You can use the word processor on your desktop to get to any document on the shared server.

Now imagine a word processor that enables you to open and view a document that resides on any computer on the Internet. You can view the document in its full glory, with formatted text and graphics. If the document makes a reference to another document (possibly residing on yet another computer), you can open that linked document by clicking the reference. That kind of easy access to distributed documents is essentially what the World Wide Web provides.

Of course, the documents have to be in a standard format, so that any computer (with the appropriate Web browser software) can access and interpret the document. And a standard protocol is necessary for transferring Web documents from one system to another.

The standard Web document format is *Hypertext Markup Language* (HTML), and the standard protocol for exchanging Web documents is *Hypertext Transfer Protocol* (HTTP). HTML documents are text files and don't depend on any specific operating system, so they work on any system from Windows and Mac to any type of UNIX and Linux.

A *Web server* is software that provides HTML documents to any client that makes the appropriate HTTP requests. A *Web browser* is the client software that actually downloads an HTML document from a Web server and displays the contents graphically.

Links and URLs

Like the pages of real books, Web pages contain text and graphics. Unlike real books, however, Web pages can include multimedia, such as video clips, sound, and links to other Web pages that can actually take you to those Web pages.

The *links* in a Web page are references to other Web pages that you can follow to go from one page to another. The Web browser typically displays these links as underlined text (in a different color) or as images. Each link is like an instruction to you — something like, "For more information, please consult Chapter 4," that you might find in a real book. In a Web page, all you have to do is click the link; the Web browser brings up the referenced page, even though that document may actually reside on a faraway computer somewhere on the Internet.

Chapter 9: Browsing the Web

The links in a Web page are referred to as hypertext links *because when you click a link, the Web browser jumps to the Web page referenced by that link.*

This arrangement brings up a question. In a real book, you might refer the reader to a specific chapter or page in the book. How does a hypertext link indicate the location of the referenced Web page? In the World Wide Web, each Web page has a special name, called a Uniform Resource Locator *(URL). A URL uniquely specifies the location of a file on a computer. Figure 9-1 shows the parts of a URL.*

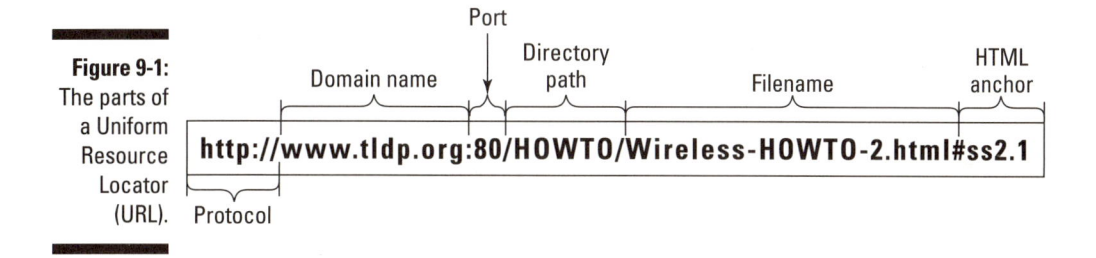

Figure 9-1: The parts of a Uniform Resource Locator (URL).

`http://www.tldp.org:80/HOWTO/Wireless-HOWTO-2.html#ss2.1`

Protocol — Domain name — Port — Directory path — Filename — HTML anchor

As Figure 9-1 shows, a URL has the following parts:

- **Protocol:** Name of the protocol that the Web browser uses to access the data from the file the URL specifies. In Figure 9-1, the protocol is `http://`, which means that the URL specifies the location of a Web page. Here are some of the common protocol types and their meanings:

  - `file://` means the URL is pointing to a local file. You can use this URL to view HTML files without having to connect to the Internet. For example, `file:///srv/www/html/index.html` opens the file `/srv/www/html/index.html` from your Linux system.

  - `ftp://` means that you can download a file using the File Transfer Protocol (FTP). For example, `ftp://ftp.purdue.edu/pub/uns/NASA/nasa.jpg` refers to the image file `nasa.jpg` from the `/pub/uns/NASA` directory of the FTP server `ftp.purdue.edu`. If you want to access a specific user account via FTP, use a URL in the following form:

    `ftp://username:password@ftp.somesite.com/`

    with the username and password embedded in the URL. (Note that the password is in plain text and not secure.)

  - `http://` means that the file is downloaded using the Hypertext Transfer Protocol (HTTP). This protocol is the well-known format of URLs for all Web sites, such as `http://www.novell.com` for Novell's home page. If the URL does not have a filename, the Web server sends a default HTML file named `index.html`. (That's the default filename for the popular UNIX-based Apache Web servers; Microsoft Windows Web servers use a different default filename.)

- `https://` specifies that the file is accessed through a Secure Sockets Layer (SSL) connection — a protocol designed by Netscape Communications for encrypted data transfers across the Internet. This form of URL is typically used when the Web browser sends sensitive information (such as a credit card number, username, and password) to a Web server. For example, a URL such as

    `https://some.site.com/secure/takeorder.html`

    may display an HTML form that requests credit card information and other personal information (such as name, address, and phone number).

- `mailto://` specifies an e-mail address that you can use to send an e-mail message. This URL opens your e-mail program from where you can send the message. For example, `mailto:webmaster@someplace.com` refers to the Webmaster at the host `someplace.com`.

- `news://` specifies a newsgroup that you can read by means of the Network News Transfer Protocol (NNTP). For example,

    `news://news.md.comcast.giganews.com/comp.os.linux.setup`

    accesses the `comp.os.linux.setup` newsgroup at the news server `news.md.comcast.giganews.com`. If you have a default news server configured for the Web browser, you can omit the news server's name and use the URL `news:comp.os.linux.setup` to access the newsgroup.

✔ **Domain name:** Contains the fully qualified domain name of the computer that has the file this URL specifies. You can also provide an IP address in this field. The domain name is not case-sensitive.

✔ **Port:** Port number that is being used by the protocol listed in the first part of the URL. This part of the URL is optional; all protocols have default ports. The default port for HTTP, for example, is 80. If a site configures the Web server to listen to a different port, the URL has to include the port number.

✔ **Directory path:** Directory path of the file being referred to in the URL. For Web pages, this field is the directory path of the HTML file. The directory path is case-sensitive.

✔ **Filename:** Name of the file. For Web pages, the filename typically ends with `.htm` or `.html`. If you omit the filename, the Web server returns a default file (often named `index.html`). The filename is case-sensitive.

✔ **HTML anchor:** Optional part of the URL that makes the Web browser jump to a specific location in the file. If this part starts with a question mark (?) instead of a hash mark (#), the browser takes the text following the question mark to be a query. The Web server returns information based on such queries.

Web servers and Web browsers

The Web server serves up the Web pages, and the Web browser downloads them and displays them to the user. That's pretty much the story with these two cooperating software packages that make the Web work.

In a typical scenario, the user sits in front of a computer that's connected to the Internet and runs a Web browser. When the user clicks a link or types a URL into the Web browser, the browser connects to the Web server and requests a document from the server. The Web server sends the document (usually in HTML format) and ends the connection. The Web browser interprets and displays the HTML document with text, graphics, and multimedia (if applicable). Figure 9-2 illustrates this typical scenario of a user browsing the Web.

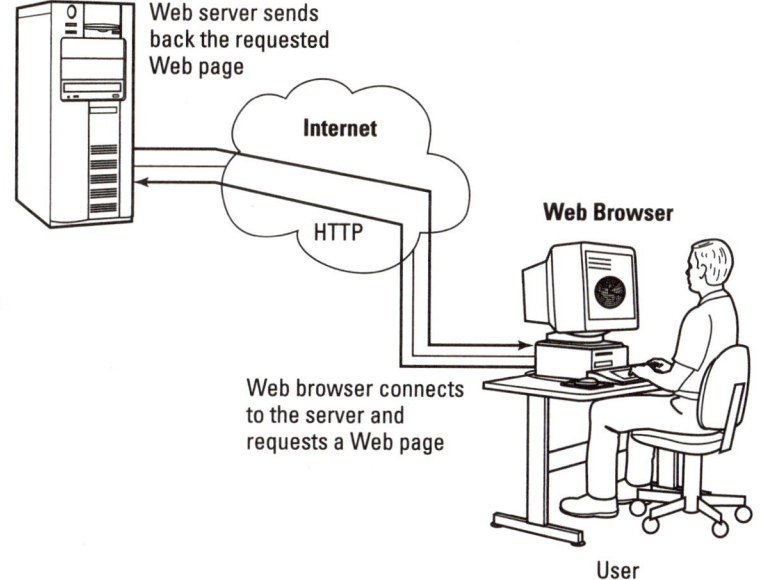

Figure 9-2:
The Web browser requests documents and the Web server sends them.

The Web browser's connection to the Web server ends after the server sends the document. When the user browses through the downloaded document and clicks another hypertext link, the Web browser again connects to the Web server named in the hypertext link, downloads the document, ends the connection, and displays the new document. That's how the user can move from one document to another with ease.

A Web browser can do more than simply "talk" HTTP with the Web server — in fact, Web browsers can also download documents using FTP and many have integrated mail and newsreaders as well.

Web Browsing in SUSE Linux

Web browsing is fun because so many of today's Web pages are so full of graphics and multimedia. Then there's the element of surprise — you can click a link and end up at an unexpected Web page. Links are the most curious (and useful) aspect of the Web. You can start at a page that shows today's weather and a click later, you can be reading this week's issue of *Time* magazine.

To browse the Web, all you need is a Web browser and an Internet connection. I assume that you've already taken care of the Internet connection (see Chapter 7 if you haven't yet set up your Internet connection), so all you need to know are the Web browsers in SUSE Linux.

Depending on the desktop — KDE or GNOME — that you elected to install in SUSE Linux, you have different choices for Web browsers:

- KDE desktop uses Konqueror as the default Web browser. Konqueror also doubles as a file manager and a universal viewer.
- GNOME provides a choice of three Web browsers: Mozilla, Epiphany, and Firefox:
    - **Mozilla:** The reincarnation of that old workhorse — Netscape Communicator — only better. Includes mail and a newsreader. The Web browser is called the Mozilla Navigator, or simply Navigator (just as it was in Netscape Communicator).
    - **Epiphany:** The GNOME Web browser that uses parts of the Mozilla code to draw the Web pages, but has a simpler user interface than Mozilla.
    - **Firefox:** Mozilla's next-generation browser that blocks popup ads, provides tabs for easily viewing multiple Web pages in a single window, and includes a set of privacy tools.

Chapter 9: Browsing the Web

> **REMEMBER:** You can easily install any of Mozilla, Epiphany, or Firefox Web browsers in KDE. See Chapter 18 for more information on how to install software in SUSE Linux.

Web Browsing with Konqueror in KDE

Konqueror is not only a file manager, but also a Web browser. Konqueror starts with a Web browser view if you start Konqueror by clicking the Web browser icon on the KDE panel (mouse over and read the help balloon to find it). On the other hand, if you start Konqueror by clicking the home folder icon (the second icon from left on the KDE panel), you can switch to a Web browser view by choosing Settings⇨Load View Profile⇨Web Browsing from Konqueror's menu.

To browse the Web using Konqueror, click the Web browser button on the KDE panel. Konqueror starts with the initial Web browser view that shows Konqueror's About page — a Web page with information about Konqueror itself, as shown in Figure 9-3.

To visit a specific Web page, simply enter the URL (the "link") in the Location bar (refer to Figure 9-3). You can type the URL without the `http://` prefix. For example, if the URL is `http://www.irs.gov`, you can simply type **www.irs.gov** in the Location bar and then press Enter. Konqueror opens the new Web page in a new tab.

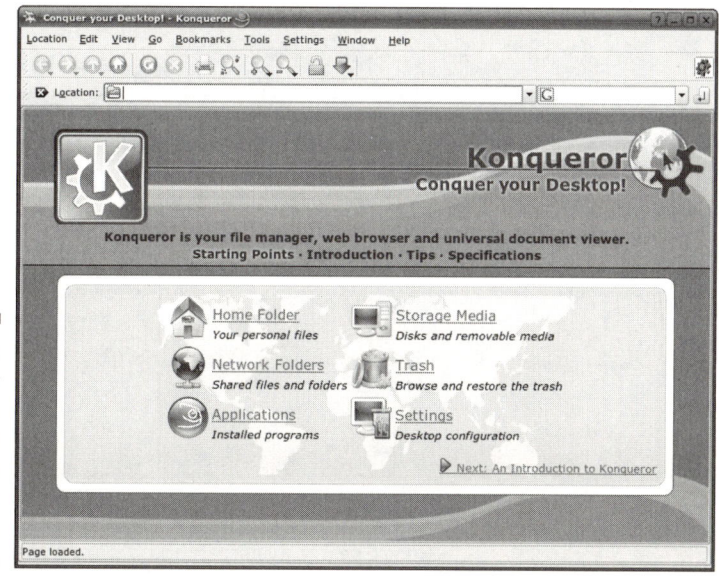

Figure 9-3: Konqueror starts with its initial Web browser view.

Part III: Doing Stuff with SUSE

To open another tab to load a new Web page, choose Location⇒New Tab from the Konqueror menu. You can then type a new URL in the Location box and that Web page appears in the new tab. Figure 9-4 shows Konqueror's Web browser view with a few Web pages loaded in different tabs (notice the tabs just below the Location field). This is called tabbed Web browsing and, as you can see, Konqueror can do tabs. By the way, you can switch between Web pages by clicking on the tabs.

Figure 9-4 shows the key parts of the Konqueror Web browser's window. Here is a quick rundown of some of the features:

- **Search:** You can perform a Google search by typing search words in the text field on the right end of the Location bar.

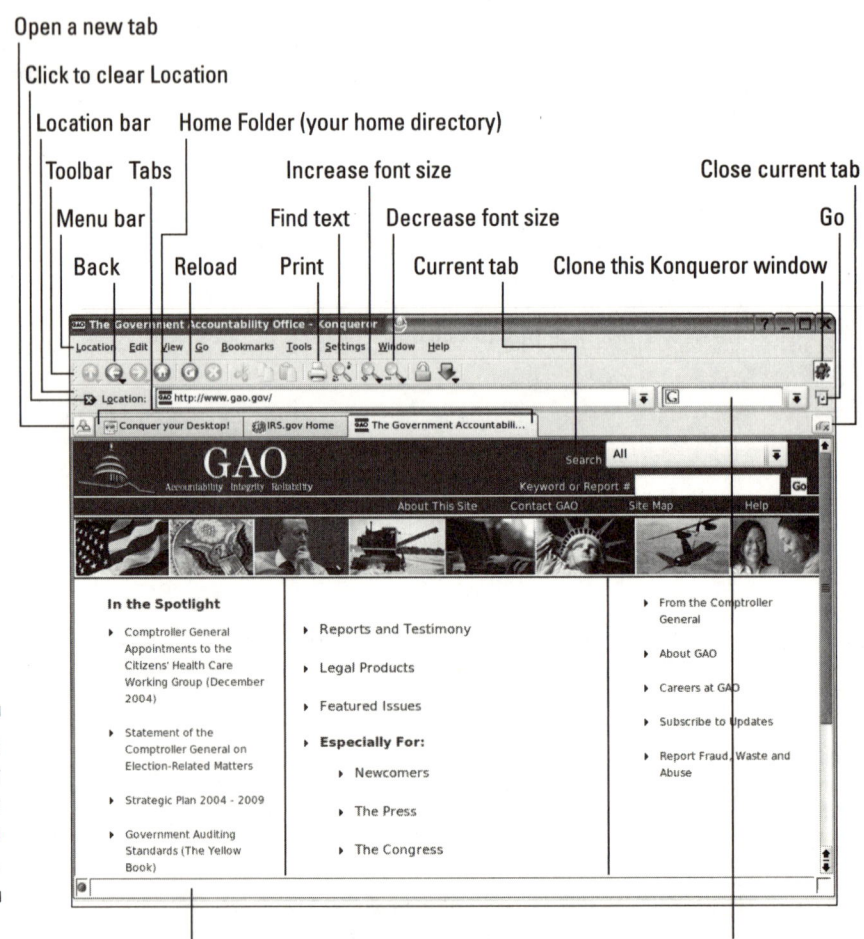

Figure 9-4: Konqueror supports tabbed Web browsing.

- **Font size:** Click the magnifying glass icon to increase or decrease the font size.
- **Tabs:** Click the button on the left end of the tabs to open a new tab, and the one on the rightmost edge to close the current tab.
- **Clone window:** Click the K button on the top right to clone the current Konqueror window, including all the tabs.
- **Location:** Type the URL in the Location bar and press Enter or click the Go button (on the right end of the Location bar) to load that URL. To clear the Location bar, click the button with an X at the left end of the Location bar.

If a Web server sends a cookie — a bit of information that a Web server wants the Web browser to save on your PC — Konqueror displays a cookie alert (see Figure 9-5). You can make your choice depending on whether you want to allow cookies from that Web site.

Figure 9-5: Konqueror asks if you want to accept cookies.

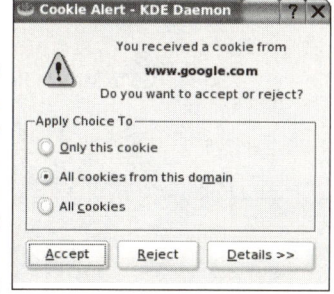

Play around with Konqueror and you will realize that it's more powerful than it first appears.

Web Browsing with Mozilla in GNOME

You can start Mozilla by choosing Main Menu⇨Internet⇨Web Browser⇨Mozilla from the GNOME desktop's top panel.

By the way, the Mozilla Web browser is also known as Mozilla Navigator. Mozilla also includes a Composer for, what else, composing (preparing) Web pages using the Hypertext Markup Language (HTML).

When Mozilla starts, it displays a browser window with a default home page. (The *home page* is a Web page that a Web browser loads when you first start it.) You can configure Mozilla to use a different Web page as the default home page.

Figure 9-6 shows a Web page from a U.S. government Web site (`www.gao.gov`), as well as the main elements of the Mozilla browser window.

Getting familiar with the Mozilla interface

The Mozilla Web browser includes lots of features in its user interface, but you can master it easily. You can turn off some of the items that make it look busy. You can also start with just the basics to get going with Mozilla and then gradually expand to areas that you haven't yet explored.

Mozilla toolbars

Starting from the top of the window, you see a menu bar with the standard menus (File, Edit, and so forth), followed by the two toolbars — the Navigation toolbar and the Personal toolbar. The area underneath the Personal toolbar is where the current Web page appears.

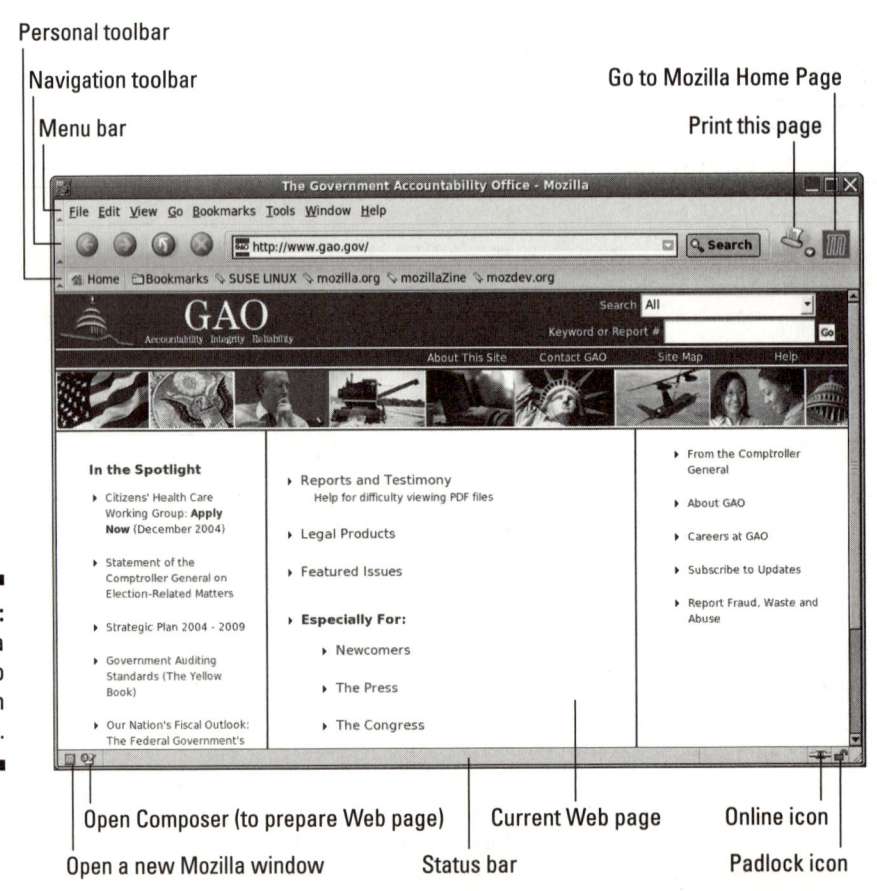

Figure 9-6: The Mozilla Web browser in action.

Callouts: Personal toolbar; Navigation toolbar; Menu bar; Go to Mozilla Home Page; Print this page; Open Composer (to prepare Web page); Open a new Mozilla window; Current Web page; Status bar; Online icon; Padlock icon

Here's what you can do with the buttons on the Navigation toolbar that appear just below the menu bar, from left to right:

- **Back:** Move to the previous Web page.
- **Forward:** Move to the page from which you may have gone backward.
- **Reload:** Reload the current Web page.
- **Stop:** Stop loading the current page.
- **Location text box:** Show the URL of the current Web page. (Type a URL in this box to view that Web page.)
- **Search:** Go to the Google Web Search page (`www.google.com`).
- **Print:** Print the current Web page. (You can also preview how the page will appear when printed.)
- **Mozilla icon:** Go to the Mozilla.org Web site (`www.mozilla.org`).

Immediately below the Navigation toolbar is the Personal toolbar with the Home and Bookmarks buttons. These two buttons serve the following purposes:

- **Home:** Takes you to the home page.
- **Bookmarks:** Displays a menu from which you can bookmark the current page as well as manage your bookmarks.

Mozilla includes a number of other links on the Personal toolbar. Clicking any of these links causes Mozilla to load the Web page corresponding to that link.

Status bar

You can think of the bar along the bottom edge of the Mozilla window as the status bar because the middle part of that area displays status information as Mozilla loads a Web page.

The left side of the status bar includes a component bar, which displays two small icons. If you want a hint about what any of these icons do, simply mouse over the button, and Mozilla displays a small balloon help message. You can click these icons to open other Mozilla windows to perform various tasks.

In the right corner of Mozilla's status bar, to the right of the status message, you see two icons. The icon on the left indicates that you're online; if you click it, Mozilla goes offline. The rightmost icon is a security padlock. Mozilla supports a secure version of HTTP that uses a protocol called *Secure Sockets Layer* (SSL) to transfer encrypted data between the browser and the Web server. When Mozilla connects to a Web server that supports secure HTTP, the security padlock appears locked. Otherwise the security padlock is open, signifying an insecure connection. The URL for secure HTTP transfers begins with `https://` instead of the usual `http://`. (Note the extra `s` in `https`.)

Mozilla displays status messages in the middle portion of the status bar. You can watch the messages in this area to see what's going on. If you mouse over a link on the Web page, the status bar displays the URL for that link.

Mozilla menus

I haven't mentioned the Mozilla menus much. That's because you can usually get by without having to go to them. Nevertheless, taking a quick look through the Mozilla menus is worthwhile so you know what each one offers. In particular, you can use the Edit➪Preferences menu to change settings such as your home page.

Changing your home page

Your *home page* is the Web page that Mozilla loads when you start it. By default, Mozilla displays a blank page. Changing the home page is easy.

First locate the page on the Web that you want to be the home page. You can get to that page any way you want. You can search with a search engine to find the page you want, you can type the URL in the Location text box, or you may even accidentally end up on a page that you want to make your home page. It doesn't matter.

When you're viewing the Web page that you want to make your home page in Mozilla, choose Edit➪Preferences from the Mozilla menu. The Preferences dialog box appears, as shown in Figure 9-7.

On the right side of Figure 9-7, notice that the Home Page radio button is selected. This option means that Mozilla Navigator displays the home page when you start it up. Then you see the URL for the home page, and underneath the address is a Use Current Page button. Click that button to make the current page your home page.

You can set a lot of other options using the Preferences window. Although I don't explain all the options, you can click around to explore everything that you can do from this window. For example, you can click the Choose File button to select a file on your local system as the home page.

Figure 9-7: Click the Use Current Page button to make the current Web page your home page.

Introducing Epiphany and Firefox

Epiphany is the Web browser that starts if you click on the Web browser icon on the GNOME desktop's top panel (mouse over each icon and read the help balloon to locate the Web browser icon). Figure 9-8 shows the initial Epiphany window showing a U.S. Government Web site.

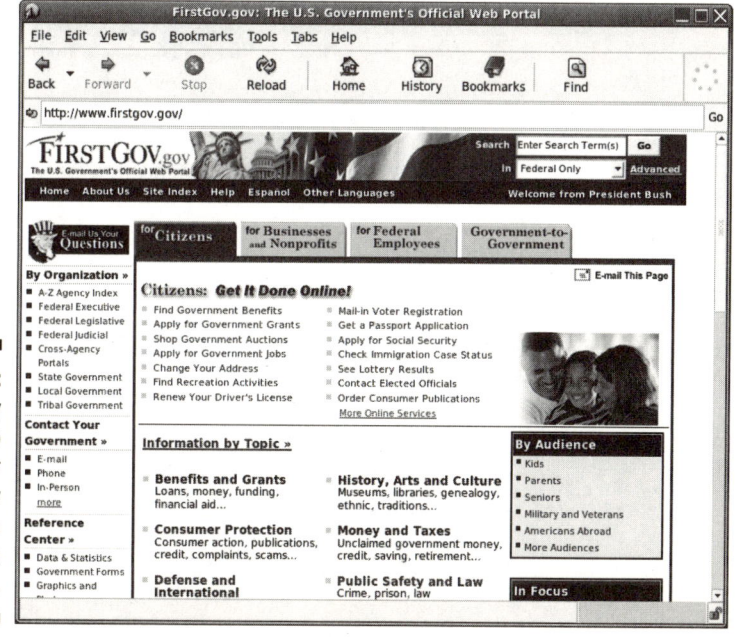

Figure 9-8: Epiphany Web browser window with a typical Web page.

If you compare Figure 9-8 with the Mozilla window in Figure 9-6, you can probably see that the Epiphany window is simpler, with just the navigation toolbar and the text entry area where you can type a new URL. Epiphany supports tabs. You can press Ctrl+T (or choose File⇨New Tab) to open a new tab where you can view a new Web page.

Firefox is the next-generation Web browser from Mozilla and, like Mozilla, Firefox is available for many different operating systems, including Linux. If you're running the GNOME desktop, Firefox is already installed on your SUSE Linux system.

To try out Firefox, choose Main Menu⇨Internet⇨Web Browser⇨Firefox Web Browser from the GNOME desktop's top panel. Figure 9-9 shows the Mozilla Firefox window showing a U.S. government Web site.

Firefox has a user interface that's similar to Mozilla. Like Epiphany, Firefox also supports tabbed browsing, which means that you can open a new tab (by pressing Ctrl+T) and view a Web page in that tab. That way, you can view multiple Web pages in a single window.

Figure 9-9:
Mozilla Firefox displaying a U.S. government Web site.

Chapter 10

E-Mailing and Instant Messaging in SUSE

In This Chapter
▶ Understanding electronic mail
▶ Taking stock of mail readers and IM (instant messaging) clients
▶ Introducing KMail
▶ Introducing Evolution
▶ Instant messaging with Kopete and GAIM

*E*lectronic mail (e-mail) is a mainstay of the Internet. E-mail is great because you can exchange messages and documents with anyone on the Internet. You can send messages anywhere in the world, and that message typically makes its way to its destination within minutes, if not seconds — something you cannot do with paper mail (also appropriately known as *snail mail*). I love e-mail because I can communicate without having to play "phone tag," in which two people can leave telephone messages for each other without ever successfully making contact.

SUSE Linux comes with several mail clients — also called mail readers — that can download mail from your Internet service provider (ISP). You can also read and send e-mail using these mail clients. In this chapter, I introduce you to the primary mail clients for the KDE and GNOME desktops. When you know one of these mail clients, you can easily use any of the mail readers.

There is yet another type of "keeping in touch" that's more in line with the twenty-first century. I'm talking about *IM* — instant messaging. IM is basically one-to-one chat, and SUSE Linux includes IM clients that can work with many instant messaging protocols such as AOL Instant Messenger (or AIM), MSN Messenger, ICQ, Jabber, Yahoo!, Gadu-Gadu, IRC (Internet Relay Chat), and SMS (Short Message Service or text messaging). I briefly describe the primary IM clients for KDE and GNOME desktops in this chapter.

Understanding E-Mail

E-mail messages are addressed to a username at a host (*host* is just a fancy name for an online computer). That means if John Doe logs in with the *username* `jdoe`, e-mail to him is addressed to `jdoe`. The only other piece of information needed to identify the recipient uniquely is the fully qualified *domain name* of the recipient's system. Thus, if John Doe's system is named `someplace.com`, his complete e-mail address becomes `jdoe@someplace.com`. Given that address, anyone on the Internet can send e-mail to John Doe.

How MUA and MTA work

The two types of mail software are

- **Mail-user agent (MUA)** is the fancy name for a mail reader — a client that you use to read your mail messages, write replies, and compose new messages. Typically, the mail-user agent retrieves messages from the mail server by using the POP3 or IMAP4 protocol. POP3 is the *Post Office Protocol Version 3,* and IMAP4 is the *Internet Message Access Protocol Version 4.* In SUSE Linux, the KDE desktop uses KMail as the mail-user agent and GNOME provides Evolution.

- **Mail-transfer agent (MTA)** is the fancy name for a mail server that actually sends and receives mail-message text. The exact method used for mail transport depends on the underlying network. In TCP/IP networks, the mail-transport agent delivers mail using the *Simple Mail-Transfer Protocol* (SMTP). You need an MTA only if your system is going to be a mail server. Specifically, you do not need an MTA if all you want to do is read and send mail via your ISP's mail server.

Figure 10-1 shows how the MUAs and MTAs work with one another when Alice sends an e-mail message to Bob. (In case you didn't know, using *Alice* and *Bob* to explain e-mail and cryptography is customary — just pick up any book on cryptography and you'll see what I mean.) And you may already know this, but the Internet is always diagrammed as a cloud — the boundaries of the Internet are so fuzzy that a cloud seems just right to represent it. (Or is it because no one knows where it starts and where it ends?)

The scenario in Figure 10-1 is typical of most people. Alice and Bob both connect to the Internet through an ISP and get and send their e-mail through their ISPs. When Alice types a message and sends it, her mail-user agent (MUA) sends the message to her ISP's mail-transfer agent (MTA) using the Simple Mail-Transfer Protocol (SMTP). The sending MTA then sends that message to the receiving MTA — Bob's ISP's MTA — using SMTP. When Bob connects to the Internet, his MUA downloads the message from his ISP's MTA using the POP3 (or IMAP4) protocol. That's the way mail moves around the Internet — from sending MUA to sending MTA to receiving MTA to receiving MUA.

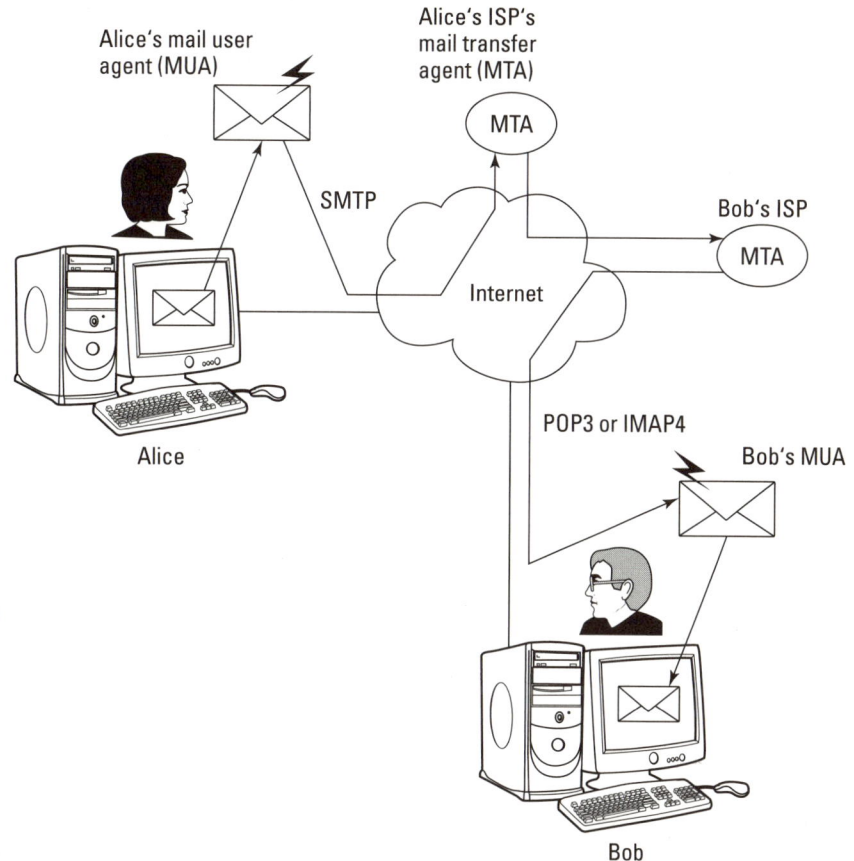

Chapter 10: E-Mailing and Instant Messaging in SUSE 157

Figure 10-1: How Alice sends e-mail to Bob (or all about MUAs and MTAs).

Mail message enhancements

Mail messages used to be plain text (and most still are), but many messages today have much more than text. Two typical new features of today's mail are

- **HTML messages:** Mail messages can be in *HTML* (Hypertext Markup Language), the language used to lay out Web pages. When you read an HTML message on a capable mail reader, the message appears in its full glory with nice fonts and embedded graphics.

- **Attachments:** Many messages today include attached files, which can be anything from documents to images. The recipient can save the attachment on disk or open it directly from the mail reader. Unfortunately, attachments are one way hackers try to get viruses and worms into your PC. (If it's any consolation, most Windows-based viruses and worms do not work in Linux.)

Part III: Doing Stuff with SUSE

WARNING! While HTML messages are nice, they are a perfect tool for hackers phishing for information. As you might know, *phishing* is a new term for hackers trying to coax personal information out of people. Often hackers send professional-looking HTML messages that might claim to be from your bank, credit card company, or eBay and ask you to click what looks like an authentic link to update your personal information. If you click the link, you typically end up at a Web site that's a sophisticated fake of a bank or a credit card site that then prompts you for information such as name, date of birth, address, bank account number, credit card number, and so on. If you are reading HTML mail, be careful of any messages that urge you to update personal information. More than likely, it's from a hacker on a phishing trip.

REMEMBER If you have an ISP account, all you need is a *mail client* (mail reader) to access your e-mail. In this case, your e-mail resides on your ISP's server and the mail reader downloads mail when you run it. You have to do some setup before you can start reading mail from your ISP's mail server. The setup essentially requires you to enter information that you get from your ISP — the mail server's name, server type (POP3, for example), your username, and your password.

E-Mailing in SUSE Linux

Each GUI desktop has a default e-mail client. The KDE desktop uses KMail and the GNOME desktop offers Evolution. In the following sections, I briefly introduce you to KMail and Evolution. All mail clients are intuitive to use, so you don't need much more than an introduction to start using them effectively.

Introducing KMail

KMail is a mail reader for KDE. To start KMail, choose Main Menu➪Internet➪ E-Mail. When you first run KMail, you get its main window, but you cannot start using it to send and receive e-mail until you have configured the mail accounts in KMail.

To configure KMail, follow these steps:

   1. **Choose Settings➪Configure KMail.**

      The Configure KMail window appears.

   2. **Click Network on the left pane of the window.**

      The Setup for Sending and Receiving Messages screen appears (see Figure 10-2).

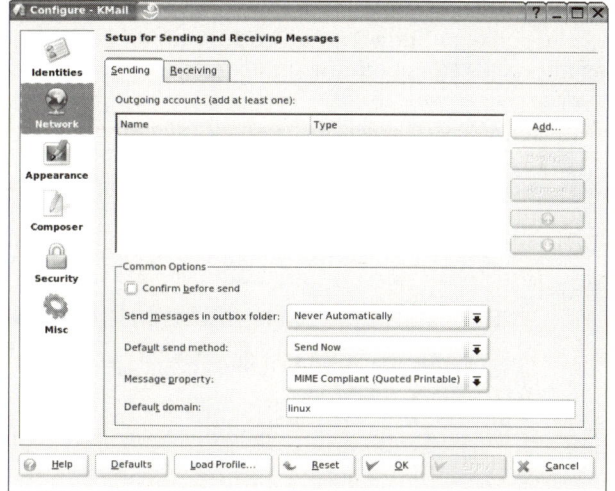

Figure 10-2: Configure e-mail accounts in the Configure KMail window.

3. **Click the Sending tab for outgoing mail and then click the Add button.**

    A dialog box prompts you for the mail-transport agent.

4. **Select the mail-transport agent and click OK.**

    Typically, for an ISP-provided mail account, you should select SMTP. A dialog box prompts you for information about the mail server.

5. **Enter the mail server's name and click OK.**

    This is the mail server that your ISP wants you to use when sending messages (for example, `smtp.comcast.net`).

6. **Click the Receiving tab for incoming mail and click Add.**

    A dialog box prompts you for the mail protocol, such as POP3 or IMAP.

7. **Select the mail protocol and click OK.**

    Most ISPs want you to use POP3 or IMAP as the mail protocol. Make your selection based on your ISP's instructions. After you click OK, a dialog box prompts for further information about your mail account.

8. **Enter the information about your ISP mail account and click OK.**

    You typically have to enter the mail server's name (for example, `mail.comcast.net`) as well as the username and password for your mail account.

9. **Click OK in the Configure KMail window.**

Part III: Doing Stuff with SUSE

After the e-mail account information is set up, you can start using KMail. The user interface is intuitive, as shown in Figure 10-3. KMail periodically checks and downloads messages from your incoming mail accounts. You can view messages as they arrive in your Inbox.

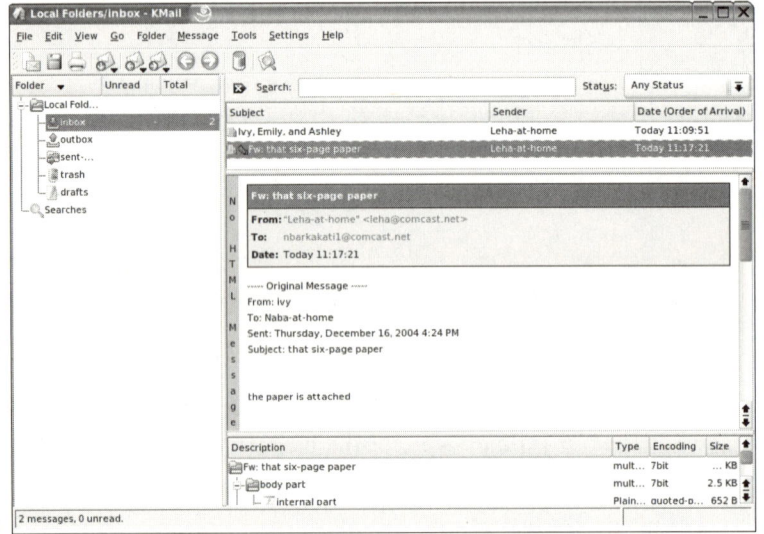

Figure 10-3: Read and manage your e-mail in KMail.

Introducing Evolution Mail

If you use the GNOME desktop, Evolution is the default e-mail client. To start Evolution, click the icon on the GNOME desktop's top panel (mouse over and read the help balloon to locate the icon) or choose Main Menu➪Office➪Evolution.

When you start Evolution for the first time, the Evolution Setup Assistant window appears, as shown in Figure 10-4.

Click Forward in the Welcome screen and the Setup Assistant guides you through the following steps:

1. **Enter your name and e-mail address in the Identity screen and click the Forward button.**

    For example, if your e-mail address is `jdoe@someplace.com`, that's what you enter.

Figure 10-4:
Evolution Setup Assistant guides you through the initial setup.

2. **Set up the options for receiving e-mail and click Forward.**

   Select the type of mail download protocol — most ISP accounts offer either POP or IMAP. Then provide the name of the mail server (for example, `mail.comcast.net`). You are prompted for the password when Evolution connects to the mail server for the first time.

3. **Provide further information about receiving e-mail — how often to check for mail and whether to leave messages on the server — and then click Forward.**

   Typically, you want to download the messages and delete them from the server (otherwise the ISP complains when your mail piles up).

4. **Set up the following options for sending e-mail and click Forward when you're done:**

    - Select the server type as SMTP.

    - Enter the name of the ISP's mail server such as `smtp.comcast.net`.

    - If the server requires you to log in, select the Server Requires Authentication check box.

    - If the server requires authentication, enter your username — the same username you use to log in to your ISP's mail server. (Often you don't have to log in to send mail; you only log in when receiving — downloading — mail messages.)

Part III: Doing Stuff with SUSE

5. **Give this mail account a descriptive name; click Forward.**

   The default name is the same as your e-mail address.

6. **Set your time zone by clicking a map; click Forward.**

7. **Click Apply to complete the Evolution setup.**

After you complete the setup, Evolution opens its main window and displays the e-mail view, as shown in Figure 10-5.

The window has a menu bar and a toolbar. The main display area is vertically divided into two panes: a narrow pane on the left (with a number of shortcut icons at the bottom), and a bigger right pane where Evolution displays information relevant to the currently selected shortcut icon. In Figure 10-5, Evolution displays the Inbox.

You can click the icons in the lower part of the left pane to switch to different views. Here's what happens when you click each of the four shortcut icons in Evolution:

- **Mail:** Switches to mail display, where you can read mail and send mail.
- **Contacts:** Opens your contact list, where you can add new contacts or look up someone from your current list.
- **Calendars:** Opens your calendar, where you can look up and add appointments.
- **Tasks:** Shows your task ("to do") list, where you can add new tasks and check what's due when.

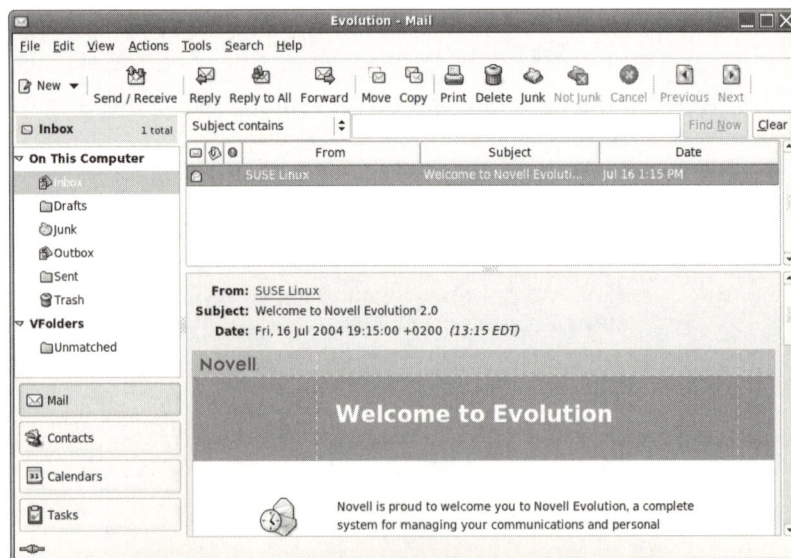

Figure 10-5: Reading mail in Evolution Mail.

As this icon summary shows, Evolution has all the necessary components of a PIM — e-mail, contacts, calendar, and task lists.

To access your e-mail, click the Mail icon and then click Inbox on the left pane. Evolution opens your inbox, as shown in Figure 10-5. If you turn on the feature to automatically check for mail every so often, Evolution prompts you for your mail password and downloads your mail. To manually download mail, just click the Send/Receive button on the toolbar (if you haven't asked Evolution to store your password, it prompts you for your mail password).

The e-mail Inbox looks very much like any other mail reader's inbox, such as the Outlook Express Inbox. Most of the time, you can click the toolbar buttons to do most anything you want to do with the e-mail messages. If you have used any GUI mail reader — from Microsoft Outlook Express to Novell GroupWise — you find Evolution's toolbar buttons familiar.

To read a message, click the message in the upper window of the Inbox and the message text appears in the lower window.

To reply to the current message, click the Reply button on the toolbar (or click Reply to All to send a reply to all the addressees). A message composition window pops up. You can write your reply and then click the Send button on the message composition window's toolbar to send the reply. Simple, isn't it?

To send a new e-mail, select New➪Mail Message on the Evolution toolbar. A new message composition window appears; you can type your message in that window, and when you're finished composing the message, click Send.

Evolution comes with extensive online help. Choose Help➪Contents from the Evolution menu and the Evolution User Guide appears in a window. You can then read the user guide in that window.

Instant Messaging in SUSE Linux

Instant messaging (IM) is kind of like a phone call in that you can communicate with others in real-time. The difference is that instead of talking, you type your messages in an IM client application. Both you and the person you are communicating with see each line of text right after you type it and press Enter. The IM client also enables you to post an Away message that lets others know that you are online but not available for conversation. Behind the scenes, instant messaging needs a central server that keeps track of all the online users and that facilitates sending the typed text between the parties engaged in messaging. That central server comes from an IM service. Some popular IM services include IRC, AIM, Yahoo! Messenger, MSN Messenger, and ICQ. You have to get an account with one of these IM services and sign in before you can exchange instant messages with others on that service. After you sign in, you can find out if your friends are online and send messages via the IM client.

There are two major IM clients in SUSE Linux. In KDE desktops, you can use Kopete, whereas GAIM is a commonly used IM client for the GNOME desktop. I briefly describe both IM clients in the following sections.

Using Kopete

Kopete — the KDE IM client — enables you to connect to many messaging services including AIM, IRC, MSN Messenger, Yahoo!, Gadu-Gadu, and SMS.

To start Kopete, choose Main Menu➪Internet➪Chat from the KDE desktop (if you have more than one messaging program installed, you have to select Kopete from a next-level menu). When you first run Kopete, you get the Configure Kopete window (see Figure 10-6), where you can enter information about your IM and other messaging service accounts.

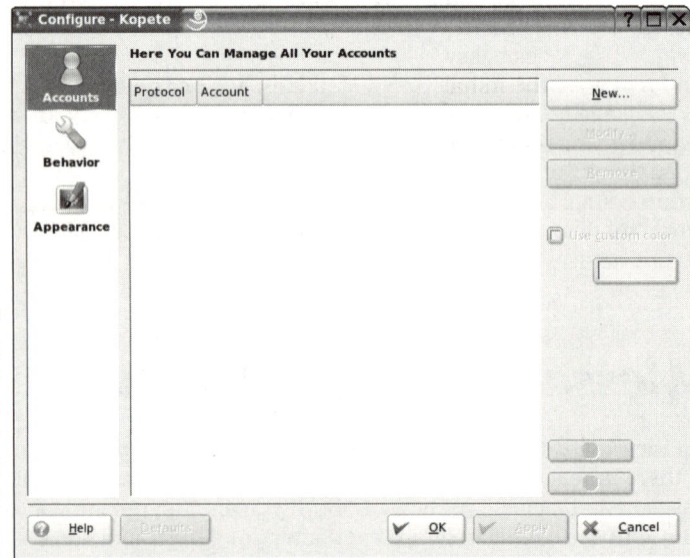

Figure 10-6: Enter information about your messaging accounts in this window.

For example, to add your AIM account information, click New and then answer and respond to the prompts from the Account Wizard. The first step is to select your messaging service. (See Figure 10-7.)

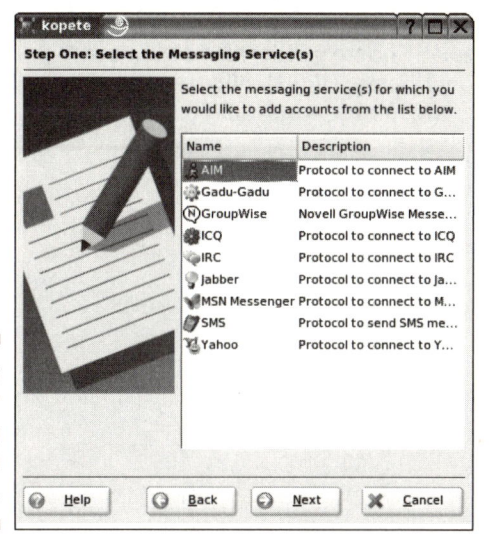

Chapter 10: E-Mailing and Instant Messaging in SUSE   *165*

Figure 10-7: Select your messaging service in this window.

Select the appropriate messaging service, such as AIM if you use AOL's instant messaging service. Then provide the AIM screen name and the password. You can also enable the option to have Kopete remember your password. If you choose that option, you're prompted to set up KWallet — the KDE Wallet System — that stores passwords and other information in an encrypted file. Figure 10-8 shows the initial screen of the KWallet setup. Just click Next, confirm that you really want to use KWallet, and enter, guess what, another password. The idea is that you'd enter that single password to open your KDE wallet that stores many more passwords and other sensitive information.

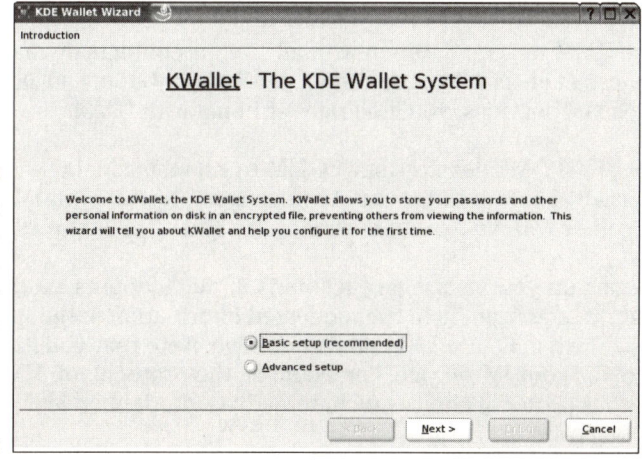

Figure 10-8: Set up KWallet to store your passwords in an encrypted file.

After you have set up your messaging service accounts, the Account Wizard closes and you get the regular Kopete window. To sign on with your messaging services and begin using Kopete, click the Connect button — the leftmost button on the toolbar — in the Kopete window. (See Figure 10-9.)

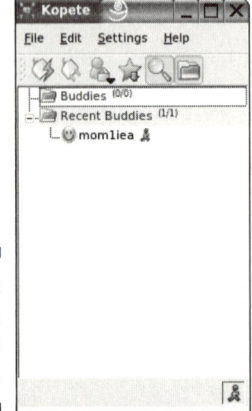

Figure 10-9: Viewing a buddy list in Kopete.

Click the magnifying glass icon to see your buddies. You see a solid smiley face icon for buddies who are online. Click on an online buddy to start chatting. Choose File⇨Add Contact to add more contacts.

Well, if you know AIM, you know what to do: Have fun IMing with Kopete!

Using GAIM

You can use GAIM to keep in touch with all of your contacts on many different IM services such as AIM, ICQ, Yahoo!, MSN, Gadu-Gadu, and Jabber. If you use any of the IM services, you'll be right at home with GAIM.

From the SUSE GNOME desktop, start GAIM by choosing Main Menu⇨Internet⇨Chat⇨GAIM Internet Messenger. The initial GAIM window appears together with an Accounts window, as shown in Figure 10-10.

Start by setting up your messaging accounts in the Accounts window. Click the Add button, and then fill in the requested information in the Add Account window, as shown in Figure 10-11, and click Save. Note that you have to select the protocol for your IM service. For example, the protocol for AIM is AIM/ICQ. Other protocol choices include Gadu-Gadu, Jabber, MSN, and Yahoo!, among others.

Chapter 10: E-Mailing and Instant Messaging in SUSE   *167*

Figure 10-10: Manage all of your IM accounts in this window.

Figure 10-11: Enter information about each IM account.

After you enter account information, the Accounts window shows all currently defined accounts. You can then select an account from the GAIM main window and click Sign On, as shown in Figure 10-12.

After GAIM logs you in, it opens the standard Buddy List window. (See Figure 10-13.)

To add buddies, choose Buddies⇨Add Buddy. In the Add Buddy window that appears, enter the screen name of the buddy and click Add. To create a new group, choose Buddies⇨Add Group. Type the name of the new group in the Add Group window that appears and then click Add.

Figure 10-12: Sign on to AIM with GAIM.

If any of your buddies are online, their names show up in the Buddy List window. To send a message to a buddy, double-click the name and a message window pops up. If someone sends you a message, a message window pops up with the message and you can begin conversing in that window.

Figure 10-13: A buddy list window in GAIM.

Chapter 11
Reading Newsgroups

In This Chapter
▶ Understanding newsgroups
▶ Reading newsgroups from your ISP using KNode and Pan
▶ Reading and searching newsgroups at some Web sites

*I*nternet newsgroups are like the bulletin board systems (BBSs) of the pre-Web age or the forums offered on online systems such as AOL and MSN. Essentially, newsgroups provide a distributed conferencing system that spans the globe. You can post articles — essentially e-mail messages to a whole group of people — and respond to articles others have posted.

Think of an Internet newsgroup as a gathering place — a virtual meeting place where you can ask questions and discuss various issues (and best of all, everything you discuss gets archived for posterity).

To participate in newsgroups, you need access to a news server — your Internet service provider (ISP) can give you this access. You also need a newsreader. SUSE Linux comes with software that you can use to read newsgroups. In this chapter, I introduce you to newsgroups and show you how to read newsgroups with KNode and Pan newsreaders. I also briefly explain how you can read and search newsgroups for free at a few Web sites.

Understanding Newsgroups

Newsgroups originated in Usenet — a store-and-forward messaging network that was widely used for exchanging e-mail and news items. Usenet works like a telegraph in that news and mail are relayed from one system to another. In Usenet, the systems are not on any network; the systems simply dial up one another and use the UNIX-to-UNIX Copy Protocol (UUCP) to transfer text messages.

Although it's a very loosely connected collection of computers, Usenet works well and continues to be used because very little expense is involved in connecting to it. All you need is a modem and a site willing to store and forward your mail and news. You have to set up UUCP on your system, but you don't need a sustained network connection; just a few phone calls are all you need to keep the e-mail and news flowing. The downside of Usenet is that you cannot use TCP/IP services such as the Web, TELNET, or FTP with UUCP.

From their Usenet origins, the newsgroups have now migrated to the Internet (even though the newsgroups are still called *Usenet newsgroups*). Instead of UUCP, the Network News Transfer Protocol (NNTP) now transports the news.

Although (for most of the online world) the news transport protocol has changed from UUCP to NNTP, the store-and-forward concept of news transfer remains. Thus, if you want to get news on your SUSE Linux system, you have to find a news server from which your system can download news. Typically, you can use your ISP's news server.

Newsgroup hierarchy

The Internet newsgroups are organized in a hierarchy for ease of maintenance as well as ease of use. The newsgroup names help keep things straight by showing the hierarchy.

Admittedly, these newsgroup names are written in Internet-speak, which can seem rather obscure at first. But the language is pretty easy to pick up with a little bit of explanation. For example, a typical newsgroup name looks like this:

```
comp.os.linux.announce
```

This name says that `comp.os.linux.announce` is a newsgroup for announcements (`announce`) about the Linux operating system (`os.linux`) and that these subjects fall under the broad category of computers (`comp`).

As you can see, the format of a newsgroup name is a sequence of words separated by periods. These words denote the hierarchy of the newsgroup. Figure 11-1 illustrates the concept of hierarchical organization of newsgroups.

To understand the newsgroup hierarchy, compare the newsgroup name with the pathname of a file (for example, `/usr/lib/X11/xinit/Xclients`) in Linux. Just as a file's pathname shows the directory hierarchy of the file, the newsgroup name shows the newsgroup hierarchy. In filenames, a slash (/) separates the names of directories; in a newsgroup's name, a period (.) separates the different levels in the newsgroup hierarchy.

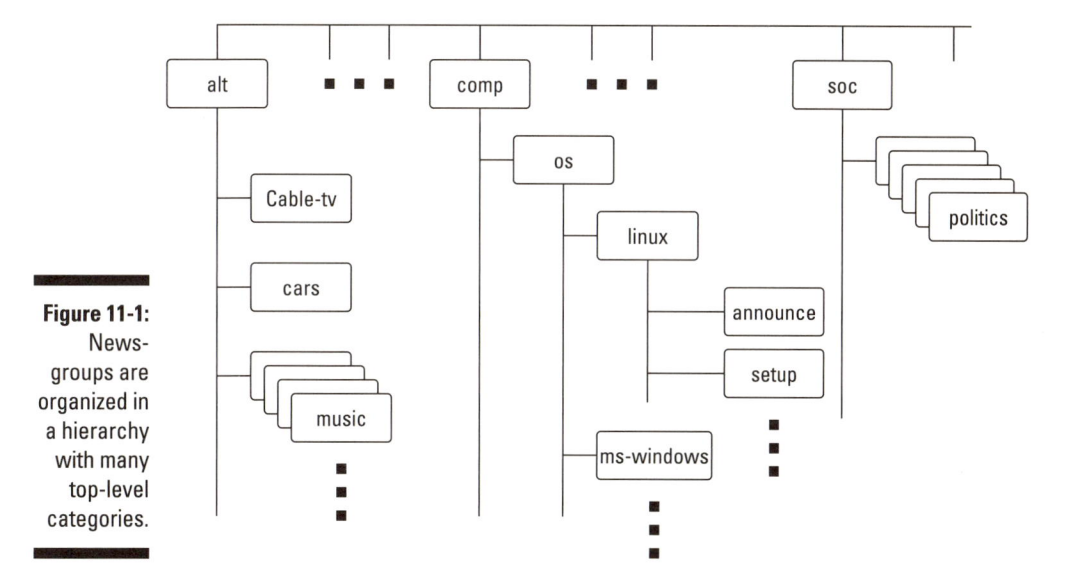

Figure 11-1: Newsgroups are organized in a hierarchy with many top-level categories.

In a newsgroup name, the first word represents the newsgroup *category*. The `comp.os.linux.announce` newsgroup, for example, is in the `comp` category, whereas `alt.books.technical` is in the `alt` category.

Top-level newsgroup categories

Table 11-1 lists some of the major newsgroup categories. You find a wide variety of newsgroups covering subjects ranging from politics to computers. The Linux-related newsgroups are in the `comp.os.linux` hierarchy.

Table 11-1	Major Newsgroup Categories
Category	**Subject**
`alt`	"Alternative" newsgroups (not subject to any rules), which run the gamut from the mundane to the bizarre
`bionet`	Biology newsgroups
`bit`	Bitnet newsgroups
`biz`	Business newsgroups
`clari`	Clarinet news service (daily news)

(continued)

Table 11-1 *(continued)*

Category	Subject
`comp`	Computer hardware and software newsgroups (includes operating systems such as Linux and Microsoft Windows)
`ieee`	Newsgroups for the Institute of Electrical and Electronics Engineers (IEEE)
`k12`	Newsgroups devoted to elementary and secondary education
`linux`	Newsgroups devoted to Linux
`misc`	Miscellaneous newsgroups
`news`	Newsgroups about Internet news administration
`rec`	Recreational and art newsgroups
`sci`	Science and engineering newsgroups
`soc`	Newsgroups for discussing social issues and various cultures
`talk`	Discussions of current issues (think "talk radio")

This short list of categories is deceptive because it doesn't really tell you about the wide-ranging variety of newsgroups available in each category. The top-level categories alone number close to a thousand, but many top-level categories are distributed only in specific regions of the world. Because each newsgroup category contains several levels of subcategories, the overall count of newsgroups can be close to 50,000 or 60,000! The `comp` category alone has more than 500 newsgroups.

Unfortunately, many newsgroups are flooded with spam, just like your e-mail Inbox, only worse because anyone can post anything on a newsgroup. Some newsgroups, called *moderated newsgroups,* offer some relief. Anyone who wants to post on a moderated newsgroup must first submit the article to a moderator — a human being — who can then decide whether to post the article or reject it. You can reduce the spam overload by browsing moderated newsgroups whenever possible.

Some Linux-related newsgroups

Typically, you have to narrow your choice of newsgroups according to your interests. If you're interested in Linux, for example, you can pick one or more of these newsgroups:

- `comp.os.linux.admin`: Information about Linux system administration.
- `comp.os.linux.advocacy`: Discussions about promoting Linux.

- `comp.os.linux.announce`: Important announcements about Linux. This newsgroup is moderated, which means you must mail the article to a moderator, who then posts it to the newsgroup if the article is appropriate for the newsgroup. (This method keeps the riff-raff from clogging up the newsgroup with marketing pitches.)
- `comp.os.linux.answers`: Questions and answers about Linux. All the Linux HOWTOs are posted in this moderated newsgroup.
- `comp.os.linux.development`: Current Linux development work.
- `comp.os.linux.development.apps`: Linux application development.
- `comp.os.linux.development.system`: Linux operating system development.
- `comp.os.linux.hardware`: Discussions about Linux and various types of hardware.
- `comp.os.linux.help`: Help with various aspects of Linux.
- `comp.os.linux.misc`: Miscellaneous Linux-related topics.
- `comp.os.linux.networking`: Networking under Linux.
- `comp.os.linux.setup`: Linux setup and installation.
- `comp.os.linux.x`: Discussions about setting up and running the X Window System under Linux.

You have to be selective about what newsgroups you read because keeping up with all the news is impossible, even in a specific area such as Linux. When you first install and set up Linux, you might read newsgroups such as `comp.os.linux.help`, `comp.os.linux.setup`, `comp.os.linux.hardware`, and `comp.os.linux.x` (especially if you run X). After you have Linux up and running, you may want to find out about only new things happening in Linux. For such information, read the `comp.os.linux.announce` newsgroup.

Reading Newsgroups from Your ISP

If you sign up with an ISP for Internet access, it can provide you with access to a news server. Such Internet news servers communicate by using the Network News Transfer Protocol (NNTP). You can use an NNTP-capable newsreader, such as KNode or Pan, to access the news server and read selected newsgroups. Using a newsreader is the easiest way to access news from your ISP's news server.

Part III: Doing Stuff with SUSE

> **WARNING!** My discussion of reading newsgroups assumes that you obtained access to a news server from your ISP. The ISP provides you the name of the news server and any username and password needed to set up your news account on the newsreader you use.

To read news, you need a *newsreader* — a program that enables you to select a newsgroup and view the items in that newsgroup. You also have to understand the newsgroup hierarchy and naming conventions (which I describe in the "Newsgroup hierarchy" section, earlier in this chapter). Now I show you how to read news from a news server.

> **REMEMBER:** If you don't have access to newsgroups through your ISP, you can try using one of the many public news servers out there. For a list of public news servers, visit NewzBot at www.newzbot.com. At this Web site, you can search for news servers that carry specific newsgroups.

Taking stock of newsreaders in SUSE Linux

Depending on the desktop — KDE or GNOME — that you run, you get a different default newsreader. Here are the two newsreaders you'd be using in SUSE Linux:

- **KNode:** A GUI newsreader that the KDE desktop offers as the default newsreader.
- **Pan:** A GUI newsreader that, according to the developer's Web site (pan.rebelbase.com), "... attempts to be pleasing to both new and experienced users." Pan is the default newsreader on the GNOME desktop.

Introducing KNode

The KDE desktop in SUSE uses KNode as its default newsreader. In SUSE, choose Main Menu⇨Internet⇨Usenet News Reader (if you have more than one news reader installed, you have to select KNode from a next-level menu).

When KNode runs for the first time, it brings up the Configure KNode dialog box, shown in Figure 11-2, through which you can configure everything needed to read newsgroups and post items to newsgroups. The left-hand side of the dialog box shows all the items that you can configure and the right-hand side is where you enter the information for the item that you have currently selected on the right-hand side.

Follow these steps to set up the news account:

1. **Enter your identification information (refer to Figure 11-2).**

Chapter 11: Reading Newsgroups

Your identification information such as name, e-mail address, and organization is used when you post a new item to a newsgroup. A dialog box appears.

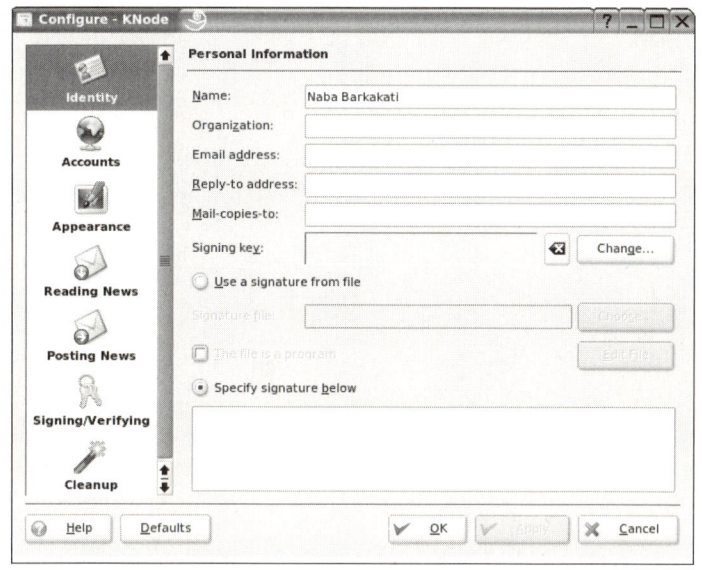

Figure 11-2:
Configure KNode from this dialog box.

2. **Click Accounts on the left pane and then click New on the Newsgroup Servers tab.**

   The New Account dialog box appears, as shown in Figure 11-3.

3. **Enter information about your news server.**

   Your ISP should have provided you with the information needed to access the news server. If the news server requires a login name and a password, check the Server Requires Authentication box to enable the User and Password fields, and enter your user information.

4. **Click OK.**

   The Configure KNode dialog box closes and you can start using KNode.

After you set up the news account, the KNode window shows the name of the news server in its left-hand side. Right-click on the server's name and select Subscribe to Newsgroups from the pop-up menu. If you have not yet subscribed to any newsgroup, a dialog box asks if you want to download a list of newsgroups. Click Yes and then a dialog box appears where you can subscribe to selected newsgroups (such as `comp.os.linux.announce`), as shown in Figure 11-4.

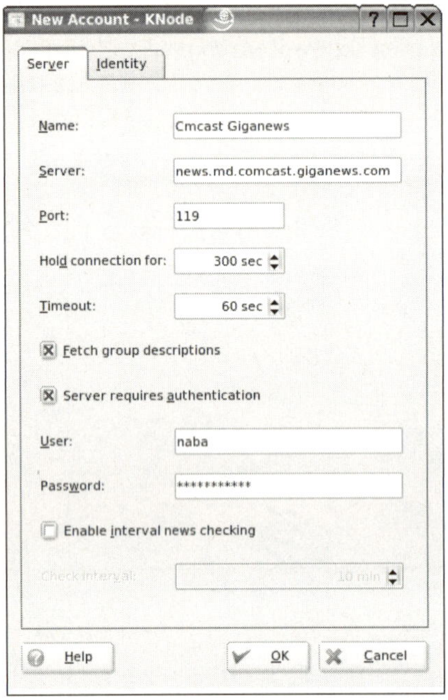

Figure 11-3: Enter information about the news server in this dialog box.

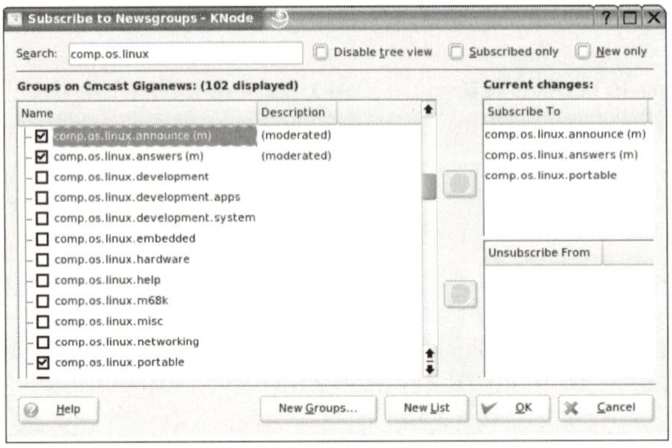

Figure 11-4: Select the newsgroups you want to read.

After you finish selecting newsgroups, click OK. The KNode window now shows the list of subscribed newsgroups. If you click on a newsgroup, KNode downloads the list of messages for that newsgroup and displays the list. You can then read the messages one by one. Just click on the subject line and the message appears in the lower pane (see Figure 11-5).

Chapter 11: Reading Newsgroups *177*

Figure 11-5 shows a typical view of the KNode window while reading an article from one of the subscribed newsgroups. The KNode user interface is similar to many other mail and newsreaders, including the Pan newsreader in GNOME.

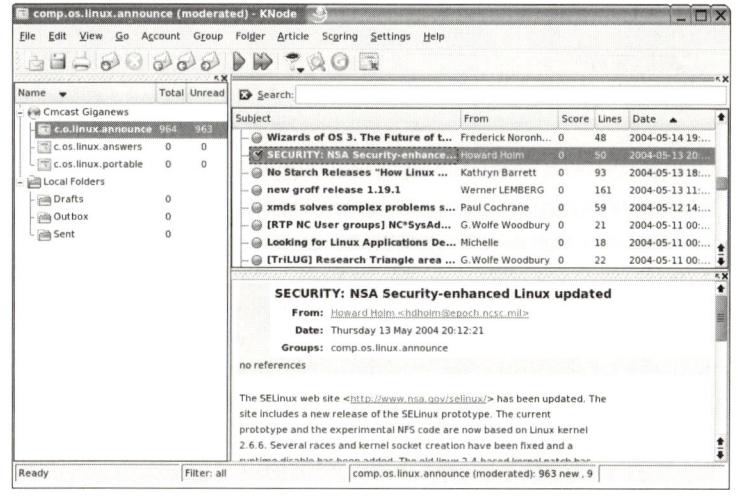

Figure 11-5: Read news items from a newsgroup in KNode.

Introducing Pan

If you have installed the GNOME desktop, Pan is your default newsreader. To start Pan, choose Main Menu➪Internet➪Usenet News Reader➪Pan Newsreader from the GNOME desktop's top panel.

When you first run Pan, the Pan Setup Wizard starts and prompts you for information. Follow these steps to complete the setup:

1. **Click Forward at the welcome message.**

   The Pan Setup Wizard prompts you for identifying information about yourself.

2. **Enter your name and e-mail address, and then click Forward.**

   The Pan Setup Wizard prompts you for information about the news server, as shown in Figure 11-6.

3. **Enter the requested information (refer to Figure 11-6) and click Forward.**

Your ISP should provide you with the news server's name as well as any username or password you need to access the newsgroups. After you click Forward, the Pan Setup Wizard prompts you for your mail server.

4. **Enter the name of the mail server that you use to send mail through your ISP account and click Forward.**

   Pan uses the mail server when you want to reply to news items.

5. **Click Save.**

   The Pan Setup Wizard saves the settings and returns to Pan.

The Pan window appears and a dialog box asks if you want to download a list of groups. Click Yes.

Pan downloads the list of newsgroups and displays it in the left-hand side of its main window, as shown in Figure 11-7. An easy way to get to your desired newsgroup is to enter the first part of the newsgroup name (for example, `comp.news.linux`) in the Find box in the toolbar and press Enter. Pan displays the newsgroups that contain the text you entered.

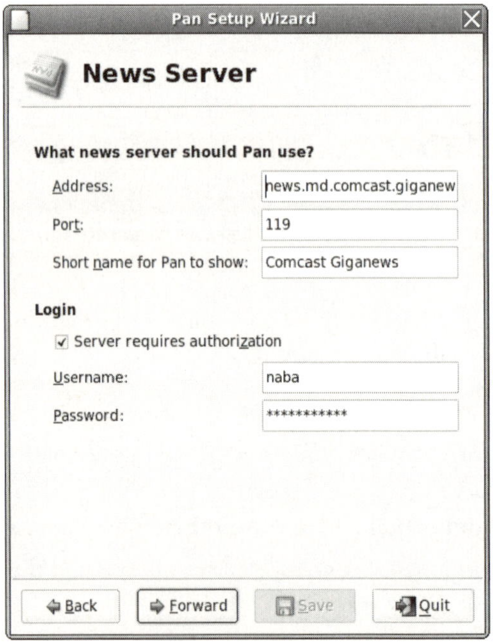

Figure 11-6: Enter information about the news server in this window in the Pan Setup Wizard.

You can then click a newsgroup to download the headers from that group. Pan displays the headers in the upper-right side of the window. You can click a header and Pan displays the contents of that news item in the lower-right part of the window. (Refer to Figure 11-7.)

Newsgroup subscriptions

Unlike magazines or newspapers, newsgroups don't require that you subscribe to them; you can read any available newsgroup on the news server. The news server's administrator may decide to exclude certain newsgroups, however; if they aren't included, you cannot read them.

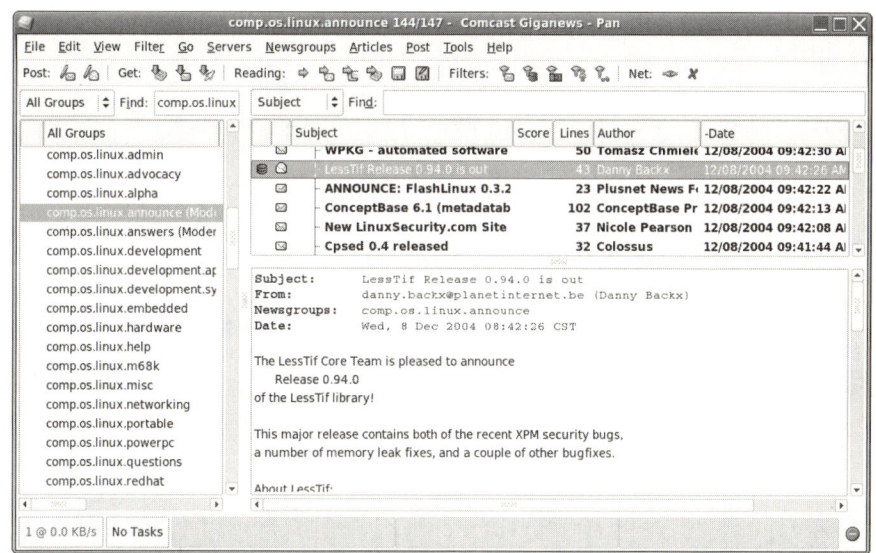

Figure 11-7: Reading a news item in Pan.

The only thing that can be called "subscribing" is when you indicate the newsgroups you routinely want to read. The news server does not receive any of this subscription information — the information is used only by the newsreader to determine what to download from the news server.

Posting news

You can use any newsreader to post a news article (a new item or a reply to an old posting) to one or more newsgroups. The exact steps for posting a news item depend on the newsreader, but posting to a newsgroup is similar to writing an e-mail message except that you are sending it to a newsgroup instead of an individual.

In KNode, click the leftmost icon on the toolbar (refer to Figure 11-5) to post to a newsgroup. To post a follow-up to the item you are currently reading, click the leftmost toolbar icon that shows an envelope with a left-pointing green arrow. If you mouse over each icon on the toolbar, a balloon help tells you what each one does.

In Pan, click the Post buttons on the left side of the toolbar (refer to Figure 11-7) to post an item to a newsgroup or post a follow-up to a message you are reading. If you mouse over the toolbar icons, a Help balloon gives you hints about each item. That should help you locate the correct buttons. When you click one of the Post buttons, a new window appears where you can compose your message and post it.

If you post an article and read the newsgroup immediately, you should see the new article, but that does not mean the article has reached other sites on the Internet. After all, your posting shows up on your news server immediately because that's where you posted the article. Because of the store-and-forward model of news distribution, the news article gradually propagates from your news server to others around the world.

The misc.test newsgroup provides a way to see whether your news posting is really getting around. If you post to that newsgroup and don't include the word *ignore* in the subject, news servers acknowledge receipt of the article by sending an e-mail message to the address listed in the Reply To field of the article's header.

Reading and Searching Newsgroups at Web Sites

If you don't have access to newsgroups through your ISP, you can still read newsgroups and post articles to newsgroups at a number of Web sites. Some of them archive old news articles and provide good search capabilities, so you can search these for articles related to some question you may have.

The best part about reading newsgroups through a Web site is that you don't even need access to a news server and you can read news from your Web browser.

Here are some Web sites that offer free access to Usenet newsgroups:

- **Google Groups** — `groups.google.com`
- **InterBulletin** — `news.interbulletin.com`
- **Mailgate** — `www.mailgate.org`
- **News2Web** — `www.news2web.com`
- **Usenet Replayer** — `www.usenet-replayer.com`

Some sites offer a Usenet newsgroup service for a fee. I don't list them here, but you can search for them with Google (`www.google.com`) — **type the search words usenet newsgroup access** to get a list of all Web sites that offer newsgroup access (including the ones that charge a fee).

One of the best places to read newsgroups, post articles, and search old newsgroup archives is Google Groups — Google's Usenet discussion forum — on the Web at `groups.google.com`. At that Web site, you can select a newsgroup to browse and you can post replies to articles posted on various newsgroups.

The best part of Google Groups is the search capability. You already know how good Google's Web search is; you get that same comprehensive search capability to locate newsgroup postings that relate to your search words. To search newsgroups, fill in the search form at `groups.google.com` and press Enter.

To browse newsgroups in Google Groups, ignore the search box and look at the list of high-level newsgroup categories such as `alt`, `comp`, and `soc`. Click the category, and you can gradually drill down to specific newsgroups. When viewing an article in Google Groups, you can click a link that enables you to post a follow-up to that article.

Chapter 12
Preparing Documents and Spreadsheets in SUSE Linux

In This Chapter
- Preparing documents in OpenOffice.org Writer
- Working with spreadsheets in OpenOffice.org Calc

*P*reparing documents and spreadsheets are the staples of the modern office. SUSE Linux comes with the OpenOffice.org (often shortened as *OO.o* or *Ooo*) suite of office applications that includes very capable word processing and spreadsheet software to help you with these tasks. Both KDE and GNOME desktops use OpenOffice.org as the primary office application suite.

In this chapter, I describe two OpenOffice.org applications — Writer for preparing documents and Calc for working with spreadsheets — in considerable detail. Writer is similar to Microsoft Word and Calc is like Microsoft Excel.

Besides Writer and Calc, OpenOffice.org also includes Impress, a presentation software package that's similar to Microsoft PowerPoint. I describe Impress in Chapter 13.

Writing with OpenOffice.org Writer

Face it: The whole world, or so it seems, uses Microsoft Office, especially Microsoft Word, to write stuff. You have to work with the world to get your job done. Until recently, the lack of a freely available and good Microsoft Office-compatible office suite may have been holding you back from using SUSE Linux as your primary desktop operating system. Well, your troubles are over. SUSE Linux comes with the OpenOffice.org office suite — a set of office productivity applications comparable to Microsoft Office and compatible with Microsoft Office as well. OpenOffice.org is installed on your system when you installed SUSE Linux.

OpenOffice.org Writer, or *Writer* for short, is at the heart of the OpenOffice.org office suite. Writer is a word processor that makes it easy for you to prepare many different types of documents on your SUSE Linux system and, best of all, share files with others who use Microsoft Word.

Typically you might work with Microsoft Word files that your co-workers and friends (and maybe even family) send you. All you have to do is save the file in a folder and open it in Writer. I provide an overview of how to open a document, work on it, and save it to a folder. Along the way, I summarize how to perform common word processing tasks with Writer.

Before your expectations go sky-high, let me caution you that if you share files between Microsoft Word and Writer, you may run into some conversion problems; some Word features may not convert fully into equivalent Writer features. However, if you share only simple documents with Microsoft Word users (or if you simply want to prepare your own nicely formatted documents), Writer should work well for you.

By the way, if you're already a proficient Microsoft Word user, you should be able to start using Writer without much trouble because much of Writer works very much like Word.

Taking stock of OpenOffice.org Writer

Before you begin using Writer, I want to give you a quick overview of its major features. When you know what you can do with Writer, you can read the subsequent sections to find out how to perform specific tasks in Writer, such as formatting tables, printing documents, and tracking changes.

You can do the following with Writer:

- Open and edit Microsoft Word files or convert Microsoft Word files to Writer format. One advantage of converting to Writer format is that Writer files are much smaller in size than corresponding Microsoft Word files.
- Save documents in many different formats including Microsoft Word 97/2000/XP, Word 95, Word 6.0, Rich Text Format (RTF), StarWriter 5.0 (as well as 4.0 and 3.0), plain text, Adobe PDF, and Web page (HTML).
- Insert graphics files of many different formats, including JPEG, GIF, ZSoft Paintbrush (PCX), TIFF, Windows BMP, Macintosh PICT, Encapsulated PostScript (EPS), Adobe Photoshop (PSD), AutoCAD DXF, and many more.
- Create tables that can include calculations and add charts that update when the table contents change.
- Perform complex page layouts with desktop publishing features such as text frames and floating frames.

Chapter 12: Preparing Documents and Spreadsheets in SUSE Linux

- Easily create and organize multiple files that make up a large project such as a book or a large report.

- Create a *mail merge* where you write a single document with generic fields and have Writer automatically create many different customized documents by filling in the specific fields (such as name, address, and phone number) from a database.

- Save versions of a document as you continue to change it, and revert to an older version if necessary.

- Compare changes and work collaboratively using the Versions system. Not only can you see what has changed and who changed it, but you can also accept or reject those changes individually (or in groups) according to certain criteria.

    A note of caution here: The versioning information doesn't export perfectly to some other formats, in particular, Microsoft Word.

- E-mail your documents directly from Writer.

- If you like, Writer can automatically complete the word you're typing by making a best guess and you can accept the choice by pressing Enter. (If this feature drives you crazy, you can simply turn it off, just as you can configure many other features in Writer.)

Writer enables you to print a Writer document directly to an Adobe Portable Document Format (PDF) file. To electronically share a document in its final form, you can print the document to a PDF file and distribute that file. Anyone can easily view and print PDF files by using the free Adobe Reader (available at www.adobe.com/products/acrobat/readstep2.html).

Getting started with Writer

The best way to learn to use Writer is to simply start using it. To start Writer, click the Writer icon on the panel (the icon showing some pieces of paper with a pen) or choose Main Menu➪Office➪Wordprocessor➪OpenOffice.org Writer in KDE or GNOME.

Writer displays its main window (Figure 12-1) with an empty document.

Using Writer is simple because it's so similar to other word processors that you've probably used, such as Microsoft Word. For example, you can type text into the blank document, format it, and save it when you're done. If you want to work on an existing document (for example, a Microsoft Word file) that you've saved on your hard drive, choose File➪Open and then pick the document from the Open dialog box. Then you can work on that document and save it in Word format, another word processing format, or in the default OpenOffice.org 1.0 Text Document format in a file with the .sxw extension.

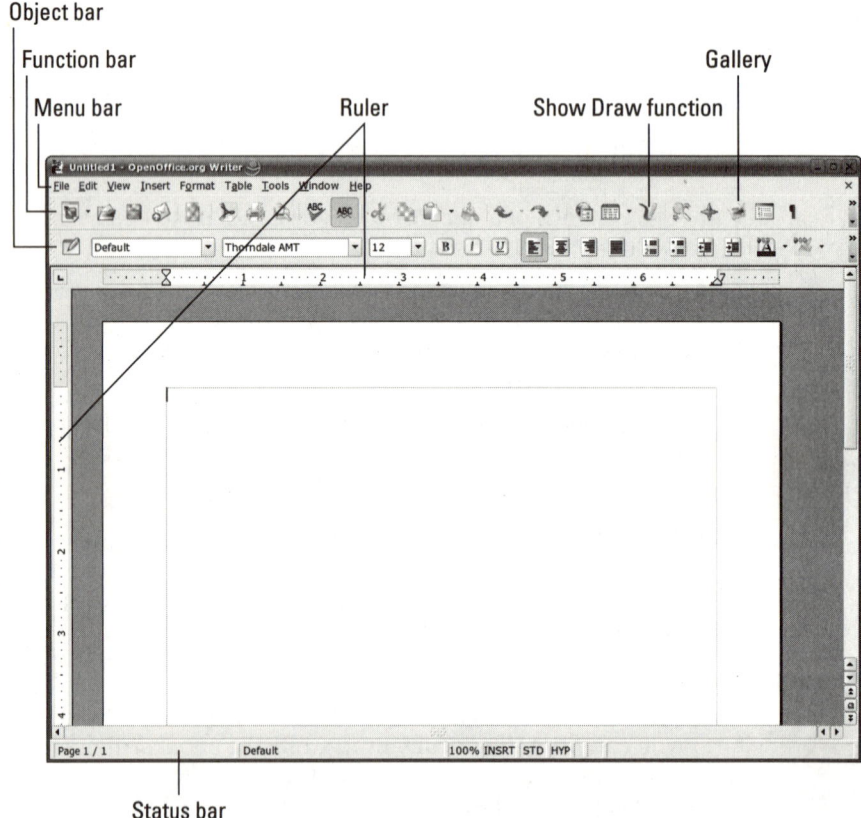

Figure 12-1: You can start typing your document in Writer's main window.

As Figure 12-1 shows, you can view the Writer window in terms of the following major parts:

- **Menu bar:** Provides the standard pull-down menus: File, Edit, Help, and so forth. Use these menus to perform all the tasks that Writer can do.
- **Function bar:** Provides buttons for performing tasks, such as opening, saving, and printing a document. You can also click icons on the function bar to open the Stylist (a list of paragraph, character, and page styles), the Navigator (a list of document parts such as headings, tables, and bookmarks), and the Gallery (a collection of predefined graphic objects such as 3D shapes, backgrounds, and bullets).
- **Object bar:** Enables you to format the document by applying styles, selecting fonts, or changing text attributes such as bold, italic, and underline. This bar changes depending on the type of object (such as plain text or graphics) that you've clicked.

- **Ruler:** Shows the page dimensions and the tab stops.
- **Status bar:** Displays the usual information about the open document, including the current page number and the total page count. You can also click elements in the status bar to change certain settings, such as the text selection mode and the zoom factor for viewing the document.

In addition to these parts, the largest part of the Writer window is the work area where your document appears. That's where you focus most of your attention.

Use tooltips to get a clue about what a particular field or button does. Mouse over a field or a button and Writer displays a small tooltip window with a brief help message. If you want more information in the tooltips, turn on extended tooltips by choosing Help⇨Extended Tips (when the check shows, the option is turned on). On the other hand, if you don't like these tooltips, toggle them off by choosing Help⇨Tips and Help⇨Extended Tips.

If you need it, help is available in Writer. Choose Help⇨Contents from the Writer menu. This brings up the OpenOffice.org Help window with help information about Writer. Click the links to view specific help information.

Setting up Writer

You don't really have to do any special setups to start using Writer. Even tasks such as printing should work right away provided you have set up a printer using the procedure described in Chapter 3. You may want to tinker with some settings, however, so that Writer works to your liking. For example, you might want to turn off AutoCorrect so that it doesn't suggest word completion, or you might want to hide some toolbars to get more workspace. You can set up most of these options from the View and Tools menus, which are located on the Menu bar (refer to Figure 12-1). In particular, you perform many of the setup tasks from the dialog box (Figure 12-2) that appears when you choose Tools⇨Options.

Preparing documents in Writer

You'll have no problem preparing documents using Writer. Typically, you can simply click to position a cursor and then type your text. To format text, select a style for the paragraph or select text and then apply formatting such as boldface or italics. In the following sections, I provide some quick tips on how to perform specific document-preparation tasks in Writer. I organize the tips into the following categories of tasks:

- Editing and reviewing documents
- Using styles and templates
- Performing page layout
- Creating and inserting graphics
- Using fields
- Working with large documents

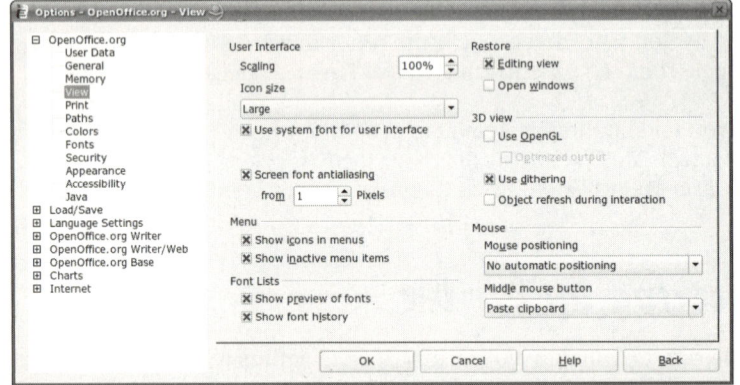

Figure 12-2: Set up many aspects of Writer from the Options dialog box.

Editing and reviewing documents

To edit a document, you have to open the file, move around within the document, insert and delete text, and save the file. You can perform most of these tasks intuitively because these steps are similar in most word processors. For that reason, I don't discuss in detail how to perform each of these tasks. Instead, in the following paragraphs, I highlight just a couple of features that you'll find particularly useful in your work.

Typically, you review changes when you collaborate with others on a document and several of you make revisions to the document. To review changes, the changes have to be tracked. Writer has features to enable change tracking (or *redlining,* as it's commonly called). With Writer, you can examine the changes, accept or reject each change, and make more editing changes — even adding comments to explain why you made a change.

Writer has other features for easily editing a document. For example, you can search and replace text — even find all occurrences of text with a specific formatting style and change each occurrence.

Most of Writer's editing and change-tracking functions are in the Edit menu (shown in Figure 12-3). Some toolbar icons provide shortcuts to the menu.

TIP

You can perform many editing tasks by clicking the toolbar icons. Just mouse over each icon and read the tooltips to see which ones enable you to make specific editing and reviewing changes.

Using styles and templates

In Writer, you can format pages, paragraphs, and blocks of text manually. For example, you can place the cursor on a paragraph, choose Format⇨Paragraph, and then format various characteristics of the paragraph (such as indentation, spacing, and borders). This paragraph-by-paragraph formatting is okay for a short document, but it can be tedious and time-consuming if you have to format hundreds of paragraphs one by one. A better approach is to define a *style* — a collection of formatting characteristics stored under a particular, usually descriptive, name. Then you can simply apply that style to all paragraphs. If you need to change any aspect of the paragraphs, simply edit the style and voilà — all paragraphs with that style get the new formatting.

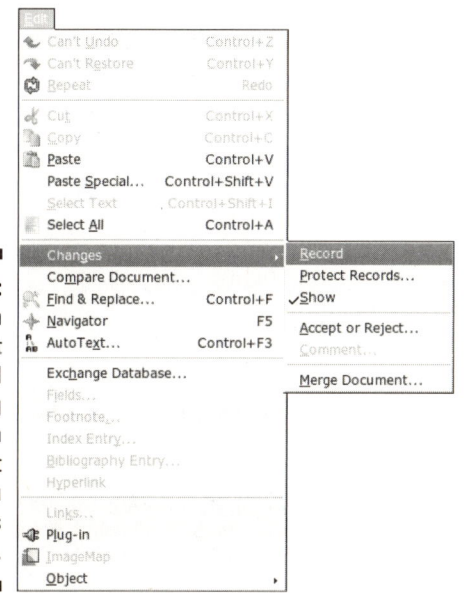

Figure 12-3: Perform most editing and reviewing tasks from the Edit menu and its submenus.

You may be familiar with paragraph and character styles in Microsoft Word, but Writer relies more on styles than Microsoft Word. Writer supports five types of styles:

- **Paragraph style:** Controls the look of a paragraph, such as the font, paragraph spacing, borders, bullets, numbering, and the style of the following paragraph.
- **Character style:** Controls the font style of selected text in a paragraph.
- **Frame style:** Controls the size and position of the frame and the text-wrapping options.
- **Page style:** Controls the page layout, including the margins, number of columns, headers, and footers.
- **Numbering style:** Controls the number or bullet character and spacing that are used for numbered or bulleted lists.

You can conveniently access and use all the document's styles in a floating window called the Stylist (Figure 12-4). Writer displays the Stylist by default, but you can show and hide it by pressing F11 (or choosing Format⇨Stylist).

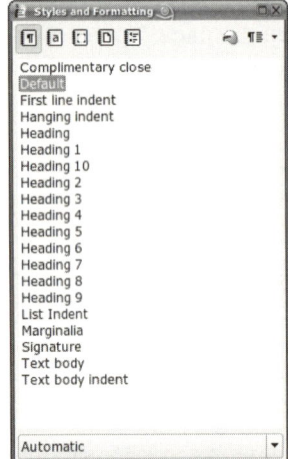

Figure 12-4: Press F11 to toggle Stylist on and off.

The Stylist makes it very easy to organize and use the styles. The five icons along the top part of the Stylist refer to the five types of styles — paragraph, character, frame, page, and numbering — from left to the right. You can click an icon to see all styles of that type. To apply a style, position the cursor where you want to apply the style and double-click the style from the Stylist. For character styles, select the text and then double-click the character style.

Chapter 12: Preparing Documents and Spreadsheets in SUSE Linux   *191*

Writer also supports templates, just as Microsoft Word does. A *template* is a special document with a collection of styles for the kinds of layouts that the document needs. You can think of a template as a model for a specific type of document. For example, you might have templates for documents such as memos, letters, fax cover sheets, envelopes, and many more.

Writer does not come with any templates, but you can create or download templates from Web sites. A Writer template for writing manuscripts using the Modern Language Association (MLA) style (see `owl.english.purdue.edu/handouts/research/r_mla.html` for more information on the MLA style), for example, is available from `www.cc.mie-u.ac.jp/~lq20106/eg5000/templates/dl/MLA-Template.stw`. You have to install the template file — `MLA-Template.stw` — before you can create documents using that template. Note that the `.stw` extension is used for OpenOffice.org template files.

To install a template file to use in Writer, follow these steps:

1. **Choose File➪Template➪Organize.**

    The Template Management dialog box (shown in Figure 12-5) appears with the My Templates folder of templates on the left side and the current list of documents on the right.

Figure 12-5: Import the template file into the My Templates template folder.

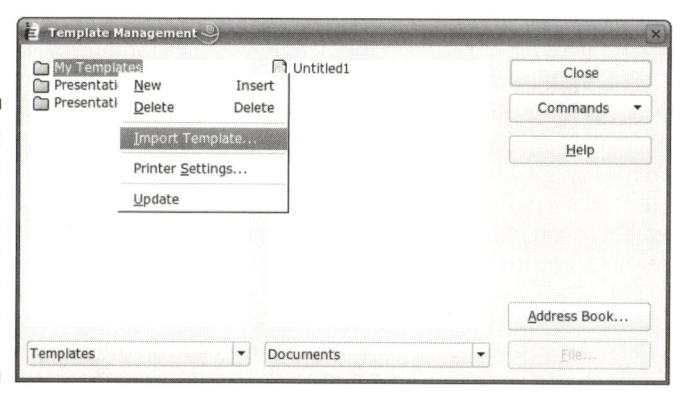

2. **Right-click the Default folder icon and select Import Template from the pop-up menu, as shown in Figure 12-5.**

    The Open dialog box appears.

3. **Navigate to the directory where you saved the template file, select the template file, and click Open.**

    The Open dialog box closes; the template now appears in the My Templates folder in the Template Management dialog box.

4. **Click Close to close the Template Management dialog box.**

To create a new document from a template you've installed, follow these steps:

1. **Choose File**⇨**New**⇨**Templates and Documents.**

   A dialog box appears.

2. **Click Templates on the left pane and then double-click the My Templates folder on the right pane.**

   You should see the templates that you have installed.

3. **Select the template you want to use and click Open.**

   A new document appears, typically with some text illustrating the selected template's styles.

4. **Erase the text in the new document and start typing what you want.**

   To view the styles in that template, open the Stylist window by pressing F11 and apply styles by double-clicking them in the Stylist.

Writer also enables you to perform many other tasks related to styles and templates. For example, you can create a style, apply a style to text, copy styles from one template to another, and so on.

Doing page layout

In Writer, page styles control the page layout, and each page can have its own style. The usual approach is to define three page styles: First Page, Left Page, and Right Page. Define the First Page style with whatever applies to the first page such as a special header and no page number. The Left Page style is the style for the even-numbered pages and the Right Page style is for odd-numbered pages. For each page style, you can also define the page style that applies to the following page. The idea would be to define Left Page as the next page style for First Page and Right Page as the style of the page that follows the Left Page style. That way, the page styles are correct for all the pages as long as you start with the First Page style. You may also want to define a Landscape page style so you can use it for pages that have to be in landscape orientation.

If you are familiar with Microsoft Word, you know that the page setup — paper size, orientation, margins, and so on — applies to all pages in the document. In Writer, a page style does not automatically apply to the entire document. Instead, each page has its own page style. Of course, you can choose to apply the same page style to all the pages. Essentially, you have more fine-grained control over page layouts in Writer.

A typical page layout task is to insert objects created in other OpenOffice.org applications, such as a Calc spreadsheet, an Impress slide, or a Draw drawing. You can insert such objects by choosing Insert➪Object➪OLE Object. Incidentally, OLE stands for Object Linking and Embedding, which is just a fancy term for the ability to create a document by adding objects like charts and drawings that are created in different applications.

When you add objects to a document, keep this caveat in mind: You can edit an object directly in the document only by using the application that originally created the object.

One object that you can insert into a Writer document is a mathematical formula, and I mean serious formulas with integral signs and Greek letters like alpha and sigma. If you're writing a scientific paper with complex equations, you'll really appreciate this feature of OpenOffice.org. Here's a typical sequence of steps to insert a formula into a Writer document (this process is similar for inserting other objects):

1. **Position the cursor and choose Insert➪Object➪Formula.**

   The user interface changes to that of OpenOffice.org Math — an application for writing mathematical formulas — and a small frame for the formula appears in the document. The formula is typeset in that frame.

2. **Select a formula type from the top two rows of the Selection window.**

   The lower rows in the Selection window show available formulas of that type. For example, the summation category (denoted by an uppercase Greek letter sigma) includes integral signs.

3. **Click a specific formula, such as an integral.**

   The Math command for this formula appears in the Commands window and parts of the formula appear in the document.

4. **Fill in the arguments for the formula.**

   As you construct the formula with commands in the Commands window, the formatted formula appears in the document (Figure 12-6).

5. **To change the font size of the formula, choose Format➪Font Size and specify the font size.**

6. **Click anywhere else in the Writer document to return to the Writer user interface.**

7. **Double-click the formula to edit it again.**

Of course, Writer has many page layout features. You can use tables, numbered and bulleted lists, and columns. Writer also supports *frames* — rectangular boxes in which you can place text, graphics, and even other frames. Using frames, you can place just about anything anywhere on the document.

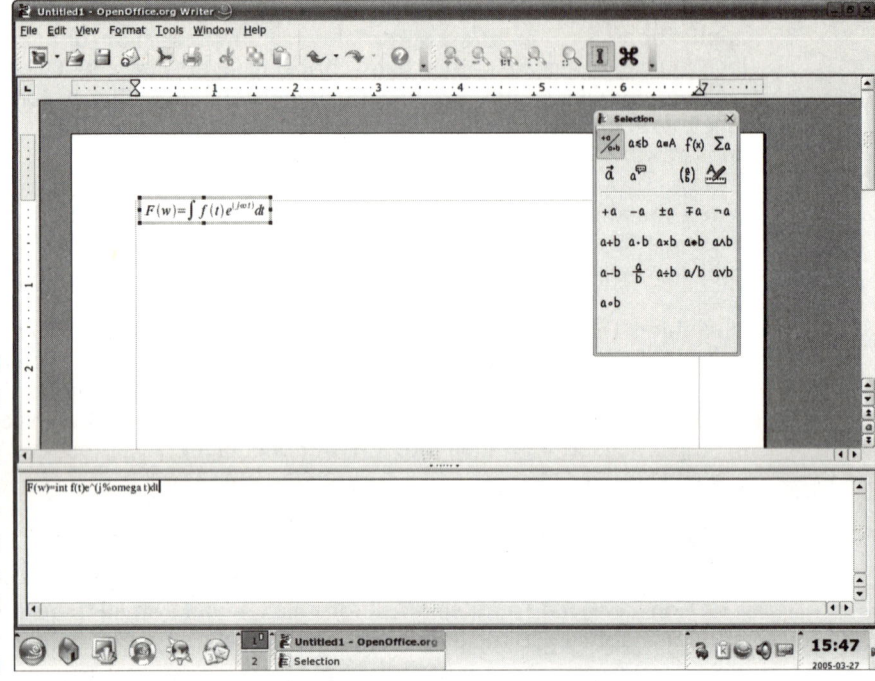

Figure 12-6: Insert a math formula into a Writer document by using the Math application.

Creating and inserting graphics

Writer includes a drawing toolbar with tools that you can use to draw in the document. You can also insert into your document both line drawings and images from files in many different formats.

To create simple diagrams in your document, click the Show Drawing Functions icon (on the right side of the function bar at the top of the Writer window) The Draw Functions toolbar appears along the bottom of the Writer window, as shown in Figure 12-7.

Figure 12-7: The Draw Functions toolbar.

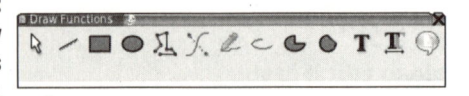

Click in the document where you want to add a diagram. Select a tool from the Draw Functions toolbar (Figure 12-7) and start drawing. To change the drawing tool, open the Draw Functions toolbar again and select another tool.

Tip: To keep the Draw Functions toolbar visible while you create a diagram, open the toolbar as usual, drag the toolbar's top part, and tear it away. The toolbar then turns into a *tearoff menu* (a small window that floats in the document window) from which you can easily select and use different drawing tools.

Writer also comes with a gallery of predefined graphics. To view the Gallery (shown in Figure 12-8), choose Tools⇨Gallery or click the Gallery icon (on the Function bar). Select from the themes along the left side of the gallery. If you see a graphic you'd like to use, drag and drop it from the gallery to the location on the document where you want to insert it. Click the Gallery icon again to hide the graphics gallery.

Using fields

Think of *fields* as bits of information that might change, but you want to call them by a name and use them in your document. For example, you might want to insert the current date and the page numbers into the header of a document. You can do so by inserting fields that refer to the date and page numbers. Some of the predefined fields (such as date and page numbers) are easy to use. Simply choose Insert⇨Fields and then select the field you want to insert.

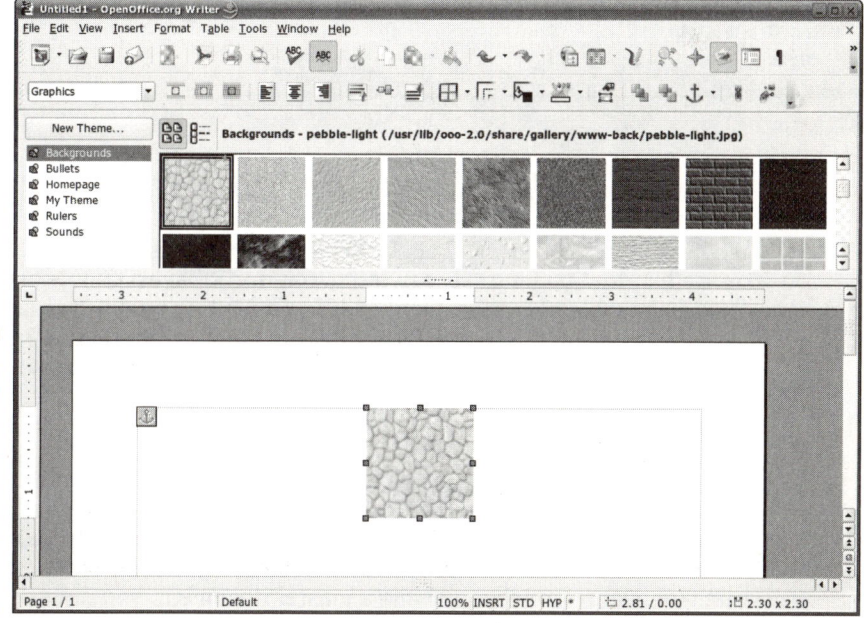

Figure 12-8: Drag and drop graphics from the gallery onto your document.

In addition to the fields you see in the Insert menu, you can pick from many more fields. Choose Insert⇨Fields⇨Other to open the Fields dialog box (Figure 12-9) where you can browse and pick other fields to use in your document. From the Fields dialog box, you can also change the format for a field. For example, you can select how the date field is shown in the document.

Another type of useful field is a *reference* or a *bookmark*. The idea is to mark a location in the document by a name and then refer to that location elsewhere by that assigned name. For example, you can insert a cross-reference to the page where that location occurs.

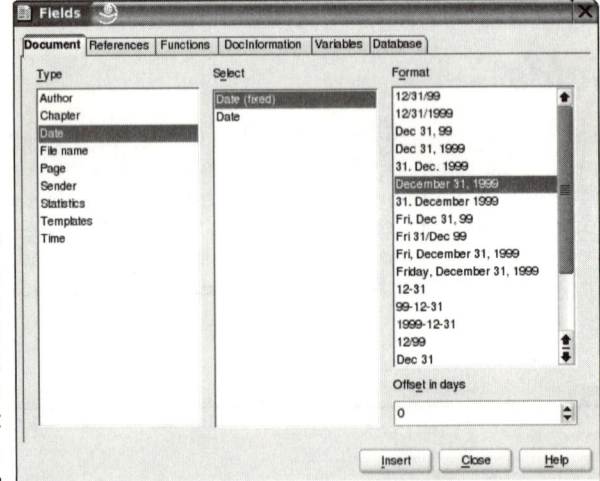

Figure 12-9: Use the Fields dialog box to pick other fields or select formats.

Working with large documents

What's a large document? Well, I consider a large document any document over a hundred pages or so. Anything that might have a couple of chapters and need a table of contents and an index definitely qualifies as a large document — for example, a book. Writer includes features to do the "usual things" you'd want to do when working with these larger, more cumbersome documents, such as creating tables of content, inserting indexes, and adding entries to indexes.

Writer also enables you to tie together several Writer files into a single large document — what Writer refers to as a *master document*. Master documents are ideal for books, for example. You can keep the chapters in separate files and then organize these files into a book by using the master document feature. For a large project involving a master document, you have to plan a little and take care of the following key steps:

1. **Create a template with the styles you need as well as any fields you plan to use.**

    For more about styles and templates, see the appropriately named section "Using styles and templates," earlier in this chapter.

 2. **Create the individual files and the master document by using the same template.**

 3. **Insert the files into the master document — that's how you combine all the individual parts into the final product.**

 4. **Add a table of contents and index and a bibliography, if needed.**

 5. **Work on the component files.**

 6. **Update the table of contents and index.**

Preparing Spreadsheets with OpenOffice.org Calc

Does the name VisiCalc mean anything to you? What about Lotus 1-2-3? I'm sure you have heard of Lotus 1-2-3, but maybe not VisiCalc — the first spreadsheet program that turned the IBM PC into a business tool. (Believe it or not, you can download and run VisiCalc even on today's PCs. Curious? For more information, visit Dan Bricklin's Web site at www.bricklin.com/history/vcexecutable.htm.)

Spreadsheet programs continue to be a staple of the office suite, and the OpenOffice.org suite is no exception. OpenOffice.org Calc, or just Calc for short, is the spreadsheet program in the OpenOffice.org suite.

All the spreadsheet programs that came after VisiCalc — from Lotus 1-2-3 to Microsoft Excel and Calc — still follow that visual model of a spreadsheet laid out in rows and columns. Of course, the newer spreadsheets (such as Excel and Calc) have many more bells and whistles, including fancy GUIs.

If you have used any other spreadsheet program, such as Microsoft Excel, you'll be right at home when you start using Calc. Therefore, I don't try to give you detailed instructions on how to use Calc; instead, I provide a quick overview and some tips on how to perform some common tasks in Calc.

Taking stock of OpenOffice.org Calc

Before describing the types of tasks you can perform in Calc, I want to highlight the key features of Calc. Calc can do all the basic spreadsheet functions you expect in a spreadsheet program. Here are some things you can do with Calc:

- Open and edit Microsoft Excel files or convert Microsoft Excel files into Calc format. Calc uses an XML format and saves files with the .SXC extension.
- Save documents in many different formats including Microsoft Excel 97/2000/XP, Excel 95, Excel 5.0, dBASE, StarCalc 5.0 (as well as 4.0 and 3.0), SYLK (an old Microsoft format), comma-separated values (CSV), and Web page (HTML).
- Use charting tools to visualize data in 2D or 3D plots.
- Insert graphics files of many different formats, including JPEG, GIF, ZSoft Paintbrush (PCX), TIFF, Windows BMP, Macintosh PICT, Encapsulated PostScript (EPS), Adobe Photoshop (PSD), AutoCAD DXF, and many more.
- Save versions of a spreadsheet as you continue to change it, allowing you to revert to an older version if necessary.
- Use styles and templates to format your spreadsheet.
- Define cells to dynamically change format depending on the value in the cell.
- Easily exchange — import and export — data with existing databases by using the DataPilot.
- Set up cells to accept values from a set of specific values or ranges of valid values.
- Lock cells so data cannot be changed inadvertently.
- Perform scenario analysis by storing multiple values in the same block of cells — and define scenarios so you can select a set of values for a specific scenario.
- Use the Goal Seek feature to determine the value of a cell that would give you a result you want from a formula.

Getting started with Calc

The best way to learn to use Calc is to simply start using it. To start Calc, choose Main Menu➪Office➪Spreadsheet in KDE (in GNOME, choose Main Menu➪Office➪Spreadsheet➪OpenOffice.org Calc). The Calc window opens with a blank spreadsheet. You can then begin typing text and numbers into the cells and use formulas to calculate whatever you want.

To familiarize yourself with Calc, take a moment to examine the tools and icons packed into Calc's main window (shown in Figure 12-10).

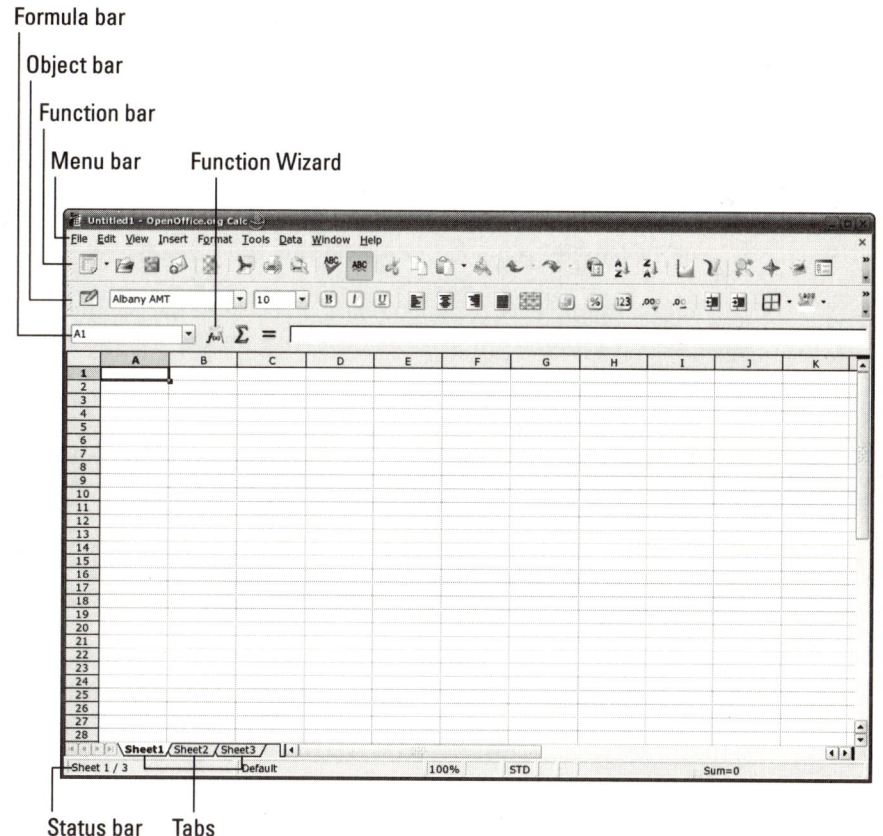

Chapter 12: Preparing Documents and Spreadsheets in SUSE Linux *199*

Figure 12-10: You can control Calc through its tool and icon bars.

(Figure labels: Formula bar, Object bar, Function bar, Menu bar, Function Wizard, Status bar, Tabs)

Notice the following major parts in the main Calc window (refer to Figure 12-10):

- **Menu bar:** Provides the standard pull-down menus: File, Edit, Help, and so forth. Use these menus to perform all the tasks that Calc can do.

- **Function bar:** Provides buttons for performing routine tasks: opening, saving, and printing a document. You can also click icons on the function bar to open the Stylist (a list of cell and page styles), the Navigator (a list of spreadsheet items such as sheets and graphics), and the Gallery (a collection of predefined graphic objects such as 3D shapes, backgrounds, and bullets).

- **Object bar:** Enables you to format the document by applying styles, selecting fonts, or changing text attributes (such as boldface, italics, and underlining). This bar changes depending on the type of object (such as plain text or graphics) you've clicked.

Part III: Doing Stuff with SUSE

 ✓ **Formula bar:** Provides a field where you can enter formulas, create sums, and launch the Function AutoPilot.

 ✓ **Tabs:** Located along the bottom of the spreadsheet, they enable you to work with different sheets in the same file.

 ✓ **Status bar:** Displays information about the current sheet (the current sheet number, the page style, and so on). You can also click various elements in the status bar to change settings, such as the text selection mode and the zoom factor for viewing the spreadsheet.

In addition to these tool and icon bars, the largest part of the Calc window is the work area where your spreadsheet appears and where you focus most of your attention.

Use the tooltips to find out what an icon or menu option does. Mouse over a menu item and Calc displays a small tooltip window with a brief help message.

Note: Curious about that Function AutoPilot icon that's pointed out in Figure 12-10? Check out the section "Calculating and charting data," later in this chapter, where I show you how to use that handy little feature.

You can configure Calc through the Tools➪Options dialog box. On the left side of the dialog box, click the plus sign (+) next to Spreadsheet. The plus sign turns to a minus sign (-) and a number of different categories of options appear (as shown in Figure 12-11). You can then click each category to configure various aspects of Calc.

Figure 12-11: Set up Calc from the Spreadsheet category in the Tools➪Options dialog box.

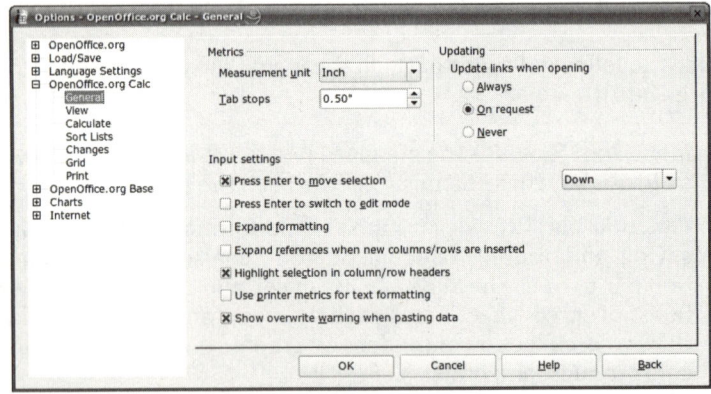

Preparing spreadsheets with Calc is a straightforward affair. Typically, you can enter text and numbers into the cells, resize the columns by dragging the vertical lines, and enter formulas to calculate the answers you need. To help you perform some common tasks in Calc, I provide some quick tips for two broad categories of tasks:

- Entering and formatting data
- Calculating and charting data

Entering and formatting data

When entering and formatting data, use Calc in the same way you use Microsoft Excel. You can type entries in cells, use formulas, and format the cells (such as specifying the type of value and the number of digits after the decimal point). The Format menu contains many of the options for formatting the spreadsheet.

After you're done entering data into a spreadsheet, save it by choosing File⇨Save As. A dialog box appears, from which you can specify the file format, the directory location, and the name of the file. You've seen similar Save As dialog boxes a thousand times before. OpenOffice.org Calc can save the file in a number of formats, including Microsoft Excel 97/2000/XP, Microsoft Excel 95, Microsoft Excel 5.0, and text file with comma-separated values (CSV).

TIP

If you want to exchange files with Microsoft Excel, save the spreadsheet in Microsoft Excel format (choose an appropriate version of Excel). Then you can transfer that file to a Windows system and open it in Microsoft Excel.

After you've saved the spreadsheet once, you can also save intermediate versions of a spreadsheet. To save a new version, choose File⇨Versions and then click Save New Version in the next dialog box.

To share a spreadsheet with people who don't use Calc or Excel, you can print the spreadsheet to a PDF file and then send that to others because anyone can easily view and print PDF files by using the free Adobe Reader (see `www.adobe.com/products/acrobat/readstep2.html`).

Calculating and charting data

To perform calculations, use formulas you normally use in Microsoft Excel. For example, use the formula SUM(D2:D6) to add up the entries from cell D2 to D6. To set cell D2 as the product of the entries A2 and C2, type **=A2*C2** in cell D2.

> To learn more about the functions available in OpenOffice.org Calc, choose Help⇨Contents. This opens the OpenOffice.org Help window, from which you can browse the functions by category and click a function to read more about it.

One interesting feature of Calc is the support for scenarios. A *scenario* is simply a collection of values for one or more cells. Scenarios are useful when you compare the effect of some cells on other calculations in the spreadsheet. For example, the monthly payment on a loan would depend on the principal, the interest rate, and the duration of the loan. You can use Calc's scenario feature to compare the monthly payments for a number of different scenarios where each scenario has a certain combination of interest rate and loan duration in months. To use scenario for this comparison, follow these steps:

1. **Set up the spreadsheet cells with labels and values for the principal, annual interest rate in percentage, and loan duration in months (refer to Figure 12-12). Calculate the monthly payment using this formula:**

   ```
   -PMT(MONTHLY_RATE;MONTHS;PRINCIPAL)
   ```

   Figure 12-12 illustrates this example. The cells in the range B5:C7 specify the principal, annual rate, and the number of months. Cell C6, with the annual interest rate, is formatted to show a percentage. Cell C11 computes the payment using the formula that you see in the formula bar. Notice that the annual rate in cell C6 has to be divided by 12 to get the monthly rate.

2. **Select the cells that you want to include in the scenario and choose Tools⇨Scenarios. For example, in Figure 12-12, select the cells in the range B5:C7.**

   The Create Scenario dialog box appears.

3. **Fill in the scenario name, and then click OK.**

   For example, the scenario shown in Figure 12-12 is named `Rate_6_5_PCT` (that's my name for the 6.5% rate scenario).

4. **Enter values into the cells — principal, interest rate, and months to repay loan.**

   The scenario name appears in a drop-down list above the cells that constitute the scenario (as shown in Figure 12-12). The cell values define what that scenario means.

5. **Repeat Steps 2, 3, and 4 for other scenarios where each scenario has a combination of principal amount, rate, and loan duration in months.**

6. **Select a scenario from the drop-down list (refer to Figure 12-12) to see the monthly payment for that scenario.**

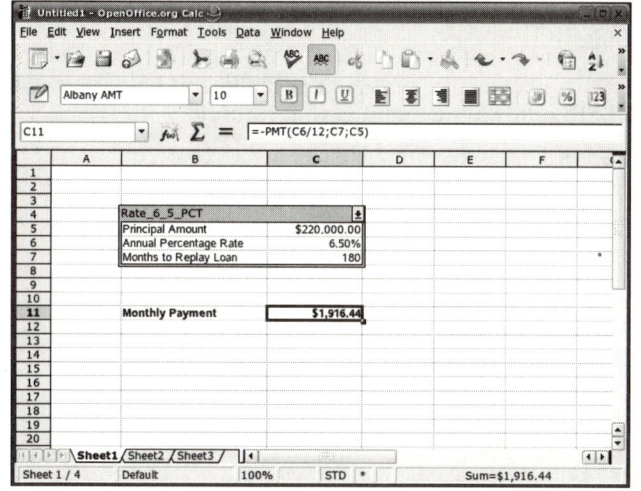

Chapter 12: Preparing Documents and Spreadsheets in SUSE Linux   203

Figure 12-12: Use scenarios to compare the effect of different sets of values on a calculation.

To figure out where a particular cell is being used in some calculation, click the cell and then choose Tools⇨Detective⇨Trace Dependents. Calc draws arrows to show where that cell is being used.

If you cannot remember a function, use the Function Wizard to build the formula in a cell. To use the Function Wizard, follow these steps:

1. **Click the Function Wizard icon (refer to Figure 12-10) on the Formula bar.**

    The Function Wizard dialog box appears.

2. **Scroll down the list of functions and double-click the function you want.**

    Doing so causes the formula and its arguments to appear (see Figure 12-13), waiting for you to specify the values to be used arguments.

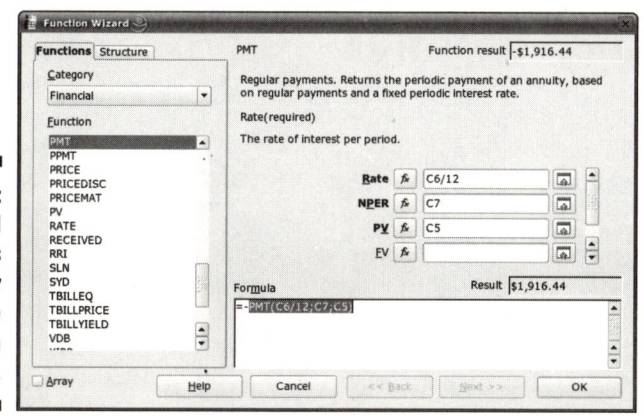

Figure 12-13: Build formulas interactively by using the Function Wizard.

3. **Click each argument and identify the cell that should be used as that argument.**

   When you specify all the arguments, the Result field (shown in Figure 12-13) shows the result of that formula.

4. **Click OK.**

   The formula appears in the spreadsheet cell.

Chapter 13

Doing Even More Office Stuff in SUSE Linux

In This Chapter

▶ Keeping track of appointments and tasks
▶ Making calculations
▶ Preparing presentations in OpenOffice.org Impress

*B*esides word processing and spreadsheets that I cover in Chapter 12, what else do you do in an office? Hmmm . . . let me see. How about keeping track of appointments and tasks? Calculating how much profit you made? And making sales pitches or some sort of presentation? In this chapter, I cover SUSE Linux applications for some of these other office tasks. The chapter begins with a quick summary of the calendar applications in KDE and GNOME. Then I describe OpenOffice.org Impress — a Microsoft PowerPoint-like presentation software package.

Keeping Track of Appointments and Tasks

If you installed KDE as your desktop, you can use Kontact — a new KDE application that integrates existing KDE applications such as the KMail mail reader and the KOrganizer calendar program into a single graphical personal information manager. To start Kontact, click the Personal Information Manager icon on the KDE panel (see Figure 13-1) or choose Main Menu⇨Office⇨Kontact.

Part III: Doing Stuff with SUSE

Figure 13-1: Start KDE Kontact by clicking the icon on the KDE panel.

Click this icon to start KDE Kontact

When Kontact starts, it usually displays the KMail application. You can, however, switch to other views by clicking the icons on the left pane of the Kontact window (refer to Figure 13-2). For example, Figure 13-2 shows Kontact after you click the Calendar icon. In this case, Kontact displays the output of KOrganizer — the KDE calendar program. The KOrganizer program displays a calendar view where you can click a date to set or view that day's schedule. Figure 13-2 shows a typical calendar.

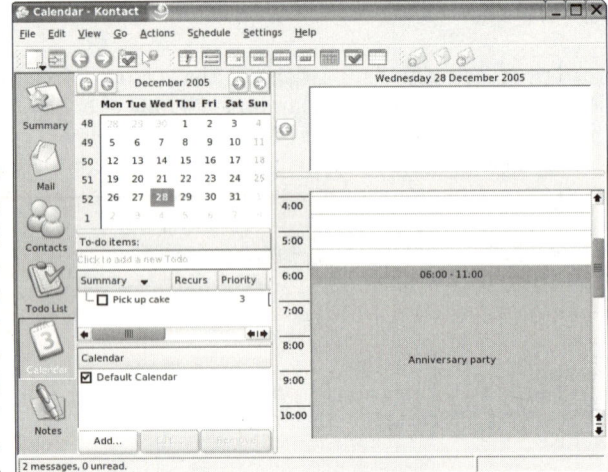

Figure 13-2: On the KDE desktop, use Kontact to store your appointments and view your calendar.

You can go to a different month or year by clicking the arrows next to the month and the year. To add a to-do item for a specific date, select the date from the calendar, click the To-do Items text box and type the description of the task.

To add appointments for a specific time, double-click the time and type a brief description of the appointment in the dialog box that appears. Click OK when you're done. After you finish adding events and appointments, choose File⇨Save to save the calendar.

Chapter 13: Doing Even More Office Stuff in SUSE Linux 207

If you installed the GNOME desktop, you can use Evolution to keep track of your calendar and tasks. Start Evolution by clicking its icon on the GNOME desktop's top panel (or choose Main Menu➪Office➪Evolution). After the Evolution window appears, click Calendars on the left pane to use the calendar, as shown in Figure 13-3.

Evolution's calendar is intuitive to use. Simply select a date and double-click a time to open the Appointment dialog box where you can type in the details of the appointment.

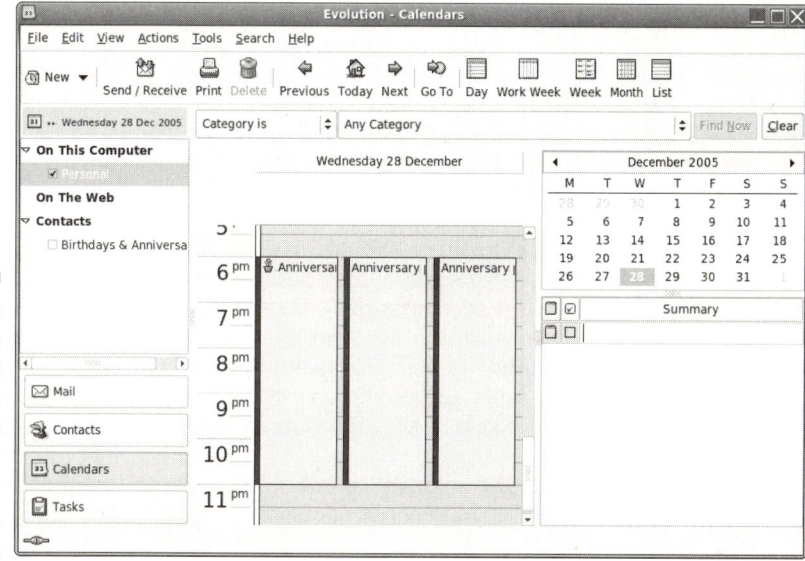

Figure 13-3: On the GNOME desktop, use Evolution as your calendar application.

Making Calculations

You have a choice of the KDE calculator or the GNOME calculator, depending on which desktop you installed. Both are scientific calculators, and you can do the typical scientific calculations, such as square root and inverse, as well as trigonometric functions, such as sine, cosine, and tangent.

To use the calculator on a KDE desktop, choose Main Menu➪Utilities➪Calculator➪KCalc. Figure 13-4 shows the KDE calculator in SUSE Linux.

You can display additional buttons by selecting options from the Settings menu. For example, choose Settings➪Trigonometric Buttons to show buttons that enable you to perform trigonometric calculations with the calculator.

If you installed the GNOME desktop, choose Main Menu➪Utilities➪Calculator➪XCalc to get a calculator.

Figure 13-4: Do your calculations in the KDE calculator.

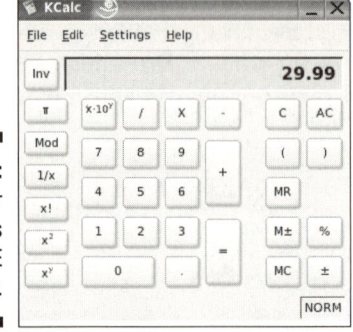

Making Presentations with OpenOffice.org Impress

It seems the business world, or should I say the whole world, is full of PowerPoint rangers — those dedicated souls who live by their PowerPoint briefing packages (slide presentations). It's hard to imagine a meeting or a conference where someone isn't vigorously making points on-screen with PowerPoint. Face it: Slide presentations are here to stay. Making presentations is a fact of life; businesspeople have come to expect office-application suites to include some sort of presentation software.

Like Microsoft Office, the OpenOffice.org office application suite comes with its own PowerPoint-like presentation software — OpenOffice.org Impress (or Impress for short). If you have used Microsoft PowerPoint and you're already familiar with its nuts and bolts — the concept of a slide, how to add text and graphics to a slide, how to organize the slides, and how to run a slide show — then you'll find it easy to get started with Impress. Because some details of how you perform basic Impress tasks may differ from the way they're done in PowerPoint, I provide some quick tips to point you in the right direction. I start with an overview of Impress and then cover some categories of common tasks that you'll likely perform in Impress.

Taking stock of OpenOffice.org Impress

You'll find that Impress can do all the usual things that presentation software such as Microsoft PowerPoint can do. For example, you can create professional-looking slide shows in Impress, using capabilities like these:

- Open and edit Microsoft PowerPoint files or convert Microsoft PowerPoint files to Impress format. One advantage of converting to Impress format is that Impress files are smaller in size than corresponding Microsoft PowerPoint files. Presentation files stored in Impress format are assigned filenames with the .sxi extension.
- Save documents in many different formats, including Microsoft PowerPoint 97/2000/XP, StarDraw 5.0 and 3.0, and StarImpress 5.0 and 4.0.
- Insert graphics and clip art from files of many different formats, including JPEG, GIF, ZSoft Paintbrush (PCX), TIFF, Windows BMP, Macintosh PICT, Encapsulated PostScript (EPS), Adobe Photoshop (PSD), AutoCAD DXF, and many more.
- Insert other OpenOffice.org documents (from programs such as Writer, Calc, and Draw) into a presentation.
- Use AutoPilot to quickly create a presentation.
- Use all the drawing tools from OpenOffice.org Draw to add drawings to the slides.
- Export a presentation to a Web Page (HTML) with or without frames. You can also export the slides in any of the supported graphics file formats.
- Use layers to separate parts of the slide so that each part can be edited or viewed separately.
- Use special effects such as animated text and graphics, sound, and slide transition effects.
- Use FontWork (Format⇨FontWork) to create various text effects such as aligning text along a curve.
- Render text in 3D.
- Save versions of a presentation as you continue to change it and revert back to an older version, if necessary.
- Add speaker's notes to each slide and create handouts.

Getting started with Impress

The best way to get comfortable using Impress is simply to start using it. To start Impress, choose Main Menu⇨Office⇨Presentation⇨OpenOffice.org Impress in KDE or GNOME.

The AutoPilot Presentation dialog box appears and guides you through the steps of starting a new presentation. From the AutoPilot Presentation dialog box, you can create an empty presentation, create a presentation from a template, or open an existing presentation. If you select an empty presentation and click Next, the AutoPilot asks you to select the slide design. Then you can click Create to open the Impress window, where you can select the layout of your first slide. After you finish laying out a slide, you can proceed to insert new slides. For each slide, you can select the layout you want.

You can open and edit Microsoft PowerPoint files in Impress. To open an existing file, choose File⇨Open and then select the file to open.

Before you start creating slides with Impress, take a moment to examine the Impress window (shown in Figure 13-5).

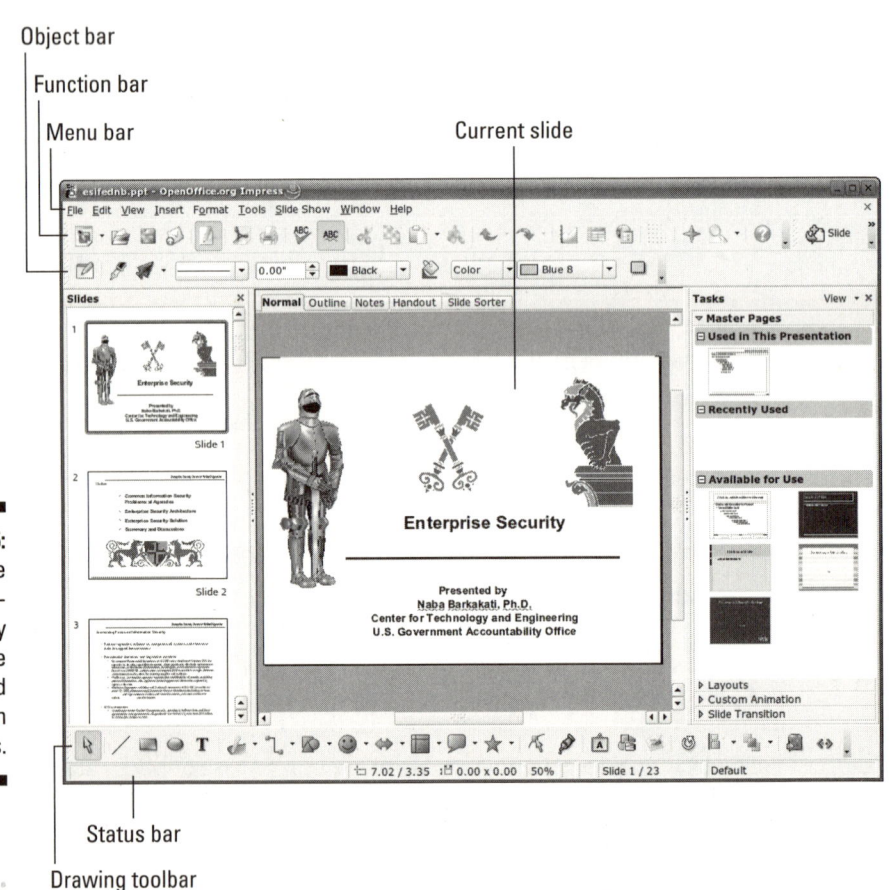

Figure 13-5: Create slide presentations by using the menus and toolbars in Impress.

Chapter 13: Doing Even More Office Stuff in SUSE Linux   211

In Figure 13-5, note the major parts of the Impress window:

- **Menu bar:** Provides the standard pull-down menus such as File, Edit, and Help for performing all the tasks that Impress can do.
- **Function bar:** Provides buttons for performing tasks such as opening, saving, and printing a document. You can also click icons on the function bar to open the Stylist, the Navigator, and the Gallery.
- **Object bar:** Enables you to format the document by applying styles, selecting fonts, or changing text attributes such as bold, italic, and underline. This bar changes according to the type of object you've clicked (for example, plain text or graphic image).
- **Drawing toolbar:** Located along the bottom of the window, it provides buttons that you can use to perform drawing tasks.
- **Rulers:** Show the vertical and horizontal page dimensions.
- **Navigation bar:** Located along the bottom of the slide, it enables you to change the views and select a slide to work with.
- **Status bar:** Displays information about the current slide such as the current slide number and the total count of slides. You can also click elements in the status bar and change settings such as the zoom factor for viewing the slide.

In addition to these tool and icon bars, you can turn on two more toolbars (when visible, these toolbars appear at the bottom of the window, above the status bar):

- Choose View➪Toolbars➪Option Bar to turn on the option bar that appears below the navigation bar. The option bar displays icons through which you perform some drawing tasks such as editing curves, showing grid lines, and indicating what happens when you click text and other objects.
- Choose View➪Toolbars➪Color Bar to turn on the color bar that appears at the bottom of the window, just above the status bar. The color bar displays colors that you can pick and use on objects. You can show or hide the color bar by clicking the downward-pointing arrow on the upper-left side of the color bar.

The largest part of the Impress window is the work area where you work on the current slide and where you focus most of your attention.

Use the tooltips to find out what an icon or menu option does. Mouse over a toolbar icon or a menu item and Impress displays a small tooltip window with a brief help message.

You don't have to set up anything to start using Impress. However, if you ever need to configure some aspects of Impress, you can do so through the Tools⇨Options and Tools⇨Configure menus. In particular, the Presentation category of the Tools⇨Options window contains the options for Impress (Figure 13-6). You should go through each of the Presentation options to see what you can configure from this window.

Figure 13-6: Set up Impress through the options in the Presentation category.

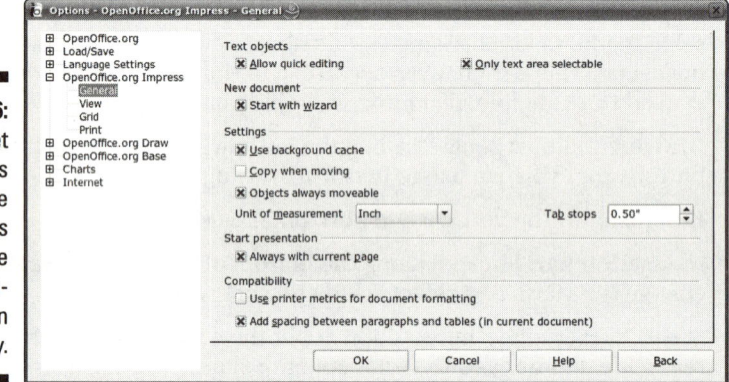

Using Impress

When you start Impress, the Presentation Wizard prompts you for the type of presentation you want. If Impress is already running, you get the Presentation Wizard when you choose File⇨New⇨Presentation. If you want a blank presentation, simply click Create in the first step of the Presentation Wizard. Impress displays a new window with a blank presentation.

To change the slide layout, pick a new layout from a gallery of layouts shown on the right side of the new Impress window. Impress then displays an empty slide with the selected layout.

Typically, a slide layout might have a title area and some text bullets. You can click and add the text to each of these areas. To insert any graphic image, choose Insert⇨Graphics and pick the graphics file you want to insert. You can draw directly on the slide by using the drawing tools from the vertical toolbar along the left side of the Impress window. To see which tool does what, move the mouse over any icon and a tooltip gives you a hint.

After you finish working on a slide, you can insert another slide by choosing Insert⇨Slide. Impress displays an Insert Slide dialog box (similar to the Modify Slide dialog box shown in Figure 13-7) and you can select the layout for the next slide.

To save a presentation, choose File⇨Save from the menu. For new documents, you have to provide a filename and select the directory to save the file.

Chapter 13: Doing Even More Office Stuff in SUSE Linux *213*

Figure 13-7: Select the presentation type from this dialog box and click Create.

That, in a nutshell, is how you create presentations in PowerPoint. In the following sections, I provide some quick tips for performing the following tasks with Impress:

- ✓ Preparing presentations
- ✓ Adding graphics and special effects
- ✓ Delivering presentations

Preparing presentations

Typically, you start with a blank slide with a specific layout. For example, the slide has a title area and a bulleted list for the points you want to make with the slide. You can click the title area, type the title, and then click the bulleted text area to start entering text. Then you add another slide and continue with the process until you finish the presentation.

If you're going to present information that's already in a Writer document, you can use the outline of that Writer document to start a presentation. The Writer document does have to follow one rule — it must use the heading styles Heading 1, Heading 2, and so on for the major sections in the document.

TIP

To create a presentation from the outline of a Writer document that uses the heading styles, open the document in Writer and choose Send➪Outline to Presentation from the Writer menu. You should see an Impress window open up with a new presentation that has slides based on the headings in the Writer document. Each Heading 1 style becomes a new slide and the Heading 2 and Heading 3 styles appear as bulleted text in the slides.

After working on the set of slides, you may want to rearrange the slides. To rearrange slides in a different order, choose View➪Slide Sorter. Impress displays an array of miniature-sized slides, arranged in a rectangular grid in the work area (as in Figure 13-8). Think of this as the slide sorter view because you can move the slides around and sort them in this view.

In the slide-sorter view shown in Figure 13-8, you can drag and drop slides into different positions and rearrange them in the order you want. To delete a slide in this view, click the slide to select it and press Delete (or choose Edit➪Delete). When prompted to confirm the deletion, you can click Yes if you really want to delete the slide. Double-click a slide to return to the usual single-slide view.

As you work on the presentation, keep in mind these concepts:

- **Master slide:** You can think of the *master slide* as the background of every slide. If you put text or other fields (such as date and page number) on the master slide, those elements appear on every slide in the presentation.

- **Layers:** You can have layers in both the master slide as well as each individual slide. Think of the layers as transparent sheets on which you place some related text and graphics. The slide is then made up of these layers superimposed on one another. You can use layers to group related information. For example, if you're drawing the plans for a house, you can put all the dimensions on a separate layer. The nice part is that you can hide or show layers easily. Just click the third icon from the left on the Navigation bar (see Figure 13-5) or choose View➪Layer.

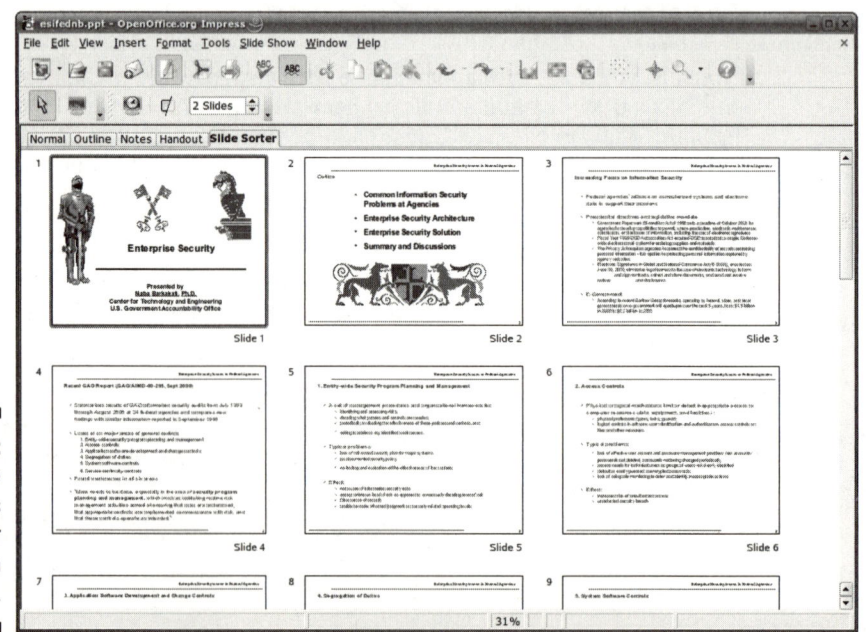

Figure 13-8: Arrange slides in this slide-sorter view in Impress.

✔ **Master notes and master handouts:** The idea is the same as that for the master slide. You can define some fields and text on the master notes or master handout; these become part of the background for your notes and handouts. The *notes* refer to the explanatory text you add to the bottom of each slide. The *handouts* are printouts of the slides — typically several miniature slides to a page — that are handed out to the audience at a briefing.

Well, I could go on and on, but you can discover its capabilities best by simply starting to use Impress.

Adding graphics and special effects

To jazz up your presentation, you might want to add graphics, charts, and other special effects to the slides. With Impress, you can do nearly everything you can think of — all you have to decide is how many bells and whistles your presentation needs. It's your call, but I recommend using these features judiciously lest they detract from your presentation's main message.

If you want to add some simple drawings to the slide, you can pick from the drawing tools on the vertical toolbar on the left side of the Impress window (refer to Figure 13-9) and start drawing on the slide. To insert an image into the slide, choose Insert➪Graphics and then select the image file you want to insert.

You can also insert charts to graphically depict data. You start by inserting a chart with dummy data, and then you edit the data as well as other features of the chart. To add a chart and edit the data, follow these steps:

1. **Choose Insert➪Chart.**

    A chart with the default chart type and dummy data appears.

2. **Resize the chart by dragging the handles around the border of the chart; then right-click the chart and select Chart Data from the pop-up menu that appears (see Figure 13-9).**

    A mini-spreadsheet appears with the dummy chart data.

3. **Edit the row and column labels and enter the data you want the chart to display.**

4. **When you're done editing the chart, click the green right arrow icon, located to the right of the toolbar, to apply the changes and close the Chart Data window.**

5. **To change the chart type, right-click the chart and select Chart Type from the pop-up menu that appears; choose a new type and click OK.**

Part III: Doing Stuff with SUSE

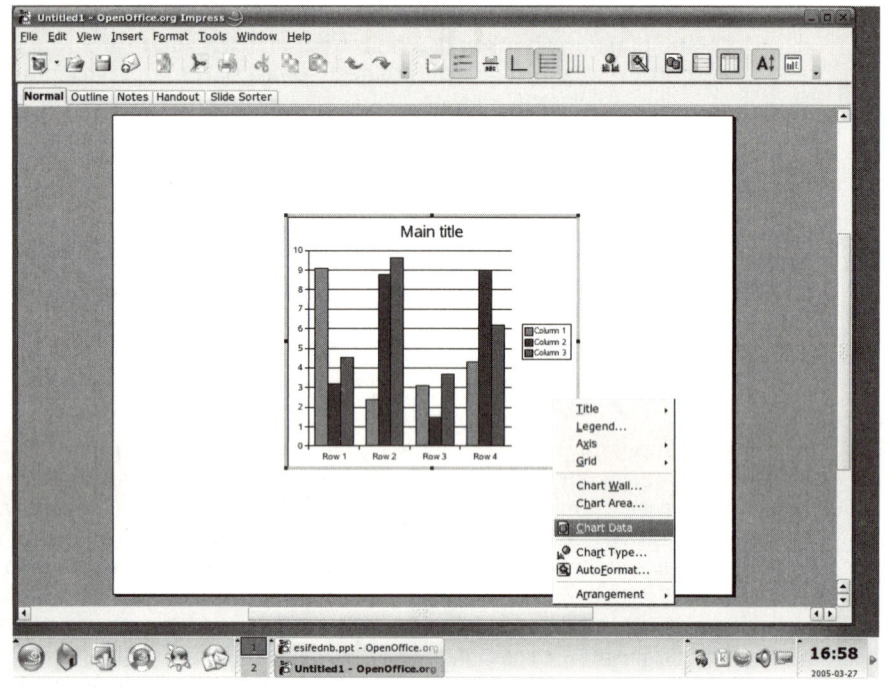

Figure 13-9: Right-click the chart to modify the data and chart type.

You can do a lot more than just add graphics and charts to your slide presentations. You can insert spreadsheets and Writer documents into a slide, add text that runs along a curve, and add special effects to various elements in a slide.

Delivering presentations

After you prepare a spectacular set of slides, you have to deliver it to your audience. This typically involves tasks such as preparing speaker's notes, running a slide show, converting the presentation into HTML for delivery via the Web, and printing handouts.

You can also print an Impress presentation directly to an Adobe Portable Document Format (.pdf) file. This makes it easy to electronically share a presentation with everyone because anyone can easily view and print .pdf files by using the free Adobe Reader.

Chapter 14

Playing Music and Burning CDs

In This Chapter
▶ Playing audio CDs
▶ Playing digital music
▶ Burning CDs and DVDs

SUSE Linux comes with several audio and video applications. You can listen to audio CDs, MP3 music (as well as other digital music files), and watch MPEG video (provided you have the decoders installed). You can also rip audio CDs and burn new CDs — both audio and data CDs. In this chapter, I introduce some of the audio applications that you can find in either KDE or GNOME desktops.

> **REMEMBER:** The video applications lack the decoders necessary to play video such as MPEG or DVD. In particular, commercial DVDs use an encryption method called Content Scrambling System (CSS) to prevent the DVD data from being copied. The open source Linux video players do not include the software to decrypt CSS and therefore cannot play DVDs.

Playing Audio CDs

SUSE Linux comes with both the GNOME or KDE CD player applications. To play an audio CD, you need a sound card, and that sound card must be configured to work in SUSE Linux. All of that should happen when you install SUSE Linux following the steps outlined in Chapter 2.

In KDE, if you insert an audio CD into the drive, a dialog box appears (see Figure 14-1) and asks whether you want to play the CD with the CD player. Click Yes.

Part III: Doing Stuff with SUSE

Figure 14-1: Play audio CDs with the KDE CD Player.

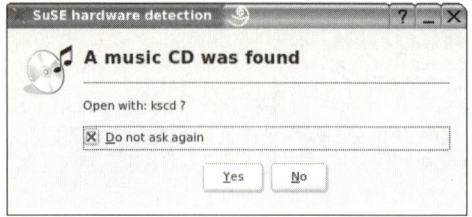

The KDE CD Player (KsCD) starts and displays the title of the CD and the name of the current track. The CD Player gets the song titles from http://freedb.freedb.org — a free open source CD database on the Internet. You need an active Internet connection for the CD Player to download song information from the CD database. After the CD Player downloads information about a particular CD, it caches that information in a local database for future use. The CD Player user interface is intuitive, and you can figure it out easily. One nice feature is that you can select a track by title. Figure 14-2 shows the KDE CD Player (KsCD) playing a track from an audio CD. To select a track by title, click the track title at the top edge of the KDE CD Player. Then select the track from the drop-down list that appears.

Figure 14-2: Play audio CDs with the KDE CD Player.

Playing audio CDs is simple in GNOME as well. Insert the audio CD into the drive and the GNOME CD Player should start automatically. If it does not, choose Main Menu⇨Multimedia⇨CD Player⇨CD Player. Click the Play/Pause button in the toolbar along the bottom (see Figure 14-3) and you should be off and running. Figure 14-3 shows the GNOME CD player in action. As with the KDE CD Player, you can click the track title for a drop-down list of all the tracks and select one that you want to play.

Figure 14-3: Play audio CDs with the GNOME CD Player.

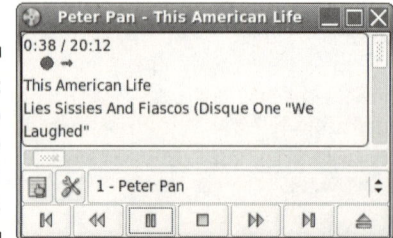

Playing Music Files

Typically, digital music files are stored in MP3 format and the filenames have an .mp3 extension. Both KDE and GNOME desktops include several applications for playing digital music.

REMEMBER: The music players can also play digital music in other formats besides MP3 such as Ogg Vorbis, FLAC (Free Lossless Audio Codec, an audio file format that is similar to MP3), and Windows WAV.

In KDE, you can use amaroK, JuK, or RealPlayer to play music. Each application is straightforward to use. To start amaroK, choose Main Menu➪Multimedia➪Audio Player➪amaroK. To play music, click the PL button in the lower-left corner of the amaroK window (see Figure 14-4). Browse the folders to locate the music file and double-click to play. Figure 14-4 shows amaroK playing an MP3 music file. Use the buttons on the toolbar along the bottom to control the music playback.

Figure 14-4: Playing MP3 music with the amaroK audio player.

To start JuK, choose Main Menu➪Multimedia–>Jukebox from the KDE desktop. JuK is short for *jukebox*. You can load a whole bunch of music files into JuK and play them one after another or in any order you want. When you first start JuK, JuK displays a dialog box that prompts you to add a folder (containing music files). After you select the folder containing music files, JuK displays the list and you can select a title and click the play button (on the toolbar) to play that music. Figure 14-5 shows JuK with a slew of MP3 files and a selected file that it's currently playing.

You can also use RealPlayer to play MP3 music in SUSE Linux. You find RealPlayer on both KDE and GNOME desktops. To start RealPlayer, choose Main Menu➪Multimedia➪RealPlayer in KDE or Main Menu➪Multimedia➪RealPlayer 10 in GNOME.

When you first start RealPlayer, the RealPlayer Setup Assistant appears and prompts you to set up RealPlayer. You have to accept a license agreement and you can also configure Mozilla helpers so that you can play audio and clips from inside the Mozilla Web browser.

Figure 14-5: Use JuK to organize your MP3 files and play them as well.

To play a music file from RealPlayer, follow these steps:

1. **Choose File**⇨**Open File.**

    The Select Files dialog box appears.

2. **Double-click to open a folder, locate the music file you want to play, and click to select the file. Then click Open.**

    RealPlayer opens the file and starts playing music (see Figure 14-6).

3. **Use the play/pause and stop buttons to control the music playing.**

Figure 14-6: Playing music in RealPlayer.

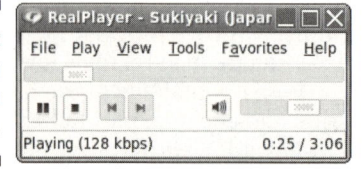

You can also listen to Internet radio stations in RealPlayer. Simply choose File⇨Open Location and enter the URL for a radio station that's broadcasting in RealAudio or streaming MP3 format. For example, to listen to BBC Radio 1, I type **http://www.bbc.co.uk/radio1/realaudio/media/r1live.ram** in the Open Location dialog box. For a directory of Internet audio feeds in MP3 and RealAudio formats, see www.janecek.com/bitcasters.html.

GNOME also comes with another music player, called XMMS, that can play many types of digital music, including MP3. XMMS can also play streaming MP3 audio from Internet sites such as those listed at www.shoutcast.com.

To start XMMS, choose Main Menu➪Multimedia➪Audio Player➪XMMS from the GNOME desktop. After XMMS starts, open a music file by choosing Window Menu➪Play File (to access the Window Menu, click the upper-left corner of the window), or by pressing L. Then select one or more music files from the Play Files dialog box. Click the Play button, and XMMS starts playing the sound file. Figure 14-7 shows the XMMS window when it's playing a sound file.

Figure 14-7: You can play MP3 music files in XMMS.

To listen to streaming MP3 audio from the Internet, choose Window Menu➪Play Location and enter the URL in the dialog box that appears.

Burning a CD/DVD

Nowadays, GUI file managers often have the capability to burn CDs. For example, GNOME's Nautilus File Manager has built-in features to burn CDs. The KDE desktop comes with K3b, which is a popular CD/DVD burning application.

Most CD burning applications are simple to use. You basically gather up the files that you want to burn to the CD or DVD and then start the burning process. Of course, for this to work, your PC must have a CD or DVD burner installed.

Burning CD/DVDs with K3b

Figure 14-8 shows the initial window of the K3b CD/DVD burning application in SUSE Linux. The upper part of the K3b window is for browsing the file system to select what you want to burn onto a CD or DVD. The upper-left corner shows the CD writer device installed; in this example, it's a CD-RW/DVD drive so that the drive can read DVDs and CDs, but burn CDs only.

Part III: Doing Stuff with SUSE

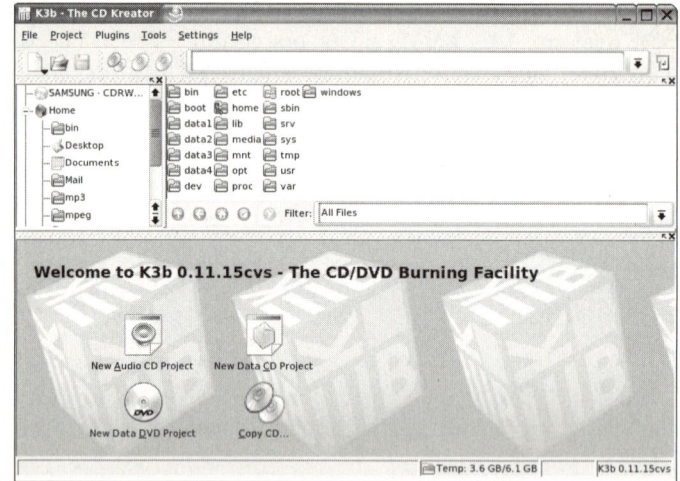

Figure 14-8: You can burn CDs and DVDs with the K3b application.

To burn a CD or DVD using K3b, you follow these high-level steps:

1. Start K3b by choosing Main Menu➪Multimedia➪CD/DVD Burning.

2. Start a new project by clicking one of the project icons shown in the lower part of the K3b window — New Audio CD Project, for example, or New Data DVD Project.

3. Add files to the project. For an audio CD, you can drag and drop MP3 files as well as audio tracks.

4. Burn the project to the CD or DVD by choosing Project➪Burn or pressing Ctrl+B (or by clicking the Burn button in the project pane of the K3b window).

As a specific example, here is how you can burn an audio CD using K3b:

1. **Click the New Audio CD Project icon on the lower pane of the K3b window — that's the project pane of K3b.**

    A project tab appears in the lower pane of the K3b window and a message tells you to drag and drop files and then click the Burn button (located in the lower-right corner of the window, as you can see in Figure 14-9).

2. **If you want to copy tracks from an audio CD, put the CD in the drive and select the CD drive from the drop-down list on the toolbar (refer to Figure 14-9).**

    K3b displays the titles of the tracks from the audio CD.

Chapter 14: Playing Music and Burning CDs 223

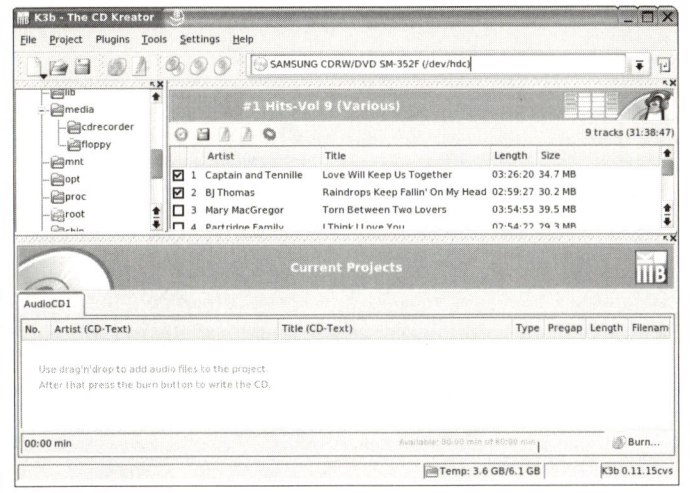

Figure 14-9: Selecting tracks to rip from an audio CD.

3. **Select the tracks you want and click the Start Ripping button — the rightmost button on the toolbar above the list of tracks (see Figure 14-9).**

   K3b then displays a CD Ripping dialog box.

4. **Click Start Ripping in the CD Ripping dialog box. When finished, click Close and eject the audio CD.**

   K3b extracts the tracks into separate files and stores them in a folder in your home directory. The folder name is based on the title of the audio CD album.

5. **Click the Home folder on the top-left pane and click the folder with the ripped audio files (look for the audio CD album's name). Select the files (they appear in the top-right pane) and drag and drop them in the lower pane.**

6. **Repeat steps 2 through 5 with other audio CD tracks. To add MP3 files, go to the folder with the MP3 files and drag and drop them in the lower pane of K3b.**

   Figure 14-10 shows a typical audio CD project with two ripped tracks and an MP3 file.

7. **When you are ready to burn the audio CD, insert a blank CD-R into the CD burner and click the Burn button.**

   K3b displays the Audio Project dialog box.

8. **Click Burn in the Audio Project dialog box.**

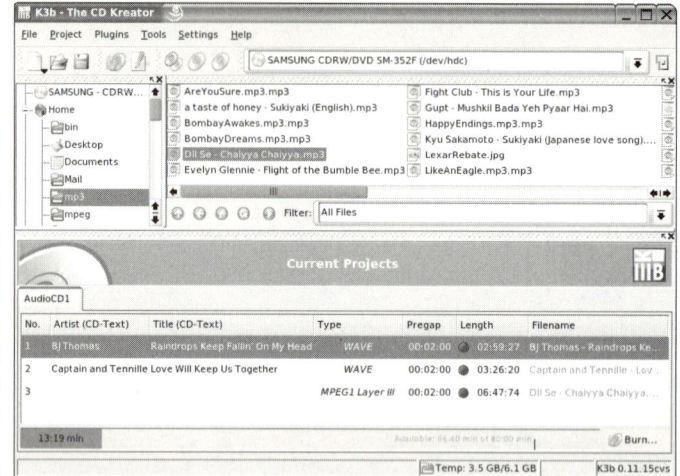

Figure 14-10: Drag and drop ripped audio CD tracks and MP3 files into the K3b project.

K3b displays the Writing Audio CD dialog box and starts burning the audio CD. When everything is done, click Close to dismiss the dialog box, as shown in Figure 14-11.

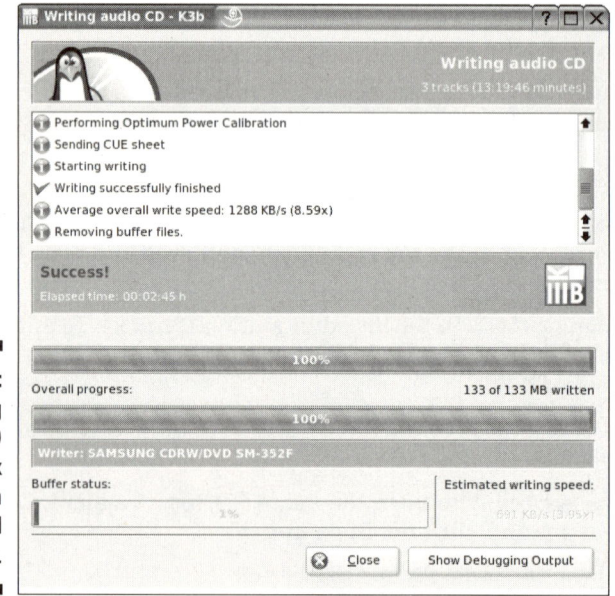

Figure 14-11: The Writing audio CD dialog box showing a successful burn.

Chapter 14: Playing Music and Burning CDs **225**

9. **You can burn more copies of the same audio CD project and when you're done, choose File➪Quit.**

To burn a CD image (ISO file) onto a blank CD-R, choose Tools➪CD➪Burn CD Image.

K3b needs the external command line programs `cdrecord` and `cdrdao` to burn CDs. K3b also needs the `growisofs` program to burn DVDs. These external programs should already be installed when you elect to install the KDE desktop during SUSE Linux installation following the steps outlined in Chapter 2.

Burning data CDs in Nautilus

If you have a CD recorder attached to your system (it can be a built-in ATAPI CD recorder or an external one attached to the USB port), you can use Nautilus from the GNOME desktop to burn data CDs. From a Nautilus object window, you can access the CD Creator built into Nautilus. Just follow these simple steps:

1. **In any Nautilus object window, choose Places➪CD Creator.**

   Nautilus opens a CD Creator object window.

   Note: If you don't have any Nautilus object windows open, just double-click the Computer icon on the desktop.

2. **From other Nautilus windows, drag and drop into the CD Creator window whatever files and folders you want to put on the CD.**

   To get to files on your computer, double-click the Computer icon to open it in Nautilus and find the files you want. Then drag and drop those file or folder icons into the CD Creator window.

3. **From the CD Creator window, choose File➪Write to CD.**

   Nautilus displays a dialog box (see Figure 14-12) where you can select the CD recorder, the write speed, and several other options, such as whether to eject the CD when done. You can also specify the CD title.

4. **Click the Write Files to CD button.**

   Nautilus burns the CD.

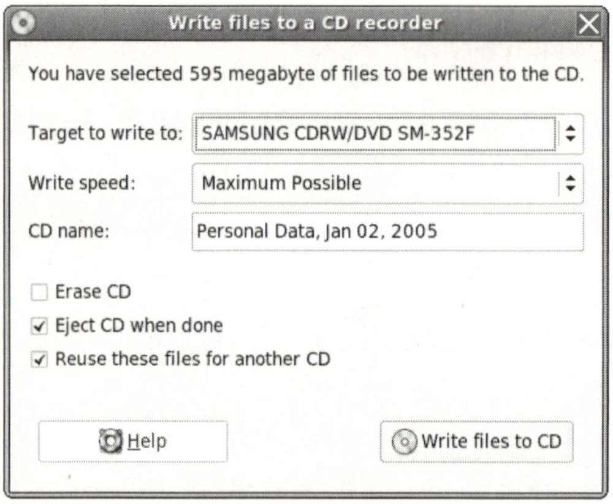

Figure 14-12: Write files to a CD recorder from GNOME's Nautilus File Manager.

Chapter 15

Working with Photos and Images

In This Chapter

▶ Downloading photos from a digital camera
▶ Scanning photos and documents
▶ Manipulating images
▶ Viewing images
▶ Viewing PDF and PostScript files

Digital cameras are all the rage nowadays. Your SUSE Linux system is the perfect place to download the photos, view them, and, if necessary, touch up the photos. You can also scan photographs or documents, provided you have a scanner attached to your PC (typically through the USB port).

SUSE Linux includes applications for working with digital cameras and scanners as well as editing images. You can use a camera application to download photos from your digital camera or simply access the camera as a USB mass storage device (just like another hard drive). The scanner application called Kooka enables you to easily scan hardcopy photos or documents and then use the images just like your digital photos.

Both KDE and GNOME desktops come with The GIMP (GNU Image Manipulation Program) — an application that enables you to view and perform image-manipulation tasks, such as photo retouching, image composition, and image creation.

For simply viewing your digital photos, you can use image viewers such as Gwenview in KDE and Eye of Gnome in GNOME. For reading PDF files or PostScript files, you can use KGhostview in KDE and GNOME PDF viewer and GGV PostScript viewer in GNOME. Both KDE and GNOME also include the well-known Adobe Acrobat Reader.

As you can see, SUSE Linux is no slouch when it comes to working with digital photos and image files of all kinds. In this chapter, I introduce you to many of the image processing applications in SUSE Linux.

Downloading Photos from a Digital Camera

The KDE desktop comes with a digital camera application called Digikam that you can use to download pictures from digital cameras as well as organize your photos in albums for easy viewing. Digikam works with many different makes and models of digital cameras. Depending on the model, the cameras can connect to the serial port or the Universal Serial Bus (USB) port.

To use Digikam with your digital camera, follow these steps:

1. **Connect your digital camera to the serial port or USB port (whichever interface the camera supports) and turn on the camera.**

2. **Start Digikam by choosing Main Menu⇨Graphics⇨Photograph⇨ Digikam from the KDE desktop.**

   Digikam's main window appears. If this is the first time, Digikam prompts you for a location where you want to keep your photos. Select a folder in your home directory and click OK.

3. **From the Digikam menu, choose Settings⇨Configure Digikam.**

   A configuration dialog box appears.

4. **Click the Cameras icon in the dialog box and click Auto-Detect. After the camera is detected, click OK.**

   If your camera is supported and the camera is configured to be in PTP (Picture Transfer Protocol) mode, the camera is detected (see Figure 15-1 for an example). If not, you can get the photos from your camera by using an alternate method that I describe after these steps.

5. **Select your camera model from the Camera menu.**

   A new window appears and, after a short while, displays thumbnails of the photos in the camera, as shown in Figure 15-2.

6. **Click the thumbnails to select the images you want to download; then choose Download⇨Download Selected to download the images. To download all images, choose Download⇨Download All.**

   Digikam then downloads the images to an album. You can view the photos in Digikam and edit the photos in The GIMP or your favorite photo editor.

To view your photo album in Digikam, click My Albums on the left-hand side of the Digikam main window and it displays thumbnail images of the photos on the right-hand window (see Figure 15-3).

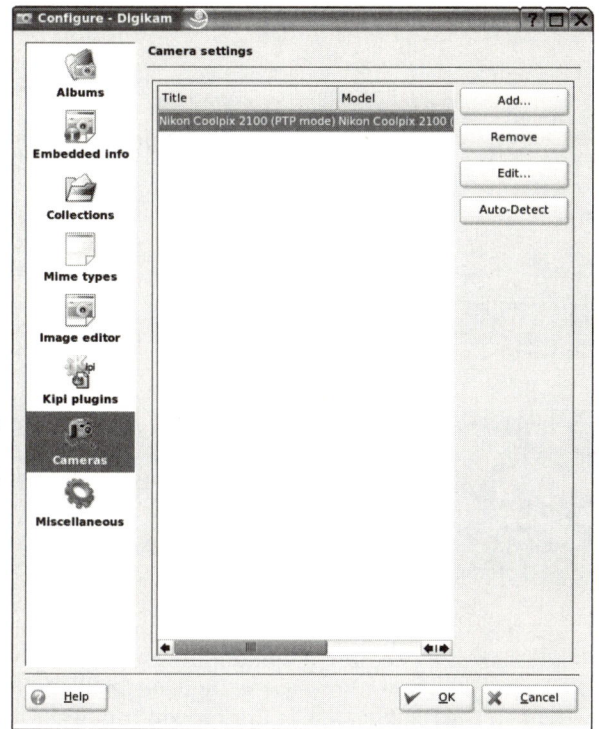

Figure 15-1: After connecting your digital camera, click Auto-Detect in this dialog box.

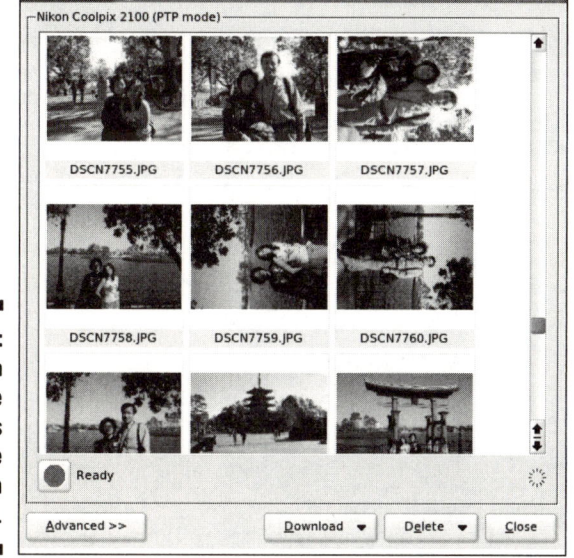

Figure 15-2: Digikam displays the thumbnails of the photos in the camera.

Part III: Doing Stuff with SUSE

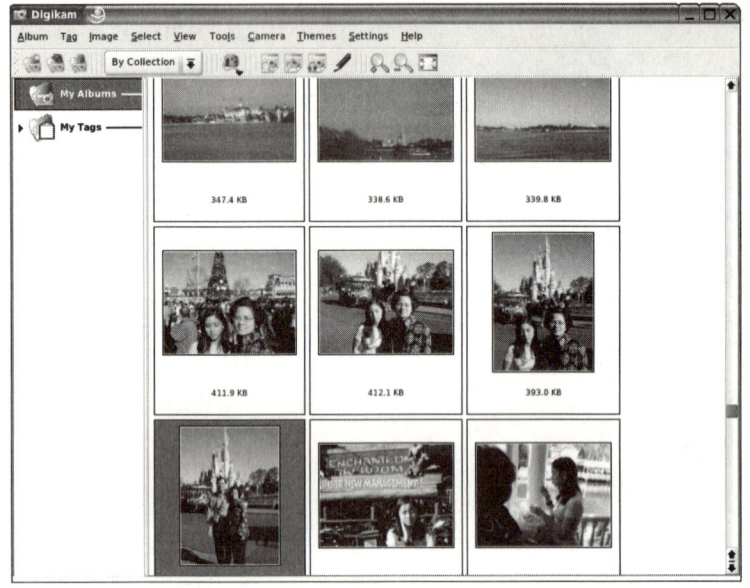

Figure 15-3: You can view your photo album in Digikam.

Digikam also includes an image editor. If you double-click a thumbnail in the photo album, Digikam opens that photo in the Digikam Image Editor, as shown in Figure 15-4. In the Digikam Image Editor, you can perform some limited image editing tasks such as rotating images or converting them to black and white or sepia.

Figure 15-4: You can touch up photos in the Digikam Image Editor.

Chapter 15: Working with Photos and Images

TIP

Don't despair if Digikam doesn't recognize your digital camera or if you are using the GNOME desktop and Digikam is not installed by default. You can still access the digital camera's storage media (compact flash card, for example) as a USB mass storage device, provided your camera supports USB mass storage. To access the images on your USB digital camera, use the following steps (by the way, I prefer transferring photos this way because I don't have to run any camera application such as Digikam):

1. **Read the camera manual and use the menu options of the camera to set the USB mode to Mass Storage.**

   If the camera doesn't support USB Mass Storage, you cannot use this procedure to access the photos. If the camera supports the Picture Transfer Protocol mode, you can use Digikam to download the pictures.

2. **Connect your digital camera to the USB port by using the cable that came with the camera, and then turn on the camera.**

   This causes SUSE Linux to detect the camera. If you are using KDE, the Konqueror file manager opens the contents of the camera in a window. In GNOME, double-click the Computer icon on the desktop; then look for a USB hard drive icon and double-click to open it. That should get you to the folders in your digital camera's memory card. The names of the folders depend on your camera model. For example, in Nikon Coolpix cameras, the photos are in folders named 100nikon, 101nikon, 102nikon, and so on, but these folders reside in another folder named dcim. Open the photo folder and you can see the thumbnail of the photos, as shown in Figure 15-5.

Figure 15-5: You can access your camera as a USB mass storage device.

3. **Click to select photos you want and copy them to your hard drive by dragging and dropping them into a selected folder.**

Part III: Doing Stuff with SUSE

4. **Close the file manager windows, turn off the camera, and disconnect the USB cable from the PC.**

Who needs a digital camera application when you can access the camera just like any other storage device?

Scanning Photos and Documents

If you have a scanner — a hardware device that enables you to obtain a digital image of any photo or document — you can use it with SUSE Linux. Typically, scanners plug into a PC's USB port. Here are the steps to follow to set up your scanner in SUSE Linux (I describe the procedures for the KDE desktop, but the steps are similar in GNOME):

1. **Plug a scanner into the SUSE Linux PC's USB port. SUSE Linux detects the scanner and displays the dialog box shown in Figure 15-6. The dialog box prompts you if you want to configure the scanner. Click Yes.**

Figure 15-6: SUSE Linux detects the scanner when you connect it to the PC.

The SUSE configuration program, YaST, starts and prompts you for the `root` password. Type the `root` password and click OK.

2. **YaST displays another dialog box (see Figure 15-7) that informs you that you can install a scanning application called Kooka. Click Yes to install the package.**

Figure 15-7: YaST asks if you want to install the scanning program Kooka.

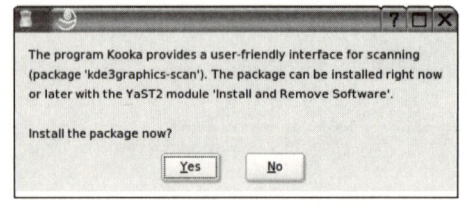

Chapter 15: Working with Photos and Images

3. **YaST then asks you for the CD (or DVD, if you have SUSE Linux on a DVD) that contains the needed package. Insert the requested CD or DVD and click OK.**

   YaST installs the software package that provides the Kooka application and then prompts you for the scanner model.

4. **Select the scanner make and model from the list (see Figure 15-8) and click Next.**

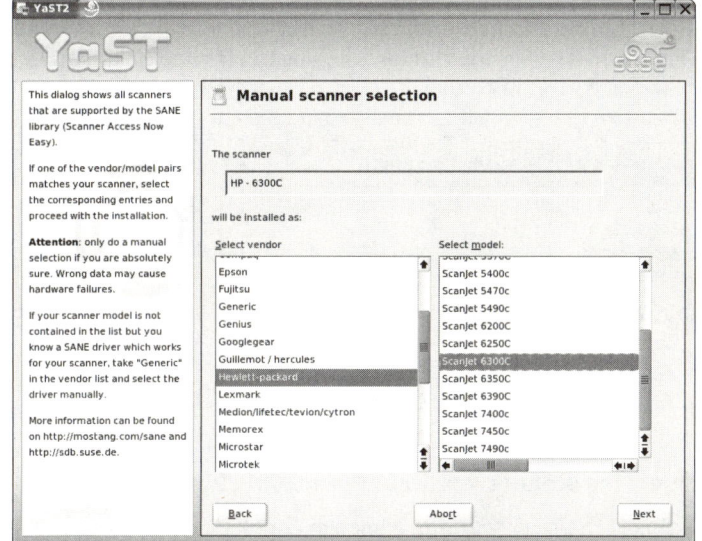

Figure 15-8: Select your scanner make and model.

5. **YaST displays your selection and asks for confirmation. Check that the scanner make and model are correct and click Next.**

6. **YaST displays a dialog box telling you that users logged in at the graphical desktop will be granted access to the scanner and asks you to disconnect and reconnect the scanner. Read the information and click OK.**

7. **YaST displays a scanner test screen. Click Next to continue.**

8. **YaST provides an overview of the scanner. Click Finish to complete installing the scanner.**

9. **A dialog box asks if you want YaST to save all settings and exit. Click Yes.**

10. **Disconnect the scanner from the USB port and reconnect it again.**

In GNOME, the steps for installing a scanner are similar except that you will be prompted to install the SANE (Scanner Access Now Easy) library — something that applications need to access the scanner. You will, of course, also have to install Kooka as well.

After you have installed the scanner, follow these steps to scan a photo (or any document) using the Kooka scanning application:

1. **Choose Main Menu⇨Graphics⇨Scanning⇨Kooka from the KDE desktop (in GNOME, open a terminal window and type** kooka).

   The scanner application called Kooka starts and displays a dialog box (Figure 15-9) showing the installed scanners and asks you to select the scanner you want to use.

   Figure 15-9: Selecting your scanner in Kooka.

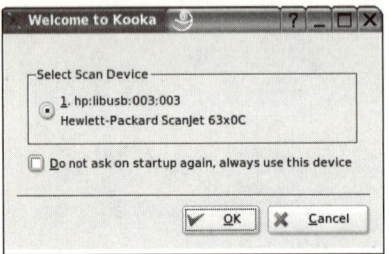

2. **Select the scanner you want to use and click OK.**

   If this is the only scanner, click the check box that says `Do not ask on startup again, always use this device`. The Kooka main window appears.

   If you don't see the Preview Scan and Final Scan buttons in the lower-left corner of the Kooka window, quit the application (choose File⇨Quit). Next open a terminal window, type **su -** and enter the `root` password. Then type **kooka**.

3. **Place the photo in the scanner.**

   Position it the way you want and close the scanner cover.

4. **Select the scan mode from the drop-down list in the scanner settings section (see Figure 15-10).**

   The scan mode depends on the document you are scanning. For color photos, select Color. Other choices include Greyscale, Halftone (for black and white images made up of dots, as in older newspaper photos), and Line Art (for black and white documents with text or line drawings).

Chapter 15: Working with Photos and Images 235

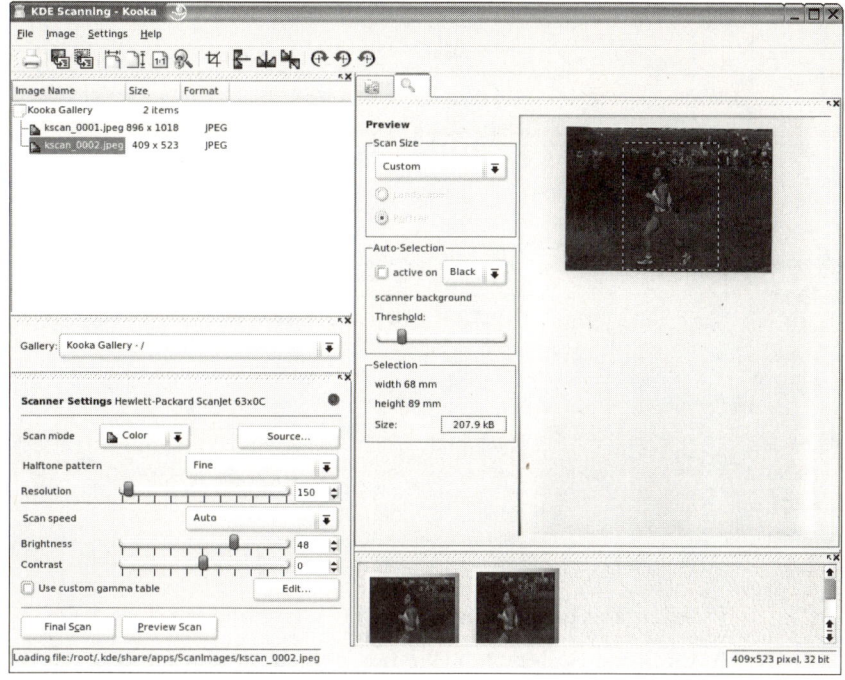

Figure 15-10: Preview the results of initial scanning in Kooka.

5. **Select the resolution (expressed in terms dots-per-inch or dpi) from the scanner settings. You can type the resolution in the text box next to the scale or click the up and down arrows to adjust the resolution.**

    Typically scanners can scan at resolutions such as 1200 dpi, but you can scan at a low resolution such as 72 dpi if you want to use the image on a Web page. For printing, the resolution should be higher — typically higher than 200 dpi.

6. **Click the Preview tab (the tab with the magnifying glass icon).**

7. **Click Preview Scan.**

    You can see the results in the Preview Scan tab (see Figure 15-10). Use the selection tool to select the part of the image you want to scan during the final scan.

8. **Click Final Scan.**

    Kooka scans the part you selected in the Preview Scan tab and displays a dialog box (see Figure 15-11), prompting you for the format in which you want to save the scanned image.

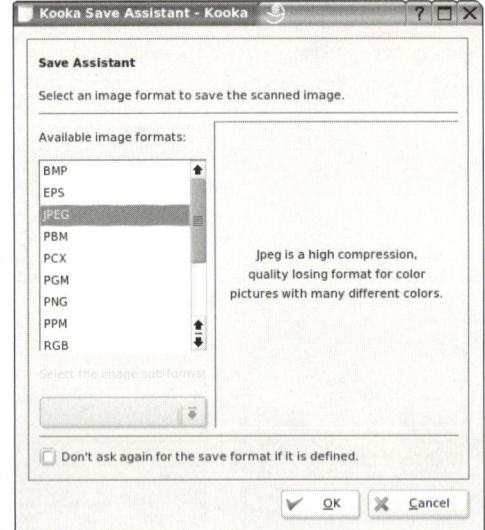

Figure 15-11: Select the image format in which you want Kooka to save the image.

9. **Select the format (such as JPEG for photos) and click OK.**
10. **Click the Gallery tab (the tab with the folder icon).**

    Kooka displays the final scanned image, as shown in Figure 15-12.

Figure 15-12: A typical view of a final scanned image in Kooka.

Chapter 15: Working with Photos and Images 237

11. **Choose File⇨Save Image to save scanned images to folders.**

    Kooka displays a Save As dialog box from which you can select the folder where you want Kooka to save the scanned images.

12. **Choose File⇨Quit when you're done using Kooka.**

> **TIP:** For help on Kooka, choose Help⇨Kooka Handbook. This opens the Kooka Manual in a new window.

Now you can use the scanned images just like other digital photos. You can also touch up the images in an image processing application such as The GIMP, which I describe next.

Editing Images with The GIMP

The GIMP is an image-manipulation program written by Peter Mattis and Spencer Kimball and released under the GNU General Public License (GPL). SUSE Linux comes with this program, although you may have to specifically select a package to install it. The GIMP is comparable to other image-manipulation programs such as Adobe Photoshop and Corel PHOTO-PAINT.

To try out The GIMP, choose Main Menu⇨Graphics⇨Image Editing in KDE or Main Menu⇨Graphics⇨Image Editing⇨The GIMP in GNOME.

When you start it for the first time, The GIMP displays a window with copyright and license information. Click the Continue button to proceed with the installation. The next screen shows the directories to be created when you proceed with a personal installation of The GIMP.

The GIMP installation involves creating a directory in your home directory and placing a number of files in that directory. This directory essentially holds information about any changes to user preferences you may make to The GIMP. Go ahead and click the Continue button at the bottom of the window. The GIMP creates the necessary directories, copies the necessary files to those directories, and guides you through a series of dialog boxes to complete the installation.

After the installation is done, click the Continue button. From now on, you don't see the installation window anymore; you have to deal with installation only when you run The GIMP for the first time.

The GIMP then loads any *plugins* — external modules that enhance its functionality. It displays a startup window that shows a message about each plugin as it loads. After finishing the startup, The GIMP displays a tip of the day in a window. You can browse the tips and click the Close button to close the Tip window. At the same time, The GIMP displays a number of windows, as shown in Figure 15-13.

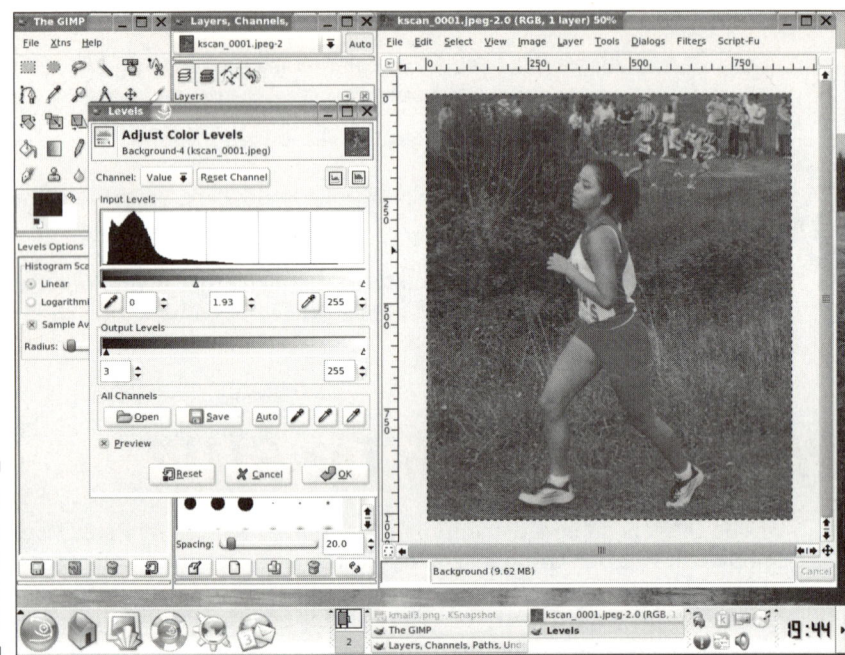

Figure 15-13: Touch up your photos with The GIMP.

These windows include a main toolbox window titled The GIMP, a Tool Options window, a Brush Selection window, and a Layers, Channels, Paths window. Of these, the main toolbox window is the most important — in fact, you can close the other windows and work by using the menus and buttons in the toolbox.

The toolbox has three menus on the menu bar:

- **The File menu** has options to create a new image, open an existing image, save and print an image, mail an image, and quit The GIMP.
- **The Xtns menu** gives you access to numerous extensions to The GIMP. The exact content of the Xtns menu depends on which extensions are installed on your system.
- **The Help menu** is where you can get help and view tips. For example, choose Help➪Help to bring up The GIMP Help Browser with online information about The GIMP.

To open an image file in The GIMP, choose File➪Open. The Open Image dialog box comes up, which you can then use to select an image file. You can change directories and select the image file that you want to open. The GIMP can read all common image-file formats, such as GIF, JPEG, TIFF, PCX, BMP, PNG, and PostScript. After you select the file and click OK, The GIMP loads the image into a new window. (Refer to Figure 15-13 to see an image after it's loaded in The GIMP, along with all the other The GIMP windows.)

Chapter 15: Working with Photos and Images

The toolbox also has many buttons that represent the tools you use to edit the image and apply special effects. You can get pop-up help on each tool button by hovering the mouse pointer over the button. You can select a tool by clicking the tool button, and you can apply that tool's effects to the image.

For your convenience, The GIMP displays a pop-up menu when you right-click the image window. The pop-up menu has most of the options from the File and Xtns menus in the toolbox. You can then select specific actions from these menus.

You can do much more than just load and view images with The GIMP, but a complete discussion of all its features is beyond the scope of this book. If you want to try the other features of The GIMP, consult The GIMP User Manual, available online at www.gimp.org/docs/.

Viewing Images

If all you want is to view your photos and other image files, you don't have to use something as powerful as The GIMP. Both KDE and GNOME come with image viewing applications.

If you installed KDE as your desktop, you can use Gwenview to view all the photos in a folder. Here are the quick steps to use Gwenview:

1. **Choose Main Menu⇨Graphics⇨Viewer⇨Gwenview.**
2. **Browse the folders from the top-left pane and select the folder that contains your photos.**

   Gwenview displays thumbnails of the photos in the right pane.

3. **Click on a thumbnail to view a larger version, as shown in Figure 15-14.**

In GNOME, use Eye of Gnome to view images. Follow these steps to use Eye of Gnome:

1. **Choose Main Menu⇨Graphics⇨Viewer⇨Image Viewer.**

   Eye of Gnome starts and displays a blank window.

2. **Click Open on the toolbar.**

   The Load Image dialog box appears.

3. **Browse and locate the folder containing images such as digital photos. Click or Ctrl+click to select one or more photos. Then click Open.**

   Eye of Gnome loads the images and displays them in a thumbnail view in the lower pane of its window (see Figure 15-15). On the upper pane, it displays a larger view of the currently selected image.

240 Part III: Doing Stuff with SUSE

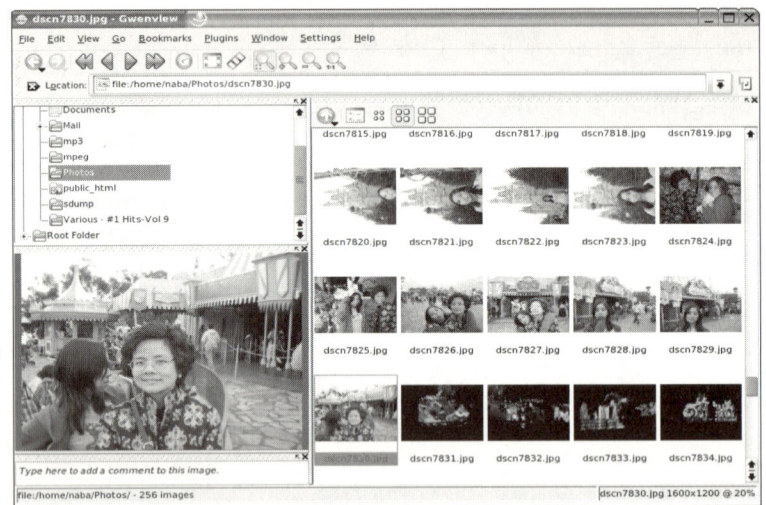

Figure 15-14: If you use KDE, view images in Gwenview.

Figure 15-15: If you are a GNOME fan, use Eye of Gnome to view images.

To the left of the larger image, Eye of Gnome displays some details about the image such as the filename, the image dimensions, and the file size. For digital photos, it displays details of the camera as well as other information such as resolution of the image and the date the photo was taken.

4. **Click the Previous and Next buttons on the toolbar to view photos or simply click on a thumbnail to view that image.**

Viewing PDF and PostScript Files

Both KDE and GNOME come with Acrobat Reader for viewing and printing PDF documents. As you might know, PDF stands for portable document format and, as the name implies, it's widely used as the format for documents that can be viewed on almost any system that has a PDF viewer. PDF files typically have .pdf extension.

To start Acrobat Reader, choose Main Menu⇨Office⇨Document Viewer in KDE and Main Menu⇨Office⇨Document Viewer⇨Acrobat Reader in GNOME.

When Acrobat Reader runs for the first time, it displays a license agreement in a dialog box. After you click Accept, Acrobat Reader starts and displays its main window. To open a PDF file, choose File⇨Open and select the file from the Open dialog box. For example, you could open the file /usr/X11R6/lib/Acrobat5/Reader/help/reader.pdf (by the way, you can get the same file by choosing Help⇨Reader Help). Figure 15-16 shows Acrobat Reader displaying its own help file.

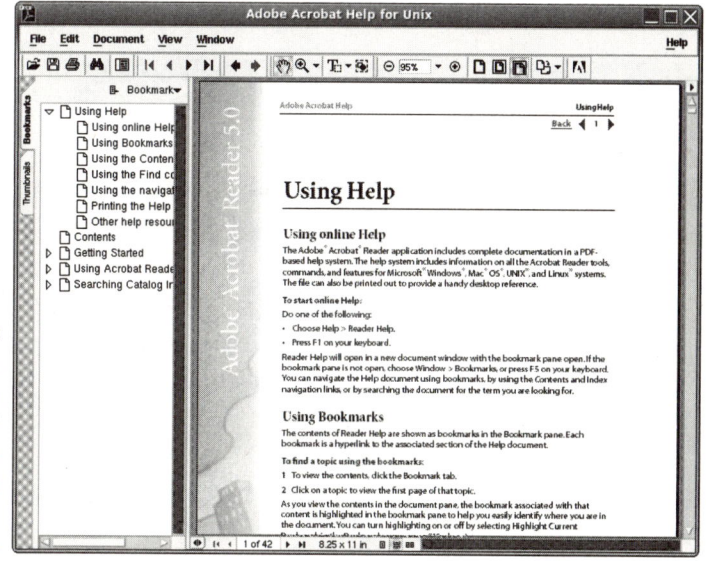

Figure 15-16: You can view PDF documents in Acrobat Reader.

KGhostscript in KDE and GGV PostScript Viewer in GNOME are ideal for viewing and printing PostScript documents. (These files typically have the .ps extension in their names.) For a long document, you can view and print selected pages. You can also view the document at various levels of magnification by zooming in or out. GGV PostScript Viewer can also open PDF files.

I describe GGV PostScript Viewer next, but you can use KGhostview in KDE in a similar manner (just choose Main Menu⇨Office⇨Document Viewer⇨KGhostview).

To run GGV PostScript Viewer, choose Main Menu⇨Graphics⇨Viewer⇨PostScript Viewer from the GNOME desktop. The GGV PostScript Viewer window appears. In addition to the menu bar and toolbar along the top edge, a vertical divide splits the main display area of the window into two parts.

To load and view a PostScript document in GGV PostScript Viewer, choose File⇨Open, or click the Open icon on the toolbar. GGV PostScript Viewer displays a dialog box. Use this dialog box to navigate the file system and select a PostScript file. You can select one of the PostScript files that come with Ghostscript. For example, open the file `tiger.ps` in the `/usr/share/ghostscript/7.07/examples` directory. (If your system has a version of Ghostscript later than 7.07, you have to use the new version number in place of 7.07.)

To open the selected file, click the Open File button in the File Selection dialog box. GGV PostScript Viewer opens the selected file, processes its contents, and displays the output in its window, as shown in Figure 15-17.

Figure 15-17:
You can view PostScript files in GGV PostScript Viewer.

Chapter 16

What's a Shell and Why Do I Care?

In This Chapter
▶ Opening terminal windows and virtual consoles
▶ Exploring the bash shell

Sometimes things just don't work. What do you do if the GUI desktop stops responding to your mouse clicks? What if the GUI doesn't start at all? You can still tell your SUSE Linux system what to do, but you have to do it by typing commands into a text screen. In these situations, you work with the *shell* — the SUSE Linux command interpreter. I introduce the bash shell (the default shell in SUSE Linux) in this chapter.

After you figure out how to work with the shell, you may even begin to like the simplicity and power of the Linux commands. And then, even if you're a GUI aficionado, someday soon you may find yourself firing up a terminal window and making the system sing and dance with two- or three-letter commands strung together by strange punctuation characters. (Hey, I can dream, can't I?)

Opening Terminal Windows and Virtual Consoles

First things first. If you're working in a GUI desktop such as GNOME or KDE, where do you type commands for the shell? Good question.

The easiest way to get to the shell is to open a *terminal* (also called *console*) window. In KDE, click the icon that looks like a monitor covered by a seashell (for a shell, get it?) to open a terminal window. In GNOME, select Programs Menu➪System➪Terminal➪Terminal and that should open up a terminal window. Now you can type commands to your heart's content.

If, for some reason, the GUI seems to be *hung* (you click and type but nothing happens), you can turn to the *virtual consoles.* (The *physical* console is the monitor-and-keyboard combination.) The idea of virtual consoles is to give you the ability to switch between several text consoles, even though you have only one physical console. Whether you are running a GUI or not, you can then use different text consoles to type different commands.

To get to the first virtual console from the GNOME or KDE desktop, press Ctrl+Alt+F1. Press Ctrl+Alt+F2 for the second virtual console, and so on. Each of these virtual consoles is a text screen where you can log in and type Linux commands to perform various tasks. When you're done, type **exit** to log out.

You can use up to six virtual consoles. In most distributions, the seventh one is used for the GUI desktop. To get back to the GUI desktop, press Ctrl+Alt+F7.

If the GUI appears to be hung, switch to a virtual console and gracefully shut down the system from that console. For example, press Ctrl+Alt+F2 and then log in as root. After that, type **shutdown -h now** to halt the system. To restart the system, type **reboot**.

Exploring the Bash Shell

If you've used MS-DOS, you may be familiar with COMMAND.COM, the DOS command interpreter. That program displays the infamous C:\> prompt. In Windows, you can see this prompt if you open a command window. (To open a command window in Microsoft Windows, choose Start⇨Run, type **cmd** in the text box, and then click OK.)

SUSE Linux comes with a command interpreter that resembles COMMAND.COM in DOS, but it can do a whole lot more. The SUSE Linux command interpreter is called a *shell.*

The default shell in SUSE Linux is bash. When you open a terminal window or log in at a text console, the bash shell is what prompts you for commands. Then, when you type a command, the shell executes your command.

In addition to the standard Linux commands, bash can execute any computer program. So you can type the name of an application (the name is usually more cryptic than what you see in GNOME or KDE menus) at the shell prompt, and the shell starts that application.

Understanding the syntax of shell commands

Because a shell interprets what you type, knowing how the shell processes the text you enter is important. All shell commands have this general format that starts with a command followed by options (some commands have no options):

```
command option1 option2 ... optionN
```

Such a single on-screen line giving a command is commonly referred to as a *command line*. On a command line, you enter a command, followed by zero or more options (or *arguments*). These strings of options — the *command line options* (or command line arguments) — modify the way the command works so that you can get it to do specific tasks.

The shell uses a blank space or a tab to distinguish between the command and options. Naturally, you help it by using a space or a tab to separate the command from the options and the options from one another.

An option can contain spaces — all you have to do is put that option inside quotation marks so that the spaces are included. For example, to search for my name in the password file, I enter the following grep command (grep is used for searching for text in files):

```
grep "Naba Barkakati" /etc/passwd
```

When grep prints the line with my name, it looks like this:

```
naba:x:1000:100:Naba Barkakati:/home/naba:/bin/bash
```

If you created a user account with your username, type the grep command with your username as an argument.

In the output from the grep command, you can see the name of the shell (/bin/bash) following the last colon (:).

The number of command line options and their format, of course, depends on the actual command. Typically, these options look like -X, where X is a single character. For example, the ls command lists the contents of a directory. You can use the -l option to see more details.

If a command is too long to fit on a single line, you can press the backslash key followed by Enter. Then, continue typing the command on the next line. For example, type the following command (press Enter after each line):

```
cat \
/etc/passwd
```

The `cat` command then displays the contents of the `/etc/passwd` file.

You can concatenate (that is, string together) several shorter commands on a single line. Just separate the commands by semicolons (;). For example, the following command

```
cd; ls -l; pwd
```

changes the current directory to your home directory, lists the contents of that directory, and then shows the name of that directory.

Combining shell commands

You can combine simple shell commands to create a more sophisticated command. For example, suppose that you want to find out whether a device file named sbpcd resides in your system's /dev directory because some documentation says you need that device file for a Sound Blaster Pro CD-ROM drive. You can use the `ls /dev` command to get a directory listing of the /dev directory, and then browse through it to see whether that listing contains sbpcd.

Unfortunately, the /dev directory has a great many entries, so you may find it hard to find any item that has sbpcd in its name. You can, however, combine the ls command with grep and come up with a command line that does exactly what you want. Here's that command line:

```
ls /dev | grep sbpcd
```

The shell sends the output of the `ls` command (the directory listing) to the `grep` command, which searches for the string sbpcd. That vertical bar (|) is known as a *pipe* because it acts as a conduit (think of a water pipe) between the two programs — the output of the first command is fed into the input of the second one.

Controlling command input and output

Most Linux commands have a common feature — they always read from the standard input (usually, the keyboard) and write to the standard output

Chapter 16: What's a Shell and Why Do I Care?

(usually, the screen). Error messages are sent to the standard error (usually to the screen as well). These three devices often are referred to as `stdin`, `stdout`, and `stderr`.

You can make a command get its input from a file and then send its output to another file. Just so you know, the highfalutin' term for this feature is *input and output redirection* or *I/O redirection*.

Getting command input from a file

If you want a command to read from a file, you can redirect the standard input to come from that file instead of from the keyboard. For example, type the following command:

```
sort < /etc/passwd
```

This command displays a sorted list of the lines in the `/etc/passwd` file. In this case, the less-than sign (`<`) redirects `stdin` so that the `sort` command reads its input from the `/etc/passwd` file.

Saving command output in a file

To save the output of a command in a file, redirect the standard output to a file. For example, type **cd** to change to your home directory and then type the following command:

```
grep typedef /usr/include/* > typedef.out
```

This command searches through all files in the `/usr/include` directory for the occurrence of the text `typedef` — and then saves the output in a file called `typedef.out`. The greater-than sign (`>`) redirects `stdout` to a file. This command also illustrates another feature of `bash`. When you use an asterisk (`*`), `bash` replaces the asterisk with a list of all filenames in the specified directory. Thus, `/usr/include/*` means *all the files in the `/usr/include` directory*.

TIP

If you want to append a command's output to the end of an existing file instead of saving the output in a new file, use two greater-than signs (`>>`) like this:

```
command >> filename
```

Saving error messages in a file

Sometimes you type a command and it generates a whole lot of error messages that scroll by so fast you can't tell what's going on. One way to see all the error messages is to save the error messages in a file so that you can see what the heck happened. You can do that by redirecting `stderr` to a file.

For example, type the following command:

```
find / -name COPYING -print 2> finderr
```

This command looks throughout the file system for files named `COPYING`, but saves all the error messages in the `finderr` file. The number 2 followed by the greater-than sign (2>) redirects `stderr` to a file.

If you want to simply discard the error messages instead of saving them in a file, use `/dev/null` as the filename, like this:

```
find / -name COPYING -print 2> /dev/null
```

That `/dev/null` is a special file — often called the *bit bucket* and sometimes glorified as the *Great Bit Bucket in the Sky* — that simply discards whatever it receives. So now you know what they mean when you hear phrases such as, "Your mail probably ended up in the bit bucket."

Typing less with automatic command completion

Many commands take a filename as an argument. To view the contents of the `/etc/passwd` text file, for example, type the following command:

```
cat /etc/passwd
```

The `cat` command displays the `/etc/passwd` file. For any command that takes a filename as an argument, you can use a `bash` feature to avoid having to type the whole filename. All you have to type is the bare minimum — just the first few characters — to uniquely identify the file in its directory.

To see an example, type **cat /etc/pas** but don't press Enter; press Tab instead. `bash` automatically completes the filename, so the command becomes `cat /etc/passwd`. Now press Enter to run the command.

Whenever you type a filename, press Tab after the first few characters of the filename. `bash` probably can complete the filename so that you don't have to type the entire name. If you don't enter enough characters to uniquely identify the file, `bash` beeps. Just type a few more characters and press Tab again.

Going wild with asterisks and question marks

You can avoid typing long filenames another way. (After all, making less work for users is the idea of computers, isn't it?)

Chapter 16: What's a Shell and Why Do I Care?

This particular trick involves using the asterisk (*) and question mark (?) and a few more tricks. These special characters are called *wildcards* because they match zero or more characters in a line of text.

If you know MS-DOS, you may have used commands such as COPY *.* A: to copy all files from the current directory to the A: drive. bash accepts similar wildcards in filenames. As you'd expect, bash provides many more wildcard options than the MS-DOS command interpreter does.

You can use three types of wildcards in bash:

- The **asterisk (*)** character matches zero or more characters in a filename. That mBeans * denotes all files in a directory.
- The **question mark (?)** matches any single character. If you type test?, that matches any five-character text that begins with test.
- A **set of characters in brackets** matches any single character from that set. The string [aB]*, for example, matches any filename that starts with a or B.

Wildcards are handy when you want to do something to a whole lot of files. For example, to copy all the files from the /media/cdrom directory to the current directory, type the following:

```
cp /media/cdrom/* .
```

Bash replaces the wildcard character * with the names of all the files in the /media/cdrom directory. The period at the end of the command represents the current directory.

You can use the asterisk with other parts of a filename to select a more specific group of files. Suppose you want to use the grep command to search for the text typedef struct in all files of the /usr/include directory that meet the following criteria:

- The filename starts with s
- The filename ends with .h

The wildcard specification s*.h denotes all filenames that meet these criteria. Thus you can perform the search with the following command:

```
grep "typedef struct" /usr/include/s*.h
```

The string contains a space that you want the grep command to find, so you have to enclose that string in quotation marks. That way, bash does not try to interpret each word in that text as a separate command line argument.

The question mark (?) matches a single character. Suppose that you have four files — image1.pcx, image2.pcx, image3.pcx, and image4.pcx — in the current directory. To copy these files to the /mnt/floppy directory, use the following command:

```
cp image?.pcx /mnt/floppy
```

Bash replaces the single question mark with any single character, and copies the four files to /mnt.

The third wildcard format — [...] — matches a single character from a specific set of characters enclosed in square brackets. You may want to combine this format with other wildcards to narrow down the matching filenames to a smaller set. To see a list of all filenames in the /etc/X11/xdm directory that start with x or X, type the following command:

```
ls /etc/X11/xdm/[xX]*
```

Repeating previously typed commands

To make repeating long commands easy for you, bash stores up to 500 old commands as part of a *command history* (basically just a list of old commands). To see the command history, type **history**. bash displays a numbered list of the old commands, including those that you entered during previous logins.

If the command list is too long, you can limit the number of old commands that you want to see. For example, to see only the ten most recent commands, type this command:

```
history 10
```

To repeat a command from the list that the history command shows, simply type an exclamation point (!), followed by that command's number. To repeat command number 3, type **!3**.

You can repeat an old command without knowing its command number. Suppose you typed more /usr/lib/X11/xdm/xdm-config a few minutes ago, and now you want to look at that file again. To repeat the previous more command, type the following:

```
!more
```

Often, you may want to repeat the last command that you just typed, perhaps with a slight change. For example, you may have displayed the contents of the directory by using the ls -l command. To repeat that command, type two exclamation points as follows:

```
!!
```

Chapter 16: What's a Shell and Why Do I Care?

Sometimes, you may want to repeat the previous command but add extra arguments to it. Suppose that `ls -l` shows too many files. Simply repeat that command, but pipe the output through the `more` command as follows:

```
!! | more
```

Bash replaces the two exclamation points with the previous command and then appends `| more` to that command.

TIP: Here's the easiest way to recall previous commands. Just press the up-arrow key and `bash` keeps going backward through the history of commands you previously typed. To move forward in the command history, press the down-arrow key.

Part IV
Becoming a SUSE Wizard

The 5th Wave — By Rich Tennant

"We're much better prepared for this upgrade than before. We're giving users additional training, better manuals, and a morphine drip."

In this part...

You may not have realized it, but you are the system administrator (or sysadmin, for short) of your SUSE Linux system. I start this Part with a chapter that introduces you to the sysadmin duties and YaST — the graphical tool through which you do all your sysadmin chores in SUSE. Then I show you how to keep your SUSE system up-to-date and how to install new software. Finally, I cover security — how to keep the bad guys out of your system (assuming your system is hooked up to the Internet).

Chapter 17

Look Ma, I'm a Sysadmin!

In This Chapter

▶ Introducing the sysadmin role
▶ Becoming `root`
▶ Introducing the YaST Control Center
▶ Starting and stopping services
▶ Managing devices
▶ Managing user accounts

*S*ystem administration, or *sysadmin* for short, refers to whatever has to be done to keep a computer system up and running; the *system administrator* (also called the *sysadmin*) is whoever is in charge of taking care of these tasks.

If you're running Linux at home or in a small office, you're most likely the system administrator for your systems. Or maybe you're the system administrator for a whole LAN full of Linux systems. No matter. In this chapter, I introduce you to basic system administration procedures and show you how to perform some common tasks. As you'll see, in SUSE Linux, you can perform most sysadmin tasks through a graphical tool called YaST. I also discuss some command lines that can be handy if, for some reason, the GUI desktop does not start.

What Does a Sysadmin Do?

So what *are* system administration tasks? My off-the-cuff reply is, "Anything you have to do to keep the system running well." More accurately, though, a system administrator's duties include the following:

- **Adding and removing user accounts.** You have to add new user accounts and remove unnecessary user accounts. If a user forgets the password, you have to change the password.
- **Managing the printing system.** You have to turn the print queue on or off, check the print queue's status, and delete print jobs if necessary.
- **Installing, configuring, and upgrading the operating system and various utilities.** You have to install or upgrade parts of the Linux operating system and other software that are part of the operating system.
- **Installing new software.** You have to install software that comes in a package format such as RPM. You also may have to download and unpack software that comes in source-code form — and then build executable programs from the source code.
- **Managing hardware.** Sometimes, you have to add new hardware and install drivers so the devices work properly.
- **Making backups.** You have to back up files, either in a Zip drive or on tape (if you have a tape drive).
- **Mounting and unmounting file systems.** When you want to access the files on a CD-ROM, for example, you have to mount that CD-ROM's file system on one of the directories in your Linux file system. You also have to mount floppy disks, in both Linux format and DOS format.
- **Automating tasks.** You have to schedule Linux tasks to take place automatically (at specific times) or periodically (at regular intervals).
- **Monitoring the system's performance.** You may want to keep an eye on system performance to see where the processor is spending most of its time, and to see the amount of free and used memory in the system.
- **Starting and shutting down the system.** Although starting the system typically involves nothing more than powering up the PC, you do have to take some care when you want to shut down your Linux system. Typically you can perform the shutdown operation by selecting a menu item from the graphical login screen. Otherwise, use the `shutdown` command to stop all programs before turning off your PC's power switch.
- **Monitoring network status.** If you have a network presence (whether a LAN, a DSL line, or cable modem connection), you may want to check the status of various network interfaces and make sure your network connection is up and running.
- **Setting up host and network security.** You have to make sure that system files are protected and that your system can defend itself against attacks over the network.
- **Monitoring security.** You have to keep an eye on any intrusions, usually by checking the log files.

Chapter 17: Look Ma, I'm a Sysadmin! 257

That's a long list of tasks! I don't cover all of them in this chapter, but this and the next three chapters describe most of these tasks. In this chapter, I focus on some of the basics by introducing you to some GUI tools, explaining how to become `root` (the superuser), and showing you how to monitor system performance, manage devices, and set up user accounts.

Becoming root, When You Must

You have to log in as `root` to perform the system administration tasks. The `root` user is the superuser and the only account with all the privileges needed to do anything in the system.

Common wisdom says you should *not* normally log in as `root`. When you're `root`, all it takes is one misstep, and you can easily delete all the files — especially when you're typing commands. Take, for example, the command `rm *.html` that you may type to delete all files that have the `.html` extension. What if you accidentally press the spacebar after the asterisk (*)? The shell takes the command to be `rm * .html` and — because * matches any filename — deletes everything in the current directory. Seems implausible until it happens to you!

If you're logged in as a normal user, how do you do any system administration chores? Well, you become `root` for the time being. If you're working at a terminal window or text-mode console, type

```
su -
```

Then enter the `root` password in response to the prompt. From this point on, you're `root`. Do whatever you have to do. To return to your usual self, type

```
exit
```

That's it! It's that easy.

Resetting a Forgotten root Password

To perform system administration tasks, you have to know the `root` password. What happens if you forget the `root` password? Not to worry: Just reboot the PC and you can reset the `root` password by following these steps:

1. **Reboot the PC (select Reboot as you log out of the GUI screen) or power up as usual.**

   Soon you see the graphical boot screen that shows the names of the operating systems you can boot. The text cursor rests on a line labeled Boot Options.

2. **If you have more than one operating system installed, use the arrow key to select SUSE Linux as your operating system.**

3. **Type the following and then press Enter:**

   ```
   single init=/bin/sh
   ```

   Linux starts up as usual but runs in a single-user mode that does not require you to log in. After Linux starts, you see the following command line prompt that ends with a hash mark (#), similar to the following:

   ```
   sh-3.00#
   ```

4. **Type the following command, and then press Enter:**

   ```
   mount / -n -o remount,rw
   ```

   This makes the `root` file system — the forward slash (/) in the `mount` command — writeable so that you can change the password (which is stored in a file in the `root` file system).

5. **Type the `passwd` command to change the `root` password as follows:**

   ```
   sh-3.00# passwd
   Changing password for user root.
   New password:
   ```

6. **Type the new `root` password that you want to use (it doesn't appear on-screen), and then press Enter.**

   The `passwd` command asks for the password again, like this:

   ```
   Re-enter new password:
   ```

7. **Type the password again, and press Enter.**

   If you enter the same password both times, the `passwd` command changes the `root` password.

8. **Type the following command and press Enter.**

   ```
   mount / -n -o remount,ro
   ```

   This remounts the `root` file system in a read-only mode.

9. **Now type /sbin/reboot to reboot the PC.**

   After SUSE Linux restarts, you can again become `root` by typing **su -** and entering the new password. When GUI utilities such as YaST prompt for the `root` password, enter the new `root` password.

Chapter 17: Look Ma, I'm a Sysadmin! *259*

> **WARNING!** Make sure that your SUSE Linux PC is *physically* secure. As these steps show, anyone who can physically access your SUSE Linux PC can simply reboot, set a new `root` password, and do whatever they want with the system.

Introducing Your New Friend, YaST

SUSE Linux comes with GUI tools for performing system administration tasks. The GUI tools prompt you for input and then run the necessary Linux commands to perform the task. You access these GUI sysadmin tools through the YaST Control Center. In this section, I briefly introduce the YaST Control Center.

To start the YaST Control Center, choose Main Menu⇨System⇨YaST from the KDE or GNOME desktop. Normally you are not logged in as `root`, so the YaST Control Center pops up a dialog box that prompts you for the `root` password, as shown in Figure 17-1. Just type the password and press Enter. If you don't want to use the utility, click Cancel.

Figure 17-1: Type the `root` password and press Enter to gain `root` privileges.

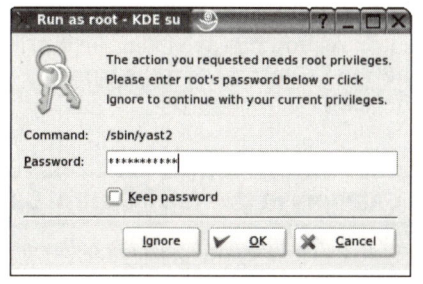

After you enter the root password, the main window of the YaST Control Center appears, as shown in Figure 17-2.

The left pane of the YaST Control Center window shows icons for the categories of tasks you can perform. The right-hand pane shows icons for specific tasks in the currently selected category. When you click an icon in the right-hand side of the YaST Control Center, a new YaST window appears and enables you to perform that task.

> **REMEMBER** By the way, when I tell you about starting a specific GUI tool from the YaST Control Center, I use the familiar menu selection notation such as YaST Control Center⇨Software⇨Install and Remove Software, which means start the YaST Control Center, click the Software category in the left pane and then click the Install and Remove Software icon from the icons that appear in the right pane. Simple enough!

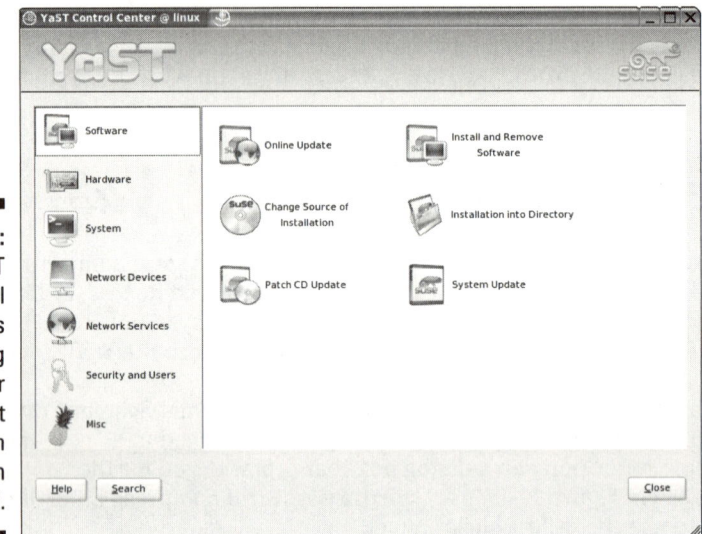

Figure 17-2: The YaST Control Center is your starting point for most sysadmin tasks in SUSE.

Table 17-1 summarizes the tasks for each of the category icons you see in the left side of the YaST Control Center. As you can see from the entries in the second column of Table 17-1, the YaST Control Center is truly one-stop shopping for all of your sysadmin chores.

Table 17-1	Tasks by Category in the YaST Control Center
This Category	**Enables You to Configure/Manage the Following**
Software	Online Update; Install and Remove Software; Change Source of Installation; Installation into Directory; Patch CD Update; System Update
Hardware	Bluetooth; CD-ROM Drives; Disk Controller; Graphics Card and Monitor; Hardware Information; IDE DMA Mode; IrDA (infrared link); Joystick; Keyboard Layout; Mouse Model; Printer; Scanner; Sound; TV Card
System	/etc/sysconfig Editor; Boot Loader Configuration; Choose Language; Create a Boot, Rescue, or Module Floppy; Date and Time; LVM (logical volume manager); Partitioner; Power Management; Powertweak Configuration; Profile Manager; Restore System; Runlevel Editor; Select Keyboard Layout; System Backup
Network Devices	DSL; Fax; ISDN; Modem; Network Card; Phone Answering Machine

This Category	Enables You to Configure/Manage the Following
Network Services	DHCP Server; DNS Server; DNS and Host Name; HTTP Server (Web server); Host Names; Kerberos Client; LDAP Client; Mail Transfer Agent; NFS Client; NFS Server; NIS Client; NIS Server; NTP Client; Network Services (inetd); Proxy; Remote Administration; Routing; Samba Client; Samba Server; TFTP Server
Security and Users	Edit and create groups; Edit and create users; Firewall; Security settings
Misc	Autoinstallation; Load Vendor Driver CD; Post a Support Query; View Start-up Log; View System Log

Starting and Stopping Services

Knowing the sequence in which Linux starts processes as it boots is important. You can use this knowledge to start and stop services, such as the Web server and Network File System (NFS). The next few sections provide you with an overview of how Linux boots and starts the initial set of processes. These sections also familiarize you with the shell scripts that start various services on a Linux system.

Understanding how Linux boots

When Linux boots, it loads and runs the core operating system program from the hard drive. The core operating system is designed to run other programs. A process named `init` starts the initial set of processes on your Linux system.

To see the processes currently running on the system, type

```
ps ax | more
```

You get an output listing that starts off like this:

```
  PID TTY      STAT   TIME COMMAND
    1 ?        S      0:01 init [5]
```

The first column, with the heading `PID`, shows a number for each process. PID stands for *process ID* (identifier) — a sequential number assigned by the

Linux kernel. The first entry in the process list, with a *process ID* (PID) of 1, is the `init` process. It's the first process, and it starts all other processes in your Linux system. That's why `init` is sometimes referred to as the "mother of all processes."

What the `init` process starts depends on the following:

- The *run level,* an identifier that identifies a system configuration in which only a selected group of processes are started.
- The contents of the `/etc/inittab` file, a text file that specifies which processes to start at different run levels.
- A number of shell scripts — sequence of Linux commands — that are executed at specific run levels.

SUSE Linux uses seven run levels — 0 through 6. Table 17-2 shows the meanings of the different run levels in SUSE Linux.

Table 17-2	Run Levels in SUSE Linux
Run Level	**Meaning**
0	Shuts down the system
1	Runs in single-user stand-alone mode (no one else can log in; you work at the text console)
2	Runs in multiuser mode without network
3	Runs in full multiuser mode with network and text-mode login
4	Unused
5	Runs in full multiuser mode with graphical login (default run level)
6	Reboots the system

The current run level, together with the contents of the `/etc/inittab` file, control which processes `init` starts in Linux. In SUSE, run level 3 is used for text-mode login screens and 5 for the graphical login screen. You can change the default run level by editing a line in the `/etc/inittab` file.

To check the current run level, type the following command in a terminal window:

```
/sbin/runlevel
```

This `runlevel` command prints an output like this:

```
N 5
```

The first character of the output shows the previous run level (N means no previous run level), and the second character shows the current run level (5). In this case, the system started at run level 5.

Trying a new run level with the init command

To try a new run level, you don't have to change the default run level in the /etc/inittab file. Type **su -** at a terminal window to become root, and then you can change the run level (and, consequently, the processes that run in Linux) by typing **init** followed by the run level.

For example, to put the system in single-user mode, type the following:

```
init 1
```

If you have never seen the single-user mode, be prepared for a surprise. It looks very similar to a system reboot and there is no GUI. All you get is a text prompt where you can type Linux commands.

If you want to try run level 3 without changing the default run level in the /etc/inittab file, enter the following command at the shell prompt:

```
init 3
```

The system ends all current processes and enters run level 3. By default, the init command waits 20 seconds before stopping all current processes and starting the new processes for run level 3.

To switch to run level 3 immediately, type the command **init -t0 3**. The number after the -t option indicates the number of seconds init waits before changing the run level.

You can also use the telinit command, which is simply a symbolic link (a shortcut) to init. If you make changes to the /etc/inittab file and want init to reload its configuration file, use the command telinit q.

To use the GUI desktop and any tools such as YaST, which you use for system administration tasks, your SUSE Linux system must be at run level 5. If you switch to a single-user mode or run level 3, you can switch to run level 5 by typing **init 5**.

Using YaST to start and stop services

To start and stop services using YaST, choose YaST Control Center⇨System⇨Runlevel Editor. YaST displays the Runlevel Editor window, as shown in Figure 17-3.

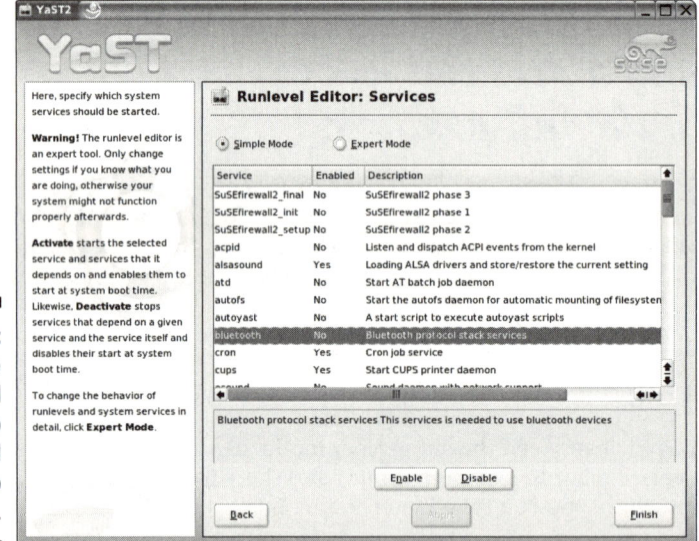

Figure 17-3: Use the Runlevel Editor to start and stop services.

The Runlevel Editor shows the list of services along with a brief description of the service and whether the service is enabled or not. You can select a service and either enable or disable it by clicking the Enable or Disable button.

If a service is enabled, clicking Disable causes YaST to stop it immediately and also change the settings so that the service is not restarted when you reboot the system. Conversely, for a currently disabled service, clicking Enable causes YaST to start it as well as ensure that the service starts when the system reboots.

Manually starting and stopping services

If YaST is not available to start and stop services, you can manually type commands in a terminal window to start and stop any service (you have to first type **su -** to become `root`). The only catch is that you have to know the name of the script that starts and stops a service. Typically, these scripts have the same name as the service and these script files are located in the /etc/init.d directory. For example, the script /etc/init.d/xinetd starts and stops the xinetd service. To restart this service manually, you would type **/etc/init.d/xinetd restart** in a terminal window.

You can enhance your system administration skills by familiarizing yourself with the scripts in the /etc/init.d directory. To see its listing, type the following command:

```
ls /etc/init.d
```

The script names give you some clue about which server the script can start and stop. For example, the bluetooth script starts and stops the processes required for Bluetooth networking services.

Checking Your System's Performance

When you're the system administrator, you must keep an eye on how well your SUSE Linux system is performing. You can monitor the overall performance of your system by looking at information such as

- Central Processing Unit (CPU) usage
- Physical memory usage
- Virtual memory (swap-space) usage
- Hard drive usage

SUSE Linux comes with a number of utilities that you can use to monitor one or more of these performance parameters. Here I introduce a few of these utilities and show you how to understand the information presented by these utilities.

Using the top utility

To view the top CPU processes — the ones that are using most of the CPU time — you can use the text mode top utility. To start that utility, type **top** in a terminal window (or text console). The top utility then displays a text screen listing the current processes, arranged in the order of CPU usage, along with various other information, such as memory and swap-space usage. Figure 17-4 shows a typical output from the top utility.

Figure 17-4: You can see the top CPU processes by using the top utility.

The `top` utility updates the display every five seconds. If you keep `top` running in a window, you can continually monitor the status of your SUSE Linux system. To quit `top`, press Q or Ctrl+C or close the terminal window.

The first five lines of the output screen (refer to Figure 17-4) provide summary information about the system. Here is what these five lines show:

- The first line shows the current time, how long the system has been up, how many users are logged in, and three *load averages* — the average number of processes ready to run during the last 1, 5, and 15 minutes.

- The second line lists the total number of processes and the status of these processes.

- The third line shows CPU usage — what percentage of CPU time is used by user processes, what percentage by system (kernel) processes, and during what percentage of time the CPU is idle.

- The fourth line shows how the physical memory is being used — the total amount, how much is used, how much is free, and how much is allocated to buffers (for reading from the hard drive, for example).

- The fifth line shows how the virtual memory (or swap space) is being used — the total amount of swap space, how much is used, how much is free, and how much is being cached.

The table that appears below the summary information (refer to Figure 17-4) lists information about the current processes, arranged in decreasing order by amount of CPU time used. Table 17-3 summarizes the meanings of the column headings in the table that `top` displays.

Table 17-3   Meanings of Column Headings in top Utility's Output

Heading	Meaning
PID	The process ID of the process
USER	Username under which the process is running
PR	Priority of the process
NI	*Nice value* of the process — the value ranges from -20 (highest priority) to 19 (lowest priority) and the default is 0 (the *nice value* represents the relative priority of the process, the higher the value the lower the priority and the nicer the process — because it yields to other processes)
VIRT	The total amount of virtual memory used by the process, in kilobytes
RES	Total physical memory used by a task (typically shown in kilobytes, but an m suffix indicates megabytes)
SHR	Amount of shared memory used by the process
S	State of the process (S for sleeping, D for uninterruptible sleep, R for running, Z for *zombies* — processes that should be dead, but are still running — or T for stopped)
%CPU	Percentage of CPU time used since last screen update
%MEM	Percentage of physical memory used by the process
TIME+	Total CPU time the process has used since it started
COMMAND	Shortened form of the command that started the process

Using the uptime command

You can use the `uptime` command to get a summary of the system's state. Just type the command like this:

```
uptime
```

It displays output similar to the following:

```
4:19pm  up 32 days, 2:52, 3 users, load average: 0.13,
       0.23, 0.27
```

This output shows the current time, how long the system has been up, the number of users, and (finally) the three load averages — the average number of processes that were ready to run in the past 1, 5, and 15 minutes. Load averages greater than 1 imply that many processes are competing for CPU time simultaneously.

The load averages give you an indication of how busy the system is.

Checking disk performance and disk usage

Linux comes with the /sbin/hdparm program that you can use to control IDE or ATAPI hard drives that are common on most PCs. One feature of the hdparm program is that you can use the -t option to determine the rate at which data is read from the disk into a buffer in memory. For example, here's the result of the command on my system:

```
/sbin/hdparm -t /dev/hda

/dev/hda:
 Timing buffered disk reads:  64 MB in  3.04 seconds = 21.05 MB/sec
```

The command requires the IDE drive's device name (/dev/hda) as an argument. If you have an IDE hard drive, you can try this command to see how fast data is read from your system's disk drive.

To display the space available in the currently mounted file systems, use the df command. If you want a more human-readable output from df, type the following command:

```
df -h
```

Here's a typical output from this command:

```
Filesystem            Size  Used Avail Use% Mounted on
/dev/hda11            6.1G  2.7G  3.5G  44% /
tmpfs                 122M   36K  122M   1% /dev/shm
/dev/hda7              43M  9.6M   32M  24% /boot
```

As this example shows, the -h option causes the df command to show the sizes in gigabytes (G) and megabytes (M).

To check the disk space being used by a specific directory, use the du command — you can specify the -h option to view the output in kilobytes (K) and megabytes (M), as shown in the following example:

```
du -h /var/log
```

Here's a typical output of that command:

```
24K     /var/log/cups
0       /var/log/news
3.3M    /var/log/YaST2
0       /var/log/samba
0       /var/log/smpppd
8.3M    /var/log
```

The `du` command displays the disk space used by each directory and the last line shows the total disk space used by that directory. If you want to see only the total space used by a directory, use the `-s` option, like this:

```
du -sh /home
751M    /home
```

Managing Hardware Devices

Use the YaST Control Center's Hardware category to access GUI tools that enable you to control various devices. Figure 17-5 shows the different types of devices you can manage from YaST Control Center⇨Hardware.

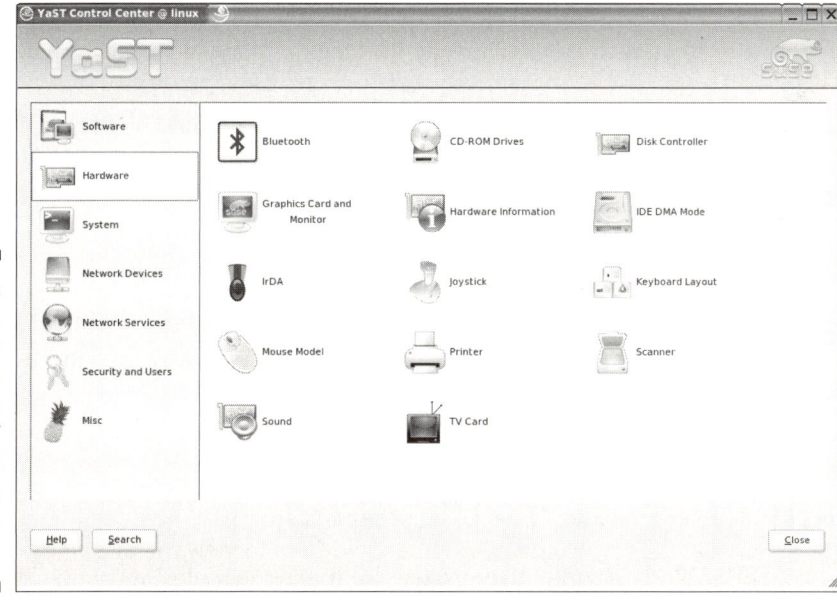

Figure 17-5: Manage hardware devices through YaST Control Center's Hardware category.

Part IV: Becoming a SUSE Wizard

For example, if you are connecting a scanner to your SUSE Linux PC, you would use YaST Control Center➪Hardware➪Scanner to set up the scanner.

As the right pane in Figure 17-5 shows, the YaST Control Center's Hardware category provides access to the following device configuration tools:

- **Bluetooth:** Enable or disable Bluetooth services and configure Bluetooth when enabled (for example, configure Bluetooth security settings).
- **CD-ROM Drives:** Mount all detected CD/DVD drives on the Linux file system.
- **Disk Controller:** Configure any configurable disk controller in the PC.
- **Graphics Card and Monitor:** Change to text-mode display or configure the X Window System. (For example, specify the graphics card and monitor type and change the display resolution and number of colors.)
- **Hardware Information:** Detect all hardware and display information about each hardware device in the system.
- **IDE DMA Mode:** Change the direct memory access (DMA) settings for disk drives and CD/DVD drives connected to the PC's IDE controller.
- **IrDA:** Configure any infrared link on the PC.
- **Joystick:** Configure a joystick connected to the sound card's joystick port. (You do not need to configure a USB joystick; just plug the joystick into the USB port and start using it.)
- **Keyboard Layout:** Specify the keyboard layout (based on the language such as UK English, US English, French, and so on).
- **Mouse Model:** Specify the type of mouse (should be detected automatically, otherwise you would have trouble getting the graphical desktop to start).
- **Printer:** Configure a printer.
- **Scanner:** Configure any scanner connected to the PC.
- **Sound:** Add a sound card or view details about a detected sound card.
- **TV Card:** Configure a TV or radio card. (These are plug-in cards capable of receiving TV or radio signals.)

Managing User Accounts

SUSE Linux is a multiuser system, so it has many user accounts. Even if you are the only user on your system, many servers require a unique username and group name. Take, for example, the FTP server. It runs under the username `ftp`. A whole host of system usernames are not for people, but just for running specific programs.

Chapter 17: Look Ma, I'm a Sysadmin! 271

Also, users can belong to one or more groups. Typically, each username has a corresponding private group name. By default, each user belongs to that corresponding private group. However, you can define other groups so that everyone belonging to a group can access a specific set of files and directories.

To create a user account in SUSE Linux, use YaST Control Center➪Security and Users➪Edit and Create Users. YaST then brings up the User and Group Administration pane, shown in Figure 17-6, where you can define new user accounts.

Notice that the pane has two radio buttons: Users and Groups (as shown in Figure 17-6). Selecting the Users radio button displays the current list of user accounts. Selecting the Groups radio button lists the names of groups. Initially, the User and Group Administration tool filters out any system users and groups. However, you can view the system users by clicking Set Filter and selecting System Users from the drop-down menu. (*System users* refer to user accounts that are not assigned to human users; rather, these user accounts are used to run various services.)

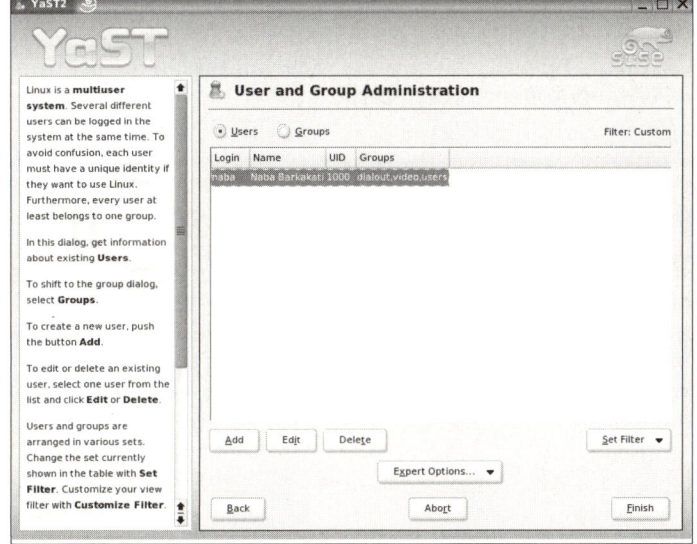

Figure 17-6: You can manage user accounts and groups from YaST.

You can add new users and groups or edit existing users and groups from the pane shown in Figure 17-6.

To add a new user account, make sure that the Users radio button is selected and click the Add button. Then enter the information requested in the Add a New Local User window, as shown in Figure 17-7.

Figure 17-7: Create a new user account by filling in the information in this YaST window.

Fill in the requested information in the window (refer to Figure 17-7), and click the Create button. The new user now appears in the list of users in the User and Group Administration pane.

You can add more user accounts, if you like. When you are done, click the Finish button in the User and Group Administration pane (refer to Figure 17-6) to create the new user accounts.

By default, YaST places all local users in a group named `users`. Sometimes you want a user to be in other groups as well, so that the user can access the files owned by that group. Adding a user to another group is easy. For example, suppose I want to add the username `naba` to the group called `wheel`. I type **su -** to become `root` and then simply type the following command in a terminal window:

```
usermod -G wheel naba
```

To remove a user account in SUSE, click the username in the list of user accounts (refer to Figure 17-6). Then click the Delete button.

Chapter 18

Updating SUSE and Adding New Software

In This Chapter

▶ Updating SUSE Linux online with YaST Online Update (YOU)

▶ Locating and installing new software using YaST

▶ Working with RPM files with the `rpm` command

*B*e it a bug fix or an enhancement, SUSE Linux often has updates that you need to install. Additionally, you may sometimes download new software. The updates come in the form of software patches, which refer to changes to existing software packages. The new software usually comes in the form of *Red Hat Package Manager* (RPM) files. Both patches and RPM files have to be installed — installing patches updates existing software and installing RPM files usually installs new software.

You can use the GUI YaST Online Update (YOU) to keep SUSE Linux updated by downloading and installing patches. On the other hand, you can use YaST Control Center⇨Software⇨Install and Remove Software to install new software (and also remove unneeded software). In case the GUI tool is not available, you can also use the `rpm` commands to install or remove software packages that come in the form of RPM files.

In this chapter, I show you how to update SUSE Linux online and how to locate and install new software using YaST. I also introduce you to the `rpm` commands that enable you to install or remove RPM software packages directly from a text console or a terminal window.

WARNING! You need a fast Internet connection (such as a DSL or cable modem) to easily update your SUSE Linux applications or download new software packages. Make sure that your Internet connection is up and running before you attempt to update your SUSE Linux system online.

Updating SUSE Linux Online

SUSE Linux comes with YOU — YaST Online Update — for online software updates. To access YOU, start YaST Control Center⇨Software⇨Online Update. This brings up the YaST Online Update window, as shown in Figure 18-1.

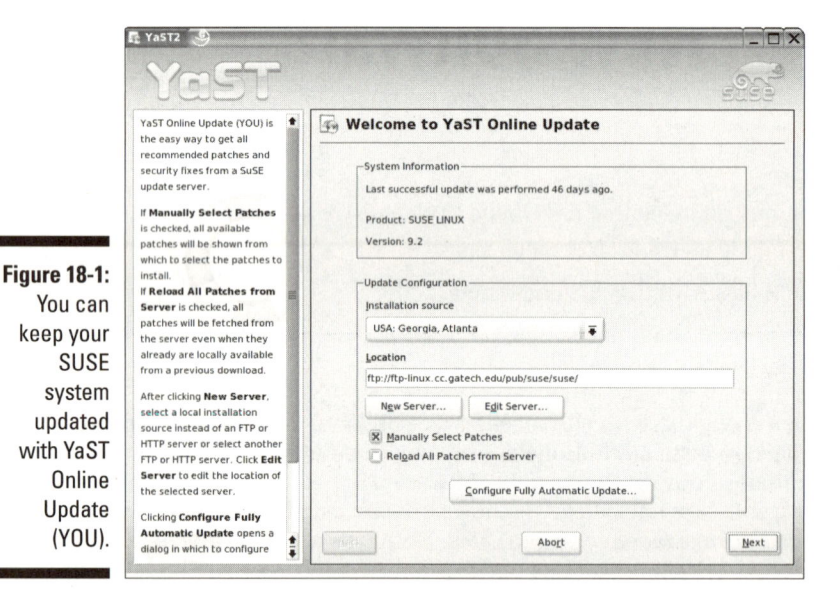

Figure 18-1: You can keep your SUSE system updated with YaST Online Update (YOU).

To set up YOU automatic updates, click the Configure Fully Automatic Update button. This brings up the YOU Automatic Mode Setup dialog box, as shown in Figure 18-2.

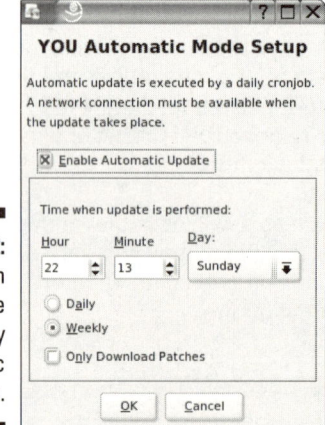

Figure 18-2: You can configure YOU for fully automatic updates.

You can then enable automatic updates by checking the Enable Automatic Update box. If you enable automatic updates, you have to specify a time of the day and frequency (daily or weekly) when you want YOU to check for any available patches and download and install them, if available. If you do not want to install the patches automatically, you can specify that YOU only download the patches and not install them. After setting the automatic update options, click OK to close the dialog box.

The next important setting for YOU is the online server from which to download the patches. To select the location, click the Installation Source drop-down menu in the YOU window (refer to Figure 18-1) and select an online server from where YOU should download the software updates. When you select a location, the full URL for the location appears in the Location text box. If you know of a new server, you can click New Server and enter the information about the new server. Typically, you can get by with the predefined set of servers that SUSE Linux provides.

After the Installation source is set, YOU is ready to update SUSE Linux. If you have configured fully automatic update, the update process would happen according to the day and time you specified in the YOU Automatic Mode Setup dialog box. Otherwise, you can manually perform an update by clicking Next in the YOU main window (refer to Figure 18-1). YOU then downloads information about any new updates in the form of a list of patches and displays them, as shown in Figure 18-3.

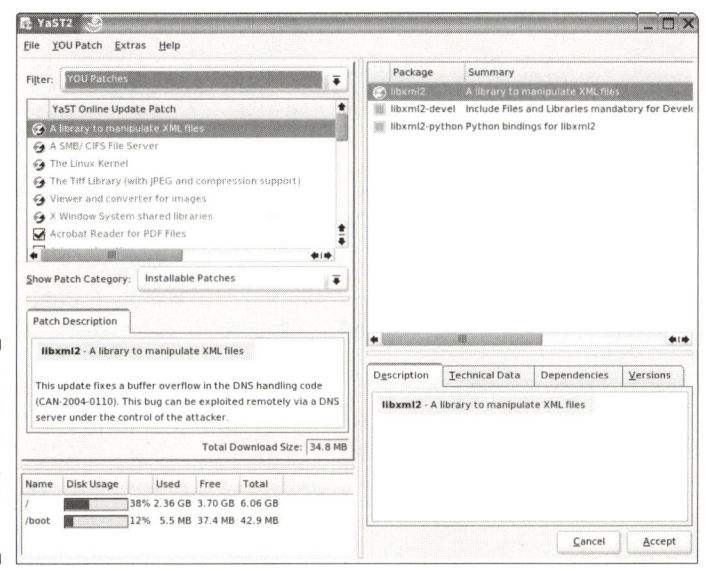

Figure 18-3: Select YOU patches and click Accept to install them.

The upper part of the left pane shows the list of YOU patches. A description of the currently selected patch appears below the list of patches. Typically, the description tells you what sort of problem the patch fixes. The right pane shows the packages updated by the patch.

Some of the critical patches are preselected for you and marked with icons denoting the type of action to be taken. You can accept the recommended selections and simply click Accept (see the lower-right corner of the window in Figure 18-3). YOU then begins to download the selected patches and installs them on your SUSE system one by one. For some patches, YOU displays a dialog box with information recommending a specific action. For example, Figure 18-4 shows a dialog box that recommends that you reboot the system after installing a patch to the Linux kernel. You can respond to these messages by clicking Install Patch as long as you understand the recommendation and plan to follow it.

Figure 18-4: For some patches, YOU prompts you with some more information.

Depending on the number and size of patches, YOU takes some time to download all the patches and install them. As YOU performs its steps, it displays the status of the patch download and installation in the window, as shown in Figure 18-5. When all patches are downloaded and installed, the Finish button is activated and you can click Finish to exit YOU.

That, in a nutshell, is how you can update your SUSE Linux system online with YOU. It's a nice and easy way to maintain your SUSE system, provided you have a high-speed Internet connection.

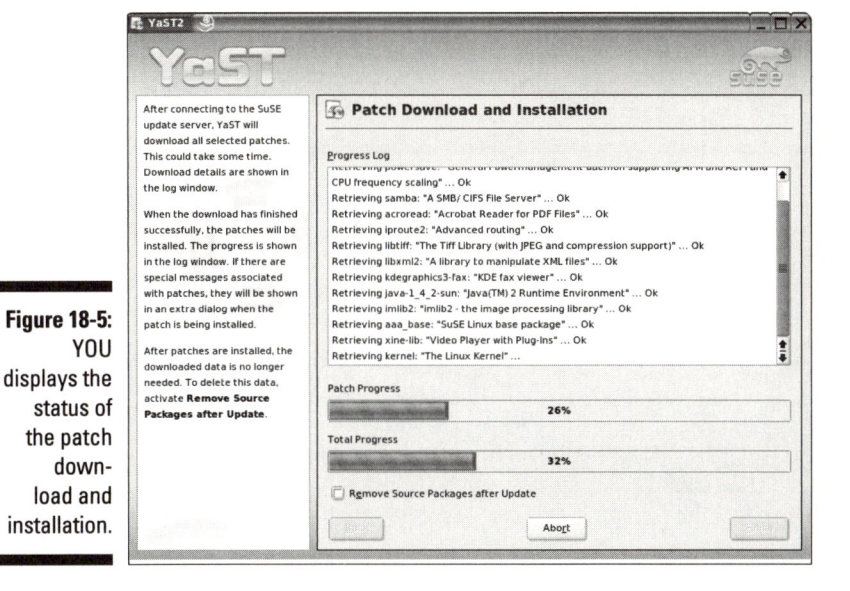

Figure 18-5: YOU displays the status of the patch download and installation.

Locating and Installing Software Using YaST

You can use YaST Control Center➪Software➪Install and Remove Software to locate specific software packages and install them. Of course, these would be software packages that were not installed as part of the SUSE Linux installation. To locate a software package and install it (as well as any other required packages), follow these general steps:

1. Start YaST Control Center➪Software➪Install and Remove Software.

2. If you know the name of the package, type in the name of the package in the Search field and click Search.

   The matching packages appear in the right pane, as shown in Figure 18-6. To install one or more packages, click to select the check mark next to the package name and then click Accept. YaST prompts you for the CD or DVD, depending on whether you had installed SUSE Linux from multiple CDs or a single DVD.

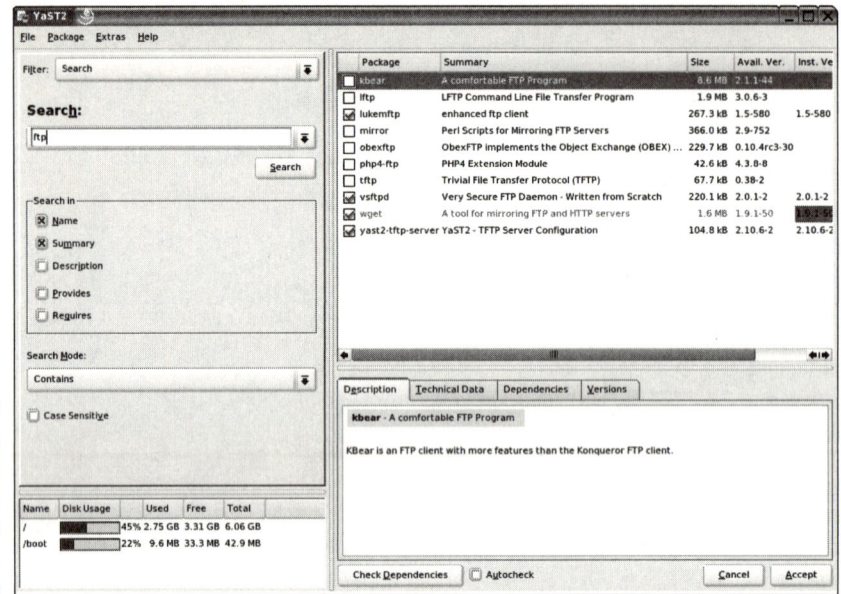

Figure 18-6:
You can search for a package by name.

3. To select groups of related packages, click the Filter drop-down list and select Selections. Then you can make a selection on the left pane and pick specific packages from the right pane (refer to Figure 18-7).

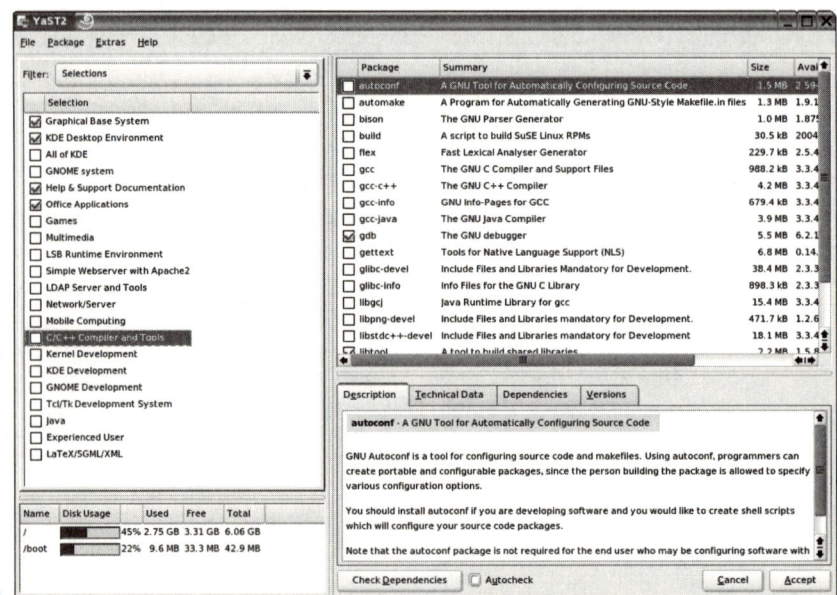

Figure 18-7:
You can make selections from groups of related packages.

Chapter 18: Updating SUSE and Adding New Software

Sometimes you may find a new software package in the form of an RPM file that you want to download and install on your SUSE Linux system. The YaST Control Center can help you install such RPM files as well.

To install one or more RPM packages using the YaST Control Center, you must first save the RPM packages in a directory and add that directory to the list of software sources. To do this, follow these steps:

1. **Download the RPM files and save them in a directory.**
2. **Start YaST Control Center⇨Software⇨Change Source of Installation.**

   The Software Source Media window appears.

3. **Choose Add⇨Local Directory in the Software Source Media window.**

   The Local Directory dialog box prompts you for the name of a directory, as shown in Figure 18-8.

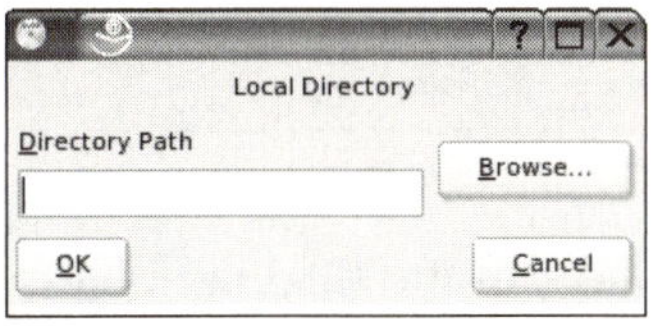

Figure 18-8: Specify the directory where the RPM files are located.

4. **Click Browse to find the directory from a dialog box or type the full pathname of the directory where the RPM files are located. Then click OK.**
5. **Click OK in response to the message that asks if you want to make the RPM files available for installation.**
6. **Click Finish in the Software Source Media window.**

After completing this step, follow these steps to install the RPM packages:

1. **Start YaST Control Center⇨Software⇨Install and Remove Software.**
2. **Click the Filter drop-down menu and select Package Groups.**

   YaST displays the names of Package Groups in the left pane and the list of packages for the currently selected package in the right pane.

3. **Scroll down the Package Groups list in the left pane and click zzz All (the last item).**

   YaST displays an alphabetic listing of all packages in the right pane, as shown in Figure 18-9.

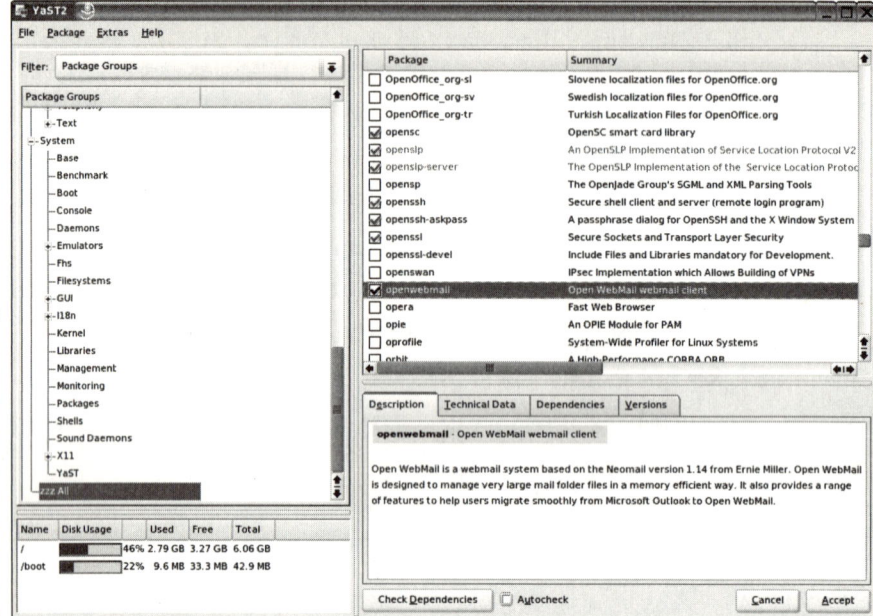

Figure 18-9: Select the RPM packages to install from the Package Group listing.

4. **In the right pane, look for the names of the RPM packages you have downloaded. Click on the check box to the left of each package name to select it for installation.**

5. **Click Accept.**

    YaST may display a dialog box informing you about other packages that will automatically be installed because these packages are needed by one or more of the RPMs you are installing. Simply click Continue to proceed with the installation. Remember that you may need to insert the SUSE Linux CDs or DVD because some of the needed packages may be on those media.

Using RPM Commands to Work with RPM Files

RPM — Red Hat Package Manager — is a format for packaging all the necessary files for a software product in a single file — called an *RPM file* or simply an *RPM*. In fact, the SUSE Linux distribution is made up of a whole lot of RPMs. If you do not have a GUI tool like the YaST Control Center handy, you can still work with RPMs through the RPM commands. You have to type these commands at the shell prompt in a terminal window or a text console. Even if you don't use the RPM commands to install or remove a package in SUSE Linux, you can still use the RPM commands to find out information about packages.

Using the RPM commands

When you install an RPM-based distribution such as SUSE Linux, the installer uses the rpm command to unpack the packages (RPM files) and to copy the contents to your hard drive.

You don't have to understand the internal structure of an RPM file, but you need to know how to use the rpm command to work with RPM files. Here are some of the things you can do with the rpm command:

- Find out the version numbers and other information about the RPMs installed on your system.
- Install a new software package from an RPM. For example, you may install a package you skipped during the initial installation. You can do that with the rpm command.
- Remove (uninstall) unneeded software you previously installed from an RPM. You may uninstall a package to reclaim the disk space, if you find that you rarely (or never) use the package.
- Upgrade an older version of an RPM with a new one.
- Verify that an RPM is in working order. You can verify a package to check that all necessary files are in the correct locations.

As you can see, the rpm command is versatile — it can do a lot of different things, depending on the options you use.

If you ever forget the rpm options, type the following command to see a list:

```
rpm --help | more
```

The number of rpm options will amaze you!

Understanding RPM filenames

An RPM contains a number of files, but it appears as a single file on your Linux system. By convention, the RPM filenames have a specific format. A typical RPM filename looks like this:

```
samba-3.0.9-2.1.i586.rpm
```

This filename has the following parts, the first three of which are separated by dashes (-):

- **Package name:** `samba`
- **Version number:** `3.0.9`
- **Release number:** `2.1`
- **Architecture:** `i586` (this package is for Intel 80586 or Pentium-compatible processors)

Usually, the package name is descriptive enough for you to guess what the RPM may contain. The version number is the same as that of the software package's current version number. Developers assign the release number to keep track of changes. The architecture is `i586` or `noarch` for the RPMs you want to install on a PC with an Intel Pentium or compatible processor.

Querying RPMs

As it installs packages, the `rpm` command builds a database of installed RPMs. You can use the `rpm -q` command to query this database to find out information about packages installed on your system.

For example, to find out the version number of an RPM installed on your system, type the following `rpm -q` command:

```
rpm -q cups
```

You see a response similar to the following:

```
cups-1.1.21-5.3
```

The response is the name of the RPM package. The name is the same as the RPM filename, except that the last part — `.i586.rpm` — isn't shown. In this case, the version part of the RPM tells you that you have `cups` (the Common UNIX Printing System) version 1.1.21 installed.

You can see a list of all installed RPMs by using the following command:

```
rpm -qa
```

You see a long list of RPMs scroll by your screen. To view the list one screen at a time, type

```
rpm -qa | more
```

If you want to search for a specific package, feed the output of `rpm -qa` to the `grep` command. For example, to see all packages with `kernel` in their names, type

```
rpm -qa | grep kernel
```

The result depends on what parts of the kernel RPMs are installed on a system.

You can query much more than a package's version number with the `rpm -q` command. By adding single-letter options, you can find out other useful information. For example, try the following command to see the files in the `cups` package:

```
rpm -ql cups
```

Here are a few more useful forms of the `rpm -q` commands to query information about a package (to use any of these `rpm -q` commands, type the command, followed by the package name):

- `rpm -qc`: Lists all configuration files in a package.
- `rpm -qd`: Lists all documentation files in a package. These are usually the online manual pages (also known as *man pages*).
- `rpm -qf`: Displays the name of the package (if any) to which a specified file belongs.
- `rpm -qi`: Displays detailed information about a package, including version number, size, installation date, and a brief description.
- `rpm -ql`: Lists all the files in a package. For some packages, you see a very long list.
- `rpm -qs`: Lists the state of all files in a package (the state of a file can be one of the following: normal, not installed, or replaced).

These `rpm` commands provide information about installed packages only. If you want to find information about an uninstalled RPM file, add the letter *p* to the command line option of each command. For example, to view the list of files in the RPM file named `samba-3.0.9-2.1.i586.rpm`, go to the directory where that file is located and then type the following command:

```
rpm -qpl samba-*.rpm
```

Of course, this command works only if the current directory *contains* that RPM file.

Two handy `rpm -q` commands enable you to find out which RPM file provides a specific file and which RPMs need a specified package. To find out the name of the RPM that provides a file, use the following command:

```
rpm -q --whatprovides filename
```

For example, to see which RPM provides the file /etc/vsftpd.conf, type

```
rpm -q --whatprovides /etc/vsftpd.conf
```

RPM then prints the name of the package that provides the file, like this:

```
vsftpd-2.0.1-2
```

If you provide the name of a package instead of a filename, RPM displays the name of the RPM package that contains the specified package.

On the other hand, to find the names of RPMs that need a specific package, use the following command:

```
rpm -q --whatrequires packagename
```

For example, to see which packages need the openssl package, type

```
rpm -q --whatrequires openssl
```

The output from this command shows all the RPM packages that need the openssl package.

Installing an RPM

To install an RPM, use the `rpm -i` command. You have to provide the name of the RPM file as the argument. If you want to view the progress of the RPM installation, use `rpm -ivh`. A series of hash marks (#) displays as the package is unpacked. For example, to install an RPM file named samba-3.0.9-2.1.i586.rpm, go the directory where the file is located and then type the following command to install it:

```
rpm -ivh samba-*.rpm
```

TIP: You don't have to type the full RPM filename — you can use a few characters from the beginning of the name followed by an asterisk (*). Make sure you type enough of the name to identify the RPM file uniquely.

If you try to install an RPM that's already installed, the `rpm -i` command displays an error message.

Removing an RPM

You may want to remove — uninstall — a package if you realize you don't really need the software. For example, if you have installed the X Window System development package but discover you're not interested in writing GUI applications, you can easily remove the package by using the `rpm -e` command.

You have to know the name of the package before you can remove it. One good way to find the name is to use `rpm -qa` in conjunction with `grep` to search for the appropriate RPM file.

For example, to remove the package named `qt3-devel`, type

```
rpm -e qt3-devel
```

To remove an RPM, you don't need the full RPM filename; all you need is the package name — the first part of the filename up to the dash (-) before the version number.

The `rpm -e` command does not remove a package that other packages need.

Upgrading an RPM

Use the `rpm -U` command to upgrade an RPM. You must provide the name of the RPM file that contains the new software. For example, if I have version 1.1.20 of `cups` (printing system) installed on my system but I want to upgrade to version 1.1.21, I download the RPM file `cups-1.1.21-5.3.i586.rpm` from a repository and use the following command:

```
rpm -U cups-1.1.21-5.3.i586.rpm
```

The `rpm` command performs the upgrade by removing the old version of the `cups` package and installing the new RPM.

TIP: Whenever possible, upgrade rather than remove the old package and install a new one. Upgrading automatically saves your old configuration files, which saves you the hassle of reconfiguring the software after a fresh installation.

Chapter 19

Securing SUSE Linux

In This Chapter

▶ Understanding host and network security issues
▶ Getting familiar with computer security terminology
▶ Practicing good host security
▶ Securing the network
▶ Keeping up with security news and updates

*I*n this chapter, I explain why you need to worry about security and give you a high-level view of how to get a handle on security. I explain the two key aspects of security — host security and network security — and introduce you to the terminology used in discussing computer security. Then I provide an overview of how to secure the host (the stand-alone PC) and the network. Finally, I end by pointing out a few resources that can help you keep up with security news and updates.

Why Worry about Security?

In today's networked world, you have to worry about your SUSE Linux system's security. For a stand-alone system, or a system used in an isolated local area network (LAN), you have to focus on protecting the system from the users and the users from one another. In other words, you don't want a user to modify or delete system files, whether intentionally or unintentionally. Also, you don't want a user destroying another user's files.

If your SUSE Linux system is connected to the Internet, you have to secure the system from unwanted accesses over the Internet. These intruders — or *crackers,* as they are commonly known — typically impersonate a user, steal or destroy information, and even deny you access to your own system (known as a *Denial of Service* or *DoS* attack).

By its very nature, an Internet connection makes your system accessible to any other system on the Internet. After all, the Internet connects a huge number of networks across the globe. In fact, the client/server architecture of Internet services, such as HTTP (Web) and FTP, rely on the wide-open network access the Internet provides. Unfortunately, the easy accessibility to Internet services running on your system also means that anyone on the Net can easily access your system.

If you operate an Internet host that provides information to others, you certainly want everyone to access your system's Internet services, such as FTP and Web servers. However, these servers often have vulnerabilities that crackers may exploit in order to cause harm to your system. You need to know about the potential security risks of Internet services — and the precautions you can take to minimize the risk of someone exploiting the weaknesses of your FTP or Web server.

You also want to protect your company's internal network from outsiders, even though your goal is to provide information to the outside world through a Web or FTP server. You can protect your internal network by setting up an Internet *firewall* — a controlled access point to the internal network — and placing the Web and FTP servers on a host outside the firewall.

Understanding Linux Security

To secure a Linux system, you have to tackle two broad categories of security issues:

- **Host security issues** that relate to securing the operating system and the files and directories on the system
- **Network security issues** that refer to the threat of attacks over the network connection

Understanding the host security issues

Here are some high-level guidelines to address host security (I cover some of these topics in detail later in this chapter):

- When installing SUSE Linux, select only the package groups that you need for your system. Don't install unnecessary software. For example, if your system is used as a workstation, you don't have to install most of the servers (Web server, news server, and so on).
- Create initial user accounts and make sure all passwords are strong enough that password-cracking programs can't "guess" them. SUSE Linux includes tools to enforce strong passwords.
- Set file ownerships and permissions to protect important files and directories.

- Use the GNU Privacy Guard (GnuPG) to encrypt or decrypt files with sensitive information and to authenticate files that you download from the Internet. GnuPG comes with SUSE Linux and you can use the `gpg` command to perform the tasks such as encrypting or decrypting a file.

- Use file integrity-checking tools, such as Tripwire, to monitor any changes to crucial system files and directories. The open source version of Tripwire (which is somewhat old) is available from www.tripwire.org. Visit www.tripwire.com for the commercial version.

- Periodically check various log files for signs of any break-ins or attempted break-ins. These log files are in the /var/log directory of your system.

- Install security updates to SUSE Linux as soon as they become available. These security updates fix known vulnerabilities in SUSE Linux. You can get these updates by using the YaST Online Update that I describe in Chapter 18.

Understanding network security issues

The issue of network security comes up as soon as you connect your organization's internal network to the Internet. You need to think of network security even if you connect a single computer to the Internet, but security concerns are more pressing when an entire internal network is opened to the world.

If you're an experienced system administrator, you already know that the cost of managing an Internet presence doesn't worry corporate management; their main concern is security. To get your management's backing for the Web site, you have to lay out a plan to keep the corporate network secure from intruders.

You may think that you can avoid jeopardizing the internal network by connecting only the external servers, such as Web and FTP servers, to the Internet. However, employing this simplistic approach isn't wise. It's like deciding not to drive because you may have an accident. Not having a network connection between your Web server and your internal network also has the following drawbacks:

- You cannot use network file transfers, such as FTP, to copy documents and data from your internal network to the Web server.

- Users on the internal network cannot access the corporate Web server.

- Users on the internal network don't have access to Web servers on the Internet. Such a restriction makes a valuable resource — the Web — inaccessible to the users in your organization.

A practical solution to this problem is to set up an Internet firewall and to put the Web server on a highly secured host outside the firewall.

In addition to using a firewall, here are some of the other steps to take to address network security (I explain these further, later in this chapter):

- Enable only those Internet services you need on a system. In particular, don't enable services that are not properly configured.
- Use Secure Shell (ssh) for remote logins. Don't use the r commands, such as rlogin and rsh.
- Secure any Internet services, such as FTP or TELNET, that you want to run on your system. Better yet, don't run them unless you need them.
- Promptly fix any known vulnerabilities of Internet services that you choose to run. You can download and install the latest security updates for SUSE Linux by using the YaST Online Update.

Getting Familiar with Computer Security Terminology

Computer books, magazine articles, and experts on computer security use a number of terms with unique meanings. You need to know these terms to understand discussions about computer security (and to communicate effectively with security vendors). Table 19-1 describes some of the commonly used computer security terms.

Table 19-1   Commonly Used Computer Security Terminology

Term	Description
Application gateway	A proxy service that acts as a gateway for application-level protocols, such as FTP, HTTP, NNTP, and SSH.
Authentication	The process of confirming that a user is indeed who he or she claims to be. The typical authentication method is a challenge-response method wherein the user enters a username and secret password to confirm his or her identity.
Backdoor	A security weakness a cracker places on a host in order to bypass security features.

Term	Description
Bastion host	A highly secured computer that serves as an organization's main point of presence on the Internet. A bastion host typically resides on the perimeter network, but a dual-homed host (with one network interface connected to the Internet and the other to the internal network) is also a bastion host.
Buffer overflow	A security flaw in a program that enables a cracker to send an excessive amount of data to that program and to overwrite parts of the running program with code in the data being sent. The result is that the cracker can execute arbitrary code on the system and possibly gain access to the system as a privileged user.
Certificate	An electronic document that identifies an entity (such as an individual, an organization, or a computer) and associates a public key with that identity. A certificate contains the certificate holder's name, a serial number, expiration date, a copy of the certificate holder's public key, and the digital signature of the Certificate Authority so a recipient can verify that the certificate is real.
Certificate Authority (CA)	An organization that validates identities and issues certificates.
Cracker	A person who breaks into (or attempts to break into) a host, often with malicious intent.
Confidentiality	Of data, a state of being accessible to no one but you (usually achieved by encryption).
Decryption	The process of transforming encrypted information into its original, intelligible form.
Denial of Service (DoS)	An attack that uses so many of the resources on your computer and network that legitimate users cannot access and use the system. From a single source, the attack overwhelms the target computer with messages and blocks legitimate traffic. It can prevent one system from being able to exchange data with other systems or prevent the system from using the Internet.
Distributed Denial of Service (DDoS)	A variant of the denial-of-service attack that uses a coordinated attack from a distributed system of computers rather than a single source. It often makes use of worms to spread to multiple computers that can then attack the target.

(continued)

Table 19-1 *(continued)*

Term	Description
Digital signature	A one-way MD5 or SHA-1 hash of a message encrypted with the private key of the message originator, used to verify the integrity of a message and ensure nonrepudiation.
DMZ	Another name for the perimeter network. (DMZ originally stood for *demilitarized zone,* the buffer zone separating the warring North and South in Korea and Vietnam.)
Dual-homed host	A computer with two network interfaces (think of each network as a home).
Encryption	The process of transforming information so it's unintelligible to anyone but the intended recipient. The transformation is done by a mathematical operation between a key and the information.
Exploit tools	Publicly available and sophisticated tools that intruders of various skill levels can use to determine vulnerabilities and gain entry into targeted systems.
Firewall	A controlled-access gateway between an organization's internal network and the Internet. A dual-homed host can be configured as a firewall.
Hash	The result when a mathematical function converts a message into a fixed-size numeric value known as a *message digest* (or *hash*). The MD5 algorithm, for example, produces a 128-bit message digest; the Secure Hash Algorithm-1 (SHA-1) generates a 160-bit message digest. The hash of a message is encrypted with the private key of the sender to produce the digital signature.
Host	A computer on a network that is configured to offer services to other computers on the network.
Integrity	Of received data, a state of being the same as originally sent (that is, unaltered in transit).
IPSec (IP Security Protocol)	A security protocol for the Network layer of the OSI Networking Model, designed to provide cryptographic security services for IP packets. IPSec provides encryption-based authentication, integrity, access control, and confidentiality.

Term	Description
IP spoofing	An attack in which a cracker figures out the IP address of a trusted host and then sends packets that appear to come from the trusted host. The attacker can send packets but cannot see responses. However, the attacker can predict the sequence of packets and essentially send commands that set up a backdoor for future break-ins.
Logic bombs	A form of sabotage in which a programmer inserts code that causes the program to perform a destructive action, such as terminating the programmer's employment, when some triggering event occurs, such as terminating the programmer's employment.
Nonrepudiation	A security feature that prevents the sender of data from being able to deny ever having sent the data.
Packet	A collection of bytes, assembled according to a specific protocol, that serves as the basic unit of communication on a network. On TCP/IP networks, for example, the packet may be referred to as an *IP packet* or a *TCP/IP packet*.
Packet filtering	Selective blocking of packets according to type of packet (as specified by the source and destination IP address or port).
Perimeter network	A network between the Internet and the protected internal network. The perimeter network (also known as DMZ) is where the bastion host resides.
Port scanning	A method of discovering which ports are open (in other words, which Internet services are enabled) on a system, performed by sending connection requests to the ports, one by one. This procedure is usually a precursor to further attacks.
Proxy server	A server on the bastion host that enables internal clients to access external servers (and enables external clients to access servers inside the protected network). There are proxy servers for various Internet services, such as FTP and HTTP.
Public-key cryptography	An encryption method that uses a pair of keys — a private key and a public key — to encrypt and decrypt the information. Anything encrypted with the public key is decrypted only with the corresponding private key, and vice versa.

(continued)

Table 19-1 *(continued)*

Term	Description
Public-Key Infrastructure (PKI)	A set of standards and services that enables the use of public-key cryptography and certificates in a networked environment. PKI facilitates tasks, such as issuing, renewing, and revoking certificates, and generating and distributing public- and private-key pairs.
Screening router	An Internet router that filters packets.
Setuid program	A program that runs with the permissions of the owner regardless of who runs the program. For example, if `root` owns a setuid program, that program has `root` privileges regardless of who started the program. Crackers often exploit vulnerabilities in setuid programs to gain privileged access to a system.
Sniffer	Synonymous with packet sniffer — a program that intercepts routed data and examines each packet in search of specified information, such as passwords transmitted in clear text.
Symmetric-key encryption	An encryption method wherein the same key is used to encrypt and decrypt the information.
Spyware	Any software that covertly gathers user information through the user's Internet connection and, usually, transmits that information in the background to someone else. Spyware can also gather information about e-mail addresses and even passwords and credit card numbers. Spyware is similar to a Trojan horse in that users are tricked into installing spyware when they install something else.
Threat	An event or activity, deliberate or unintentional, with the potential for causing harm to a system or network.
Trojan horse	A program that masquerades as a benign program, but, in fact is a backdoor used for attacking a system. Attackers often install a collection of Trojan horse programs that enable the attacker to freely access the system with `root` privileges, yet hide that fact from the system administrator. Such collections of Trojan horse programs are called *rootkits*.
Virus	A self-replicating program that spreads from one computer to another by attaching itself to other programs.
Vulnerability	A flaw or weakness that may cause harm to a system or network.

Term	Description
War-dialing	Simple programs that dial consecutive phone numbers looking for modems.
War-driving	A method of gaining entry into wireless computer net works using a laptop, antennas, and a wireless network card that involves patrolling locations to gain unauthorized access.
Worm	A self-replicating program that copies itself from one computer to another over a network.

Practicing Good Host Security

Host is the techie term for your Linux system — especially when you use it to provide services on a network. But the term makes sense even when you think of the computer by itself; it's the host for everything that runs on it — the operating system and all the applications. A key aspect of computer security is to secure the host.

In this section, I take you through a few key steps to follow in securing your SUSE Linux host. These steps include installing operating system updates (following steps that I outline in Chapter 18), protecting passwords, and protecting the files and directories.

Making passwords expire

Obviously, leaving passwords lying around where anyone can get at them — even if they're encrypted — is bad security. So instead of storing passwords in the /etc/passwd file (which any user can read), Linux now stores them in a shadow password file, /etc/shadow. Only the superuser (root) can read this file.

The /etc/shadow file also includes fields that control when each password expires. You can use the chage command to change the password-expiration information. For starters, you can check a user's password-expiration information by using the chage command with the -l option, as follows (in this case, you have to be logged in as root):

```
chage -l root
```

This command displays expiration information, including how long the password lasts and how often you can change the password.

If you want to ensure that the user is forced to change a password every 90 days, you can use the `-M` option to set the maximum number of days that a password stays valid. For example, to make sure that user `naba` is prompted to change the password in 90 days, I log in as `root` and type the following command:

```
chage -M 90 naba
```

You can use the command for each user account to ensure that all passwords expire when appropriate, and that all users must pick new passwords.

Protecting files and directories

One important aspect of securing the host is to protect important system files — and the directories that contain these files. You can protect the files through the file ownership and through the permission settings that control who can read, write, or (in case of executable programs) execute the files.

The default Linux file security is controlled through the following settings for each file or directory:

- User ownership
- Group ownership
- Read, write, execute permissions for the owner
- Read, write, execute permissions for the group
- Read, write, execute permissions for others (everyone else)

Viewing ownerships and permissions

You can see these settings for a file when you look at the detailed listing with the `ls -l` command. For example, type the following command to see the detailed listing of the `/etc/inittab` file:

```
ls -l /etc/inittab
```

The resulting listing looks something like this:

```
-rw-r--r--  1 root root 2926 Nov 12 20:11 /etc/inittab
```

In Chapter 6, I explain how to interpret the first ten characters on that line. For now, you should know that the set of nine characters, starting with the second one, describes the file permissions for user, group, and others. The third and fourth fields show the user and group that own this file. In this case, both user and group names are the same: `root`.

Chapter 19: Securing SUSE Linux

Changing file ownerships

You can set the user and group ownerships with the `chown` command. For example, if the file `/dev/hda` should be owned by the user `root` and the group `disk`, type the following command as `root` to set up this ownership:

```
chown root.disk /dev/hda
```

To change the group ownership alone, use the `chgrp` command. For example, here's how you can change the group ownership of the file `ledger.out` from whatever it was earlier to the group named `accounting`:

```
chgrp accounting ledger.out
```

Changing file permissions

You may need to change a file's permission settings to protect it from others. Use the `chmod` command to change the permission settings of a file or a directory.

To use `chmod` effectively, you have to specify the permission settings. A good way is to *concatenate* one or more letters from each column of Table 19-2, in the order shown (Who/Action/Permission).

Table 19-2   File Permission Codes

Who	Action	Permission
u user	+ add	r read
g group	- remove	w write
o others	= assign	x execute
a all	s set user ID	

For example, to give everyone read access to all files in a directory, pick a (for *all*) from the first column, + (for *add*) from the second column, and r (for *read*) from the third column to come up with the permission setting a+r. Then use the whole set of options with `chmod`, like this:

```
chmod a+r *
```

On the other hand, to permit everyone to read and execute one specific file, type

```
chmod a+rx filename
```

> **TIP**
>
> Suppose you have a file named `mystuff` that you want to protect. You can make it accessible to no one but you if you type the following commands, in this order:
>
> ```
> chmod a-rwx mystuff
> chmod u+rw mystuff
> ```
>
> The first command turns off all permissions for everyone, and the second command turns *on* the read and write permissions for the owner (you). Type **ls -l** to verify that the change took place. (You see a permission setting of `-rw-------`.)

Another way to specify a permission setting is to use a three-digit sequence of numbers. In a detailed listing, the read, write, and execute permission settings for the user, group, and others appear as the sequence

```
rwxrwxrwx
```

with dashes in place of letters for disallowed operations. Think of `rwxrwxrwx` as three occurrences of the string `rwx`. Now assign the values r=4, w=2, and x=1 (use zero for a missing letter — one that appears as a dash). To get the value of the sequence `rwx`, simply add the values of r, w, and x. Thus, `rwx` = 7 (4+2+1). Using this formula, you can assign a three-digit value to any permission setting. For example, if the user can read and write the file but everyone else can only read the file, the permission setting is `rw-r--r--` (that's how it appears in the listing), and the value is 644 because `rw-` is 4+2, which is 6 and `r--` is just 4 (for r alone). Thus, if you want all files in a directory to be readable by everyone but writable only by the user, use the following command:

```
chmod 644 *
```

Setting default permission

What permission setting does a file get when you (or a program) create a new file? The answer is in what is known as the user file-creation mask that you can see and set using the `umask` command.

Type **umask**, and it prints out a number showing the current file-creation mask. The default setting is different for the `root` user and other normal users. For the `root` user, the mask is set to 022, whereas the mask for normal users is 002. To see the effect of this file-creation mask and to interpret the meaning of the mask, follow these steps:

1. **Log in as `root` and type the following command:**

    ```
    touch junkfile
    ```

    This command creates a file named `junkfile` with nothing in it.

2. **Type** ls -l junkfile **to see that file's permissions.**

    You see a line similar to the following:

    ```
    -rw-r--r--  1 naba users 0 2005-01-30 16:23 junkfile
    ```

    Interpret the numerical value of the permission setting by converting each three-letter permission in the first field (excluding the very first letter) into a number between 0 and 7. For each letter that's present, the first letter gets a value of 4, second letter is 2, and the third is 1. For example, rw- translates to 4+2+0 (because the third letter is missing) or 6. Similarly, r-- is 4+0+0 = 4. Thus the permission string -rw-r--r-- becomes 644.

 3. **Subtract the numerical permission setting from 666 and what you get is the** umask **setting.**

    In this case, 666 – 644 results in an umask of 022.

Thus, an umask of 022 results in a default permission setting of 666 – 022 = 644. When you rewrite 644 in terms of a permission string, it becomes rw-r--r--.

To set a new umask, type **umask** followed by the numerical value of the mask. Here is how you go about it:

 1. **Figure out what permission settings you want for new files.**

    For example, if you want new files that can be read and written only by the owner and by nobody else, the permission setting looks like this:

    ```
    rw-------
    ```

 2. **Convert the permissions into a numerical value by using the conversion method that assigns 4 to the first field, 2 to the second, and 1 to the third.**

    Thus, for files that are readable and writable only by their owner, the permission setting is 600.

 3. **Subtract the desired permission setting from 666 to get the value of the mask.**

    For a permission setting of 600, the mask becomes 666 – 600 = 066.

 4. **Use the** umask **command to set the file-creation mask:**

    ```
    umask 066
    ```

A default umask of 022 is good for system security because it translates to files that have read and write permission for the owner and read permissions for everyone else. The bottom line is that you don't want a default umask that results in files that are writable by the whole wide world.

Checking for set user ID permission

Another permission setting called set user ID (or `setuid` for short) can be a security hazard. When the `setuid` permission is enabled, the file executes under the user ID of the file's owner. In other words, if an executable program is owned by `root` and the `setuid` permission is set, no matter who executes that program, it runs as if `root` is executing it. This permission means that the program can do a lot more (for example, read all files, create new files, and delete files) than what a normal user program can do. Another risk is that if a `setuid` program file has some security hole, crackers can do a lot more damage through such programs than through other vulnerabilities.

You can find all `setuid` programs with a simple `find` command (remember to type **su -** to become `root`):

```
find / -type f -perm +4000 -print
```

You see a list of files such as the following:

```
/bin/su
/bin/ping
/bin/eject
/bin/mount
... lines deleted ...
```

Many of the programs have the `setuid` permission because they need it, but check the complete list and make sure that there are no strange `setuid` programs (for example, `setuid` programs in a user's home directory).

If you want to see how these permissions are listed by the `ls` command, type **ls -l /usr/bin/passwd** and you see the permission settings:

```
-rwsr-xr-x  1 root shadow 80036 2004-10-02 05:08 /usr/bin/passwd
```

The `s` in the owner's permission setting (`rws`) tells you that the `setuid` permission is set.

Securing the Network

To secure your SUSE Linux system, you have to pay attention to both host security and network security. The distinction between the two types of security is somewhat arbitrary because securing the network involves fixing up things on the host that relate to what Internet services your system offers. In this section, I explain how you can secure the Internet services (mostly by not offering unnecessary services), how you can use a firewall to stop unwanted network packets from reaching your network, and how to use Secure Shell for secure remote logins.

Securing Internet services

For an Internet-connected Linux system (or even one on a LAN that's not connected to the Internet), a significant threat is the possibility that someone could use one of many Internet services to gain access to your system. Each service — such as mail, Web, or FTP — requires running a server program that responds to client requests arriving over the TCP/IP network. Some of these server programs have weaknesses that can allow an outsider to log in to your system — maybe with `root` privileges. Luckily, Linux comes with some facilities that you can use to make the Internet services more secure.

> **WARNING!** Potential intruders can employ a *port-scanning tool* — a program that attempts to establish a TCP/IP connection at a port and to look for a response — to check which Internet servers are running on your system. Then, to gain access to your system, the intruders can potentially exploit any known weaknesses of one or more services.

Turning off stand-alone services

To provide Internet services such as Web, mail, and FTP, your Linux system has to run server programs that listen to incoming TCP/IP network requests. Some of these servers are started when your system boots, and they run all the time. Such servers are called *stand-alone servers*. The Web server and mail server are examples of stand-alone servers.

Another server, called `xinetd`, starts other servers that are configured to work under `xinetd`. Some servers can be configured to run stand-alone or under a superserver such as `xinetd`. For example, the `vsftpd` FTP server can be configured to run stand-alone or to run under the control of `xinetd`.

> **TIP** You can turn the servers on or off by using the `chkconfig` command. For example, to turn off the FTP service, type **chkconfig vsftpd off**.

Configuring the Internet superserver

In addition to stand-alone servers such as a Web server or mail server, there is another server — `xinetd` — that you have to configure separately. The `xinetd` server is called *Internet superserver* because it can start other servers on demand.

The `xinetd` server reads a configuration file named `/etc/xinetd.conf` at startup. This file, in turn, refers to configuration files stored in the `/etc/xinetd.d` directory. The configuration files in `/etc/xinetd.d` tell `xinetd` which ports to listen to and which server to start for each port. Type **ls /etc/xinetd.d** to see a list of the files in the `/etc/xinetd.d` directory on your system. Each file represents a service that `xinetd` can start. To turn off any of these services, type **chkconfig *filename* off** where *filename* is the name of the configuration file in the `/etc/xinetd.d` directory. After you turn any of these services on or off, you must restart the `xinetd` server; otherwise, the changes don't take effect. To restart the `xinetd` server, type **/etc/init.d/xinetd restart**. This command stops the `xinetd` server and then starts it again. When it restarts, it reads the configuration files, and the changes take effect.

Configuring TCP wrapper security

A security feature of `xinetd` is its use of a feature called *TCP wrapper* to start various services. The *TCP wrapper* is a block of code that provides an access-control facility for Internet services, acting like a protective package for your message. The TCP wrapper can start other services, such as FTP and `vnc` (a server that enables other computers to view and interact with your computer's graphical desktop); but before starting a service, it consults the `/etc/hosts.allow` file to see whether the host requesting service is allowed that service. If nothing appears in `/etc/hosts.allow` about that host, the TCP wrapper checks the `/etc/hosts.deny` file to see if it denies the service. If both files are empty, the TCP wrapper provides access to the requested service.

Here are the steps to follow to tighten the access to the services that `inted` or `xinetd` are configured to start:

1. **Use a text editor to edit the `/etc/hosts.deny` file, adding the following line into that file:**

    ```
    ALL:ALL
    ```

    This setting denies all hosts access to any Internet services on your system.

2. **Edit the `/etc/hosts.allow` file and add to it the names of hosts that can access services on your system.**

    For example, to enable only hosts from the 192.168.1.0 network and the `localhost` (IP address 127.0.0.1) to access the services on your system, place the following line in the `/etc/hosts.allow` file:

    ```
    ALL: 192.168.1.0/255.255.255.0 127.0.0.1
    ```

3. **If you want to permit access to a specific Internet service to a specific remote host, you can do so by using the following syntax for a line in `/etc/hosts.allow`:**

    ```
    server_program_name: hosts
    ```

Here `server_program_name` is the name of the server program, and `hosts` is a comma-separated list of hosts that can access the service. You may also write `hosts` as a network address or an entire domain name, such as `.mycompany.com`.

Using Secure Shell (SSH) for remote logins

SUSE Linux comes with the *Open Secure Shell* (OpenSSH) software that uses public-key cryptography to authenticate users and to encrypt the communication between two hosts, so users can securely log in from remote systems and copy files securely.

In this section, I briefly describe how to use the OpenSSH software in SUSE Linux. The OpenSSH software is installed during SUSE Linux installation. OpenSSH uses public-key encryption where the sender and receiver both have a pair of keys — a public key and a private key. The public keys are freely distributed, and each party knows the other's public key. The sender encrypts data by using the recipient's public key. Only the recipient's private key can then decrypt the data.

To use OpenSSH, you first need to start the `sshd` server and then generate the host keys. Here's how:

- If you want to support SSH-based remote logins on a host, start the `sshd` server on your system. Type **ps ax | grep sshd** to see if the server is already running. If not, in a terminal window type **su -** to become `root`, and turn on the SSH service.

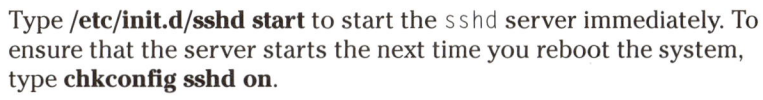

  Type **/etc/init.d/sshd start** to start the `sshd` server immediately. To ensure that the server starts the next time you reboot the system, type **chkconfig sshd on**.

- Generate the host keys with the following command:

  ```
  ssh-keygen -d -f /etc/ssh/ssh_host_key -N ''
  ```

  The `-d` flag causes the `ssh-keygen` program to generate DSA keys, which the SSH2 protocol uses. If you see a message saying that the file `/etc/ssh/ssh_host_key` already exists, that means that the key pairs were generated during SUSE Linux installation. In that case, press **n** to avoid overwriting the keys and continue to use the existing file.

A user can now log in from a remote system using the ssh command (assuming that the remote system also runs Linux). From a Windows system, a user can run a program such as putty that supports SSH.

For example, to log into my account on a SUSE Linux system from another Linux system on the network, I type

ssh 192.168.0.6 -l naba

Here I identify the remote host by its IP address (192.168.0.6). When prompted for the password, I enter the password. After that, I can have a secure login session with the remote host. (The information sent between the two systems is encrypted.)

Setting up a simple firewall

A *firewall* is a network device or host with two or more network interfaces — one connected to the protected internal network and the other connected to unprotected networks, such as the Internet. The firewall controls access to and from the protected internal network.

If you connect an internal network directly to the Internet, you have to make sure that every system on the internal network is properly secured — which can be nearly impossible because just one careless user can render the entire internal network vulnerable. A firewall is a single point of connection to the Internet: You can direct all your efforts toward making that firewall system a daunting barrier to unauthorized external users. Essentially, a firewall is like a protective fence that keeps unwanted external data and software out and sensitive internal data and software in. (See Figure 19-1.)

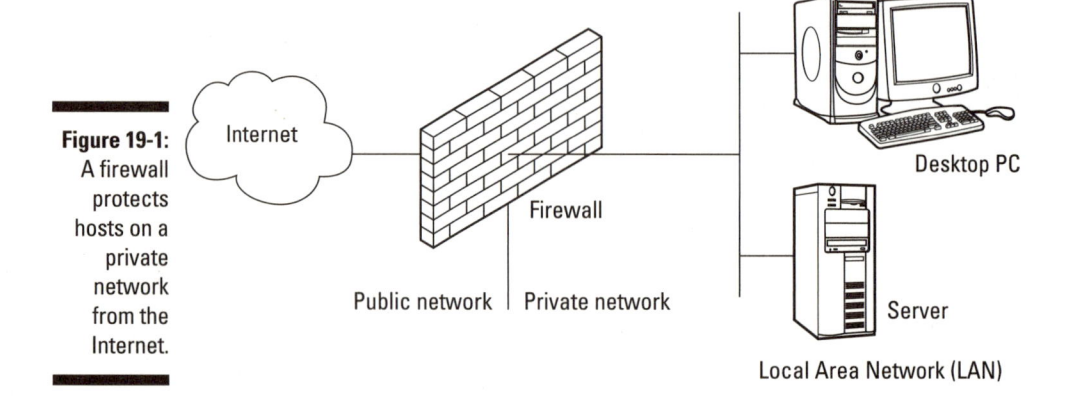

Figure 19-1: A firewall protects hosts on a private network from the Internet.

The firewall runs software that examines the network packets arriving at its network interfaces and takes appropriate actions based on a set of rules. The idea is to define these rules so that they allow only authorized network traffic

Chapter 19: Securing SUSE Linux **305**

to flow between the two interfaces. Configuring the firewall involves setting up the rules properly. A configuration strategy is to reject all network traffic and then enable only a limited set of network packets to go through the firewall. The authorized network traffic would include the connections necessary to enable internal users to do things such as visiting Web sites and receiving electronic mail.

Your SUSE Linux system comes with built-in packet-filtering capability that provides a simple firewall. The Linux kernel's built-in packet-filtering capability is handy when you don't have a dedicated firewall between your Linux system and the Internet. This is the case, for example, when you connect your Linux system to the Internet through a DSL or cable modem. You can essentially have a packet-filtering firewall inside your Linux system, sitting between the kernel and the applications.

SUSE Linux includes a GUI tool to turn on a packet filtering firewall. To set up a firewall, follow these steps:

1. **Choose Main Menu⇨System⇨YaST to start the YaST Control Center.**

   The YaST Control Center window appears.

2. **Choose YaST Control Center⇨Security and Users⇨Firewall.**

   YaST opens the Firewall Configuration Basic Settings window (see Figure 19-2) that you can use to configure the firewall in four steps. If you had already set up a firewall when you installed SUSE Linux, YaST takes you to a firewall configuration screen from where you can stop or reconfigure the firewall.

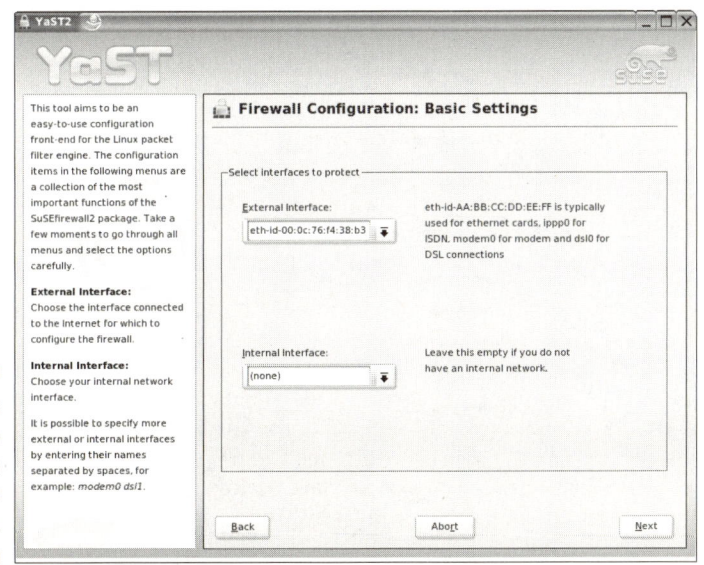

Figure 19-2: Specify the network interfaces to protect.

306 Part IV: Becoming a SUSE Wizard

3. **Select the network interfaces to protect (see Figure 19-2). Click Next.**

   YaST displays the Firewall Configuration Services window, as shown in Figure 19-3.

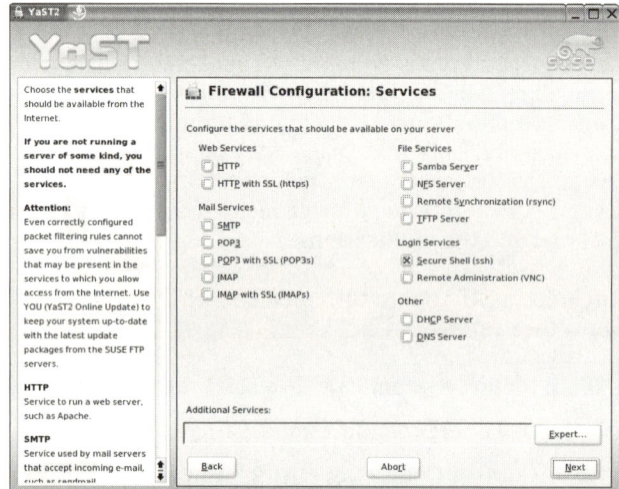

Figure 19-3: Specify the services to allow.

4. **Select services (such as Samba and Secure Shell) that your SUSE system should be allowed to provide (see Figure 19-3). Click Next.**

   YaST displays the Firewall Configuration Features window, as shown in Figure 19-4.

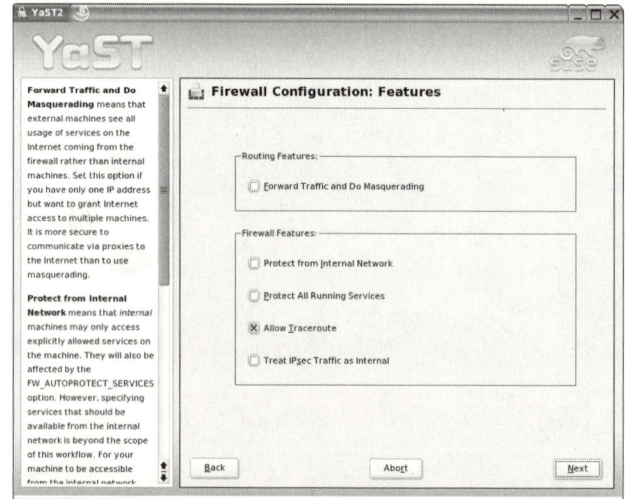

Figure 19-4: Specify the other features of the firewall.

5. **Enable other features (see Figure 19-4) such as forwarding packets between network interfaces (if your PC has more than one network interface). Click Next.**

   YaST displays the Firewall Configuration Logging Options window, as shown in Figure 19-5.

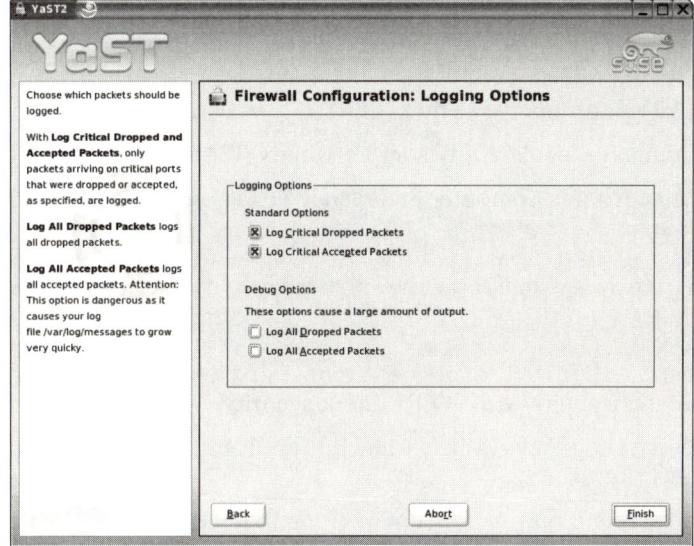

Figure 19-5: Specify the logging options for the firewall.

6. **Turn on different levels of logging (see Figure 19-5). Click Finish to turn on the firewall.**

Using NATs

Network Address Translation (NAT) is an effective tool that enables you to "hide" the network addresses of an internal network behind a firewall. In essence, NAT allows an organization to use private network addresses behind a firewall while still maintaining the ability to connect to external systems through the firewall.

TIP

You can implement NAT by purchasing a NAT router that can connect your internal network to a DSL or cable modem. I describe NAT routers in Chapter 7.

Keeping Up with Security News and Updates

To keep up with the latest security alerts, you may want to visit one or more of the following sites on a daily basis:

- Novell's online Linux security support Web site at `www.novell.com/linux/security/securitysupport.html`
- CERT Coordination Center (CERT/CC) at `www.cert.org`
- Computer Incident Advisory Capability (CIAC) at `www.ciac.org/ciac`
- United States Computer Emergency Readiness Team (US-CERT) at `www.us-cert.gov`

If you have access to Internet newsgroups, you can periodically browse the following:

- `comp.security.announce`: A moderated newsgroup that includes announcements from CERT about security.
- `comp.security.linux`: A newsgroup that includes discussions of Linux security issues.
- `comp.security.unix`: A newsgroup that includes discussions of UNIX security issues, including items related to Linux.

If you prefer to receive regular security updates through e-mail, you can also sign up for (subscribe to) various mailing lists:

- **FOCUS-LINUX:** Fill out the form at `www.securityfocus.com/subscribe` to subscribe to this mailing list focused on Linux security issues.
- **US-CERT National Cyber Alert System:** Follow the directions at `www.us-cert.gov` to subscribe to this mailing list. The Cyber Alert System features four categories of security information through its mailing lists:
    - Technical Cyber Security Alerts provide technical information about vulnerabilities in various common software products.
    - Cyber Security Alerts are sent when vulnerabilities affect the general public. They outline the steps and actions that nontechnical home and corporate computer users can take to protect themselves from attacks.
    - Cyber Security Bulletins are biweekly summaries of security issues and new vulnerabilities along with patches, workarounds, and other actions that users can take to help reduce the risk.
    - Cyber Security Tips offer advice on common security issues for nontechnical computer users.

Part V
The Part of Tens

The 5th Wave — By Rich Tennant

In this part...

Here we go again — yet another Top Ten list . . . No, wait . . . a whole slew of Top Ten lists! It's the signature part of the *For Dummies* series. Hey, I can't argue with success!

I begin with a selected set of frequently asked questions (or FAQs, as everyone calls them) about SUSE Linux. Next comes the ten best things about SUSE. Then I present ten good resources for finding out more about SUSE. Finally, I end with the ten most frequently used SUSE Linux commands.

Chapter 20

Ten Frequently Asked Questions about SUSE

In This Chapter

▶ What does SUSE stand for?

▶ Where can I find answers to SUSE Linux questions?

▶ When is the next SUSE release?

▶ Can I get ISO files for SUSE Linux from the Internet?

▶ How do I do an FTP install of SUSE Linux?

▶ How can I auto-login into KDE as another user?

▶ How can I reboot after an apparent crash?

▶ How do I schedule a command to run every 30 minutes?

▶ How can I find all the huge files on my system?

▶ Where can I find SUSE RPMs?

If you are new to SUSE Linux, you probably have lots of questions about SUSE (even if you already know Linux). I had questions when I first started using SUSE Linux, and I have been using Linux since 1991. Frequently Asked Questions — FAQs — are the time-honored solution to providing answers to common questions about a specific subject. In this chapter, I present ten such frequently asked questions about SUSE Linux. These are the questions that, in my opinion, are likely to be asked by beginners and experienced Linux users alike. I hope you find an answer or two that help you do your job with SUSE Linux.

What Does SUSE Stand for and How Do You Pronounce It?

The acronym SUSE came from the German name *Software und System Entwicklung* (Software and System Development). SUSE is pronounced *soo-suh*.

The distribution was originally referred to by a mixed case name: SuSE. Now, however, the distribution's name is written in all uppercase: SUSE. Eventually, SUSE's origins as an acronym will probably be forgotten and it will be thought of as a name that doesn't stand for anything at all.

How Can I Find Answers to My SUSE Linux Questions?

You can find helpful information about SUSE Linux at many online resources. Start with `www.suse.com`. Choose Support⇨knowledgebase from that Web page's menu. Then select SUSE as the product, type in one or more keywords, and click Search Now.

If you don't find the answer at `www.suse.com`, try searching newsgroups through the Advanced Groups Search on Google Groups:

```
http://groups.google.com/advanced_group_search?hl=en
```

Type the search terms you prefer. You can even set the date ranges for the articles to search.

If the newsgroup search does not give you the answer, do a Linux search on Google by visiting the search page at

```
http://www.google.com/linux
```

Type the search words and press Enter or click Google Search. For SUSE-specific answers, type **SUSE** in addition to the search words.

If you also want to search the SUSE mailing lists, visit `www.google.com` and type **lists site:lists.suse.com** followed by the search words. For example, to search for `DVD movie player` you would type **lists site:lists.suse.com DVD movie player** into the search field.

One of these online searches should get you the answer to your question. If not, you can post a question at one of the forums such as `www.suseforums.com` that are listed in Chapter 22.

When Is the Next SUSE Linux Release?

Everyone wants to know the answer to this question, including myself! Of course, the correct answer is, "Whenever Novell decides to release it." Based on past history, however, a new SUSE release seems to appear about every six months.

Can I Get ISO Files for SUSE Linux from the Internet?

When Novell releases a new version of SUSE Linux, it's initially available only as a commercial product. However, about eight weeks after the release date of the latest version, Novell makes available for free the ISO image files for that version. Novell also offers the necessary files on its FTP server from where you can perform an FTP install.

How Do I Do an FTP Install of SUSE Linux?

Say that you have this book in hand, but a later version of SUSE Linux is now available for FTP install. Instead of installing the version on the companion CD or DVD, you can easily do an FTP install.

To install SUSE Linux from one of many FTP servers that mirror the latest SUSE distribution, you have to perform the following major steps:

1. Download the SUSE boot image from the FTP server and burn a CD with that image.
2. Make a note of the FTP server's IP address and the directory where the SUSE distribution's files are located.
3. Boot the PC with the boot CD and then type a command at the boot prompt to begin an FTP install from the FTP server that you identify by its IP address.

If you have a PC that runs Windows and has a high-speed Internet connection, you can use that PC to download the boot image and burn the boot CD. You can also use the PC to look up the IP address of the FTP server.

You also need to know the name of the network card installed in your PC because you have to manually load the driver before you can start the SUSE FTP install. You can find the FTP server's IP address when you download the SUSE installer's boot image. I explain the steps in this section.

Part V: The Part of Tens

Installing SUSE from an FTP server can take two hours or more over a typical broadband DSL or cable modem connection to the Internet. Follow these steps to do an FTP install from an FTP server over the Internet:

1. **Use a Web browser to open the list of FTP servers at `www.suse.com/us/private/download/ftp/int_mirrors.html` and find an FTP server near you that's marked `complete` (that means the server has the complete SUSE distribution and all updates).**

   The list of servers is organized by country and it includes both FTP and HTTP (Web) servers. Go to the country nearest yours and pick the nearest server that's marked `complete`.

   In a terminal window, type **ping** followed by the name of the FTP server (for example, **mirror.mcs.anl.gov**). You'll then see the IP address of the FTP server on the next line (for example, 140.221.9.138). Write down that IP address for use later on. If you are performing this step in Microsoft Windows, you also use the `ping` command, but type the command in a Command Prompt window (choose Start⇨Run and type **cmd** and press Enter).

2. **Click your FTP server link and find the directory that contains the `boot.iso` file — that's the SUSE installer's boot image.**

   The directory depends on the version of SUSE. For example, for version 9.2, the `boot.iso` file is in the FTP server's `pub/suse/i386/9.2/boot/` directory. The file is several tens of megabytes in size.

3. **Download the `boot.iso` file and save it.**

4. **Burn the `boot.iso` image onto a CD.**

   Use your PC's CD burner application to burn the ISO image named `boot.iso`.

5. **Go to the PC on which you want to do the SUSE FTP install, insert the boot CD, and restart the PC.**

   If your PC isn't set up to boot from the CD/DVD drive, you have to enter SETUP (by pressing a key such as F2 as the PC powers up) and change the order of the boot devices.

   The PC reboots and, after a few moments, a text screen displays a screen with a number of options. Use the arrow keys to move between list items and the buttons on the screen.

6. **Use the arrow keys to select the Manual Installation option and press Enter.**

   The installer shows a list of languages.

7. **Select the language and press Enter.**

   The installer displays a list of keyboard maps — the language-dependent layouts for the keyboard.

Chapter 20: Ten Frequently Asked Questions about SUSE 315

8. **Select the keyboard language and press Enter.**

   The installer displays the Main menu.

9. **Use the arrow keys to select Kernel Modules (Hardware Drivers) and press Enter.**

   The installer displays a list of choices that includes options to load driver modules as well as view names of loaded modules.

10. **Use the arrow keys to select Load Network Card Modules and press Enter.**

    The installer displays a list of network driver modules, organized by the name of the network card.

11. **Use the arrow keys to select your network card and press Enter.**

    The installer prompts for any parameters for the driver. Press Enter if there are no parameters. If all goes well, the installer successfully loads the network driver module and displays a message. Press Enter to continue.

12. **Press the right-arrow key to select Back and press Enter.**

    You will be back at the Main menu.

13. **Use arrow keys to select Start Installation/System and press Enter. On the next screen, select Start Installation/Update and press Enter.**

    The installer displays a list of source mediums — this is where you indicate where the installer can find the files it needs to perform the installation.

14. **Select Network as the source medium and press Enter.**

    The installer prompts you for the network protocol.

15. **Select FTP as the network protocol and press Enter.**

    A dialog box prompts you to determine whether to configure the network automatically by using the Dynamic Host Configuration Protocol (DHCP). If your network uses DHCP as most do, select Yes and press Enter. Otherwise, you have to enter the IP address and the name server's IP address at this step. The installer then prompts for the IP address of the FTP server.

16. **Enter the IP address of the FTP server that you found in Step 1 (for example, enter** 140.221.9.138 **for the FTP server** mirror.mcs.anl.gov**).**

    The installer prompts you if you want to use a username and password to connect to the FTP server. Because the FTP servers support anonymous FTP — which means anyone can log in with the username anonymous — select No and press Enter. The installer also prompts if you want to use an HTTP proxy. Unless your PC is behind a proxy (which may be the case at some organizations), select No and press Enter. The installer then prompts for the name of the directory where the SUSE files are located.

17. **Enter the name of the directory on the FTP server where the SUSE Linux files are located and press Enter.**

    The directory name would be the parent directory of the location where you found the `boot.iso` file in Step 1. For example, if the `boot.iso` file is in `pub/suse/i386/9.2/boot/`, you should type **pub/suse/i386/9.2/** and press Enter.

    The installer displays a message informing you that it is loading data into ramdisk (which refers to an area of memory that acts as a hard drive). When the installer finishes downloading data, the YaST (that's what the SUSE installer is called) installer starts and displays its initial GUI screen.

    From this point on, the installation steps are the same as the ones for a CD/DVD install, which I explain in Chapter 2. You should jump to the point where the YaST installer displays its initial GUI screen.

How Can I Auto-Login into the KDE Desktop as Another User?

If yours is the only user account on your SUSE Linux system and you use the KDE desktop, you are probably accustomed to the convenience of auto-login. Basically, you just power up SUSE Linux and you are automatically logged into the KDE desktop.

You might face the question of changing the auto-login to another user if you have defined additional user accounts on your SUSE Linux system (for example, for your spouse or kids). If you want the auto-login to use another user account, it's easy to make that change from the KDE desktop by following these steps:

1. **Choose Main Menu⇨Control Center.**

    The KDE Control Center starts.

2. **Click System Administration in the left pane.**

    Icons for several system administration categories appear in the left pane.

3. **Click Login Manager in the left pane.**

    Login Manager options appear in tabs in the right pane.

Chapter 20: Ten Frequently Asked Questions about SUSE 317

4. **Click Administrator Mode.**

   A dialog box prompts you for the root password.

5. **Type the root password and click OK.**

   Login Manager options reappear with everything enabled (because you have entered administrator mode).

6. **Click the Convenience tab.**

   The Convenience tab's options appear, as shown in Figure 20-1. The Enable Auto-Login box is checked and you can see the username for which the auto-login is enabled.

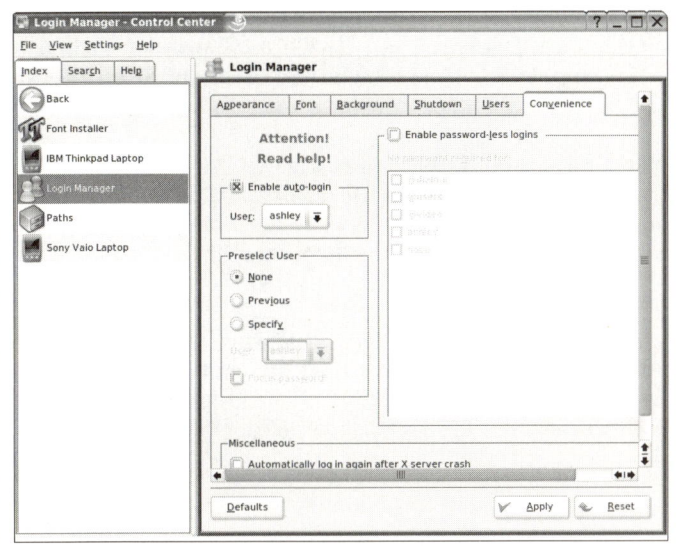

Figure 20-1: From KDE Center's Login Manager you can enable auto-login for a user.

7. **Click the User drop-down menu and select the user account that you want to use for auto-login.**

   If the Enable Auto-Login box is not checked, click on it until it shows a check mark.

WARNING! Although auto-login is convenient, it's definitely not good for security. You should enable auto-login only if you are using the SUSE Linux system in a safe environment such as your home. Turn auto-login off from the Convenience tab mentioned in Step 6.

If My System Crashes, Can I Press the Reset Button to Reboot?

Even though your mouse or keyboard seems to be dead, this does not necessarily mean that everything in your system has crashed. Therefore, you should not immediately reach for the reset button.

In case it's the GUI desktop that's hung, press Ctrl+Alt+Backspace to kill the X server and restart it. If this works, you should see a graphical login screen from which you can log in again.

If restarting X does not help, press **Ctrl+Alt+F2** and see if you can get a text console with a login prompt. If you see the login prompt, login with your username and password. Then type **su -** and type the `root` password to become `root`. After that, type **reboot** to safely reboot the PC.

If you don't get a text console by pressing Ctrl+Alt+F2, try to log into the system from another machine on the network (type **ssh** followed by your SUSE Linux system's IP address). You can become `root` by typing **su -** and then type **reboot** to reboot the PC. Of course, this last option works only if you have multiple PCs in a local area network.

If nothing works, just wait some time, make sure that there is no hard drive activity (many PCs have a light that blinks when the hard drive is active; the hard drive also makes noise that you may be able to hear), and then press the reset button.

How Can I Schedule a Command to Run Every 30 Minutes?

You can run a command or a script (which is a file containing other commands) every so often by using `crontab`. You schedule recurring jobs by placing job information in a file with a specific format and submitting this file with the `crontab` command. A program called `crond` checks the job information every minute and executes the recurring jobs at the specified times. Because the `crond` runs recurring jobs, such jobs are also referred to as *cron jobs*.

To submit a `cron` job, follow these steps:

Chapter 20: Ten Frequently Asked Questions about SUSE

1. **Prepare a shell script (or an executable program in any programming language) that can perform the recurring task you want to perform.**

   You can skip this step if you want to execute an existing program periodically.

2. **Prepare a text file with information about the times when you want the shell script or program (from Step 1) to execute, and then submit this file by using** `crontab`.

   You can submit several recurring jobs with a single file. Each line with timing information about a job has a standard format with six fields — the first five specify when the job runs, and the sixth and subsequent fields constitute the actual command that runs. For example, here is a line that executes the `myjob` shell script in a user's home directory every 30 minutes:

   ```
   0,30 * * * * $HOME/myjob
   ```

3. **Suppose the text file** `jobinfo` **(in the current directory) contains the job information. Submit this information to** `crontab` **with the following command:**

   ```
   crontab jobinfo
   ```

That's it! You are set with the `cron` job. From now on, the `cron` job runs at regular intervals (as specified in the job information file), and you receive mail messages with the output from the job.

To verify that the job is indeed scheduled, type the following command:

```
crontab -l
```

The output of the `crontab -l` command shows the `cron` jobs currently installed in your name. To remove your `cron` jobs, type **crontab -r**.

How Can I Find All the Huge Files on My SUSE Linux System?

You can type a one-line incantation to do this job for you. Here are the steps:

1. **If you are at a graphical desktop such as KDE or GNOME, open a terminal window.**

2. **Type** `su -` **and then enter the** `root` **password to become** `root`.

3. **Now type the following command (change 50000k, which stands for 50,000KB or about 50MB, to whatever you consider to be a large file):**

   ```
   find / -xdev -type f -size +50000k -ls | sort -n -k 7,7 >
           bigfiles
   ```

   This command line starts with the `find` command to find the files whose size exceeds 50,000KB (that's what the option `-size +50000k` means). The part after the vertical bar (|) sorts the files by size, and `> bigfiles` means the output is saved in a file named `bigfiles` in the current directory. The end result is that the list of large files, sorted by size, would be in a file named `bigfiles` in the current directory. To view the list, type **more bigfiles**.

Where Can I Find More SUSE RPMs?

Software for SUSE Linux is usually distributed in the form of RPM files. That's why it's common to refer to the software as RPM. You would want to find RPMs that are meant for SUSE Linux (as opposed to RPMs meant for Red Hat or Fedora). One good place to look for SUSE RPMs is the Packman site at the following URL:

```
http://packman.links2linux.org/
```

This site organizes the RPMs by category such as Finance, Games, Graphics, Internet, Multimedia, and so on. You can browse the RPMs by category or search by keyword. After downloading an RPM file, you can install it by using YaST or the `rpm` command (see Chapter 18 for more information).

In addition to the Packman site, here are three more Web sites where you can search for RPMs:

```
http://rpm.pbone.net/
http://www.rpmseek.com/
http://rpmfind.net/
```

Try them in the order listed, but start with the Packman site first.

Chapter 21

The Ten Best Things about SUSE

In This Chapter
- YaST
- Great hardware detection
- Easy installation
- YaST Online Update (YOU)
- Automatic mounting of Windows partition and USB memory stick
- Auto-login at the KDE desktop
- Support for laptops (power management)
- Easy access to Windows shares
- Cute gecko mascot
- SUSE's increasing popularity

I am often asked by friends and acquaintances what's so great about SUSE Linux and why should they consider using it (or perhaps switch to it from another Linux distribution). I have gotten into the habit of listing what you might call the selling points of SUSE Linux. When I began writing this book, I decided to list some of these points in a chapter in the obligatory Parts of Ten that adorns every *For Dummies* book. This is that chapter — with a list of what I think are the ten best things about SUSE.

YaST — The Super Sysadmin Tool

One of the best things about SuSE Linux is YaST — Yet Another Setup Tool — the system setup and configuration tool that makes SUSE Linux easy to install and maintain. If you have installed SUSE Linux, you have already used YaST. For any sysadmin task from configuring hardware to installing new software, YaST is the tool you use.

You typically encounter YaST in the form of the YaST Control Center — a GUI tool from which you can launch various other YaST modules that are meant for specific tasks such as installing software, configuring hardware, managing a network, or setting up security. In Chapter 17, I introduce the YaST Control Center and the various sysadmin tasks you can perform through the control center.

If you are at a text console, you can still use YaST — through its command line. For example, to install an RPM from a command-line, type **/sbin/yast -i** followed by the name of an RPM package.

YaST used to be proprietary software, but in 2004, Novell released YaST under the GNU General Public License (GPL) — the same open source license that governs Linux itself.

Detects All Hardware (Well, Nearly All!)

One of the best things about SUSE Linux is that it detects nearly all hardware during installation and setup. For all detected hardware, SUSE Linux loads any drivers needed to access the hardware and takes care of any configuration steps such as adding entries in the /etc/fstab configuration file and creating subdirectories in the /media directory where a storage device could be mounted. The excellent hardware detection means that you can usually install SUSE Linux on most PCs without any trouble.

If you add hardware after you install SUSE Linux, you can connect the hardware to the PC, power it on, and then run the appropriate hardware configuration module from the YaST Control Center (see Chapter 17 for more on the YaST Control Center).

Smooth and Easy Installation

SUSE Linux installation is neither oversimplified nor unnecessarily complex — it's just right. With its hardware detection capabilities and the YaST GUI tool, an average user can easily handle the SUSE Linux installation. The installer makes easy even a potentially complex step as resizing the Windows partition on the hard drive to make room for SUSE Linux. All you have to do is indicate the size of the Windows partition and the installer takes care of shrinking the size of the partition.

Instead of guiding the user through a set sequence of installation screens, the installer presents all the options in a single screen. Then all you need to change are the items that need changing such as the time zone and maybe the software selection between the KDE or GNOME desktop. The installer handles all other configurations after installing the minimal system and rebooting. All in all, SUSE Linux installation is smooth and easy.

I Love YOU — YaST Online Update

YaST Online Update, or YOU for short, makes it easy to keep your SUSE Linux system updated. All you need is a high-speed Internet connection. YOU can then download the latest software updates from an online server of your choice. You can set it up to automatically download and install updates or just download and then you can manually install the updates. I describe YOU in Chapter 18.

Automatic Mounting of My Windows Partitions and USB Memory Stick

If you have Windows partitions, SUSE Linux automatically mounts them so you can easily access files in your Windows partition. For example, in a dual boot Windows XP/SUSE Linux system, you probably find the Windows XP partition mounted at /windows directory in the Linux file system. If for some reason Linux does not mount the Windows XP partition automatically, you can become root by typing **su -** and then mount it by typing **mount /dev/hda2 /windows** because the Windows XP partition is usually the second partition on the hard drive (of course, this applies only if your PC has Windows XP installed).

When you plug in a USB memory stick into a USB port, SUSE Linux detects it and mounts it in a directory in the /media directory. After plugging in, you can access a USB memory stick by clicking the My Computer icon on the desktop and then clicking the hard drive icon labeled /dev/sda1 — that's the device name assigned to the USB memory stick.

Automatic Login at the KDE Desktop

Automatically logging in to the KDE desktop is not good for security, but it's convenient when your SUSE Linux system is in a secure environment such as your home. After you boot the system, SUSE Linux automatically logs you in and you can start at the KDE desktop.

By the way, if you are in an office with other people and want to turn this feature off, choose Main Menu⇨Control Center from the KDE desktop. Then choose Control Center⇨System Administration⇨Login Manager. Click Administrator Mode and enter the `root` password. Then click the Convenience tab and click to turn off the Enable Auto-Login check box.

Good Support for Laptops

SUSE Linux continues to improve upon some features that are important to laptop users. When you run your laptop on its battery, you want to conserve power by shutting down various parts of the system when you are not doing work. SUSE Linux can do this through its support for ACPI (Advanced Configuration and Power Interface). You can access the power management module from an icon on the panel (it's the icon that looks like an electric plug). From this module's menu, you can see how much battery life is remaining and suspend the system to the disk so that you can resume later without having to go through a lengthy system reboot.

Easy Browsing of Windows Shares

Click Network Browsing on the KDE desktop in your SUSE Linux system and the network browser automatically detects and shows you the Windows workgroups in your local area network. You can then browse the shared folders by clicking on a workgroup and then on icons for specific Windows PCs. You can easily copy documents from the Windows shares to your SUSE Linux system or open them using Linux software such as OpenOffice.org Writer.

That Cute Gecko Mascot

You know what I mean. Take a look at the KDE or GNOME desktop (or go to `www.suse.com`) and you can see the cute gecko mascot that has come to represent SUSE Linux the world over. Good thing Novell didn't do anything to the mascot after acquiring SUSE. You have to agree — it's a cute mascot.

SUSE's Increasing Popularity

Don't you just love to be part of a trend? I do. SUSE is on the rise and we can ride high — at least, while the ride lasts. SUSE Linux is already popular in Europe and is continuing to improve. SUSE Linux's fortunes are on the rise following Novell's acquisition of Germany's SUSE Linux AG for $210 million. SUSE Linux is poised for more growth in the U.S. marketplace, helped in part by IBM's $50 million investment in Novell as part of the SUSE acquisition deal. Recently, Novell announced that SUSE's YaST installation and configuration tool will become open source, licensed under the GNU General Public License. All these recent developments have generated a distinct "buzz" around SUSE Linux as the up and coming Linux distribution for everyone from home users to enterprise servers. And the nice thing is that you and I — we — are part of the crowd that's contributing to SUSE's popularity.

Chapter 22

Ten Great Web Sites for SUSE Maniacs

In This Chapter

▶ www.suse.com

▶ portal.suse.com/sdb/en/index.html

▶ distrowatch.com/table.php?distribution=suse

▶ www.suseforums.net

▶ www.linuxquestions.org/questions/f60

▶ www.linuxforums.org/forum/forum-36.html

▶ www.linux-laptop.net/

▶ packman.links2linux.org

▶ www.tldp.org/

▶ www.linuxhq.com/guides/

*I*n this age of the Internet, we look to Web sites when we need any information about virtually anything. For SUSE maniacs — those of us always trying to find the latest news and information about SUSE Linux and things related — there are enough Web sites out there to satisfy everyone's information needs. From all the available SUSE and Linux-related Web sites, I have culled ten Web sites that I consider most useful for SUSE Linux users. I present these ten Web sites in this chapter.

http://www.suse.com

For anything related to SUSE Linux, you've got to start here — the official SUSE Linux Web site. You will be redirected to the SUSE Linux page at www.novell.com/linux/suse/. You can browse this Web site for latest news about SUSE Linux, Novell's Linux products, and the support and services Novell offers.

From Novell's SUSE Linux page, you can search the SUSE knowledgebase — click Support and select knowledgebase. Search the knowledgebase for answers to your SUSE Linux questions.

http://portal.suse.com/sdb/en/index.html

This is the English page at the SUSE portal. If you want to use the site in other languages such as German, French, or Spanish, click the appropriate link along the top of the page.

The SUSE portal gives you access to the SUSE support database (or SDB, for short). You can search the SDB by keyword or browse the database by category. There is a link to the main SUSE FTP server (`ftp.suse.com/pub`) as well as a list of mirror sites from which you can download SUSE Linux.

From the SUSE portal, you can also access and search the SUSE Linux hardware database to see information about how well SUSE Linux supports a specific hardware device such as a graphics card, networking card, printer, modem, and so on.

http://distrowatch.com/table.php?distribution=suse

This Web page provides summary information about the latest SUSE Linux release as well as lots of links to news, reviews, forums, and documentation about SUSE. By following links at this Web site, you can also buy SUSE Linux on CDs and DVDs at a reasonably low cost (this can be convenient if you don't have high-speed Internet access and cannot easily download huge ISO files).

http://www.suseforums.net

This is an online forum for SUSE Linux. You can register as a user for free and then post questions or search the forums for previously posted questions and answers. You can browse the forum without registering.

http://www.linuxquestions.org/questions/f60

LinuxQuestions.org has a number of forums on Linux, including one for SUSE Linux. I show the URL that takes you directly to the SUSE Linux forum.

You can browse and search the forums for answers to questions on topics such as installation, networking, and security. To post a question on the forum, you must register as a member (you don't have to pay to become a member).

http://www.linuxforums.org/forum/forum-36.html

This is another SUSE online forum where you can search for answers to your SUSE Linux questions. As with other forums, you have to register and log in before you can post your questions. You also must log in before you can search the forums. You can, however, browse the postings at the forum without logging in as a registered user.

http://www.linux-laptop.net/

This Web site chronicles the experiences of many users who have installed various Linux distributions (including many versions of SUSE Linux) on their laptops. You can browse the information by the make and model of laptops. The information is useful if you are considering installing SUSE Linux on a laptop.

http://packman.links2linux.org

From this site, you can download software for SUSE Linux — in the form of RPMs — from this Web site. You can browse the RPMs by category, look at a complete index, or search by keyword.

http://www.tldp.org/

This is the famous Linux Documentation Project Web site. Here you can find links to HOWTO documents, guides, Frequently Asked Questions (FAQs), man pages with help on Linux commands, the Linux Gazette magazine, and much more. This site is not SUSE-specific; rather, it provides general Linux information. Nevertheless, it's a treasure trove of information for anyone who wants to learn Linux.

http://www.linuxhq.com/guides/

This Web page offers a collection of guides on Linux topics such as getting started, system and network administration, and programming. You can browse the guides and tutorials. Who knows? You may very well find a guide that addresses exactly what you want to know.

Chapter 23
Ten Most Commonly Used SUSE Commands

In This Chapter
- apropos
- man
- ls
- cat
- grep
- locate
- chmod
- rpm
- tar
- pico

One of these days, you'll become a SUSE Linux expert, and then you'll want to use cryptic commands for everything. Yeah, right! Seriously: Sometimes you do end up having to use some Linux commands either because you are stuck at a text console (X is on the fritz) or there's no quick way in a GUI to do what you want. I'm going to show you the ten most commonly used SUSE Linux commands. (I didn't do a survey to find the ten most-used commands — these are simply the ones I use most often.)

Linux commands are case-sensitive and all commands are in lowercase. Of course, directory and filenames can be in mixed case.

Before I forget . . . if you are wondering where you use these commands, you type these commands at a shell prompt in a text console or in a terminal window, which you can open from the GUI desktop. See Chapter 16 for more information about shells and the syntax of commands.

apropos: Finding Commands Based on a Keyword

Sometimes you might be at a loss to find a command that does something specific like how to print from the command line. That's when you can turn to the lifesaver command — `apropos`. The `apropos` command looks up the keyword in a database of all online manual pages (called *man pages*) and displays all Linux commands whose description contains the keyword.

The syntax of the `apropos` command is the following:

```
apropos keyword
```

This command displays all Linux commands whose `man` pages include *keyword*. By the way, I don't show the `more` command as a top ten command, but you often need to use `more` to view output one page at a time. In this case, if the output of `apropos` is too long, simply type a vertical bar followed by **more** (**| more**) after the `apropos` command. For example, type **apropos print | more** and see what you get. Press the spacebar to continue.

As much as `apropos` can be useful, when you try `apropos` with a simple keyword such as `find`, you may end up with a long listing of `man` pages because the word *find* appears in many man pages. Your best bet is to try `apropos` with as unique a keyword as possible. For example, to look up commands that relate to MP3 files, try typing **apropos MP3**. Here's what I get when I type **apropos MP3** on my SUSE Linux system:

```
plaympeg (1)         - MPEG audio (MP3) and video (MPEG-1) player
normalize-mp3 (1)    - adjust levels of mp3 or ogg files by running normal-
                       ize(1), then re-encoding
```

What you get on your system might be different, but, as you can see, `apropos` displays the commands related to a keyword.

man: Reading Online Man Page

The `man` command is for viewing online manual pages (also called *man pages*). The simplest form of the `man` command looks like this:

```
man commandname
```

This causes `man` to display the `man` page (think of it as the online help) for the command you specify by *commandname*. For example, if you want to know how to use the `man` command itself, type **man man**.

When you first read a `man` page, it can be somewhat daunting because a typical `man` page has lots of information. However, after a while, you get the idea how they are organized and which parts you need to read to understand what the command does.

You can use `man` in combination with `apropos`. First, use `apropos` to look up the commands for a keyword. Then select the command that seems most appropriate and use `man` to look up the description of that command.

TIP: Use the `man` command to read the `man` page of each of the Linux commands I list in this chapter. That way, you'll become familiar with these oft-used commands.

ls: Listing Files and Directories

The `ls` command displays the contents of a specified directory. If you omit the directory name, `ls` displays the contents of the current directory. By default, `ls` does not list files whose names begin with a period (.); to see all files, type `ls -a`. You can see full details of files (including size, user and group ownership, and read-write-execute permissions) with the `ls -l` command.

cat: Feeding Input to Commands

The `cat` command is deceptive when you find out what it does literally — it copies the contents of a file to the standard output (which means the text console or the terminal window). So what's so great about it? Well, to see why `cat` is useful, you have to use `cat` together with the output redirection feature of the shell. Basically, you can feed the output of `cat` as input to other commands. For example, suppose you have several MP3 files that you want to consolidate into a single big MP3 file. You can type the following `cat` command to perform that task:

```
cat *.mp3 > bigone.mp3
```

This command concatenates all the files with names ending in .mp3 and creates the `bigone.mp3` file in the current directory. Incidentally, that greater-than sign (>) is the output redirection character that causes the output of the `cat` command to go to the `bigone.mp3` file.

You can use `cat` to make an ISO image file of any CD. Assuming that the CD-ROM drive's device name is `/dev/cdrom`, just type the following `cat` command to create the ISO image file named `cdimage.iso` (you can use any filename you want):

```
cat /dev/cdrom > cdimage.iso
```

How's that for a multipurpose tool?

grep: *Searching for Text in Files*

If you have used Linux (or any variant of UNIX) for a while, you probably know about the `grep` command, which enables you to search files for a pattern of strings. Here is a typical use of `grep` to locate all files that have any occurrences of the string `ethernet` or `Ethernet` — on any line of all files with names that end in `.h`:

```
cd /usr/include
grep "[eE]thernet" *.h
```

The last command finds all occurrences of `ethernet` or `Ethernet` in the files with names ending in `.h`.

The `grep` command's "[eE]thernet" argument is known as a regular expression, a pattern that matches a set of strings. You construct a regular expression with a small set of operators and rules that resemble the ones for writing arithmetic expressions. A list of characters inside brackets ([...]), for example, matches any single character in the list. Thus, the regular expression "[eE]thernet" is a set of two strings, as follows:

```
ethernet Ethernet
```

There are many more ways to construct regular expressions, but I won't go into that. Even if you don't know much about regular expressions, you can use `grep` perfectly well to search for a specific sequence of characters in one or more text files. Later on, you can gradually learn more complex search patterns.

Setting aside the regular expressions for the time being, here is the syntax of a typical use of `grep`:

```
grep [options] pattern  files
```

This `grep` command searches for the *pattern* in the specified *files*, and [*options*] denote one or more single-character options that begin with a hyphen. Here are the options and their meanings:

-N (where N is a number) displays N lines around the line containing the pattern.

-c shows the number of lines that contain the search pattern.

-f reads options from a specified file.

-i ignores case.

-l displays the filenames that contain the pattern.

-n displays a line number next to lines that contain the pattern.

-q returns a status code but does not display any output.

-v displays the lines that do not contain a pattern.

-w matches only whole words.

locate: Finding Files and Directories the Easy Way

The `locate` command searches a database of filenames for any name that matches a specified pattern. If you are not sure about the location of a file, just type `locate` followed by a part of the filename. For example, here's how you can search for the XF86Config file:

```
locate XF86Config
```

This causes `locate` to display all file or directory names that contain XF86Config in their names.

I love the `locate` command. I use it all the time whenever I want to check if a certain file exists somewhere in my system. Sometimes a huge number of files and directories might contain the search word. You can send the output of `locate` through more by typing **locate *keyword* | more** and browsing the output a page at a time. Another trick is to send the output through the `grep` command and look for some other word that helps you find a specific file. For example, when I want to see if there is a binary (executable) file with rpm in its name, I type **locate rpm | grep bin** because I know that the binary files would be in a directory whose name contains bin (for example, /bin, /usr/bin or /sbin, and so on).

The `locate` command isn't installed by default in SUSE Linux.

chmod: Changing Permissions

You use the `chmod` command to change the permission settings of one or more files. The syntax is as follows:

```
chmod [-cfvR] perm files
```

The command changes the permission settings of *files* to what you specify in the *perm* argument. The characters within square brackets are the options and they have the following meanings:

- `-c` lists only files whose permissions have changed.
- `-f` stops any error message displays.
- `-v` verbosely displays permission changes.
- `-R` recursively changes permissions of files in all subdirectories.

To use `chmod` effectively, you have to learn how to specify the permission settings. One way is to concatenate one letter from each column of the following table in the order shown (Who/Action/Permission):

Who	Action	Permission
u user	+ add	r read
g group	- remove	w write
o others	= assign	x execute
a all	s set user ID	

For example, to give everyone read access to all files in a directory, type **chmod a+r ***. On the other hand, to permit everyone to execute a specific file, type **chmod +x filename**.

Another way to specify a permission setting is to use a three-digit sequence of numbers. In a detailed listing of a file that you get when you use the command `ls -l`, the read, write, and execute permission settings for the user, group, and others appear as the sequence rwxrwxrwx (with dashes in place of letters for disallowed operations). Think of rwxrwxrwx as three occurrences of the string rwx. Now, assign the values:

r = 4

w = 2

x = 1

- = 0

With these numerical assignments, to get the value of the sequence rwx, simply add the values of r, w, and x. Thus, rwx = 4+2+1 = 7. Similarly, rw- would be 4+2+0 = 6.

Using this formula, you can assign a three-digit value to any permission setting. For example, if the user can read and write the file but everyone else can only read the file, the permission setting is rw-r--r-- (that's how it appears in the listing shown by ls -l), and the value is 644. Thus, if you want all files in a directory to be readable by everyone but writable by only the user, type **chmod 644 ***.

rpm: Taming RPM Packages

The rpm command is useful because most SUSE software comes in RPM files. You can use the rpm command to install these files and find out information about packages that are already installed. I cover the rpm command in Chapter 18.

tar: Packing and Unpacking Archives

The tar command creates an archive file that can contain other directories and files and (optionally) compress the archive for efficient storage. The tar command can write the archive to a specified device such as a floppy, or you can use tar to package a whole set of files and directories in a single file. In fact, many software packages are distributed in the form of a compressed tar file.

The command syntax of the tar program is as follows:

```
tar options destination source
```

Here, *options* are usually specified by a sequence of single letters, with each letter specifying what tar should do. *destination* is the device name of the backup device. And *source* is a list of file or directory names denoting the files to back up. Optionally, you can add a hyphen prefix for the options.

For example, suppose you want to archive the contents of the /etc/X11 directory in a file. To do this, type the following command:

```
tar zcvf /tmp/etcX11bkup.tar.gz /etc/X11
```

The tar command displays a list of filenames as each file is copied to the compressed tar archive. In this case, the options are zcvf, the destination is etcX11bkup.tar.gz (in the /tmp directory), and the source is the /etc/X11 directory (which implies all its subdirectories and their contents). The z option causes `tar` to compress the archive. The c option creates an archive, f specifies the filename, and v instructs `tar` to be verbose (which means show lots of information as it works).

REMEMBER

I show `.tar.gz` as the file extension for the archive file because that's the customary way to indicate that it's a compressed `tar` archive. For an uncompressed `tar` archive, the customary file extension is `.tar`. The `.gz` part is added when the z option is used to compress the archive. The `.gz` comes from `gzip` — the Linux command to compress a file. Sometimes compressed `tar` archives also use the `.tar.Z` extension.

Open source software source files are typically distributed in compressed `tar` archives. These files with the `.tar.gz` or `.tar.Z` extension are often referred to as a *compressed tarball*. If you want the software, you have to download the compressed tarball, unpack it, and build it.

To view the contents of the compressed tarball `/tmp/etcX11bkup.tar.gz` that you created earlier, type the following command:

```
tar ztf /tmp/etcX11bkup.tar.gz
```

You should see a list of the filenames (each begins with `/etc/X11`) indicating what's in the backup. In this `tar` command, the t option lists the contents of the `tar` archive and z takes care of uncompressing the archive.

To extract the files from a tarball, follow these steps:

1. Change the directory to `/tmp` by typing this command:

    ```
    cd /tmp
    ```

2. Type the following command:

    ```
    tar zxvf etcX11bkup.tar.gz
    ```

    This `tar` command uses the x option to extract the files from the archive stored in the tarball `etcX11bkup.tar.gz`.

If you check the contents of the `/tmp` directory, you should see that the `tar` command creates an `etc/X11` directory tree in `/tmp` and extracts all the files from the `tar` archive into that directory.

That gives you an idea of how the `tar` command is used. Now you know what to do to a tarball, if you ever come across one!

pico: Editing Text Files

The `pico` command runs a text editor that comes with SUSE Linux. It's easier to learn than the `vi` and `ed` text editors and handy when you need to edit text configuration files.

> **TIP**
> If you plan to edit any system configuration file (such as `/etc/fstab`), start by making a backup copy of the file. For example, to save a copy of the `/etc/fstab` file, become `root` by typing **su -** and then type **cp /etc/fstab /etc/fstab.saved**. After editing the original `/etc/fstab` file, if you have any problems, you can revert back to the saved version by typing **cp /etc/fstab.saved /etc/fstab**.

To edit a file with `pico` (or create a new text file), just type **pico *filename*** in a terminal window. Figure 23-1 shows the typical text-mode display of the `pico` editor.

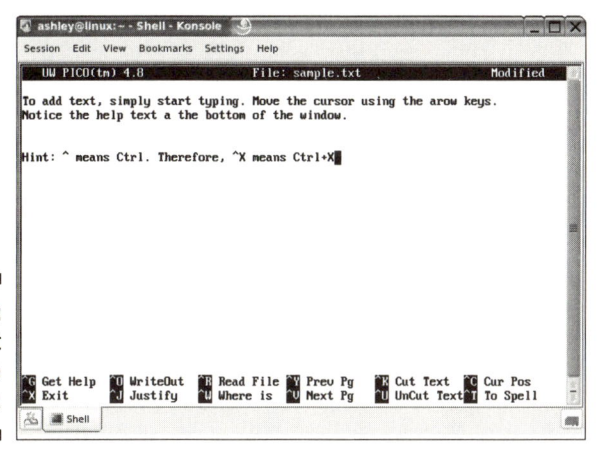

Figure 23-1: Edit text files in the `pico` editor.

To add text, simply start typing. You can move the cursor by using the arrow keys. The last two lines (see the bottom of the window in Figure 23-1) give you hints about other `pico` commands. For example, to save the file, press Ctrl+O (hold down the Ctrl key and then press O). To exit, press Ctrl+X. I'm confident that you can practice with `pico` and learn it fairly quickly.

Appendix
About the DVD-ROM

In This Appendix
- System requirements
- DVD installation instructions
- What you'll find on the DVD
- Troubleshooting

This book's companion DVD includes a Special Edition of SUSE Linux to get you started on your Linux journey. This appendix briefly describes the DVD and tells you how to get started with the installation.

System Requirements

Make sure that your computer meets the minimum system requirements shown in the following list. If your computer doesn't match up to most of these requirements, you may have problems using the software and files on the DVD:

- A PC with an Intel Pentium or compatible processor running at 400 MHz or faster for graphical installation
- At least 192MB of total RAM installed on your computer for graphical installation (256MB recommended)
- At least 520MB free space on your hard drive for a minimal installation; 5GB of free space recommended if you plan to install most packages, so that you can try out everything covered in this book
- A DVD-ROM drive
- A graphics card and a monitor capable of displaying at least 256 colors
- A sound card
- Ethernet network interface card (NIC) or modem

DVD Installation Instructions

To install SUSE Linux from the companion DVD, follow these steps (consult Chapter 2 for details.):

1. **Check whether your PC's hardware, such as graphics card, network card, and SCSI card, work in SUSE Linux. If not, try to find Linux drivers for the device.**

   To check if your PC's hardware is compatible with SUSE Linux, visit the SUSE Linux Hardware Database at `hardwaredb.suse.de`. If you download any Linux drivers for any device, you should burn them onto a CD for safekeeping.

2. **Set up your PC to boot from the CD/DVD drive (to do this, you have to enter SETUP as your PC powers up).**

3. **Boot your PC with the DVD.**

4. **Select Installation from the initial boot screen and press Enter.**

   The SUSE Linux installer — YaST — runs and displays graphical screens through which you perform the installation steps. Respond to the questions and choices as the installation program takes you through the initial installation steps. Here are some key steps:

   - Review the hard drive partitioning that YaST recommends. If you have Microsoft Windows (any version) installed on your hard drive, YaST can reduce the size of the Windows partition and make space for SUSE Linux. You don't need any other partitioning software.
   - Set the local time zone.
   - If you want, change the software selection from the default KDE desktop to the GNOME desktop.

5. **YaST reboots the system after the initial installation and continues with further installation and configuration of SUSE Linux.**

   After installing more packages, YaST continues with configuration of the system. Here are a few key configuration steps that you have to go through:

   - Configure the Ethernet network, if any. Typically, you configure the network automatically by using DHCP.
   - Set the `root` password.
   - Add a user account (you would typically log in using this account).
   - Configure hardware such as a graphics card, sound card, and printers.

What You'll Find on the DVD

This section provides a summary of the software and other goodies you find on the DVD. If you need help installing the items provided on the DVD, refer back to the installation instructions in the preceding section.

Shareware programs are fully functional, free, trial versions of copyrighted programs. If you like particular programs, register with their authors for a nominal fee and receive licenses, enhanced versions, and technical support.

Freeware programs are free, copyrighted games, applications, and utilities. You can copy them to as many PCs as you like — for free — but they offer no tech support.

GNU software is governed by its own license, which is included in the folder of the GNU software. There are no restrictions on the distribution of GNU software. See the GNU license at the root of the DVD or at the back of this book for details. As required by the GNU license, Novell makes the SUSE Linux source code available. You can download the source code for SUSE Linux from the following URL:

```
ftp://ftp.suse.com/pub/suse/i386/9.2/suse/src/
```

Trial, demo, or *evaluation* versions of software are usually limited by time or functionality (such as not letting you save a project after you create it).

The DVD includes a Special Edition of SUSE Linux. The Special Edition is similar to the personal edition that SUSE used to sell in versions prior to 9.2. The version of SUSE Linux on the companion DVD includes all the basics:

- Your choice of KDE or GNOME graphical desktop environments
- Konqueror Web browser and file manager
- Multimedia tools for playing CDs and DVDs, burning CDs, and ripping audio CDs
- Office software in the form of the much-acclaimed OpenOffice.org suite
- Photo and graphics editing software such as The GIMP, and much more

In short, the Special Edition of SUSE Linux that accompanies this book gives you everything you need for a typical home or small office computer.

SUSE does offer a commercial version of SUSE Linux, called the professional edition, that includes many servers; software development tools; additional word processing, database, and spreadsheet programs; and many more extra programs. The Special Edition is smaller and is geared to the home user who doesn't need everything else that the professional edition includes.

Troubleshooting

If you have difficulty installing or using the materials on the companion DVD, consult the detailed installation instructions in Chapter 2.

If you still have trouble with the DVD-ROM, please call the Wiley Product Technical Support phone number: (800) 762-2974. Outside the United States, call 1(317) 572-3994. You can also contact Wiley Product Technical Support through the Internet at www.wiley.com/techsupport. Wiley Publishing will provide technical support only for installation and other general quality control items; for technical support on the applications themselves, consult the program's vendor or author.

To place additional orders or to request information about other Wiley products, please call (800) 225-5945.

Index

• Symbols and Numerics •

* (asterisk) wildcard character, 249
? (question mark) wildcard character, 249–250
. (single dot) current directory, 95
[ ] (square brackets) wildcard format, 250
~ (tilde) home directory, 95
. . (two dots) parent directory, 95
0-6 run levels, 262
10BaseT Ethernet, 124–125
100BaseT Ethernet, 124–125
802.11a wireless Ethernet standard, 129
802.11b wireless Ethernet standard, 128–129
802.11g wireless Ethernet standard, 129

• A •

AbiWord, 57
absolute pathname, 94
administration. *See* system administration
Adobe Acrobat Reader, 60–61, 185, 241
ADSL (Asymmetric DSL), 110
alternative newsgroups, 171
amaroK audio player, 59, 219
Apache Web server, 16
application gateway, 290
Applixware Office, 15
appointments. *See* calendars
`apropos` command, 332
art newsgroups, 172
asterisk (*) wildcard character, 249
Asymmetric DSL (ADSL), 110
attachments (e-mail), 157
audio CDs
  burning, 59, 221–225
  ejecting, 48
  inserting, 48
  playing, 48, 59, 217–218
  ripping, 59
audio players, 59, 219–221
authentication, 290
automatic command completion, 248
automatic login, 316–317, 324

• B •

backdoor, 290
backups
  CDs, 225–226
  `tar` program, 20
`bash` shell
  automatic command completion, 248
  capabilities, 244
  combining commands, 246
  command line, 49, 245
  command line options, 50, 245
  command syntax, 245–246
  controlling command input and output, 246–247
  defined, 13, 48
  repeating commands, 250–251
  saving error messages, 247–248
  wildcard characters, 249–250
bastion host, 291
`/bin` directory, 83
biology newsgroups, 171
bitnet newsgroups, 171
Bluetooth wireless technology, 20
`/boot` directory, 83
boot loader, 27, 30, 39–40
booting
  defined, 30, 39–40
  DVD/CD-ROM drive, 26
  `init` process, 261–262
browsers. *See* Web browsers
buffer overflow, 291
burning CDs/DVDs, 59, 221–225
business newsgroups, 171

SUSE Linux 9.3 For Dummies

• C •

CA (Certificate Authority), 291
cable modem, 107–108, 114–119
Cable Modem Termination System (CMTS), 116
cabling, 124
Calc, 57–58, 197–200
calculators, 207–208
calendars
  Evolution, 57–58, 207
  Kontact, 57–58, 205–206
`cat` command, 333–334
`cd` command, 94, 99
CD Creator (Nautilus), 225
CD player application, 59, 217–218
CD-ROM drive, 25
CDs
  burning, 59, 221–225
  ejecting, 48
  inserting, 48
  playing, 48, 59, 217–218
  ripping, 59
central processing unit (CPU), 9–10, 17
CERT Coordination Center (CERT/CC) Web site, 308
Certificate Authority (CA), 291
certificates, 291
`chage` command, 295–296
changing
  directories, 94, 99
  file ownerships, 297
  file permissions, 297–298, 336–337
  run levels, 263
charts, 215–216
chat (instant messaging), 56, 163
checking current run level, 262–263
`chkconfig` command, 301
`chmod` command, 297–298, 336–337
`chown` command, 297
CIAC (Computer Incident Advisory Capability) Web site, 308
Clarinet news service, 171
CMTS (Cable Modem Termination System), 116
CodeWeavers CrossOver Office, 15
combining commands, 246
command line, 49, 245
command line interface, 13

command line options, 50, 245
commands. *See commands by name*
Computer Incident Advisory Capability (CIAC) Web site, 308
computer newsgroups, 172
confidentiality, 291
configuring
  dialup modem, 121–122
  Ethernet LAN, 125–126
  firewall, 304–307
  hardware, 269–270
  Internet superserver, 301–302
  peripheral devices, 19–20
  printers, 45–47
  SUSE Linux, 21–22, 35–37
  TCP wrapper security, 302–303
connecting peripheral devices, 19–20
connecting to the Internet. *See* Internet connection
copying
  directories, 98
  files, 87, 93, 98
`cp` command, 98
CPU (central processing unit), 9–10, 17
crackers, 287, 291
creating
  directories, 88, 93, 99
  presentations, 212–213
  slides (presentations), 212
  spreadsheets, 201
  templates (Writer documents), 191
  user accounts, 271–272
  Writer documents, 185–186
`cron` jobs, 318–319
CrossOver Office (CodeWeavers), 15
cryptography, 293
current directory, 94
customizing
  GNOME, 78–79
  KDE, 75–76
Cyber Alert System, 308

• D •

Dan Bricklin's Web site, 197
DDoS (Distributed Denial of Service) attack, 291
decoders, 58
decrypting files, 289, 291

Index

default permission, 298–299
default run level, 31
deleting
  directories, 87, 93, 99–100
  files, 87, 93, 99
  RPM files, 285
  slides (presentations), 214
  user accounts, 272
Denial of Service (DoS) attack, 287, 291
detecting hardware, 322
/dev directory, 83
development environment, 16–17
df command, 102–103
Dia graphics application, 60–61
dialup networking, 107–108, 119–122
digital camera
  Digikam interface, 60–61, 228–230
  downloading photos, 228–229
  USB Mass Storage, 231–232
digital music files, playing, 219–220
digital signature, 292
Digital Subscriber Line (DSL)
  Asymmetric DSL (ADSL), 110
  availability, 109
  comparison with other connection methods, 107–108
  costs, 108
  data-transfer rates, 106–107
  distance limits, 107
  DSL modem, 108–109
  equipment, 107
  Ethernet hub, 113
  how it works, 108–109
  ISDN DSL (IDSL), 110
  loop length, 109
  NAT router, 112–114
  PPP over Ethernet (PPPoE), 114
  Symmetric DSL (SDSL), 110
  typical setup, 110–114
directories
  absolute pathname, 94
  /bin directory, 83
  /boot directory, 83
  browsing, 86, 89–92
  changing, 94, 99
  copying, 98
  creating, 88, 93, 99
  current directory, 94
  defined, 81

  deleting, 87, 93, 99–100
  /dev directory, 83
  disk-space usage, 103
  /etc directory, 83
  finding, 100–101, 335
  /home directory, 84, 95
  /lib directory, 84
  listing, 95–98, 333
  /media directory, 84
  /mnt directory, 84
  moving, 99
  /opt directory, 84
  parent directory, 95
  /proc directory, 84
  relative directory name, 94
  renaming, 88, 93
  /root directory, 81, 83–84
  /sbin directory, 84
  /srv directory, 84
  /sys directory, 84
  /tmp directory, 84
  /usr directory, 84
  /var directory, 84
  viewing, 85–87, 89–91
disk partition, 23
disk-space usage, 102–103
display adapter, 25
Distributed Denial of Service (DDoS) attack, 291
distributions of Linux, 11–12
distrowatch.com Web site, 328
DMZ, 292
document scanning, 232–237
documentation, 17
documents. *See* Writer documents
domain names, 156
DoS (Denial of Service) attack, 287, 291
downloading
  patches, 273, 275–277
  photos from digital camera, 228–229
  RPMs, 329
  SUSE Linux, 328
  SUSE Linux source code, 343
  templates (Writer documents), 191
Draw, 60–61
DSL (Digital Subscriber Line). *See* Digital Subscriber Line
du command, 102–103, 269
dual-homed host, 292

DVD (included in book)
  freeware programs, 343
  shareware programs, 343
  SUSE Linux installation, 342
  system requirements, 341
  troubleshooting, 344
DVD/CD-ROM drive, 25
DVDs
  burning, 59, 221–225
  ejecting, 48
  inserting, 48
  playing, 48

• E •

editing
  files, 339
  photos, 230
  Writer documents, 188–189
802.11a wireless Ethernet standard, 129
802.11b wireless Ethernet standard, 128–129
802.11g wireless Ethernet standard, 129
ejecting CDs/DVDs, 48
e-mail
  attachments, 157
  domain names, 156
  Evolution, 160–163
  how it works, 156
  HTML messages, 157–158
  KMail, 56, 158–160
  mail-transfer agent (MTA), 156–157
  mail-user agent (MUA), 156–157
  Novell Evolution, 56
  phishing, 158
encrypting files, 289, 292
engineering newsgroups, 172
Epiphany Web browser, 146, 153–154
error messages, 247–248
/etc directory, 83
Ethernet cards, 123–125
Ethernet hub, 113
Ethernet LAN
  cabling, 124
  configuring, 125–126
  data-transfer rates, 124
  defined, 123
  Internet connection, 126–127
  mixing and matching computers, 128

100BaseT Ethernet, 124–125
10BaseT Ethernet, 124–125
wireless access, 124, 128–134
Evolution
  calendar, 56–58, 207
  e-mail, 160–163
Excel (Microsoft), 197
execute (x) permission, 97
expiration dates for passwords, 295–296
exploit tools, 292
Eye of GNOME image viewer, 60–61, 239–240

• F •

fax viewer, 60–61
fields in Writer documents, 195–196
file managers
  Konqueror, 85–88
  Nautilus, 88–93
file sharing, 20
file systems
  backups, 20
  defined, 20, 81
  mounting, 19, 101–102
  sharing, 20
  SUSE Linux, 81–84
  unmounting, 101–102
file-creation mask, 298–299
filenames, 82
files
  browsing, 86, 89–92
  copying, 87, 93, 98
  decrypting, 289, 291
  deleting, 87, 93, 99
  editing, 339
  encrypting, 289, 292
  finding, 82, 100–101, 335
  integrity, 292
  integrity-checking tools, 289
  listing, 96–98, 333
  moving, 87, 92–93, 99
  ownerships, 296–297
  pathnames, 82–83
  permissions, 97, 296–300, 336–337
  renaming, 88, 93, 99
  searching text, 334–335
  symbolic link, 97
  viewing, 85–87, 89–92

Index 349

find command, 100–101
finding
  directories, 100–101, 335
  files, 82, 100–101, 335
  large files, 319–320
  RPMs, 320
  software, 277–278
Firefox Web browser, 146, 154
firewall
  configuring, 304–307
  defined, 21, 288, 292
  NAT (Network Address Translation), 307
FOCUS-LINUX mailing list, 308
folders. *See* directories
forums, 328–329
Free Software Foundation (FSF), 14
FTP server, 16
function keys (SUSE installer boot screen), 28

• G •

GAIM IM client, 166–168
gecko mascot, 324
GGV PostScript Viewer, 60–61, 241–242
GIMP (GNU Image Manipulation Program)
  features, 15, 60–61
  installing, 237
  opening image files, 238
  plugins, 237
  toolbox, 238–239
  User Manual, 239
GNOME (GNU Network Model Environment)
  calculator, 207
  CD player application, 59, 217–218
  Clipboard tool, 44
  clock, 44
  context menus, 67–68
  customizing, 78
  desktop icons, 44, 67
  features, 14–15
  help, 17
  hide panel, 44
  home folder, 44
  icon context menus, 68–69
  initial screen, 40–41
  launcher applets, 77
  logging in, 40–41

  logging out, 45
  Main Menu, 43–45, 70–73
  panels, 43, 67, 69–70, 77
  personal information manager, 44
  power management tool, 44
  SUSE Hardware tool, 44
  SUSE Help Center, 44
  SUSE Watcher, 44
  terminal program, 44
  terminal window, 93, 243
  virtual console, 243
  volume control, 44
  Web browser, 44
  Workspace Switcher, 44
GNOME PDF Viewer, 60–61
GNOME Web site, 77
GnomeMeeting videoconferencing, 57
GNU General Public License (GPL), 12, 14
GNU Image Manipulation Program (GIMP). *See* GIMP
GNU Network Model Environment (GNOME). *See* GNOME
GNU Privacy Guard (GnuPG), 289
GNU Project, 14
GNU software, 13
Gnumeric, 57
Google Groups Web site, 181
GPL (GNU General Public License), 12, 14
graphical user interface (GUI), 14
graphics
  presentations, 215–216
  Writer documents, 194–195
graphics applications, 60–61
grep command, 50, 334–335
Grip, 59
groups, 271–272
GRUB boot loader, 30, 39–40
GUI (graphical user interface), 14
Gwenview image viewer, 60–61, 239–240

• H •

hackers, 158
handouts (presentations), 215
hard drive, 18, 25
hardware compatibility, 26
hardware configuration, 37, 269–270
hardware (defined), 9
hardware detection, 322

SUSE Linux 9.3 For Dummies

hardware requirements, 24–26
hash, 292
`hdparm` program, 268–269
help, 17
history of commands, 250
`/home` directory, 84, 95
host, 292
host security issues, 288–289, 295
hot plugs, 20
HTML e-mail messages, 157–158
HTML (Hypertext Markup Language), 142
HTTP (Hypertext Transfer Protocol), 142
hypertext links, 143

• I •

ICMP (Internet Control Message Protocol), 136
IDSL (ISDN DSL), 110
IEEE (Institute of Electrical and Electronics Engineers)newsgroups, 172
`ifconfig` command, 135–136
IM clients
　GAIM, 166–168
　Kopete, 164–166
IM (instant messaging), 56, 163
image applications, 60–61
image editors
　Digikam Image Editor, 230
　The GIMP, 60–61, 237–239
image viewers, 60–61, 239–240
Impress, 57–58, 208–212
`init` command, 263
`init` process, 261–262
`innd` news server, 16
inserting CDs/DVDs, 48
inserting slides (presentations), 212
installing
　GIMP (GNU Image Manipulation Program), 237
　patches, 273, 275–277
　RPM files, 279–280, 284
　security updates, 289
　software, 30, 277–278
installing SUSE Linux
　boot loader, 27
　booting from the DVD/CD-ROM drive, 26
　from CD or DVD, 26–27
　from companion DVD, 342

disk partition, 23
ease of, 322–323
FTP server, 313–316
hardware compatibility, 26
hardware configuration, 37
hardware requirements, 24–26
laptops, 329
release notes, 37
screen resolution, 28
step-by-step directions, 23–24
SUSE installer boot screen, 27–28
Windows partition, 31–33
YaST graphical installer, 24, 28–38
instant messaging (IM), 56, 163
Institute of Electrical and Electronics Engineers (IEEE) newsgroups, 172
integrity (of data), 292
InterBulletin Web site, 181
Internet connection
　cable modem, 107–108, 114–119
　dialup modem, 107–108, 119–122
　Digital Subscriber Line (DSL), 106–114
　Ethernet LAN, 126–127
　firewall, 21
　security risks, 287–288
　testing, 35
Internet Control Message Protocol (ICMP), 136
Internet (defined), 105–106
Internet Protocol (IP), 106
Internet radio stations, 220
Internet service provider (ISP), 107
Internet services
　list of, 16
　security, 301
Internet superserver, 301–302
IP (Internet Protocol), 106
IP routing table, 136
IP spoofing, 293
IP telephone, 57
IPSec (IP Security Protocol), 292
ISDN DSL (IDSL), 110
ISO image files, 313
ISP (Internet service provider), 107

• J •

juK audio player, 59, 219–220

Index

• K •

K-12 newsgroups, 172
Kaffeine video player, 59
K3b CD/DVD burning application, 59, 221–225
KDE (K Desktop Environment)
  Application Starter, 74
  automatic login, 316–317, 324
  calculator, 207–208
  CD player application, 217–218
  Clipboard tool, 44
  clock, 44
  context menus, 67–68
  Control Center, 75–76
  customizing, 75–76
  desktop icons, 44, 67
  Desktop Pager, 44
  features, 14–15
  help, 17
  hide panel, 44
  home folder, 44
  icon context menus, 68–69
  initial screen, 40, 74
  logging in, 40–41
  logging out, 45
  Main Menu, 43–45, 70–73
  moving windows, 74
  panels, 43, 67, 69–70, 74
  personal information manager, 44
  power management tool, 44
  resizing windows, 74
  SUSE Hardware tool, 44
  SUSE Help Center, 44
  SUSE Watcher, 44
  terminal program, 44
  terminal window, 93, 243
  virtual console, 243
  volume control, 44
  Web browser, 44
KDE Web site, 74
kdetv TV player, 59–60
kernel, 11–12
keyboard
  compatibility of different types, 25
  layout, 30
KFax fax viewer, 60–61
KGhostview, 60–61, 241–242
kino video editor, 59–60

KMail, 56, 158–160
KNode newsreader, 57, 174–177
knowledgebase (SUSE Linux Web site), 312, 328
Konqueror file manager, 85–88
Konqueror Web browser, 88, 146–149
Kontact Personal Information Manager, 57–58, 205–206
Kooka scanning application, 234–237
Kopete IM client, 164–166
KsCD, 59
KWallet, 165

• L •

LAN (local area network)
  Ethernet cabling, 123–126
  Ethernet cards, 123–125
  Internet connection, 127
  mixing and matching computers, 128
  wireless access, 128–134
language settings, 31
laptop support, 324, 329
layers (slides), 214
LDAP (Lightweight Directory Access Protocol), 36
/lib directory, 84
links (Web pages), 142–143
Linux distributions, 11–12
Linux Documentation Project Web site, 330
Linux kernel, 11–12
Linux newsgroups, 172–173
Linux security newsgroups, 308
Linuxhq.com Web site, 330
LinuxQuestions.org Web site, 329
listing
  directories, 95–98, 333
  files, 96–98, 333
local area network (LAN). *See* LAN
locate command, 101, 335
log files, 289
logging in
  KDE/GNOME, 40–41
  root user, 257
logging out of KDE/GNOME, 45
logic bombs, 293
loop length, 109
Lotus 1-2-3, 197
ls command, 95–98, 296, 333

• M •

mail clients, 155
Mailgate Web site, 181
mailing lists, 308, 312
mail-transfer agent (MTA), 156–157
mail-user agent (MUA), 156–157
`man` command, 17, 332–333
man pages (manual pages), 17, 332–333
master handouts (presentations), 215
master notes (presentations), 215
master slide (presentations), 214
`/media` directory, 84
memory, 10, 17, 25
microprocessor, 9–10, 17
Microsoft Excel, 197
Microsoft Office, 183
Microsoft PowerPoint, 58
Microsoft Word, 184
miscellaneous newsgroups, 172
`mkdir` command, 99
`/mnt` directory, 84
mode installation setting, 30
modems
  cable modem, 107–108, 114–119
  dialup modem, 107–108, 119–122
  drivers, 26
  DSL modem, 108–109
  soft modems, 26
  war-dialing, 295
moderated newsgroups, 172
monitor, 25
monitoring performance, 265–269
`more` command, 51
`mount` command, 19, 101–102
mounting
  file systems, 19, 101–102
  USB memory stick, 323
  Windows partition, 323
mouse, 25, 30
moving
  directories, 99
  files, 87, 92–93, 99
Mozilla Web browser, 146, 149–153
MTA (mail-transfer agent), 156–157
MUA (mail-user agent), 156–157
multimedia applications, 58–60
multitasking operating system, 10–11
multiuser operating system, 10–11

music files, playing, 219–220
`mv` command, 99

• N •

NAT (Network Address Translation), 112, 307
NAT router, 112–114
Nautilus file manager
  browsing files/folders, 89–92
  CD Creator, 225–226
  copying files, 93
  creating folders, 93
  deleting files/folders, 93
  features, 88–89
  moving files, 92–93
  renaming files/folders, 93
  viewing files/folders, 89–92
Network Address Translation (NAT), 112, 307
network authentication methods, 36
Network Information System (NIS), 36
network interface card (NIC), 25
network interfaces, 135–136
Network News Transfer Protocol (NNTP), 170
network protocols, 15
network security issues, 289–290
network settings, 35
networking, 15, 20–21
new releases, 312–313
news readers, 57
news server, 16
newsgroups
  categories, 171–173
  hierarchy, 170–171
  how they work, 169–170
  Linux security, 308
  posting news, 179–180
  reading, 173–181
  searching, 181
  subscriptions, 179
newsreaders
  KNode, 57, 174–177
  Pan, 174, 177–179
News2Web Web site, 181
NIC (network interface card), 25
NIS (Network Information System), 36

Index

NNTP (Network News Transfer Protocol), 170
nonrepudiation, 293
notes (presentations), 215
Novell Evolution
  calendar, 56–58, 207
  e-mail, 160–163
Novell Web site, 308

• O •

office applications, 57–58
100BaseT Ethernet, 124–125
online documentation, 17
online forums, 328–329
Open Secure Shell (OpenSSH), 303–304
open source (defined), 11
Open Source Initiative Web site, 11
OpenOffice.org
  Calc, 57–58, 197–200
  Draw, 60–61
  features, 15
  Impress, 57–58, 208–212
  Writer, 57, 184–187
operating system (defined), 10–11
/opt directory, 84
organizer, 57–58. *See also* calendars
ownerships (of files), 296–297

• P •

packet filtering, 293, 305
packet sniffers, 294
packets (defined), 293
Packman Web site, 320, 329
Pan newsreader, 57, 174, 177–179
parent directory, 95
partitioning, 30
passwords
  expiration dates, 295–296
  resetting the root password, 257–258
  "strong" passwords, 288
patches, 273, 275–277
pathnames, 82–83
PDF viewers, 60–61, 241
performance monitoring, 265–269
perimeter network, 293
peripheral devices, 17, 19–20

permissions
  changing, 297–298, 336–337
  default permission, 298–299
  execute (x), 97
  read (r), 97
  set user ID permission, 300
  viewing, 296
  write (w), 97
phishing, 158
photo editors
  Digikam Image Editor, 230
  GIMP, 60–61, 237–239
photos
  downloading from digital camera, 228–229
  editing, 230
  scanning, 232–237
  viewing, 228–229, 239–240
pico text editor, 339
ping command, 136–137
PKI (Public-Key Infrastructure), 294
playing
  audio CDs, 48, 59, 217–218
  DVDs, 48, 59
  Internet radio stations, 220
  multimedia files, 58
  music files, 219–220
  streaming audio, 220–221
  TV, 59–60
popularity of SUSE Linux, 325
port scanning, 293
port-scanning tool, 301
posting news articles, 179–180
PostScript viewers, 60–61, 241–242
PowerPoint (Microsoft), 58
PPP over Ethernet (PPPoE), 114
presentation applications
  Microsoft PowerPoint, 58
  OpenOffice.org Impress, 57–58, 208–212
presentations, 212–216
printer configuration, 45–47
printing PDF/PostScript documents, 241–242
/proc directory, 84
processes
  init process, 261–262
  starting, 264–265
  stopping, 264–265
processor speed, 25

productivity applications, 15
proxy server, 293
`ps` command, 51
public-key cryptography, 293
Public-Key Infrastructure (PKI), 294
`pwd` command, 94

• Q •

querying RPM files, 282–284
question mark (?) wildcard character, 249–250

• R •

radio stations, 220
RAM (Random Access Memory), 17, 25
read (r) permission, 97
reading man pages (manual pages), 332–333
reading newsgroups
　KNode newsreader, 57, 174–177
　Pan newsreader, 174, 177–179
　Web sites, 180–181
RealPlayer 10, 59, 219–220
rearranging slides (presentations), 214
rebooting, 318
recreational newsgroups, 172
Red Hat Package Manager (RPM) files. *See* RPM files
relative directory name, 94
release notes, 37
remote logins, 290, 303–304
removing. *See* deleting
renaming
　directories, 88, 93
　files, 88, 93, 99
repeating commands, 250–251
resetting the `root` password, 257–258
resolution of the screen, 28
reviewing Writer documents, 188–189
ripping CDs, 59
`rm` command, 99
`rmdir` command, 99–100
`/root` directory, 81, 83–84
`root` password, resetting, 257–258
`root` user, 35, 41, 257
`route` command, 136

routing table, 136
`rpm` command, 281–285, 320, 337
RPM (Red Hat Package Manager) files
　downloading, 329
　filenames, 281–282
　finding, 320
　installing, 279–280, 284
　querying, 282–284
　uninstalling, 285
　upgrading, 285
run levels
　changing, 263
　checking current run level, 262–263
　default run level, 31
　starting, 264–265
　stopping, 264–265
　0-6 run levels, 262
`runlevel` command, 262–263
Runlevel Editor (YaST), 264

• S •

Samba, 20
SANE (Scanner Access Now Easy), 234
saving
　error messages, 247–248
　presentations, 212
`/sbin` directory, 84
scanning photos/documents, 232–237
science newsgroups, 172
screen resolution, 28
screening router, 294
scripts, 49
SCSI controller, 25
SDB (SUSE support database), 328
SDSL (Symmetric DSL), 110
searching
　man pages (manual pages), 332
　newsgroups, 181
　text in files, 334–335
Secure Shell (SSH), 303–304
security
　application gateway, 290
　authentication, 290
　backdoor, 290
　bastion host, 291
　buffer overflow, 291
　Certificate Authority (CA), 291
　certificates, 291

Index

confidentiality, 291
crackers, 287, 291
cryptography, 293
Cyber Alert System, 308
decrypting files, 289, 291
Denial of Service (DoS) attack, 287, 291
digital signature, 292
Distributed Denial of Service (DDoS) attack, 291
DMZ, 292
dual-homed host, 292
encrypting files, 289, 292
exploit tools, 292
file integrity, 289
firewall, 288, 292, 304–307
hash, 292
host, 292
host security issues, 288–289, 295
integrity (of data), 292
Internet, 287–288
Internet services, 301
Internet superserver, 301–302
IP spoofing, 293
IPSec (IP Security Protocol), 292
log files, 289
logic bombs, 293
mailing lists, 308
Network Address Translation (NAT), 307
network security issues, 288–290
news, 308
newsgroups, 308
nonrepudiation, 293
packet filtering, 293, 305
packets, 293
passwords, 288, 295–296
perimeter network, 293
port scanning, 293
proxy server, 293
public-key cryptography, 293
Public-Key Infrastructure (PKI), 294
remote logins, 290, 303–304
screening router, 294
setuid program, 294
sniffers, 294
spyware, 294
stand-alone servers, 301
symmetric-key encryption, 294
TCP wrappers, 302–303
threats, 294

Trojan horses, 294
updates, 289, 308
viruses, 294
vulnerabilities, 294
war-dialing, 295
war-driving, 295
wireless networks, 130
worms, 295
Sendmail: Mail server, 16
set user ID permission, 300
setuid program, 294
setuid programs, 300
sharing files, 20
shell. *See* bash shell
shell commands, 49–50
shell scripts, 49
shielded twisted-pair cables, 124
shutting down, 52–53
Simple Mail-Transfer Protocol (SMTP), 156
single dot (.) current directory, 95
slides (presentations), 212–216
SMTP (Simple Mail-Transfer Protocol), 156
sniffers, 294
social issues newsgroups, 172
soft modem, 26
software
  finding, 277–278
  installing, 30, 277–278
software development, 16–17
software patches
  downloading, 273, 275–277
  installing, 273, 275–277
sound card, 26
source code, 343
speaker's notes (presentations), 216
spreadsheet programs
  Calc, 57–58, 197–200
  Lotus 1-2-3, 197
  Microsoft Excel, 197
  VisiCalc, 197
spreadsheets, 201–204
spyware, 294
square brackets ([ ]) wildcard format, 250
/srv directory, 84
SSH (Secure Shell), 303–304
sshd Internet server, 16
sshd server, 303–304
Stallman, Richard, creator of the GNU Project, 14

356 SUSE Linux 9.3 For Dummies

stand-alone server security, 301
StarOffice (Sun Microsystems), 15
starting
 processes, 264–265
 SUSE Linux, 39–40
stopping processes, 264–265
streaming audio, 220–221
"strong" passwords, 288
subscribing to newsgroups, 179
Sun Microsystems StarOffice, 15
SUSE installer boot screen, 27–28
SUSE knowledgebase, 328
SUSE Linux
 configuring, 21–22, 35–37
 development history, 311
 downloading, 328
 gecko mascot, 324
 growth in U.S. market, 1
 ISO image files, 313
 new releases, 312–313
 online forums, 328–329
 popularity, 325
 pronunciation, 311–312
 shutting down, 52–53
 source code, 343
 starting, 39–40
 updates, 273, 308
 version numbers, 13
SUSE Linux Hardware Database, 26
SUSE Linux installation. *See* installing SUSE Linux
SUSE Linux Professional, 1
SUSE Linux Web site, 12, 327–328
SUSE portal Web site, 328
SUSE support database (SDB), 328
symbolic link, 97
Symmetric DSL (SDSL), 110
symmetric-key encryption, 294
/sys directory, 84
system administration
 defined, 18, 255
 managing users/groups, 271–272
 resetting the root password, 257–258
 root user, 257
 tasks, 255–257
 YaST Control Center, 259–261

system installation setting, 30
system requirements for companion DVD, 341
system users, 271

• T •

tar command, 337–338
tar program, 20
TCP wrappers, 302–303
TCP/IP (Transmission Control Protocol/Internet Protocol), 15
telinit command, 263
templates (Writer documents), 189, 191–192
Temporal Key-Integrity Protocol (TKIP), 130
10BaseT Ethernet, 124–125
terminal window, 93, 243
testing
 Internet connection, 35
 IP routing table, 136
 network connections, 136–137
 network interfaces, 135–136
threats to security, 294
tilde (~) home directory, 95
time zone, 30
TKIP (Temporal Key-Integrity Protocol), 130
/tmp directory, 84
top utility, 265–267
Totem Movie Player, 59
Transmission Control Protocol/Internet Protocol (TCP/IP), 15
Tripwire file integrity-checking tool, 289
Trojan horses, 294
troubleshooting the DVD, 344
TV players, 59–60
two dots (. .) parent directory, 95

• U •

umask command, 298–299
uname command, 50–51
Uniform Resource Locator (URL), 143–145
uninstalling RPM files, 285
United States Computer Emergency Readiness Team (US-CERT) Web site, 308

Universal Serial Bus (USB) interface, 20
`unmount` command, 102
unmounting file systems, 101–102
unshielded twisted-pair cables, 124
updates
  security, 289, 308
  YaST Online Update (YOU), 273–277, 323
upgrading RPM files, 285
`uptime` command, 267–268
URL (Uniform Resource Locator), 143–145
USB memory stick, 323
USB (Universal Serial Bus) interface, 20
`US-CERT National Cyber Alert System` mailing list, 308
US-CERT (United States Computer Emergency Readiness Team) Web site, 308
Usenet newsgroups. *See* newsgroups
Usenet Replayer Web site, 181
user accounts, 271–272
`/usr` directory, 84

• V •

`/var` directory, 84
vector drawing, 60–61
version numbers, 12–13
video card, 25
video editors, 59–60
video players, 59
videoconferencing, 57
viewing
  directories, 85–87, 89–92
  files, 85–87, 89–92
  man pages (manual pages), 332–333
  ownerships, 296
  PDF documents, 241
  permissions, 296
  photos, 228–229, 239–240
  PostScript documents, 241–242
  slides (presentations), 214
virtual consoles, 244
viruses, 294
VisiCalc, 197
`vsftpd` FTP server, 16
vulnerabilities, 294

• W •

`w` (write) permission, 97
wallpaper
  GNOME, 78–79
  KDE, 75–76
war-dialing, 295
war-driving, 295
Web browsers
  defined, 141
  Epiphany, 146, 153–154
  Firefox, 146, 154
  GNOME, 43–44, 56
  how they work, 145–146
  KDE, 42, 44, 56
  Konqueror, 88, 146–149
  Mozilla, 146, 149–153
Web pages
  HTML (Hypertext Markup Language), 142
  links, 142–143
  Uniform Resource Locator (URL), 143–145
Web servers, 142, 145–146
Web sites. *See* Web sites by name
WEP (Wired Equivalent Privacy), 130
Wi-Fi Alliance Web site, 129
Wi-Fi Protected Access (WPA), 130
wildcard characters, 249–250
Wiley Product Technical Support, 344
Windows partition, 31–33, 323
Windows shares, 324
win-modem, 26
Wired Equivalent Privacy (WEP), 130
wireless networks
  access points, 130–132
  Bluetooth wireless technology, 20
  Ethernet standards, 124, 128–129
  war-driving, 295
  Wired Equivalent Privacy (WEP), 130
  wireless network cards, 130–134
Word (Microsoft), 184
word processing, 57–58
worms, 295
WPA (Wi-Fi Protected Access), 130
write (`w`) permission, 97
Writer, 57, 184–187
Writer documents

creating, 185
editing, 188–189
fields, 195–196
graphics, 194–195
large documents, 196–197
master documents, 196–197
page layouts, 192–194
paragraph formatting, 189
presentation outlines, 213
reviewing, 188–189
styles, 189–190
Stylist, 190
templates, 189, 191–192

• X •

x (execute) permission, 97
X Window System, 14
xinetd server, 301–302
XMMS audio player, 59, 220–221

• Y •

YaST
  command line, 322
  Control Center, 259–261, 322
  Ethernet configuration, 125–126
  finding software, 277–278
  firewall configuration, 305–307
  GNU General Public License (GPL), 322
  hardware configuration, 269–270
  installing RPM files, 279–280
  installing software, 277–278
  installing SUSE Linux, 24, 28–38
  modem configuration, 121–122
  printer configuration, 45–47
  Runlevel Editor, 264
  scanner configuration, 232–233
YaST Online Update (YOU), 273–277, 323

• Z •

0-6 run levels, 262

GNU General Public License

Version 2, June 1991
Copyright © 1989, 1991 Free Software Foundation, Inc.
59 Temple Place - Suite 330, Boston, MA 02111-1307, USA

Everyone is permitted to copy and distribute verbatim copies of this license document, but changing it is not allowed.

Preamble

The licenses for most software are designed to take away your freedom to share and change it. By contrast, the GNU General Public License is intended to guarantee your freedom to share and change free software – to make sure the software is free for all its users. This General Public License applies to most of the Free Software Foundation's software and to any other program whose authors commit to using it. (Some other Free Software Foundation software is covered by the GNU Library General Public License instead.) You can apply it to your programs, too.

When we speak of free software, we are referring to freedom, not price. Our General Public Licenses are designed to make sure that you have the freedom to distribute copies of free software (and charge for this service if you wish), that you receive source code or can get it if you want it, that you can change the software or use pieces of it in new free programs; and that you know you can do these things.

To protect your rights, we need to make restrictions that forbid anyone to deny you these rights or to ask you to surrender the rights. These restrictions translate to certain responsibilities for you if you distribute copies of the software, or if you modify it.

For example, if you distribute copies of such a program, whether gratis or for a fee, you must give the recipients all the rights that you have. You must make sure that they, too, receive or can get the source code. And you must show them these terms so they know their rights.

We protect your rights with two steps: (1) copyright the software, and (2) offer you this license which gives you legal permission to copy, distribute and/or modify the software.

Also, for each author's protection and ours, we want to make certain that everyone understands that there is no warranty for this free software. If the software is modified by someone else and passed on, we want its recipients to know that what they have is not the original, so that any problems introduced by others will not reflect on the original authors' reputations.

Finally, any free program is threatened constantly by software patents. We wish to avoid the danger that redistributors of a free program will individually obtain patent licenses, in effect making the program proprietary. To prevent this, we have made it clear that any patent must be licensed for everyone's free use or not licensed at all.

The precise terms and conditions for copying, distribution and modification follow.

Terms and Conditions for Copying, Distribution and Modification

0. This License applies to any program or other work which contains a notice placed by the copyright holder saying it may be distributed under the terms of this General Public License. The "Program", below, refers to any such program or work, and a "work based on the Program" means either the Program or any derivative work under copyright law: that is to say, a work containing the Program or a portion of it, either verbatim or with modifications and/or translated into another language. (Hereinafter, translation is included without limitation in the term "modification".) Each licensee is addressed as "you".

Activities other than copying, distribution and modification are not covered by this License; they are outside its scope. The act of running the Program is not restricted, and the output from the Program is covered only if its contents constitute a work based on the Program (independent of having been made by running the Program). Whether that is true depends on what the Program does.

1. You may copy and distribute verbatim copies of the Program's source code as you receive it, in any medium, provided that you conspicuously and appropriately publish on each copy an appropriate copyright notice and disclaimer of warranty; keep intact all the notices that refer to this License and to the absence of any warranty; and give any other recipients of the Program a copy of this License along with the Program.

You may charge a fee for the physical act of transferring a copy, and you may at your option offer warranty protection in exchange for a fee.

2. You may modify your copy or copies of the Program or any portion of it, thus forming a work based on the Program, and copy and distribute such modifications or work under the terms of Section 1 above, provided that you also meet all of these conditions:

    a) You must cause the modified files to carry prominent notices stating that you changed the files and the date of any change.

    b) You must cause any work that you distribute or publish, that in whole or in part contains or is derived from the Program or any part thereof, to be licensed as a whole at no charge to all third parties under the terms of this License.

    c) If the modified program normally reads commands interactively when run, you must cause it, when started running for such interactive use in the most ordinary way, to print or display an announcement including an appropriate copyright notice and a notice that there is no warranty (or else, saying that you provide a warranty) and that users may redistribute the program under these conditions, and telling the user how to view a copy of this License. (Exception: if the Program itself is interactive but does not normally print such an announcement, your work based on the Program is not required to print an announcement.)

These requirements apply to the modified work as a whole. If identifiable sections of that work are not derived from the Program, and can be reasonably considered independent and separate works in themselves, then this License, and its terms, do not apply to those sections when you distribute them as separate works. But when you distribute the same sections as part of a whole which is a work based on the Program, the distribution of the whole must be on the terms of this License, whose permissions for other licensees extend to the entire whole, and thus to each and every part regardless of who wrote it.

Thus, it is not the intent of this section to claim rights or contest your rights to work written entirely by you; rather, the intent is to exercise the right to control the distribution of derivative or collective works based on the Program.

In addition, mere aggregation of another work not based on the Program with the Program (or with a work based on the Program) on a volume of a storage or distribution medium does not bring the other work under the scope of this License.

3. You may copy and distribute the Program (or a work based on it, under Section 2) in object code or executable form under the terms of Sections 1 and 2 above provided that you also do one of the following:

    a) Accompany it with the complete corresponding machine-readable source code, which must be distributed under the terms of Sections 1 and 2 above on a medium customarily used for software interchange; or,

    b) Accompany it with a written offer, valid for at least three years, to give any third party, for a charge no more than your cost of physically performing source distribution, a complete machine-readable copy of the corresponding source code, to be distributed under the terms of Sections 1 and 2 above on a medium customarily used for software interchange; or,

    c) Accompany it with the information you received as to the offer to distribute corresponding source code. (This alternative is allowed only for noncommercial distribution and only if you received the program in object code or executable form with such an offer, in accord with Subsection b above.)

    The source code for a work means the preferred form of the work for making modifications to it. For an executable work, complete source code means all the source code for all modules it contains, plus any associated interface definition files, plus the scripts used to control compilation and installation of the executable. However, as a special exception, the source code distributed need not include anything that is normally distributed (in either source or binary form) with the major components (compiler, kernel, and so on) of the operating system on which the executable runs, unless that component itself accompanies the executable.

    If distribution of executable or object code is made by offering access to copy from a designated place, then offering equivalent access to copy the source code from the same place counts as distribution of the source code, even though third parties are not compelled to copy the source along with the object code.

4. You may not copy, modify, sublicense, or distribute the Program except as expressly provided under this License. Any attempt otherwise to copy, modify, sublicense or distribute the Program is void, and will automatically terminate your rights under this License. However, parties who have received copies, or rights, from you under this License will not have their licenses terminated so long as such parties remain in full compliance.

5. You are not required to accept this License, since you have not signed it. However, nothing else grants you permission to modify or distribute the Program or its derivative works. These actions are prohibited by law if you do not accept this License. Therefore, by modifying or distributing the Program (or any work based on the Program), you indicate your acceptance of this License to do so, and all its terms and conditions for copying, distributing or modifying the Program or works based on it.

6. Each time you redistribute the Program (or any work based on the Program), the recipient automatically receives a license from the original licensor to copy, distribute or modify the Program subject to these terms and conditions. You may not impose any further restrictions on the recipients' exercise of the rights granted herein. You are not responsible for enforcing compliance by third parties to this License.

7. If, as a consequence of a court judgment or allegation of patent infringement or for any other reason (not limited to patent issues), conditions are imposed on you (whether by court order, agreement or otherwise) that contradict the conditions of this License, they do not excuse you from the conditions of this License. If you cannot distribute so as to satisfy simultaneously your obligations under this License and any other pertinent obligations, then as a consequence you may not distribute the Program at all. For example, if a patent license would not permit royalty-free redistribution of the Program by all those who receive copies directly or indirectly through you, then the only way you could satisfy both it and this License would be to refrain entirely from distribution of the Program.

    If any portion of this section is held invalid or unenforceable under any particular circumstance, the balance of the section is intended to apply and the section as a whole is intended to apply in other circumstances.

    It is not the purpose of this section to induce you to infringe any patents or other property right claims or to contest validity of any such claims; this section has the sole purpose of protecting the integrity of the free software distribution system, which is implemented by public license practices. Many people have made generous contributions to the wide range of software distributed through that system in reliance on consistent application of that system; it is up to the author/donor to decide if he or she is willing to distribute software through any other system and a licensee cannot impose that choice.

    This section is intended to make thoroughly clear what is believed to be a consequence of the rest of this License.

8. If the distribution and/or use of the Program is restricted in certain countries either by patents or by copyrighted interfaces, the original copyright holder who places the Program under this License may add an explicit geographical distribution limitation excluding those countries, so that distribution is permitted only in or among countries not thus excluded. In such case, this License incorporates the limitation as if written in the body of this License.

9. The Free Software Foundation may publish revised and/or new versions of the General Public License from time to time. Such new versions will be similar in spirit to the present version, but may differ in detail to address new problems or concerns.

    Each version is given a distinguishing version number. If the Program specifies a version number of this License which applies to it and "any later version", you have the option of following the terms and conditions either of that version or of any later version published by the Free Software Foundation. If the Program does not specify a version number of this License, you may choose any version ever published by the Free Software Foundation.

10. If you wish to incorporate parts of the Program into other free programs whose distribution conditions are different, write to the author to ask for permission. For software which is copyrighted by the Free Software Foundation, write to the Free Software Foundation; we sometimes make exceptions for this. Our decision will be guided by the two goals of preserving the free status of all derivatives of our free software and of promoting the sharing and reuse of software generally.

NO WARRANTY

11. BECAUSE THE PROGRAM IS LICENSED FREE OF CHARGE, THERE IS NO WARRANTY FOR THE PROGRAM, TO THE EXTENT PERMITTED BY APPLICABLE LAW. EXCEPT WHEN OTHERWISE STATED IN WRITING THE COPYRIGHT HOLDERS AND/OR OTHER PARTIES PROVIDE THE PROGRAM "AS IS" WITHOUT WARRANTY OF ANY KIND, EITHER EXPRESSED OR IMPLIED, INCLUDING, BUT NOT LIMITED TO, THE IMPLIED WARRANTIES OF MERCHANTABILITY AND FITNESS FOR A PARTICULAR PURPOSE. THE ENTIRE RISK AS TO THE QUALITY AND PERFORMANCE OF THE PROGRAM IS WITH YOU. SHOULD THE PROGRAM PROVE DEFECTIVE, YOU ASSUME THE COST OF ALL NECESSARY SERVICING, REPAIR OR CORRECTION.

12. IN NO EVENT UNLESS REQUIRED BY APPLICABLE LAW OR AGREED TO IN WRITING WILL ANY COPYRIGHT HOLDER, OR ANY OTHER PARTY WHO MAY MODIFY AND/OR REDISTRIBUTE THE PROGRAM AS PERMITTED ABOVE, BE LIABLE TO YOU FOR DAMAGES, INCLUDING ANY GENERAL, SPECIAL, INCIDENTAL OR CONSEQUENTIAL DAMAGES ARISING OUT OF THE USE OR INABILITY TO USE THE PROGRAM (INCLUDING BUT NOT LIMITED TO LOSS OF DATA OR DATA BEING RENDERED INACCURATE OR LOSSES SUSTAINED BY YOU OR THIRD PARTIES OR A FAILURE OF THE PROGRAM TO OPERATE WITH ANY OTHER PROGRAMS), EVEN IF SUCH HOLDER OR OTHER PARTY HAS BEEN ADVISED OF THE POSSIBILITY OF SUCH DAMAGES.

END OF TERMS AND CONDITIONS

Limited Warranty: (a) WPI warrants that the Software and Software Media are free from defects in materials and workmanship under normal use for a period of sixty (60) days from the date of purchase of this Book. If WPI receives notification within the warranty period of defects in materials or workmanship, WPI will replace the defective Software Media. (b) WPI AND THE AUTHORS(S) OF THIS BOOK DISCLAIM ALL OTHER WARRANTIES, EXPRESS OR IMPLIED, INCLUDING WITHOUT LIMITATION IMPLIED WARRANTIES OF MERCHANTABILITY AND FITNESS FOR A PARTICULAR PURPOSE, WITH RESPECT TO THE SOFTWARE, THE PROGRAMS, THE SOURCE CODE CONTAINED THEREIN, AND/OR THE TECHNIQUES DESCRIBED IN THIS BOOK. WPI DOES NOT WARRANTY THAT THE FUNCTIONS CONTAINED IN THE SOFTWARE WILL MEET YOUR REQUIREMENTS OR THAT THE OPERATION OF THE SOFTWARE WILL BE ERROR FREE. © This limited warranty gives you specific legal rights, and you may have other rights that vary from jurisdiction to jurisdiction.

Holborn Books Ltd
Passfield Business Centre
Lynchborough Road
Passfield, Hampshire
GU30 7SB
Fax 01428 751919

www.holbornbooks.co.uk/suse

Save £ 22!

SUSE has a convincing offer for all *SUSE Linux 9.3 For Dummies* readers who want to benefit from the full performance range of SUSE LINUX with Internet, office, image, sound, video, and network functionalities: instead of paying £ 64.95 for the full package, this coupon entitles *SUSE Linux 9.3 For Dummies* readers to obtain the update edition for only £ 42.95 and save £ 22! **Any more questions?** Please feel free to contact james@holbornbooks.co.uk or the information hotline 01428 751414.

Please send me:

___ units of the latest update edition of SUSE LINUX Professional for £ 42.95 per unit (no additional shipping fees).

Name

Company

Street

City/postcode

Phone

Fax

The update eligibility is only valid with this coupon.

☐ By credit card:
   ☐ Visa   ☐ Eurocard   ☐ Amex

Card no.   Expiration date

☐ By direct debit (UK only):

Sort code

Account no.

☐ By invoice (only for regular Holborn Books customers, large companies, government agencies, and schools)

Would you like to receive information about new versions, availability, and attractive prices by e-mail?
☐ Yes   ☐ No

E-mail

Order the latest update edition of SUSE LINUX Professional now — with more than 1,000 applications on five CDs and two double-sided DVDs.

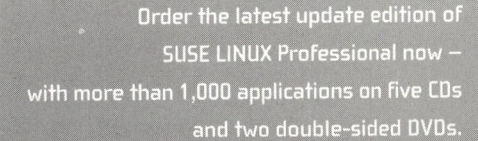

The package price includes 60 days of installation support and the detailed, easy-to-understand Administration Guide.

SUSE
A NOVELL BUSINESS

Jump in! Everything you need to get started with Linux.

The new SUSE LINUX Professional 9.3 provides everything you need for home computing and computing on the go. It includes a secure, stable and reliable Linux operating system, plus e-mail, an office suite, Web browsing, multimedia, graphical software, instant messaging and digital-photo organizing. It even has the latest tools for Web hosting and home networking. It is the complete Linux solution you've been looking for. Jump in today! Visit www.novell.com/suselinux to learn more and to order your copy of SUSE LINUX Professional 9.3.

SUSE
A NOVELL BUSINESS

Novell.

©2005 Novell is a registered trademark of Novell, Inc. in the United States and other countries. SUSE is a registered trademark of SUSE LINUX Products GmbH, a Novell business.